Evolution of APA Regime

Evolution of APA Regime

Kuldeep Sharma

Wolters Kluwer

Published by:
Kluwer Law International B.V.
PO Box 316
2400 AH Alphen aan den Rijn
The Netherlands
E-mail: international-sales@wolterskluwer.com
Website: lrus.wolterskluwer.com

Sold and distributed by:
Wolters Kluwer Legal & Regulatory U.S.
7201 McKinney Circle
Frederick, MD 21704
United States of America
E-mail: customer.service@wolterskluwer.com

ISBN 978-94-035-3551-7

e-Book: ISBN 978-94-035-3552-4
web-PDF: ISBN 978-94-035-3553-1

About the Author

Kuldeep Sharma, an erstwhile officer of the Indian Revenue Service, has worked for over thirty years in the Income Tax Department, wherein he has had the opportunity to work at multiple levels in Direct Taxes, i.e., in field dispensations as well as tax policy department under the aegis of Central Board of Direct Taxes (CBDT) and has garnered wide experience in taxation of corporates and non-corporates (including individuals).

The last ten years of his service were completely dedicated to the field of International Taxation and Transfer Pricing (IT&TP), wherein he has accredited himself in a variety of roles, involving transfer pricing audits, processing of Advance Pricing Agreements or Arrangements (APAs). For four years, he has worked in the Foreign Tax and Tax Research Division of CBDT, wherein, apart from handling policy issues related to non-residents, Country-by-Country Reporting, Tax Treaty Negotiations and complex APA, Mutual Agreement Procedure (MAP) cases, he has been actively engaged in matters involving Base Erosion and Profit Shifting (BEPS) and the Multilateral Convention to Implement Tax Treaty Related Measures to Prevent Base Erosion and Profit Shifting (MLI).

He has travelled extensively internationally and attended important events on tax, which includes representing the country during plenary meetings at Organisation for Economic Co-operation and Development (OECD), Paris. Also, he has attended a number of seminars, workshops and meetings on IT&TP.

Presently, he is actively engaged in writing books on IT&TP wherein he has shared his deep insights and experience in the niche areas of taxation. His maiden book titled *MLI Made Easy* was published by Wolters Kluwer, the Netherlands in April 2021 and has been widely appreciated.

About the Author

Kuldeep Sharma holds BSc (Physics) Hons. as well as an MBA (Finance). His years of practical experiences in Direct Taxes have enabled him to successfully achieve the status of ADIT Graduate accredited by the Chartered Institute of Taxation, UK.

For any clarification, he may be contacted at cooldip.sharma@gmail.com.

Table of Contents

List of Figures

List of Tables

List of Abbreviations

ACAP	Accelerated Competent Authority Procedure, USA
ACR	Annual Compliance Report
AE	Associated Enterprise
AITA	Adjustment of International Taxes Act, Korea
ALP	Arm's-Length Price
AMP	Advertisement, Marketing and Promotion
ANAF	National Agency for Fiscal Administration, Romania
AO	Assessing Officer
AoA	Authorized OECD Approach
APA	Advance Pricing Agreement or Arrangement
APMA	Advance Pricing and Mutual Agreement, USA
APPT	Prior Transfer Pricing Agreement
ATO	Australian Taxation Office
ATR	Advance Tax Ruling, the Netherlands
BAPA	Bilateral Advance Pricing Agreement or Arrangement
BEPS	Base Erosion and Profit Shifting
CA	Competent Authority
CASD	Competent Authority Services Division, CRA
CBDT	Central Board of Direct Taxes, India
CCRA	Canada Customs and Revenue Agency
CIT R	Corporate Income Tax Regulations, Spain
CPM	Comparable Profits Method
CRA	Canada Revenue Agency
CTA	Covered Tax Agreement
DEMPE	Development, Enhancement, Maintenance, Protection and Exploitation
DGCI	Directorate-General for Taxation, Portugal

DGT	Director General of Taxation, Indonesia
DPT	Diverted Profits Tax
DTA	Dutch Tax Authority
DTAA	Double Taxation Avoidance Agreement
DTT	Double Taxation Treaty
EC	European Commission
ESOP	Employee Stock Option Plan
EU	European Union
FAQ	Frequently Asked Questions
FAR	Functions Performed, Assets Utilized and Risks Assumed
FIRS	Federal Inland Revenue Service, Nigeria
FSC	Financial Services Company
FT&TR	Foreign Tax and Tax Research
FTA	French Tax Administration
FTS	Federal Tax Service, Russia
G20	Group of Twenty (Argentina, Australia, Brazil, Canada, China, France, Germany, India, Indonesia, Italy, Japan, Mexico, Russia, Saudi Arabia, South Africa, South Korea, Turkey, United Kingdom, United States, and the European Union)
HMRC	HM Revenue and Customs, UK
IC	Information Circulars, Canada
IP	Intellectual Property
IRAS	Inland Revenue Authority of Singapore
IRC Code	Corporate Income Tax Code, Portugal
IRD	Inland Revenue Department, New Zealand
IRS	Internal Revenue Service, USA
IT	Information Technology
ITAT	Income Tax Appellate Tribunal
ITeS	Information Technology-Enabled Services
LCITA	Law for the Coordination of International Tax Affairs, Korea
LSAs	Location-Specific Advantages
MAP	Mutual Agreement Procedure
MAPA	Multilateral Advance Pricing Agreement or Arrangement
MIRA	Maldives Inland Revenue Authority
MLI	Multilateral Convention to Implement Tax Treaty Related Measures to Prevent Base Erosion and Profit Shifting
MNC	Multinational Corporation
MNE	Multinational Enterprise
MTC	Model Tax Convention
NATA	National Agency for Tax Administration, Romania
NTA	National Tax Agency, Japan

NTS	National Tax Service, Korea
OECD	Organisation for Economic Co-operation and Development
PE	Permanent Establishment
PLI	Profit Level Indicator
PMU	APA Program Management Unit, ATO
PS LA	Law Administration Practice Statement, ATO
PTA	Portuguese Tax Authority
QA	Quality Assurance
RTB	Regional Taxation Bureau, Japan
RTC	Russian Tax Code
SARS	South African Revenue Service
SAT	State Administration of Tax, Mexico
SAT	State Administration Taxation, China
SME	Small and Medium Enterprise
STA	Swedish Tax Agency
TAA	Tax Administration Act, New Zealand
TIOPA	Taxation (International and Other Provisions) Act 2010, UK
TNMM	Transactional Net Margin Method
TP	Transfer Pricing
TPM	Transfer Pricing Method/Methodology
TPO	Transfer Pricing Officer
TSO	Tax Services Office
UAPA	Unilateral Advance Pricing Agreement

Preface

Globalization aims to benefit individual economies around the world by making markets more efficient, increasing competition, and spreading wealth more equally. Developing countries have the market and natural resources to attract capital and technology from Multinational Corporations (MNCs) for various greenfield and brownfield projects. In the process of investing in developing countries, tax uncertainty has been one of the major concerns for investors. APAs dispel tax uncertainty and ensure certainty as brought out very vehemently in this book.

The book clearly brings out the many benefits of an APA programme which is visualized as a preferred dispute prevention mechanism for taxpayers the world over. While drafting the book, an effort has been made to highlight the evolution of APA programme worldwide in a manner which will be found useful by a wide array of stakeholders, i.e., tax officers, tax professionals, tax advisors, taxpayers, academicians and others (such as law students) in any part of the academic world.

As far as the structure of the book is concerned, it is divided into seven chapters. *Chapter 1* is introductory and provides definition of APAs, their brief history, types of APAs, broad terms agreed in an APA and the main steps involved in an APA process. *Chapter 2* provides information on the benefits of the APA programme as well as a comparative study of APAs and other dispute resolution mechanisms like MAP, safe harbour. As is the case in any programme, APAs come with their own share of limitations which are also discussed at length in this chapter. *Chapter 3* describes APA programme of twenty-five jurisdictions in detail, namely, Australia, Canada, China, France, Germany, India, Indonesia, Ireland, Japan, Korea, Mexico, the Netherlands, New Zealand, Nigeria, Poland, Portugal, Romania, Russia, Singapore, Spain, Sweden, Thailand, UK, US and Vietnam. *Chapter 4* covers experience sharing in the course of the APA rollout programme in India, in respect of certain key issues noticed at ground level, so as to make readers well aware of such important aspects. These key elements include constituents/components of cost base in respect of captive entities performing functions solely for Associated Enterprises (AEs), Advertisement, Marketing and Promotion (AMP)/Development, Enhancement, Maintenance, Protection and Exploitation (DEMPE) related issues, treatment of Permanent Establishment (PE) related international transactions under India's APA programme, location savings and joint site visits. Discussions have also been made in this chapter over tendency of appellate authorities in applying APA rulings to non-APA years (period). *Chapter 5* covers experience sharing in the course of rollout of APA programme worldwide, in respect of certain key issues noticed at ground level. These elements include APAs for small and medium enterprises (SMEs) in Canada, France, Germany, Korea, the Netherlands and US. Schemes like abbreviated procedure for renewal of APAs prevalent in Germany and US are also discussed. The chapter discusses that where there is agreement between the taxpayer and both tax administrations that a PE does exist, the attribution of profit to that PE may be the subject of an APA in Ireland. Elaborate discussions have been made in respect of APA programme in the Netherlands about the significance of economic nexus prior to grant of APAs and release of anonymized APA summaries. An important facet found in the APA programme of Poland is grant of unilateral APAs for domestic affiliated entities, whereas, for UK-to-UK oil-related ring-fenced trades, APAs are specifically provided for in its legislation. *Chapter 6* discusses factors influencing speedier processing of APAs and suggestions on further improvement in the APA programme. This chapter also discusses that recourse to APAs shall increase with more opening up of economies and with the implementation of BEPS reports. The chapter concludes with a discussion on the impact of COVID-19 on APAs and OECD's Guidance thereon. *Chapter 7* provides summary of APA programmes discussed under Chapter 3, discussion on exchange of APA rulings as a mechanism to tackle BEPS concerns with more concluding remarks, *inter alia*, highlighting the filing of a large number of APA applications by the taxpayers as a testimony to their confidence in the APA programme.

The dates (period) of statistical data discussed in this book pertaining to various jurisdictions are duly mentioned at appropriate and relevant places.

Acknowledgements

The seeds of this book were sown when I wrote an extended essay titled 'Evolution of Advance Pricing Agreement (APA) Regime in India' in the course of my ADIT graduation programme for the Chartered Institute of Taxation, UK. The extended essay that I wrote and successfully cleared was dedicated to the APA programme in India, whereas this book is an extension of that thesis and covers worldwide jurisdictions where APA programme is popular and at an advanced stage with elaborate discussions on various significant aspects of APAs.

I will credit my colleagues and friends in the OECD and Tax Administrations across the world, particularly in the Tax Administration in India for their constant encouragement and guidance in the field of APA and Transfer Pricing. My considerably longish stints in the APA Delhi team and Foreign Tax & Tax Research Division, CBDT, New Delhi have helped me tremendously in developing a deep insight and experience in this field, which I have extensively shared in this book. This book, therefore, has a liberal dose of experience sharing, has practical viewpoints and observations at appropriate places, in addition to elaborate discussion on legal aspects of APA and Transfer Pricing concerning a number of jurisdictions.

I would like to extend my profound gratitude to my family which has been my constant pillar of support and has gladly permitted me to devote time meant for them to my academic pursuits. In addition, I would like to acknowledge that my elder daughter, Ms Raunicka Sharma, a BBA-LLB student from Symbiosis Law School, Noida, India, provided insights into the contours of the book, data collection and research, including its final proofreading, whereas, my younger daughter, Ms Paavnieka Sharma (student of Class XI), designed the tables and figures of the book.

My association with Wolters Kluwer began with my maiden literary venture titled *MLI Made Easy*. I would like to express my sincere gratitude to the Wolters Kluwer team for readily agreeing to continue with our association through my second venture titled *Evolution of APA Regime*. These publications may not have been possible without the confidence and faith Wolters Kluwer had in me.

Glossary

Advance Pricing Arrangement or Agreement (APA)	An arrangement that determines, in advance of controlled transactions, an appropriate set of criteria (e.g., method, comparables and appropriate adjustments thereto, critical assumptions as to future events) for the determination of the transfer pricing for those transactions over a fixed period of time.
APA process	The series of formal or informal steps described in regulations or established by the APA team during the course of its evaluation of an APA request that are involved in reaching an APA, including steps relating to pre-filing meeting.
APA request	A request for a unilateral, bilateral, or multilateral APA submitted by an applicant.
APA term	The time period consisting of all APA years.
Arm's-length price (ALP)	Price charged in a controlled transaction between two related parties should be the same as that in a transaction between two unrelated parties in the open market.
Arm's-length principle	It is set forth in Article 9 of the OECD Model Tax Convention as follows: where 'conditions are made or imposed between the two enterprises in their commercial or financial relations which differ from those which would be made between independent enterprises, then any profits which would, but for those conditions, have accrued to one of the enterprises, but, by reason of those conditions, have not so accrued, may be included in the profits of that enterprise and taxed accordingly'.
Associated enterprises	Two enterprises are associated enterprises with respect to each other if one of the enterprises meets the conditions of Article 9, subparagraph 1a) or 1b) of the OECD Model Tax Convention with respect to the other enterprise. Associated enterprises are enterprises under common control. This will generally be the case where the same persons participate directly or indirectly in the management, control or capital of both enterprises.

Bilateral APA	Bilateral APAs involve two tax administrations and taxpayers of the respective two jurisdictions.
Cancellation of APA	Cancelling an APA means that the terms of an APA are no longer effective for a period commencing after the start of the period covered by the APA. Where Revenue cancels an APA, the effective date of cancellation is determined by reference to the event that led to the cancellation. The taxpayer's position, for the period from the effective date of cancellation, is the same as if the APA had never been agreed. APA is treated as being effective and in force only up to the cancellation date and not for the whole of the proposed APA period.
Compliance Report	The report prepared by the taxpayer for each APA year demonstrating the taxpayer's compliance with the covered method(s) and APA terms and conditions.
Controlled transactions	Transactions between two enterprises that are associated enterprises with respect to each other.
Compensating adjustment	An adjustment in which the taxpayer reports a transfer price for tax purposes that is, in the taxpayer's opinion, an arm's-length price for a controlled transaction, even though this price differs from the amount actually charged between associated enterprises. This adjustment is to be made before the tax return is filed.
Corresponding adjustment	An adjustment to the tax liability of the associated enterprise in a second tax jurisdiction made by the tax administration of that jurisdiction, corresponding to a primary adjustment made by the tax administration in a first tax jurisdiction, so that the allocation of profits by the two jurisdictions is consistent.
Covered transaction	The international transaction or transactions for which the agreement has been entered into.
Critical assumptions	Factors and assumptions which are so critical and significant that neither party entering into an agreement will continue to be bound by the agreement if any of the factors or assumptions are changed.
Functional analysis	The analysis aimed at identifying the economically significant activities and responsibilities (functions) undertaken, assets used or contributed, and risks assumed by the parties to the transactions.
Independent enterprises	Two enterprises are independent enterprises with respect to each other if they are not associated enterprises with respect to each other.
International transaction	A transaction between two or more associated enterprises, either or both of whom are non-residents.
Multilateral APA	Multilateral APAs involve more than two tax administrations and taxpayers of the respective jurisdictions.
Multinational enterprise (MNE)	A company that is part of an MNE group.
Multinational enterprise group (MNE group)	A group of associated companies with business establishments in two or more countries.

Mutual agreement procedure	A means through which tax administrations consult to resolve disputes regarding the application of double tax conventions. This procedure, described and authorized by Article 25 of the OECD Model Tax Convention, can be used to eliminate double taxation that could arise from a transfer pricing adjustment.
Operating expense	Costs incurred in a financial year by a taxpayer in relation to the international transaction during the course of its normal operations.
Pre-filing meeting	A meeting/conference held between the taxpayer and the APA team before an APA request is filed.
Position paper	A document prepared by a CA and shared with its counterpart, wherein the entire analysis of the APA application is captured to enable the two authorities to understand and evaluate each other's position on the case under consideration so as to arrive at a consensus, common ground and/or a negotiated settlement. The position paper is subject to the confidentiality restrictions of the relevant double tax treaty.
Profit Level Indicator (PLI)	A measure of a company's profitability that is used to compare comparables with the tested party. A PLI may express profitability in relation to: (i) sales, (ii) costs or expenses, or (iii) assets.
Revision of APA	It means that the taxpayer and tax administrations still have the benefit of the APA for the whole of the proposed period, albeit different terms apply before and after the revision date.
Revocation of APA	Revoking an APA means that the terms of an APA are no longer effective for any part of the period specified in the APA. Where an authority revokes an APA, the taxpayer's position is the same as if the APA had never been agreed. Revocation is retroactive to the first day of the period covered by the APA. Revocation has the effect that the taxpayer is treated as if the APA had never been entered into.
Rollback of APA	Rollback of APA refers to the applicability of the methodology of determination of ALP, or the ALP, to be applied to the international transactions which had already been entered into in a period prior to the period covered under an APA, as under certain circumstances and subject to certain conditions, an APA in respect of future tax years may be rolled back and used as an appropriate transfer pricing method for past open tax years.
Safe harbour	A provision in the tax law, regulations or guidelines stating that transactions falling within a certain range will be accepted by the tax authorities without further investigation.
Site visit	Visit to the applicant's business premises by the APA team in the course of the APA process on a day and time mutually decided in advance by the applicant and the APA team.

Tested Party	When applying a CPM, RPM or TNMM, it is necessary to choose the party to the transaction for which a financial indicator (markup on costs, gross margin, or net profit indicator) is tested. The choice of the tested party should be consistent with the functional analysis of the transaction. As a general rule, the tested party is the one to which a transfer pricing method can be applied in the most reliable manner and for which the most reliable comparables can be found; i.e., it will most often be the one that has the less complex functional analysis.
Transfer pricing	The general term for the pricing of cross-border, intra-group transactions in goods, intangibles or services.
Uncontrolled transactions	Transactions between enterprises that are independent enterprises with respect to each other.
Unilateral APA	An advance pricing arrangement may be unilateral involving one tax administration and a taxpayer in that jurisdiction.

Executive Summary

1. Tax uncertainty, particularly, in the field of Transfer Pricing has been an area of immense concern to the MNCs. Various measures for providing certainty to the MNCs have been taken by tax authorities across the world to ameliorate the situation, so as to facilitate economic activity and seamless transfer of investments and technologies. Among various steps taken, introduction of APA scheme has attracted tremendous interest among the MNCs. The scope of the book is to understand evolution of APA scheme over time across various countries. In this process, elaborate discussions have been made about the history, structure, progress made and future of APA regimes across the globe.

2. If the transfer pricing notion can be seen as an art, the APA represents an essential painting. The APAs are so named because pricing methodologies are agreed in advance in relation to the covered transactions. APAs provide greater certainty for the taxpayer on the taxation of certain cross-border transactions and are considered by the taxpayers as the safest way to avoid double taxation, especially where they are bilateral or multilateral.

3. A brief history of APAs is provided in paragraphs 5-8 of Chapter 1. The system of APAs was first introduced in Japan in 1987, followed by US in 1991. As for the rest of the countries where APA programme has been adopted, Australia initiated the programme in 1991. Subsequently, the APA programme was introduced in July 1993 in Canada, whereas New Zealand adopted APAs in 1994. After the 1995 OECD report on transfer pricing further promoted APAs, Spain adopted it in 1995, Korea and Mexico adopted the APA system in 1997, followed by China in 1998. UK, France and the Netherlands adopted APAs in 1999, whereas Germany adopted it in 2000. The APA programme in Italy and Singapore was initiated in 2003, followed by Poland, Romania in 2006 and Portugal in 2008. In Indonesia, Sweden and Thailand APAs were first stipulated in the respective countries in 2010. In India, Nigeria and Russia, the APA programme was introduced in 2012. Vietnam introduced the APA programme in 2014, followed by Ireland in 2016. As of now, Maldives has the distinction of being the latest jurisdiction to introduce the APA Regulations with effect from 16 March 2021.

4. The three types of APAs available to taxpayers, i.e., unilateral, bilateral and multilateral and their characteristics are discussed in paragraphs 11 and 12 of Chapter 1 followed by discussions on broad terms of the APA in paragraph 13 and primary steps involved in processing of APAs in paragraph 14 of Chapter 1.

5. The key advantages of APA programme are discussed in depth in paragraphs 15-19 of Chapter 2, followed by discussions as to how APAs score over other dispute resolution mechanisms like MAP and safe harbour in paragraphs 20-22 of Chapter 2. As is the case in any programme, APAs come with their own share of limitations, which are discussed in paragraphs 23 and 24 of Chapter 2.

6. The worldwide APA programmes are discussed in detail in Chapter 3. Such discussions have been made in respect of the following jurisdictions, which offers a fair mix of developed and developing countries, and most importantly, the APAs have progressed fairly well in a majority of these countries, so as to provide a fair idea about the evolution of APA regime:

(1) Australia (paragraphs 26-43)
(2) Canada (paragraphs 44-70)
(3) China (paragraphs 71-91)
(4) France (paragraphs 92-110)
(5) Germany (paragraphs 111-131)
(6) India (paragraphs 132-174)
(7) Indonesia (paragraphs 175-212)
(8) Ireland (paragraphs 213-247)
(9) Japan (paragraphs 248-266)
(10) Korea (paragraphs 267-280)
(11) Mexico (paragraphs 281-290)
(12) The Netherlands (paragraphs 291-303)
(13) New Zealand (paragraphs 304-323)
(14) Nigeria (paragraphs 324-345)
(15) Poland (paragraphs 346-367)
(16) Portugal (paragraphs 368-394)
(17) Romania (paragraphs 395-416)
(18) Russia (paragraphs 417-434)
(19) Singapore (paragraphs 435-457)
(20) Spain (paragraphs 458-474)
(21) Sweden (paragraphs 475-487)
(22) Thailand (paragraphs 488-499)
(23) UK (paragraphs 500-534)
(24) US (paragraphs 535-580)
(25) Vietnam (paragraphs 581-605)

7. A striking feature noticed in the APA regime in various countries is that the procedures and provisions are similar in most countries with minor variations. Some of the prominent features of the APA programme in various jurisdictions are summarized in paragraph 606 of Chapter 3.

8. An in-depth sharing of India's APA programme has been done in Chapter 4 involving the following key elements:

- Constituents/components of cost base in respect of captive entities performing functions solely for AEs (refer paragraphs 609-611);
- Handling of complex issues on intangibles pertaining to AMP and such brand promotion (DEMPE) activities (refer paragraphs 612-619);
- Treatment of PE related International Transactions (refer paragraphs 620-621);
- Location Savings (refer paragraphs 622-625);
- Joint site visits (refer paragraphs 626-627); and
- Practice adopted by appellate authorities in applying APA rulings to non-APA years (period) (refer paragraphs 628-632).

9. The following key elements of APA programmes in practice the world over have been analysed in Chapter 5:

- Rollback available compulsorily on Risk Assessment Basis under the Australian APA Programme (refer paragraphs 634-637);
- Flexibility allowed under the Canadian APA programme to relieve double taxation (refer paragraphs 638-639);
- APAs for small businesses under the Canadian APA programme (refer paragraphs 640-644);
- Treatment of Location-Specific Advantages in China (refer paragraphs 645-647);
- APAs for SMEs under the French APA programme (refer paragraphs 648-649);
- APAs for SMEs and abbreviated procedure for renewal of APAs under the German APA programme (refer paragraphs 650-653);
- APAs for PEs under the Irish APA programme (refer paragraphs 654-655);
- APAs for SMEs under the Korean APA programme (refer paragraphs 656-657);
- APAs for SMEs under the APA programme of the Netherlands (refer paragraphs 658-659);
- Significance of economic nexus prior to grant of APAs and release of anonymized APA summaries in the Netherlands (refer paragraphs 660-662);
- Unilateral APAs for domestic affiliated entities under the APA programme of Poland (refer paragraph 663);
- APAs for certain domestic transactions under the APA programme of UK (refer paragraphs 664-665);
- APAs for small businesses and abbreviated APAs under the US APA programme (refer paragraphs 666-668).

10. Discussions have been made in paragraphs 669-671 of Chapter 6 in regard to factors influencing speedier processing of APAs. Suitable suggestions for improvement in the APA programme have been made in paragraphs 672-684 so as to iron out certain shortcomings which shall go a long way to enable this programme achieve its desired objectives. Paragraph 685 in Chapter 6 discusses that South Africa has released a discussion paper on APAs. As of now, Maldives has the distinction of being the latest jurisdiction to introduce the APA Regulations with effect from 16 March 2021, as discussed in detail in paragraphs 686-692. Recourse to APAs is destined to increase in the post-BEPS era as brought out in discussions in paragraphs 693-701 of Chapter 6. Also, APAs will be provided more impetus and would be a preferred dispute prevention recourse for MNCs with more opening up of economies as discussed in paragraphs 702-708 of Chapter 6. Impact of COVID-19 on APAs and OECD's guidance to this effect are discussed in paragraphs 709-712.

11. Chapter 7 is the concluding chapter of the book. Paragraphs 714-721 of Chapter 7 provide a synopsis of the APA programmes analysed in various jurisdictions in Chapter 3. COVID-19 has prompted jurisdictions to move online in regard to their interactions with APA applicants, as discussed in paragraphs 722-723. In terms of BEPS Action 5 minimum standard, exchange of APA rulings has provided another dimension to the benefits of APA programme, as availability of timely and targeted information about such rulings has immense potential to better equip tax authorities to quickly identify risk areas in their respective jurisdictions so as to curb BEPS. This augurs well for the APA programme and is another milestone in its evolution process. APAs have provided jurisdictions with an excellent platform to fostering a non-adversarial tax regime in their fight against BEPS.

CHAPTER 1
Introduction

If the transfer pricing notion can be seen as an art, the Advance Pricing Agreement or Arrangement (APA) represents an essential painting. The APAs are so named because transfer pricing methodologies are agreed in advance in relation to the covered transactions. APAs provide greater certainty for the taxpayer on the taxation of certain cross-border transactions and are considered by the taxpayers as the safest way to avoid double taxation, especially where they are bilateral or multilateral. The system of APAs was first introduced in Japan in 1987, followed by US in 1991. As for the rest of the countries where APA programme has been adopted, Australia initiated the programme in 1991. Subsequently, the APA programme was introduced in July 1993 in Canada, whereas New Zealand adopted APAs in 1994. After the 1995 Organisation for Economic Co-operation and Development report on transfer pricing further promoted APAs, Spain adopted it in 1995, Korea and Mexico adopted the APA system in 1997, followed by China in 1998. UK, France and the Netherlands adopted APAs in 1999, whereas Germany adopted it in 2000. The APA programme in Italy and Singapore was initiated in 2003, followed by Poland, Romania in 2006 and Portugal in 2008. In Indonesia, Sweden and Thailand APAs were first stipulated in the respective countries in 2010. In India, Nigeria and Russia, the APA programme was introduced in 2012. Vietnam introduced the APA programme in 2014, followed by Ireland in 2016. As of now, Maldives has the distinction of being the latest jurisdiction to introduce the APA Regulations with effect from 16 March 2021.

1. Chanakya, a very celebrated Indian Scholar who lived around the third century BC, in his treatise called Chanakya Neeti Shastra,[1] has *inter alia* observed as below:

> Taxation should not be a painful process for the people. There should be leniency and caution while deciding the tax structure. Ideally, governments should collect taxes like a honeybee, which sucks just the right amount of honey from the flower so that both can survive.

1. Refer Chanakya_Niti-Shastra http://www.krishnapath.org/Library/Chanakya_Niti-Shastra.pdf accessed on 11 August 2019.

The above teachings of Chanakya are perfectly imbibed in the Advance Pricing Agreement (APA) regime, wherein the taxpayers are made to agree by the Tax Administrations in advance to pay taxes for future years concerning complex matters of Transfer Pricing (TP). APA, also referred to as Advance Pricing Arrangement, in certain jurisdictions, therefore, lends benefits to both Tax Administrations and taxpayers as, on the one hand, it is a very convenient mechanism for Tax Administrations enabling tax collection without any litigation, whereas, on the other hand, the taxpayers derive tax certainty and are able to function in a non-adversarial tax regime.

2. *Definition*: The Organisation for Economic Co-operation and Development (OECD) Transfer Pricing Guidelines for Multinational Enterprises (MNEs) and Tax Administrations define[2] an APA as an arrangement that determines, in advance of controlled transactions, an appropriate set of criteria (e.g., method, comparables and appropriate adjustments thereto, critical assumptions as to future events) for the determination of the transfer pricing for those transactions over a fixed period of time.

3. *Definition*: The United Nations Practical Manual on Transfer Pricing for Developing Countries (2017) define[3] APA as an arrangement in respect of certain specified transactions that determines in advance the appropriate criteria for determining transfer pricing. The agreement may be made by the taxpayer unilaterally with the tax administration or may be a bilateral or multilateral agreement involving the tax administrations of other countries.

4. If the transfer pricing notion can be seen as an art, the APA represents an essential painting.[4] These APAs are so named because pricing methodologies are agreed in advance in relation to certain types of transactions, often called the 'covered transactions'. APAs provide greater certainty for the taxpayer on the taxation of certain cross-border transactions and are considered by the taxpayers as the safest way to avoid double taxation, especially where they are bilateral or multilateral.[5]

1.1 HISTORY OF APAs IN BRIEF

5. In the 1980s, owing to rapid development of globalization of business activities, the need to address income shifting through transactions between a corporation and its foreign related entity/entities increased. Some foreign countries had already been prepared to address such income shifting. Therefore, Japan introduced transfer pricing taxation in March 1986 to realize proper international taxation under a common

2. Refer para. 4.134 of OECD Transfer Pricing Guidelines for Multinational Enterprises and Tax Administrations (July 2017).
3. Refer Glossary of the United Nations Practical Manual on Transfer Pricing for Developing Countries (2017) accessed on 11 August 2019.
4. Refer Article by Zahra Mulachella titled 'International – Improving the Effectiveness of the International Advance Pricing Agreement Process' https://research.ibfd.org/#/doc?url=/collections/itpj/html/itpj_2018_02_int_3.html accessed on 2 September 2020.
5. Refer para. B.1.7.11 of the United Nations Practical Manual on Transfer Pricing for Developing Countries (2017) accessed on 11 August 2019.

framework with foreign countries. The system of APA was first introduced in Japan[6] in 1987, making Japan the first country in the world to implement such a procedure. It was developed to ensure proper and smooth enforcement of transfer pricing regulation.

6. The oldest concept[7] of transfer pricing itself is believed to have been introduced in the US in the early 1920s, and around the 1960s, the US tax authority (the Internal Revenue Service, or IRS) created a rule for international transactions. Since the issuance of Regulation 482 in 1968 and some regulations thereafter, the US has established its transfer pricing regulations, with the issuance of a procedural rule of the arm's-length standard and its application. Also, in 1968, the OECD commenced a study on transfer pricing, and in 1979, it produced several versions of guidelines on transfer pricing for MNEs (OECD Guidelines).[8] With regard to the transfer pricing issue, the IRS noted a tax-free transfer in some transactions and requested a comprehensive study on transfer pricing that finally resulted in a white paper in 1988, which conveyed that there was a lack of transfer pricing documentation and information available for the tax administration. Thereafter, the US IRS adopted the APA system in 1991. The US APA programme[9] began modestly and informally, but since 2000 its evolution has seen increasing levels of formality and detail highlighted by the promulgation of Revenue Procedure 2004-40, 2004-2 C.B. 50 (1 July 2004), the release of Revenue Procedure 2006-9, 2006-1 C.B. 278 (19 December 2005), the 2012 merger of the US APA programme with that portion of the office of the US competent authority (CA) that resolves transfer pricing cases under the Mutual Agreement Procedures (MAPs) of the US' bilateral income tax conventions, and the issuance of Revenue Procedure 2015-41, 2015-35 I.R.B. 263 (12 August 2015). Revenue Procedure 2015-41 is generally effective for APA requests submitted after August 2015, and while it updates and supersedes prior Revenue Procedures relating to the APA programme, it is substantively similar to its predecessors. Nevertheless, Revenue Procedure 2015-41 significantly increased APA filing requirements; its formality and the level of detail required perhaps appropriately reflecting Base Erosion and Profit Shifting (BEPS) and the other developments in international taxation, transfer pricing, and mandatory information disclosure and sharing. The increased complexity of the international tax world is also acknowledged by the Revenue Procedure's clear preference for Bilateral Advance Pricing Agreements or Arrangements (BAPAs) or Multilateral Advance Pricing Agreements or Arrangements (MAPAs), as well as the potential need to consider 'interrelated' issues and other 'coverable issues' such as CA issues arising under the business profits and associated

6. Refer APA Program Report 2007, National Tax Agency http://www.drtp.ca/wp-content/uploads/2015/02/APA_Program_Report_2007.pdf accessed on 11 August 2019.
7. Refer Article by Zahra Mulachella titled 'International – Improving the Effectiveness of the International Advance Pricing Agreement Process' https://research.ibfd.org/#/doc?url=/collections/itpj/html/itpj_2018_02_int_3.html accessed on 2 September 2020.
8. Refer OECD, Transfer Pricing and Multinational Enterprises (OECD 1979), International Organizations' Documentation IBFD.
9. Refer Article by Mark Thomas, Kristina Novak and Cym Lowell titled 'United States – Evolution of Advance Pricing Agreement Processes: Current and Future Experience in the United States' https://research.ibfd.org/#/doc?url=/collections/itpj/html/itpj_2018_02_us_1.html accessed on 2 September 2020.

enterprises (AEs) articles of US tax treaties and the determination of the income effectively connected with the conduct of a trade or business within the US.

7. The US was a party to the world's first bilateral APA in March 1991, along with Australia and Apple Computer.[10]

8. As for the rest of the countries where APA programme has been adopted, Australia initiated the programme in 1991. Subsequently, the APA programme was introduced in July 1993 in Canada, whereas New Zealand adopted APAs in 1994. After the 1995 OECD report on transfer pricing further promoted APAs, Spain adopted it in 1995, Korea and Mexico adopted the APA system in 1997, followed by China in 1998. UK, France and the Netherlands adopted APAs in 1999, whereas Germany adopted it in 2000. The APA programme in Italy and Singapore was initiated in 2003, followed by Poland, Romania in 2006 and Portugal in 2008. In Indonesia, Sweden and Thailand, APAs were first stipulated in the respective countries in 2010. In India, Nigeria and Russia, the APA programme was introduced in 2012. Vietnam introduced the APA programme in 2014, followed by Ireland in 2016. As of now, Maldives has the distinction of being the latest jurisdiction to introduce the APA Regulations with effect from 16 March 2021. The year-wise introduction of APA programme in various countries is provided in Figure 1.

10. Refer Apple Computers Australia Pty Ltd, Historic transfer pricing agreement reached between Apple Computer, the Australian Taxation Office and US Internal Revenue Service, Media Information, Frenchs Forest NSW (5 March 1991).

Figure 1 Year of Introduction of APA Programme in Various Countries

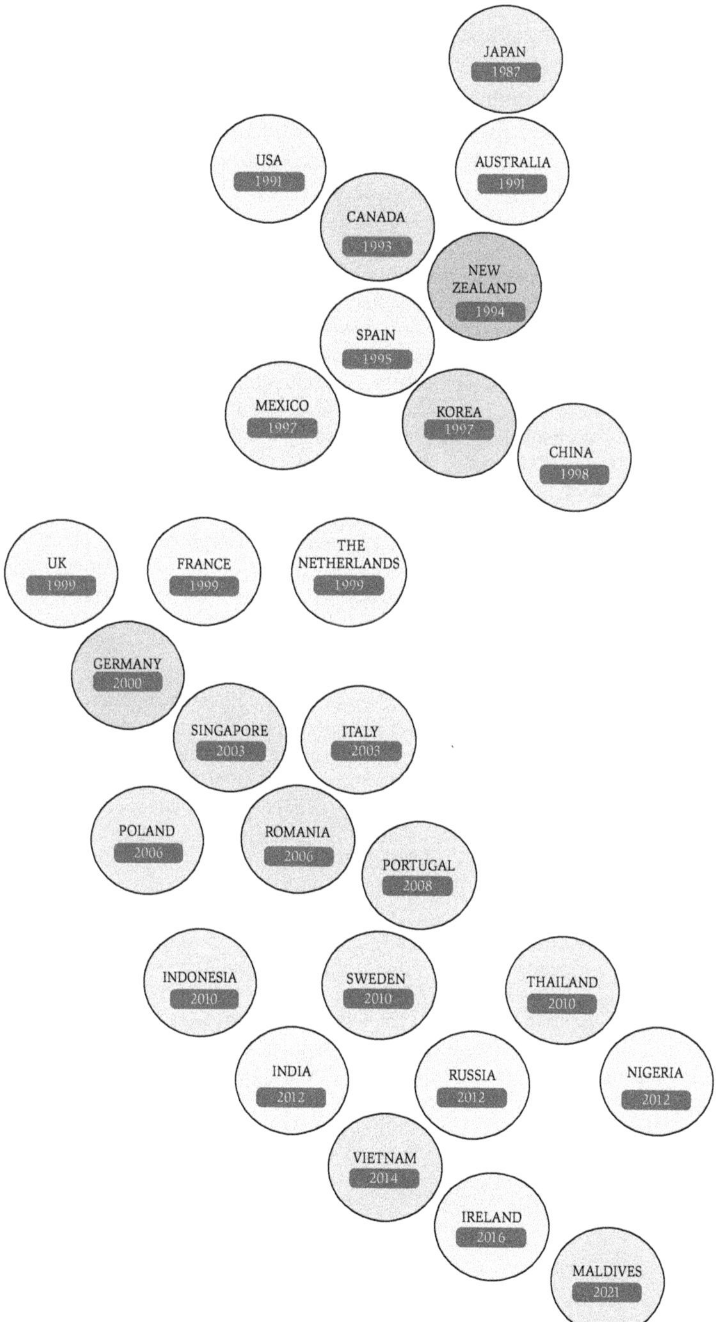

1.2 OECD'S TRANSFER PRICING GUIDELINES ISSUED IN 1995 AND 1999 (ON APAs)

9. In the chapter titled 'Administrative Approaches to Avoiding and Resolving Transfer Pricing Disputes', the OECD Transfer Pricing Guidelines, 1995[11] *inter alia* examined various administrative procedures that could be applied to minimize transfer pricing disputes and to help resolve them when they do arise between taxpayers and their tax administrations, and between different tax administrations. Among various measures, OECD *inter alia* recommended introduction of APAs. With regard to APAs, the OECD Transfer Pricing Guidelines, 1995 *inter alia* stated as below:

- An advance pricing arrangement ('APA') is an arrangement that determines, in advance of controlled transactions, an appropriate set of criteria (e.g., method, comparables and appropriate adjustments thereto) for the determination of the transfer pricing for those transactions over a fixed period of time. An APA is formally initiated by a taxpayer and requires negotiations between the taxpayer and one or more tax administrations. APAs are intended to supplement the traditional administrative, judicial, and treaty mechanisms for resolving transfer pricing issues. They may be most useful when traditional methods fail or are difficult to apply.
- APAs involving the competent authority of a treaty partner should be considered within the scope of the mutual agreement procedure in Article 25 of the OECD Model Tax Convention (MTC), even though such arrangements are not expressly mentioned there. Paragraph 3 of that Article provides that the competent authorities shall endeavour to resolve by mutual agreement any difficulties or doubts arising as to the interpretation or application of the Convention.
- At present, only a few OECD Member Countries have experience with APAs. Those countries which do have some experience seem to be satisfied so far, so that it can be expected that under the appropriate circumstances the experience with APAs will continue to expand. The success of APA programs will depend on the care taken in determining the proper degree of specificity for the arrangement based on critical assumptions, the proper administration of the program, and the presence of adequate safeguards to avoid the pitfalls, in addition to the flexibility and openness with which all parties approach the process.
- There are some continuing issues regarding the form and scope of APAs that require greater experience for full resolution and agreement among Member countries, such as the question of unilateral APAs. Whilst it is too early to make a final recommendation whether the expansion of such programmes should be encouraged, it seems likely that in certain circumstances they will aid in resolving transfer pricing disputes. The Committee on Fiscal Affairs intends to monitor carefully any expanded use of APAs and to promote greater consistency in practice among those countries that choose to use them.

11. Refer OECD's Transfer Pricing Guidelines, 1995 http://www.oecd.org/officialdocuments/publicdisplaydocumentpdf/?cote=OCDE/GD(95)31&docLanguage=En accessed on 11 August 2019.

10. In October 1999, the OECD[12] published an update to the 1995 OECD Transfer Pricing Guidelines for MNEs and Tax Administrations. This update was in the form of a new Annex to the Guidelines that provided guidance on conducting advance pricing arrangements under the Mutual Agreement Procedure (MAP APAs). The Annex became an integral part of the Guidelines as shown by the decision of the OECD Council to amend its original recommendation concerning the Guidelines in 1995 so as to incorporate the new guidance in this Annex. The OECD update of 1999 goes on to state that APA as an approach was relatively novel at the time the 1995 Guidelines were adopted by the OECD Council, and so the Committee on Fiscal Affairs stated in paragraph 4.161 of the Transfer Pricing Guidelines that it intended 'to monitor carefully any expanded use of APAs and to promote greater consistency in practice amongst those countries that choose to use them'. Further, it was stated at 4.163 of the Guidelines that, 'wherever possible, an APA should be concluded on a bilateral or multilateral basis between competent authorities through the mutual agreement procedure of the relevant treaty'. The publication of this Annex was intended as a response to both the above recommendations and was also intended to make the MAP APA process more transparent, more efficient and produce more consistent results. Further, the publication of 1999 guidance helped the efforts of the Committee on Fiscal Affairs to associate non-OECD member countries with the 1995 Guidelines.

1.3 TYPES OF APAs

11. The three types of APAs available to taxpayers are unilateral, bilateral and multilateral in nature, and taxpayers have the option to choose/apply for them at their discretion. These three types are broadly explained hereunder and in Figure 2:

(1) Unilateral APA – An APA may be unilateral involving one tax administration and a taxpayer in that jurisdiction. It is an APA in which the covered issue(s), covered method(s), and APA terms and conditions are not premised upon an underlying CA resolution.
(2) Bilateral APA – Bilateral APAs involve two tax administrations and taxpayers of the respective two jurisdictions. It is an APA in which the covered issue(s), covered method(s), and APA terms and conditions are premised on an underlying CA resolution reached between a CA and a foreign CA.
(3) Multilateral APA – Multilateral APAs involve more than two tax administrations and taxpayers of the respective jurisdictions. It is an APA in which the covered issue(s), covered method(s), and APA terms and conditions are premised on one or more underlying CA resolutions reached between a CA and more than one foreign CA.

12. Refer OECD Releases 1999 update to OECD Transfer Pricing Guidelines for Multinational Enterprises and Tax Administrations http://www.oecd.org/tax/transfer-pricing/guidelinesforapa.htm accessed on 11 August 2019.

12. For Unilateral Advance Pricing Agreements (UAPAs), there is no requirement for any underlying CA resolution; however, for BAPA and MAPA, OECD TP Guidelines 1995 provide that APAs involving the CA of a treaty partner should be considered within the scope of the MAP in Article 25 of the OECD MTC, even though such arrangements are not expressly mentioned there. Paragraph 3 of Article 25 provides that the CAs shall endeavour to resolve by mutual agreement any difficulties or doubts arising as to the interpretation or application of the Convention. In France, Germany, the Netherlands, Portugal, etc., the agreements between tax authorities defining the rules for distributing the tax base are concluded, with the primary aim of avoiding double taxation, on the basis of Article 25(3) of the OECD MTC. As a result, BAPA/MAPA can only be concluded with States with which these countries have signed a Double Taxation Avoidance Agreement (DTAA), including a provision of the type of Article 25(3) of the OECD MTC. On the other hand, there are countries like India which hold the view that provision of the type of Article 9(2) of the OECD MTC is essential for having BAPA/MAPA.

Figure 2 Characteristics of Unilateral, Bilateral and Multilateral APAs

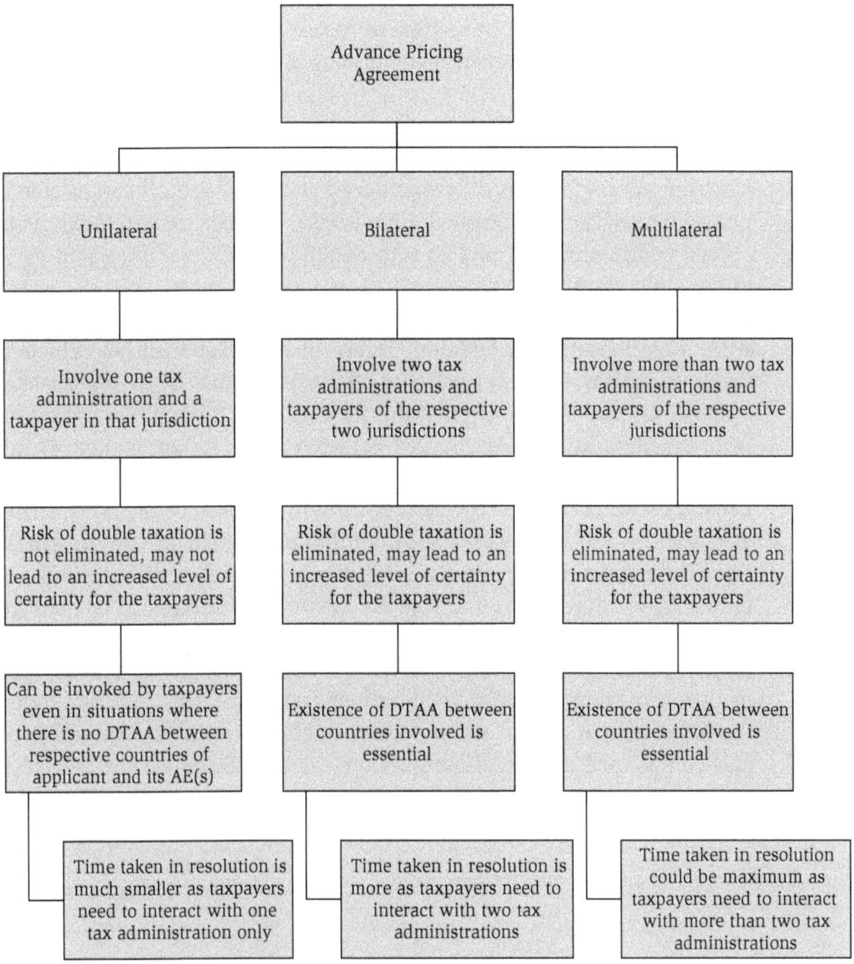

1.4 CONTENTS AND TERMS AGREED IN AN APA

13. The terms that are typically agreed between the tax administrations and the applicants in an APA are *inter alia* explained hereunder and highlighted in Figure 3:

(1) Nature of the covered transaction(s) is agreed at the outset in the APA. Covered transactions refer to the international transaction or transactions for which the APA is being entered into.

(2) Term for which the APA will be effective (including any rollback period) is clearly set out in the APA. The APA term refers to the time period consisting of all APA years. Rollback of APA refers to the applicability of the

methodology of determination of arm's-length price (ALP), or the ALP, to be applied to the international transactions which had already been entered into in a period prior to the period covered under an APA, as under certain circumstances, an APA in respect of future tax years may be rolled back and used as an appropriate transfer pricing method (TPM) for past open tax years.

(3) TPM used is agreed in the APA. It refers to the methodology by which the arm's-length principle is applied to determine the ALP of a transaction.

(4) Determination of ALP is duly mentioned in the APA. ALP means that the price charged in a controlled transaction between two related parties should be the same as that in a transaction between two unrelated parties in the open market.

(5) Details of compensating adjustments, if any, are clearly outlined in the APA. Compensating adjustment refers to an adjustment in which the taxpayer reports a transfer price for tax purposes that is, in the taxpayer's opinion, an ALP for a controlled transaction, even though this price differs from the amount actually charged between AEs. This adjustment is to be made before the tax return is filed.

(6) Critical assumptions are agreed upon by the parties to the APA. Critical assumptions are the factors and assumptions which are so critical and significant that neither party entering into an agreement will continue to be bound by the agreement if any of the factors or assumptions is changed.

(7) Taxpayer annual reporting requirements are outlined in the APA. A taxpayer that has entered into an APA is required to file an annual report demonstrating the extent of its compliance with the terms and conditions of the APA and that critical assumptions remain relevant. The Annual Report and compliance of critical assumptions by the taxpayers are duly monitored by the APA authorities.

Figure 3 Broad Terms Agreed in an APA

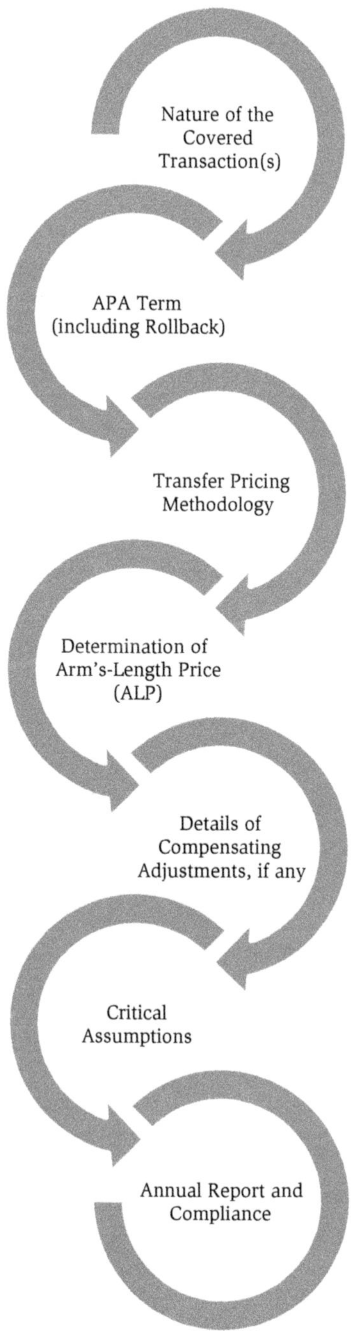

1.5 STEPS INVOLVED IN PROCESSING OF APAs

14. A striking characteristic of the APA programme across the world is that the process involved in finalization and signing of an APA is almost similar in all jurisdictions, with minor variations from country to country. Though the APA process prevalent in various countries is discussed in detail under Chapter 3, the distinct steps and stages are mentioned hereunder and in Figure 4:

(i) pre-filing stage (an optional step for applicants in certain jurisdictions);
(ii) filing of a formal APA application (as per the prescribed list of information and set of documents);
(iii) evaluation of APA application by tax jurisdictions and negotiation of APA between tax administration and an applicant for unilateral APA and between CAs involved in situations of bilateral and multilateral APAs;
(iv) formal agreement between tax administration and an applicant for unilateral APA and between CAs involved in situations of bilateral and multilateral APAs; and
(v) annual reporting and compliance of critical assumptions of an APA by the taxpayers and monitoring by the tax administrations.

Figure 4 Steps Involved in Processing of APAs

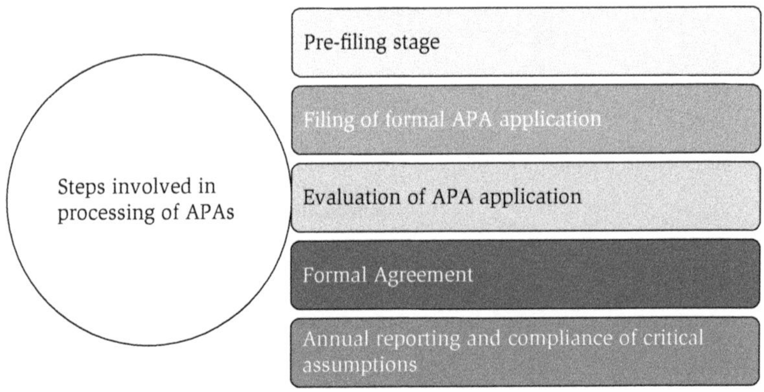

CHAPTER 2
Utility and Limitation of APAs

APAs offer a number of benefits for tax administrations and taxpayers alike and provide an opportunity for both tax administrations and taxpayers to consult and cooperate in a non-adversarial spirit and environment. APAs are an excellent dispute prevention mechanism and score over other dispute resolution mechanisms like MAP and safe harbour. As is the case in any programme, APAs come with their own share of limitations as unlike bilateral or multilateral APAs, the use of unilateral APAs may not lead to an increased level of certainty for the taxpayer involved and a reduction in economic or juridical double taxation for the MNE group.

2.1 UTILITY OF APAs

15. The key advantages[13] of APAs as stated in the United Nations Practical Manual on Transfer Pricing for Developing Countries (2017) are summarized as below:

(a) One of the key advantages of adopting an APA system is that uncertainty can be eliminated through enhancement of predictability of the taxation of international transactions. Developing countries thus have a good opportunity to obtain access to the existing documentation which is relevant to their local operations.
(b) A second advantage is that APAs can provide an opportunity for both tax administrations and taxpayers to consult and cooperate in a non-adversarial spirit and environment.
(c) As a third advantage, an APA may prevent costly and time-consuming examinations and litigation of major transfer pricing issues for taxpayers and tax administrations.

---

13. Refer para. B.8.10.2 of the United Nations Practical Manual on Transfer Pricing for Developing Countries (2017).

(d) Fourth, the disclosure and information aspects of an APA programme as well as the cooperative attitude under which an APA can be negotiated may assist tax administrations in gaining insight into complex international transactions undertaken by MNEs.

16. The key advantages[14] of APAs as stated in the OECD Transfer Pricing Guidelines (2017) are summarized as below:

(a) An APA programme can assist taxpayers by eliminating uncertainty through enhancing the predictability of tax treatment in international transactions. Provided the critical assumptions are met, an APA can provide the taxpayers involved with certainty in the tax treatment of the transfer pricing issues covered by the APA for a specified period of time. In some cases, an APA may also provide an option to extend the period of time to which it applies. When the term of an APA expires, the opportunity may also exist for the relevant tax administrations and taxpayers to renegotiate the APA. Because of the certainty provided by an APA, a taxpayer may be in a better position to predict its tax liabilities, thereby providing a tax environment that is favourable for investment.
(b) APAs can provide an opportunity for both tax administrations and taxpayers to consult and cooperate in a non-adversarial spirit and environment. The opportunity to discuss complex tax issues in a less confrontational atmosphere than in a transfer pricing examination can stimulate a free flow of information among all parties involved for the purpose of coming to a legally correct and practicably workable result. The non-adversarial environment may also result in a more objective review of the submitted data and information than may occur in a more adversarial context (e.g., litigation). The close consultation and cooperation required between the tax administrations in an APA programme also lead to closer relations with treaty partners on transfer pricing issues.
(c) An APA may prevent costly and time-consuming examinations and litigation of major transfer pricing issues for taxpayers and tax administrations. Once an APA has been agreed, fewer resources may be needed for subsequent examination of the taxpayer's return because more information is known about the taxpayer. The APA process itself may also present time savings for both taxpayers and tax administrations over the time that would be spent in a conventional examination.
(d) Bilateral and multilateral APAs substantially reduce or eliminate the possibility of juridical or economic double or non-taxation since all the relevant countries participate. By contrast, unilateral APAs do not provide certainty in the reduction of double taxation because tax administrations affected by the transactions covered by the APA may consider that the methodology adopted

14. Refer Part F.3 under Chapter IV of the OECD Transfer Pricing Guidelines (2017).

does not give a result consistent with the arm's-length principle. In addition, bilateral and multilateral APAs can enhance the MAP by significantly reducing the time needed to reach an agreement since CAs are dealing with current data as opposed to prior-year data that may be difficult and time-consuming to produce.

(e) The disclosure and information aspects of an APA programme as well as the cooperative attitude under which an APA can be negotiated may assist tax administrations in gaining insight into complex international transactions undertaken by MNEs. An APA programme can improve knowledge and understanding of highly technical and factual circumstances in areas such as global trading and the tax issues involved. The development of specialist skills that focus on particular industries or specific types of transactions will enable tax administrations to give better service to other taxpayers in similar circumstances. Through an APA programme, tax administrations have access to useful industry data and analysis of pricing methodologies in a cooperative environment.

17. Benefits of APA programme recorded by some countries are as below:

(a) In Australia,[15] APAs are negotiated in a cooperative environment in which the Australian Taxation Office (ATO), the taxpayer and the tax treaty partner in a bilateral APA use best endeavours to agree on a TPM that will result in what will be treated as an arm's-length amount of consideration or profits to each related party in relation to their international related party dealings. An APA:
- provides a taxpayer with certainty on an appropriate TPM, enhancing the predictability of the tax treatment of the taxpayer's international related party dealings;
- eliminates or substantially reduces the risk of double taxation arising from international related party dealings (particularly where the APA is bilateral);
- is prospective, but methodologies under an APA may be used subject to agreement, to resolve issues in years prior to the APA. For example, a taxpayer may seek an APA following a risk review but prior to an audit commencing, and the APA methodology may be agreed to be applied to years that would otherwise be subject to audit;
- provides a possible solution to situations where there is no realistic alternative way of both avoiding double taxation and ensuring that all profits are correctly determined and taxed at the appropriate time;
- provides taxpayers with a more flexible approach to obtaining approval for a novel methodology that is particularly appropriate to their circumstances;

15. Refer PS LA, Australia https://www.ato.gov.au/law/view/document?docid=PSR/PS20111/NAT/ATO/00001#P6 accessed on 11 August 2019.

- reduces compliance cost to the taxpayer by eliminating the risk of transfer pricing risk review or audit and the imposition of penalties by taking a different practical approach to the application of the arm's-length principle;
- reduces the record-keeping burden as taxpayers know in advance which records are required to be kept to substantiate the application of the APA approach to ascertaining pricing or profits relating to the covered international related party dealings;
- allows a taxpayer to predict costs and expenses, including tax liabilities more accurately.

(b) In Canada,[16] APA benefits include long-term time savings, efficient resolution of recurring complex matters, greater certainty about transfer pricing issues, potential application of findings to past years, and the minimization of global risk.

(c) In France,[17] the benefits of APA are stated to be as below:

> The objective of the prior agreement procedure is to constitute an instrument of legal certainty. The prior transfer pricing agreement stabilizes the fiscal environment for multinational companies. It gives French or foreign companies who so wish the opportunity to obtain from the tax authorities an agreement on the method for determining the transfer pricing which will apply to their future intra-group transactions. This system is intended to apply in particular when the implementation of the arm's length principles poses significant problems of reliability and accuracy or when the specific conditions in which transactions are carried out are unusually complex. It enables preventive resolution of the difficulties encountered by multinational companies while ensuring that the method adopted in compliance with tax legislation complies with the principles applicable in terms of OECD TP Guidelines. Given its bilateral nature, the prior agreement eliminates the risk of double taxation while preserving the tax base of the States which are parties to the agreement.

(d) In Germany,[18] tax authorities conduct APA procedures, the intention being to reach mutual agreements if possible, in order to resolve in advance potential disputes on transfer prices arising between enterprises and the various countries' tax authorities, and to avoid the twofold financial burden or double taxation (respectively) they threaten to cause. APAs aim to achieve greater legal certainty for businesses and greater efficiency in transfer pricing audits.

16. Refer IC 94-4R dated 16 March 2001 https://www.canada.ca/en/revenue-agency/services/forms-publications/publications/ic94-4/international-transfer-pricing-advance-pricing.html accessed on 9 February 2021.
17. Refer Administrative Guidelines https://bofip.impots.gouv.fr/bofip/1053-PGP.html/identifiant=BOI-SJ-RES-20-10-20180718 accessed on 11 August 2020.
18. Refer Ministry of Finance Ordinance of 5 October 2006 – Information on Bi or multilateral mutual agreement procedures under double taxation agreements for reaching Advance Pricing Agreements ('APA') in Germany https://www.oecd.org/ctp/dispute/47655669.pdf accessed on 11 August 2020.

(e) In Ireland,[19] the benefits of the APA programme are stated as below:

- A bilateral APA provides certainty to taxpayers that, as long as the terms and conditions of the APA are satisfied, the transfer pricing issues covered by the APA will not be subject to audit adjustments by the tax authorities of either country which is party to the APA.
- The purpose of an APA is to prevent disputes between a tax administration and the taxpayer with respect to the specific transaction(s) covered by the APA and to avert the risk of double taxation or taxation not in accordance with the relevant double tax treaty. An APA provides taxpayers with certainty about their TPMs and may prevent examinations and litigation of major transfer pricing issues that would be costly and time-consuming for both taxpayers and tax administrations. It also provides an opportunity for tax administrations and taxpayers to cooperate with each other in a non-adversarial environment.

(f) New Zealand[20] recognizes the following benefits in its APA programme:

> Advance pricing agreements have proven extremely useful as a robust upfront means of dealing with transfer pricing risk, especially the more complex issues that arise. APAs lock in compliant outcomes by agreeing on the criteria for transfer prices in advance of transactions occurring. They can eliminate the need for potentially costly post-lodgement reviews and audits. They are not only a faster and clearer route to multilateral tax certainty, but also give the wider community more confidence in the compliance of MNEs.

(g) In Singapore,[21] the benefits of seeking APAs include:

- APAs may provide an efficient and effective way to resolve transfer pricing issues through intergovernment negotiation and cooperation between taxpayers and CAs;
- APAs provide certainty through prescribed guidance on the determination of acceptable transfer prices between related parties;
- rollback of APAs relieves double taxation occurring in the audited FYs when an agreement on the appropriate transfer pricing adjustments is reached between Inland Revenue Authority of Singapore (IRAS) and the relevant foreign CA;
- bilateral and multilateral APAs eliminate double taxation risks when taxpayers comply with the APA terms and conditions agreed between IRAS and the relevant foreign CAs; and
- APAs avoid lengthy transfer pricing audits and penalty payments.

19. Refer Ireland's Bilateral Advance Pricing Agreement Guidelines 2016, Part 35-02-07 https://www.revenue.ie/en/tax-professionals/tdm/income-tax-capital-gains-tax-corporation-tax/part-35/35-02-07.pdf accessed on 19 March 2021.
20. Refer New Zealand – Compliance Focus – 2019 https://www.ird.govt.nz/-/media/project/ir/home/documents/international/multinational-enterprises---compliance-focus-documents/compliance-focus---2019.pdf accessed on 6 March 2021.
21. Refer IRAS e-Tax Guide: Transfer Pricing Guidelines (Fifth Edition), section 8.28 https://www.iras.gov.sg/irashome/uploadedFiles/IRASHome/e-Tax_Guides/etaxguide_Income%20Tax_Transfer%20Pricing%20Guidelines_5th.pdf accessed on 09/08/2019.

(h) In Thailand,[22] objective of APAs is stated to avoid any potential disputes, or problems of double taxation caused by transfer pricing reassessment, for which the taxpayer may apply for bilateral APA in order to:
    - ensure APA is consistent with the Revenue Code;
    - avoid and eliminate double taxation according to Double Tax Agreements signed between Thailand and other jurisdictions;
    - prevent tax avoidance and evasion;
    - enhance knowledge and understanding between the taxpayer and the tax authority;
    - indicate certain tax liabilities.

(i) In US,[23] the APA Program is designed to resolve actual or potential transfer pricing disputes in a principled, cooperative manner, as an alternative to the traditional adversarial process. An APA is a binding contract between the IRS and a taxpayer by which the IRS agrees not to seek a transfer pricing adjustment under IRC § 482 for a covered transaction if the taxpayer files its tax return for a covered year consistent with the agreed TPM. The main advantages of APAs are controlling risk and increasing predictability.

(j) In Vietnam,[24] the benefits of seeking APAs are stated to be to improve the effectiveness of tax management, reduce the cost of compliance to tax law, determine market prices in related transactions that suit the nature of the business, generate profits in order to pay income tax, prevent double taxation and fiscal evasion, and minimize disputes over market prices in related party transactions.

18. At ground level, after interacting with numerous APA applicants, in addition to the above-mentioned benefits, the following benefits are also observed:

(a) *Expert members in APA team*: Taxpayers feel assured when APA teams comprise of experts in various field like law, statistics and economics, as against Transfer Pricing Officers (TPOs) who are relatively less experienced. APAs give global insight to solve complex problems of transfer pricing arising out of international transactions.

(b) *Easy for the start-up enterprises*: APAs may be particularly helpful in the case of start-up enterprises. Start-up enterprises require set-up time in the initial phase of business. So, in the initial years, it may end up in making very low profit or even losses. It will be a hardship for the taxpayer if a transfer pricing adjustment is imposed on the enterprise on the criteria that the transaction is

22. Refer Thailand's Guidance on APA process https://www.rd.go.th/publish/fileadmin/download/GUIDANCE-ON-APA-PROCESS-EN.pdf accessed on 26 March 2021.
23. Refer USTransferPricing.com http://www.ustransferpricing.com/APA.html accessed on 11 August 2019.
24. Refer para. 2 of Article 5 of Circular No. 201/2013/TT-BTC https://vanbanphapluat.co/circular-no-201-2013-tt-btc-application-of-advance-pricing-agreements-to-tax-administration accessed on 26 March 2021.

not at arm's length. APA can address this situation by including a provision of term test. Term test refers to testing of an international transaction over a period of time rather than examining it on a year-to-year basis. This relieves the taxpayer from the hassles of transfer pricing compliance for every year and from potential litigations.

(c) *APAs encourage free flow of trade, investment and technologies*: On having attained certainty on tax front through APAs, Multinational Corporations (MNCs) are encouraged to augment worldwide trade and invest in developing economies. This is evident on perusal of a variety of articles as below:

(i) In an article[25] published in *BusinessLine* on the signing of three more unilateral APAs in India, it was stated that:

> The signing of these three APAs underscores the success of the programme in India as a dispute resolution mechanism. APAs show that the government is keen to reduce litigation and improve the environment for investment.

(ii) In an article[26] titled 'How advance pricing agreement helps India-Singapore business ties' published in *liveMint*, it was *inter alia* stated as below:

> Businesses have also accepted the APA programme as an effective tool to avoid protracted litigation, resolve complex transfer pricing issues and obtain certainty on the transfer pricing front. Companies in Singapore having their presence in India can use the APA as a remedial measure to avoid tax disputes and concentrate their time and resources in efficiently conducting their business.

(iii) In an article[27] published in *Financial Express* titled 'Advance pricing agreement: Certainty in uncertain times', it was *inter alia* stated as below:

> The government stands to gain through reduced disputes, redirection of scarce administration resources, collecting their fair share of tax and boosting the country's attractiveness to investors by providing a definite and predictable policy regime.

25. Article published on 3 April 2015 http://www.thehindubusinessline.com/economy/cbdt-signs-3-more-advance-pricing-agreements/article7065018.ece accessed on 11 August 2019.
26. Refer Article authored by Vikas Vasal, Grant Thornton India. Updated: 16 March 2018 https://www.livemint.com/Opinion/wsAuF2Ea39oCEfmz6JpdEO/How-advance-pricing-agreement-helps-India-Singapore-business.html accessed on 11 August 2019.
27. Refer Article by Ashwin Vishwanathan published on 17 December 2020 titled 'Advance pricing agreement: Certainty in uncertain times' https://www.financialexpress.com/opinion/advance-pricing-agreement-certainty-in-uncertain-times/2151462/ accessed on 20 February 2021.

(iv) In an article[28] published in CMS Law-Now, Poland titled 'The legislative amendment creates new opportunities for using advance pricing agreement (APA) solution and offers a chance for quicker resolution of disputes relating to double taxation in Poland', it was *inter alia* stated as below:

> An application for an APA decision can be submitted by a foreign investor planning investment in Poland.

(v) In an article[29] published in Lexology, Indonesia titled 'Advance pricing agreements in Indonesia', it was *inter alia* stated as below:

> The advantages of an APA can include:
> - reducing the uncertainty and enhanced predictability arising from related-party transactions conducted in the future;
> - providing certainty concerning the transfer pricing method to be applied to particular transactions;
> - lowering the ongoing compliance costs and reporting requirements once the APA has been agreed;
> - reducing the risk of double taxation, especially in the case of BAPAs;
> - avoiding costly and time-consuming litigation or examinations;
> - a better understanding of the business on the part of the DGT; and
> - the opportunity to establish or improve relationship with the DGT in a non-adversarial environment.

19. The various benefits of APA programme are summarized in Figure 5.

28. Refer Article published on 29 November 2019 titled 'The legislative amendment creates new opportunities for using advance pricing agreement (APA) solution and offers a chance for quicker resolution of disputes relating to double taxation in Poland' https://www.cms-lawnow.com/ealerts/2019/11/the-legislative-amendment-creates-new-opportunities?cc_lang=en accessed on 20 February 2021.
29. Refer Article published on 9 September 2019 titled 'Advance Pricing Agreements in Indonesia' https://www.lexology.com/library/detail.aspx?g=6e1910bb-5612-480b-a4b9-92b4b9412c82 accessed on 20 February 2021.

Figure 5 Benefits of APA Programme

Enhancement of predictability of the taxation of cross-border international transactions among associate enterprises.	Foster non-adversarial spirit and environment between tax administration and taxpayers.	Prevent costly and time-consuming examinations and litigation of major transfer pricing issues.
Assist tax administrations in gaining insight into complex international transactions undertaken by MNEs.	Taxpayers are in a better position to predict their tax liabilities, thereby providing a tax environment that is favourable for investment.	Bilateral and multilateral APAs substantially reduce or eliminate the possibility of juridical or economic double or non-taxation since all the relevant countries participate.
Provides taxpayers with a more flexible approach to obtain approval for a novel methodology that is particularly appropriate to their circumstances.	Reduces the record-keeping burden as taxpayers know in advance which records are required to be kept to substantiate the application of the APA approach.	Rollback of APAs relieves double taxation occurring in the past audited years when an agreement on the appropriate transfer pricing adjustments is reached between tax administration and taxpayers.
APAs may be particularly helpful in case of start-up enterprises which require set up time in initial phase of business. APAs can address this situation by including a provision of term test.	APAs encourage free flow of trade, investment and technologies.	Tax administrations stand to gain through reduced disputes, redirection of scarce administration resources and collecting their fair share of tax.

2.2 APAs AND OTHER DISPUTE RESOLUTION MECHANISMS

20. While APAs are part of dispute prevention mechanism, taxpayers have the option to choose dispute resolution mechanisms like MAP. Taxpayers may also opt for safe harbour rules which provide circumstances in which eligible taxpayers may elect to follow a simple set of prescribed transfer pricing rules in connection with clearly and carefully defined transactions, or may be exempted from the application of the general transfer pricing rules. A comparative study of these procedures is conducted hereunder.

2.2.1 APA Versus MAP

21. MAP derives its legal basis and application through Article 25 of the DTAAs. In certain situations, as stated below, taxpayers find taking recourse to APAs is more beneficial than taking the MAP route:

(a) In a MAP process initiated by the taxpayers, CAs interact through Article 25 of the DTAA and post discussions, they enter into an agreement first, and thereafter, they inform the taxpayers about the agreement so reached. Hence, at that stage, the taxpayers have no other option but to either accept or reject the proposal. However, in the APA process, the taxpayers are constantly engaged with the CAs and any agreement reached is well within their knowledge and has their tacit consent. Thus, under APA, the taxpayers are generally well informed about the status of their cases.

(b) MAP is invoked by taxpayers only after completion of tax audits, following which; tax demand is raised by tax authorities which puts an additional burden on the former. On the other hand, APAs apply to the future years, i.e., before tax audits are even started (with an added option for rollback at the discretion of taxpayers), which provides tax certainty to taxpayers in advance.

(c) Taxpayers apply for MAP for completed tax audits which generally relate to very few years, whereas APAs apply to up to five future years and rollback years, as well (at the discretion of taxpayers). Thus, most of the times, APAs allow more years to be covered as a dispute prevention mechanism vis-à-vis MAP proceedings.

(d) There is another dimension to APAs involving unilateral APAs (UAPA), which can be invoked by taxpayers even in situations where there is no DTAA between countries involved. MAP proceedings are impossible to apply when there is no DTAA between countries involved.

(e) Further, time taken in resolution of UAPAs is much smaller (as taxpayers need to interact with one tax administration only) in comparison to resolutions expected through MAP (as it may involve series of interactions between CAs of countries involved to reach an understanding), which may prompt taxpayers to adopt UAPAs more often.

2.2.2 APA Versus Safe Harbour

22. Safe harbour refers to circumstances in which eligible taxpayers may elect to follow a simple set of prescribed transfer pricing rules in connection with clearly and carefully defined transactions, or may be exempted from the application of the general transfer pricing rules. In the former case, prices established under such rules would be automatically accepted by the tax administrations that have expressly adopted such rules. These elective provisions are often referred to as 'safe harbor'.[30] Safe harbour has some inherent deficiencies which can be overcome by applying APAs instead. Factors which make APAs score over safe harbour are briefly discussed hereunder:

(i) A safe harbour might require the use of a particular method when the taxpayer could otherwise have determined that another method was the most appropriate method under the facts and circumstances. Such an occurrence could be considered as inconsistent with the arm's-length principle, which requires the use of the most appropriate method. On the other hand, adoption of arm's-length principle is the core principle in APAs, as in APAs, one can identify the most appropriate method; arrive at an appropriate Profit Level Indicator (PLI)/margin for each international transaction separately.

(ii) Safe harbours involve a trade-off between strict compliance with the arm's-length principle and administrability. They are not tailored to fit exactly the varying facts and circumstances of individual taxpayers and transactions. This challenge is overcome by applying APAs instead.

(iii) Tax administrations may also be concerned over the ability of taxpayers to opt in and out of a safe harbour, depending on whether the use of the safe harbour is favourable to the taxpayer in a particular year. This gives unpredictability to application of safe harbour route over a longer period of time. On the other hand, APAs provide enough predictability on revenue stream to the tax administrations, as the APA period(s) in most countries range up to five years at a stretch (with an option for rollback), with an added option for renewal (at the discretion of taxpayers).

(iv) One major concern raised by a safe harbour is that it may increase the risk of double taxation and double non-taxation, whereas, under bilateral and multilateral APAs, these risks get subdued and eliminated.

(v) Preferential tax treatment under safe harbour regimes for a specific category of taxpayers potentially entails discrimination and competitive distortions. This is evident in certain cases involving specific international transactions with turnover restrictions getting covered under safe harbour. This discrimination is best avoided by applying APAs as generally all types of international transactions with no turnover restrictions get covered under this regime.

2.3 LIMITATIONS OF APAs

23. As is the case with any programme, APAs come with their own share of limitations. Some of them are discussed hereunder:

30. Refer para. 4.101 of OECD Transfer Pricing Guidelines for Multinational Enterprises and Tax Administrations (July 2017).

(a) In unilateral APAs, the risk of potential double taxation remains given that the methodology agreed by the taxpayer with the tax administration of a country may not necessarily be accepted by the counterparty tax administration. This risk may increase after the unilateral APAs are exchanged with the tax administration of counterparty based on the minimum agreed standards in relation to Action 5[31] Report of the OECD/G20 BEPS Project.
(b) There is no time limit for renewal of APA. The APA scheme in most jurisdictions has come out with the renewal procedures but does not specify any time limit for the completion of the renewal process. Instead, the scheme in most jurisdictions rolls out similar procedures for renewal (except, e.g., in Germany & US where the tax authorities may permit the submission of an abbreviated APA request) as at the time of entering into the original agreement. This leads to consumption of additional time and efforts of the taxpayer.
(c) There are some restrictions regarding granting the benefit of the rollback of the APA. One such limitation is in regard to non-availability of the rollback in respect of an international transaction for a rollback year if the determination of ALP of the said international transaction for the said year has been the subject matter of an appeal before the Appellate Tribunal and the Appellate Tribunal has passed an order disposing of such appeal at any time before signing of the agreement, as is the case in India.
(d) A sudden downturn in business may lead to violation of critical assumptions. APAs, if not implemented in the right manner, may dilute the advantages associated to it. The fulcrum of the entire mechanism lies on the critical assumptions regarding the future market conditions in determination of the price. If the assumptions are not precise it may result in much hassle for both the taxpayers and the tax authorities. For instance, in the event of an economic slowdown, the determination of ALPs by the methods determined by the APA may not show proper results. Consider a situation where there is significant change in the economic characterization of the taxpayer. This may render the methods agreed in APA redundant. Either existing APA shall need to be revised or a new APA would need to be entered into. This may lead to additional cost and compliance issues for the taxpayer and may result in outflow of substantial resources, time and money. Unfortunately, this situation has occurred recently as with margins under pressure due to COVID-19-led business discontinuity, multinationals are looking to exit or renegotiate APAs. Many multinationals and captive centres of MNEs have reached out to tax experts seeking a legal opinion on how they can exit or renegotiate APAs signed with tax authorities.[32]

31. Refer BEPS Action 5 Report https://read.oecd-ilibrary.org/taxation/countering-harmful-tax-practices-more-effectively-taking-into-account-transparency-and-substance-action-5-2015-final-report_9789264241190-en#page1 accessed on 11 August 2019.
32. Refer Article published on 29 April 2020 titled 'Covid 19 impact: MNCs look to exit, renegotiate APAs' https://economictimes.indiatimes.com/news/company/corporate-trends/mncs-look-to-exit-renegotiate-apas/articleshow/75436398.cms?from=mdr accessed on 20 February 2021.

(e) Confidentiality concerning trade secrets, customer list, market strategies, R&D, innovation in technologies, etc. is at risk of disclosure/leakage, as APA involves sharing of lot of confidential and strategic information with tax authorities.

(f) In February 2014,[33] the European Commission (EC) notified three Member States that the Commission was launching investigations to determine whether their tax authorities had provided illegal State aid to an MNE through an APA. The notified governments and MNEs were Ireland (Apple), the Netherlands (Starbucks), and Luxembourg (Fiat). The EC notifications argued, however, that these APAs had been used for a different purpose: to stretch the law and provide a tax benefit to a specific MNE by artificially lowering its taxable profits and its tax payments. A tax benefit received by a firm from a European Union (EU) Member State, if the benefit provides a specific and discriminatory advantage to the firm, is considered a fiscal subsidy that is illegal under EU competition policy. After investigating the cases, the EC concluded in all three cases that the APA did constitute illegal State aid and demanded that the tax benefit be repaid. As of August 2018, the EC had three open investigations of State aid involving APAs granted to IKEA by the Netherlands (EC, 2017b, 18 December), McDonald's by Luxembourg (EC, 2015, 3 December), and Gibraltar companies without an adequate evaluation to grant tax exemption (EC, 2017c, 26 October). The EC has determined that State aid was provided and ordered recovery of the aid in six closed investigations involving APAs: Apple by Ireland (EC, 2016c), Starbucks by the Netherlands (EC, 2015b), Fiat Finance and Trade by Luxembourg (EC, 2015a), Amazon by Luxembourg (EC, 2017a), Engie (formerly GDF Suez) by Luxembourg (EC, 2018), and Belgian taxpayers under the Belgian 'excess profit' tax ruling system (EC, 2016b).

24. The key disadvantages[34] of APAs as stated in the OECD Transfer Pricing Guidelines (2017) are summarized as below:

(a) Unlike bilateral or multilateral APAs, the use of unilateral APAs may not lead to an increased level of certainty for the taxpayer involved and a reduction in economic or juridical double taxation for the MNE group. If the taxpayer accepts an arrangement that over-allocates income to the country entering into the APA in order to avoid lengthy and expensive transfer pricing enquiries or excessive penalties, the administrative burden shifts from the country providing the APA to other tax jurisdictions.

(b) A problem with a unilateral APA is the issue of unavailability of corresponding adjustments.

33. Refer Article titled 'Transfer pricing and state aid: the unintended consequences of advance pricing agreements' (Authors: Lorraine Eden and William Byrnes) https://unctad.org/en/PublicationChapters/diae2018d4a3.pdf accessed on 11 August 2019.

34. Refer Part F.4 under Chapter IV of the OECD Transfer Pricing Guidelines (2017).

(c) Another possible disadvantage would arise if an APA involved an unreliable prediction on changing market conditions without adequate critical assumptions. To avoid the risk of double taxation, it is necessary for an APA programme to remain flexible because a static APA may not satisfactorily reflect arm's-length conditions.
(d) An APA programme may initially place a strain on transfer pricing audit resources, as tax administrations will generally have to divert resources earmarked for other purposes (e.g., examination, advising, litigation, etc.) to the APA programme.
(e) Care should therefore be taken with interpreting the results of previously concluded APAs as being representative across all markets.
(f) The balance of compliance resources may be particularly difficult to achieve since an APA programme tends to require highly experienced and often specialized staff.
(g) The taxpayer must provide detailed information relating to its transfer pricing and satisfy any other requirements imposed for the verification of compliance with the terms and conditions of the APA. At the same time, the taxpayer is not sheltered from normal and routine examinations by the tax administration on other issues. An APA also does not shelter a taxpayer from examination of its transfer pricing activities. The taxpayer may still have to establish that it has complied in good faith with the terms and conditions of the APA, that the material representations in the APA remain valid, that the supporting data used in applying the methodology were correct, that the critical assumptions underlying the APA are still valid and are applied consistently, and that the methodology is applied consistently.
(h) An APA programme cannot be used by all taxpayers because the procedure can be expensive and time-consuming and small taxpayers generally may not be able to afford it. This is especially true if independent experts are involved. APAs may therefore only assist in resolving mainly large transfer pricing cases. In addition, the resource implications of an APA programme may limit the number of requests a tax administration can entertain.

CHAPTER 3
APA Programme Across the Globe

The worldwide APA programmes are discussed in detail in respect of twenty-five jurisdictions, namely, Australia, Canada, China, France, Germany, India, Indonesia, Ireland, Japan, Korea, Mexico, the Netherlands, New Zealand, Nigeria, Poland, Portugal, Romania, Russia, Singapore, Spain, Sweden, Thailand, UK, US and Vietnam. A striking feature noticed in the APA regime in various countries is that the procedures and provisions are similar in most countries with minor variations. The discussions highlight that APAs have progressed fairly well in a majority of these countries and provide a fair idea about the evolution of APA regime.

3.1 DISCUSSION ON APA REGIMES IN VARIOUS COUNTRIES

25. The primary focus of this treatise is to understand the history, structure, progress made and future of APA regimes across the globe. Apart from availability of unilateral APAs in most countries, tax administrations prefer entering into bilateral and multilateral APAs (bilateral and multilateral APAs substantially reduce or eliminate the possibility of juridical or economic double or non-taxation since all the relevant countries participate); hence, it is expedient to understand the worldwide APA programmes in detail. Such discussions have been made in this chapter in respect of the following jurisdictions, which offers a fair mix of developed and developing countries, and most importantly, the APAs have progressed fairly well in a majority of these countries, so as to provide a fair idea about the evolution of APA regime:

(1) Australia
(2) Canada
(3) China
(4) France
(5) Germany
(6) India

(7) Indonesia
(8) Ireland
(9) Japan
(10) Korea
(11) Mexico
(12) The Netherlands
(13) New Zealand
(14) Nigeria
(15) Poland
(16) Portugal
(17) Romania
(18) Russia
(19) Singapore
(20) Spain
(21) Sweden
(22) Thailand
(23) UK
(24) US
(25) Vietnam

3.2 APA REGIME IN AUSTRALIA

26. The relevant provisions governing the APA regime in Australia[35] are contained in Law Administration Practice Statement 2015/4 (PS LA 2015/4)[36] and guidance issued from time to time. The CA in charge of the APA programme in Australia is ATO. According to PS LA 2015/4, requests are more likely to be accepted if transfer pricing issues are complex; there is reasonable uncertainty as to how transfer pricing rules are to apply to the facts of the case and there is a high probability of double taxation without an APA. Thus, the ATO may be less likely to enter into an APA where one or more of the following indicators are present:

- the actual conditions are simple or routine with arm's-length conditions being relatively certain;
- the value of the cross-border dealings is not material;
- the cross-border dealings to be covered by the APA are only a small portion in terms of value of the total cross-border dealings;
- the proposed APA would not ensure there is alignment between true economic activity and profit outcomes in Australia;

35. Refer DLA Piper – APA and MAP Country Guide 2019 https://www.dlapiper.com/en/us/insights/publications/2019/03/apa-and-map-country-guide-2019/ accessed on 11 August 2020.
36. Refer ATO-PS LA 2015/4 https://www.ato.gov.au/law/view/document?DocID = PSR/PS20154/NAT/ATO/00001&PiT = 99991231235958#P21.

- collateral issues exist that affect the ATO's ability to enter into the proposed APA;
- the arrangements that are the subject of the proposed APA appear to lack commerciality or be primarily tax-driven. For example, the proposed APA covers activities which involve structures, restructuring or 'greenfields arrangements', where the commercial benefits to the Australian entity are questionable.

27. Unilateral, bilateral, and multilateral APAs are available in Australia, and the critical dates negotiated with the ATO during the early engagement stage (i.e., pre-filing stage) will determine the date from which the APA will commence. There is a five-year maximum term for an APA. There is no filing fee under the Australian APA regime.

3.2.1 Rollback

28. Decisions on availability of rollback of APA are made by the ATO on a risk assessment basis.

3.2.2 APA Team

29. According to PS LA 2015/4, ATO officials, who effectively form a multidisciplinary team, contribute to the development of APAs. In performing their role, each staff member is required to focus on using a pragmatic approach to develop an APA. Entering into an APA not only enables all parties to mitigate potential transfer pricing risks but also delivers mutual benefits such as cost savings and enhanced relationships over the term of the APA.

30. The APA team leader has overall responsibility for the APA request. Specific roles and responsibilities of the APA team leader include:

- analysing the APA proposal and seeking further information to support the APA request in the early engagement stage, if required;
- communicating the ATO position, reasoning and status of the APA application to the taxpayer;
- determining if a flexible approach to the APA process is appropriate and developing a tailored APA case plan for the early engagement and APA application stages;
- being accountable for the APA team actively managing the request and application, ensuring milestones, time frames and assurance and reporting requirements are met;
- involving and coordinating the input of technical specialists or other senior ATO staff, as required;
- undertaking analysis and evaluation of the taxpayer's APA request or application, including performing a functional analysis;

- requesting quality assurance (QA) panels, as required, to consider the progress of the APA request;
- developing the negotiation parameters subsequent to the recommendation of the QA panel;
- negotiating the terms and conditions of unilateral APAs with the taxpayer and assisting the CA in negotiations of bilateral APAs, within the set parameters;
- providing written justification to the QA panel where the APA team leader has decided not to follow the QA panel's recommendation and this decision has been approved by the relevant APA team's Assistant Commissioner;
- coordinating the resolution of collateral issues with the APA process;
- drafting the content of the APA agreement for signing by the CA.

31. The APA team performs the day-to-day activities of developing the APA. The members of the team assist the APA team leader in carrying out the tasks involved in developing an APA.

32. An economist from the ATO's Economist Practice assists the APA team leader, the APA team and, where applicable, the CA to critically analyse whether the taxpayer's proposed actual conditions are likely to be consistent with arm's-length conditions. More specifically, an economist may assist by:

- evaluating the related party transactions in the context of the taxpayer's business, industry and global value chain;
- analysing the arrangement's important functions, assets and risks and other factors of comparability that may affect arm's-length conditions;
- advising on the TPM (and its application) that best achieves consistency with the OECD Guidelines;
- where necessary, selecting and applying the most appropriate TPM and performing related benchmarking analyses;
- identifying any other economic aspects that may affect the alignment of a taxpayer's Australian economic activity with its profit outcomes.

The extent of involvement of an economist is determined on a case-by-case basis in accordance with PS LA 2013/2 Economic Advice and the Economist Practice.

33. The CA is authorized to enter into a bilateral or multilateral APA. The CA negotiates the terms of the APA with the CA of the relevant tax treaty partner within the parameters set by the APA team leader. In a unilateral APA, an ATO staff member, authorized as a CA, but acting in the capacity as an ATO employee, can endorse the decision of the APA team leader and sign the APA. The CA's role is to ensure that the APA is consistent with the negotiation parameters and is otherwise an acceptable outcome. The CA will also support the APA team leader by providing analysis and advice on the resolution of the case, in particular the negotiation process. If there is disagreement between the APA team leader and the CA, the matter is escalated to the Head of the APA Program Management Unit (PMU) or the Head of the APA Program, as appropriate.

34. The PMU has overarching responsibility for the administration of APAs. This includes:

- allocating an APA request to an APA team;
- identifying participants, convening and chairing the triage and APA request review workshops;
- determining whether the request can progress past the triage and APA request review workshops;
- forming and chairing the QA panel for each APA request;
- recommending negotiation parameters to the APA team leader at the QA panel;
- assisting the APA team in deciding whether a case is suitable for a flexible approach;
- convening workshops to monitor the progress of an APA request and to assist teams in resolving any issues or to make key decisions.

The Head of the PMU reviews decisions regarding suitability for an APA, if required.

3.2.3 APA Process

35. The APA process in Australia has three stages:

- Stage 1 – early engagement.
- Stage 2 – APA application.
- Stage 3 – monitoring compliance.

An APA request enters an early engagement stage before progressing to a formal APA application. Once the formal APA application is received, it passes into the APA application stage. After the parties have entered into an APA, there is a further stage of monitoring compliance. Stages 1 and 2 consist of a number of steps. It may be necessary for the ATO to repeat certain steps where insufficient information is provided to support the APA request. An overview of APA Process in Australia is provided in Figure 6.

Figure 6 Overview of APA Process in Australia

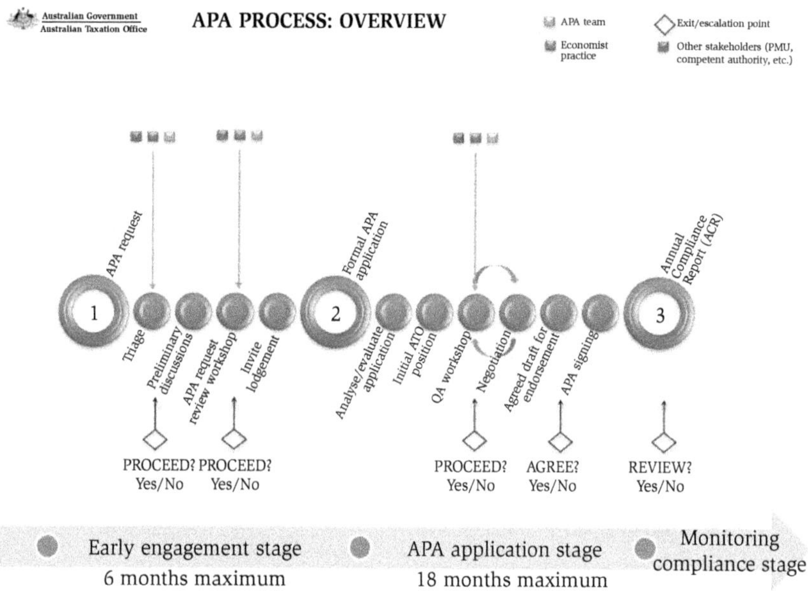

Source: ATO – PS LA 2015/4 https://www.ato.gov.au/law/view/document?DocID=PSR/PS20154/NAT/ATO/00001&PiT=99991231235958#P21.

3.2.4 Pre-filing (Early Engagement)

36. Pre-filing in Australia is called early engagement. Anonymous pre-filing is not available in Australia. An early engagement form containing an outline of the proposed APA must be completed so as to include:

- name and tax residence country of parties involved;
- explanation of how Australian operations fit into global group structure;
- role of Australian entity within the global value chain;
- cross-border dealings covered;
- extent of all cross-border dealings;
- TP methodology proposed;
- proposed term of the APA;
- collateral issues;
- critical dates;
- global group structure (as optional additional information); and
- role of Australian entity in the MNE (as optional additional information).

37. If the request for a pre-filing conference is accepted, preliminary discussions will explore avenues for the appropriate treatment of cross-border dealings and any collateral issues. A request review workshop will follow, and the taxpayer will be invited to lodge a formal APA application.

3.2.5 APA Application and Agreement

38. At the time of preparing the formal APA application, the level of documentation must allow the ATO to ascertain the following aspects:

- actual conditions relevant to the cross-border dealings;
- arm's-length conditions relevant to the cross-border dealings;
- particulars of the TP method used and comparable circumstances relevant to identifying those arm's-length conditions;
- expected result of the proposed method;
- critical assumptions;
- information agreed to in the early engagement stage or as required; and
- regarding bilateral APAs: information requests made by the Double Taxation Treaty (DTT) partner(s) in relation to the APA application and copies of any information supplied by the foreign entity to the DTT partner(s).

39. After negotiating the terms and conditions of a proposed APA with the relevant parties, the parties will reach an agreement, *inter alia*, on the following matters:

- the names, addresses and countries of residence for taxation purposes of the parties to the APA;
- terms of the APA;
- the cross-border dealings covered by the APA;
- the agreed TPM and how it is to be applied;
- the arm's-length amount, rate, range or other arm's-length outcome;
- critical assumptions, any breach of which need to be notified to the ATO in writing;
- a definition of each of the key terms in the APA;
- a statement of the accounting standards on which the taxpayer's financial statements are based, for example, Australian International Financial Reporting Standards;
- procedures for making a compensating adjustment, if necessary.

3.2.6 Annual Compliance Report

40. In respect of APAs signed, the ATO has provided elaborate Monitoring & Compliance procedures. The taxpayer must lodge the Annual Compliance Report (ACR) to the ATO for the duration of the APA. The details to be included in the ACR are provided by ATO on a case-by-case basis. Generally, the ACR should include the following:

- analysis of compliance with the APA, including the information and calculations demonstrating the outcome of the application of arm's-length methodology;
- details of any compensating adjustments made and how they were carried out in the income tax return; and
- has there been a breach of any critical assumptions.

3.2.7 Renewal of APA

41. Applications for the renewal of APAs are required to be lodged six months before expiry. An APA renewal request will go through the same stages as the initial APA request, unless the ATO considers that a streamlined process is more appropriate. According to PS LA 2015/4, this is more likely when:

- there have been no material changes to cross-border dealings or the role of the Australian entity within the global value chain;
- there are no proposed changes to the existing APA; and
- it is unlikely that there will be material changes to dealings covered under the renewed APA.

In the streamlined process, the ATO will consider the following aspects:

- whether an APA is still appropriate;
- the previous APA's arm's-length outcomes;
- any material changes to the covered dealings;
- the updated benchmarks are appropriate; and
- evidence of compliance with the existing APA.

3.2.8 Statistics

42. Statistics in respect of APA requests received and resolved in various years in Australia are provided in Table 1.

Table 1 Number of APA Requests Received and Resolved in Various Years in Australia

Category	*2011-2012*	*2012-2013*	*2013-2014*	*2014-2015*	*2015-2016*	*2016-2017*	*2017-2018*	*2018-2019*	*2019-2020*
Total active APAs at 30 June	156	166	175	148	131	114	110	116	117
Total APAs completed	54	36	35	31	41	16	24	31	27
Completed multilateral APAs	–	–	–	–	–	–	1	–	–
Completed bilateral APAs	22	26	14	19	22	6	12	14	12
Completed unilateral APAs	32	10	21	12	19	10	11	17	15
Renewals	32	18	10	15	29	12	15	17	16
New APAs	22	18	25	16	12	4	9	14	11
APA in progress total	66	63	58	74	107	106	106	77	75

Source: Key APA statistics for each income year (as at 30 June) by ATO https://www.ato.gov.au/business/international-tax-for-business/in-detail/advance-pricing-arrangements/?page = 13.

3.2.9 Ready Reckoner on Availability of Article 9(2), BAPA and Rollback Provisions

43. Australia allows unilateral, bilateral and multilateral APAs, as well as rollback of APAs. A ready reckoner on existence of Article 9(2) to relieve economic double taxation in DTAAs between Australia and various countries and the presence of BAPA and rollback provisions in the legislation of Australia's treaty partners is provided in Table 2 by analysing the following database:

- status of Article 9(2) as provided under OECD MTC, 2017 in the DTAA[37] between Australia and respective treaty partner;
- if not already present, whether Article 9(2) shall get introduced through the Multilateral Convention to Implement Tax Treaty Related Measures to Prevent Base Erosion and Profit Shifting (MLI)[38] in such DTAAs;
- the country MAP/Dispute Resolution profiles[39] of the respective treaty partners available on the OECD website.

Table 2 Ready Reckoner on Availability of Article 9(2), BAPA and Rollback Between Australia and Treaty Partners

S. N.	*Treaty Partner*	*Date of Signature of DTAA*	*Does Article 9(2) Already Exist?*	*If No, Will It Come Through MLI?*	*Does the Treaty Partner Have BAPA?*	*Does the Treaty Partner Have Rollback?*
1	Austria	08.07.1986	Yes *	–	Yes	Yes
2	Belgium	13.10.1977	Yes *	–	Yes	Yes
3	Canada	21.05.1980	Yes *	–	Yes	Yes
4	Chile	10.03.2010	Yes	–	Yes	Chilean tax legislation does not expressly provide for rollback of APAs
5	China	17.11.1988	Yes *	–	Yes	Yes
6	The Czech Republic	28.03.1995	Yes *	–	Yes	No

37. Refer IBFD Tax Research Platform https://research.ibfd.org accessed on 8 February 2021.
38. Refer OECD – Signatories and Parties to the MLI http://www.oecd.org/tax/treaties/beps-mli-signatories-and-parties.pdf accessed on 8 February 2021.
39. Refer MAP profiles on www.oecd.org https://www.oecd.org/tax/dispute/country-map-profiles.htm accessed on 8 February 2021.

S. N.	*Treaty Partner*	*Date of Signature of DTAA*	*Does Article 9(2) Already Exist?*	*If No, Will It Come Through MLI?*	*Does the Treaty Partner Have BAPA?*	*Does the Treaty Partner Have Rollback?*
7	Denmark	01.04.1981	Yes *	–	Yes	Yes
8	Finland	20.11.2006	Yes *	–	No formal programme. But can be considered based on MAP article	Can be considered
9	France	20.06.2006	No **	Yes	Yes	No
10	Germany	12.11.2015	Yes	–	Yes	Yes
11	Hungary	29.11.1990	Yes *	–	Yes	Yes
12	India	25.07.1991	Yes *	–	Yes	Yes
13	Indonesia	22.04.1992	Yes *	–	Yes	Yes @
14	Ireland	31.05.1983	Yes ***	–	Yes	Yes
15	Italy	14.12.1982	No	Yes	Yes	No
16	Japan	31.01.2008	Yes *	–	Yes	Yes
17	Korea	12.07.1982	Yes ****	–	Yes	Yes
18	Malaysia	20.08.1980	Yes *	–	Yes	Yes
19	Mexico	09.09.2002	Yes	–	Yes	Yes
20	The Netherlands	17.03.1976	Yes	–	Yes	Yes
21	New Zealand	26.06.2009	Yes *	–	Yes	Yes
22	Norway	08.08.2006	Yes *	–	Yes	Yes
23	Poland	07.05.1991	Yes *	–	Yes	No
24	Romania	02.02.2000	Yes *	–	Yes	No
25	Russia	07.09.2000	Yes *	–	Yes	No
26	Singapore	11.02.1969	Yes *****	–	Yes	Yes
27	The Slovak Republic	24.08.1999	Yes *	–	Yes	Yes
28	South Africa	01.07.1999	Yes *	–	No	No
29	Spain	24.03.1992	Yes *	–	Yes	Yes
30	Sweden	14.01.1981	Yes *	–	Yes	Yes
31	The Swiss Confederation	30.07.2013	Yes	–	Yes	Yes
32	Thailand	31.08.1989	Yes *	–	Yes	Yes #
33	Turkey	28.04.2010	Yes *	–	Yes	Yes
34	United Kingdom	21.08.2003	Yes *	–	Yes	Yes
35	US	06.08.1982	Yes	–	Yes	Yes

S. N.	*Treaty Partner*	*Date of Signature of DTAA*	*Does Article 9(2) Already Exist?*	*If No, Will It Come Through MLI?*	*Does the Treaty Partner Have BAPA?*	*Does the Treaty Partner Have Rollback?*
36	Vietnam	13.04.1992	Yes *	-	Yes	No

* Such provisions are in Article 9(3) of the DTAA.
** Such provisions are not as per Article 9(2) of the OECD MTC, 2017 in entirety.
*** Such provisions are in Article 10(4) of the DTAA.
**** Such provisions are in Article 9(5) of the DTAA.
***** Such provisions are in Article 6(3) of the DTAA.
@ Indonesia's Dispute Resolution Profile (last updated on 1 September 2016) states that rollback of APA is not permissible under the Indonesian APA programme. However, under the revised Ministry of Finance Regulation No. 22/PMK.03/2020, rollback is available in Indonesia.
# On perusal of Thailand's Dispute Resolution Profile (last updated on 1 June 2020), it is mentioned that rollback of APAs is provided for in the bilateral APA programme. However, Guidance on APA process issued by the Revenue Department of Thailand is silent on this issue.

3.3 APA REGIME IN CANADA

44. The Canada Customs and Revenue Agency (CCRA) has an APA Program to help taxpayers determine appropriate TPMs for transactions or arrangements they participate in with non-resident persons with whom they do not deal at arm's length. The Competent Authority Services Division (CASD) of the International Tax Directorate at Headquarters administers the APA programme.

45. The provisions pertaining to Tax Avoidance are contained in Part XVI of the Canadian Income Tax Act, whereas provisions pertaining to Transfer Pricing are contained in section 247 of Part XVI.1 of the Act. The relevant provisions governing the APA regime in Canada[40] are contained in Canada Revenue Agency (CRA) Information Circulars IC 94-4R, IC 94-4RSR, and TPM-11. CRA IC 94-4R[41] dated 16 March 2001 provides that any taxpayer subject to transfer pricing rules in section 247 of the Canadian Income Tax Act may request for an APA. The purpose of IC 94-4 is to explain how to apply for and obtain an APA for Canadian income tax purposes and give guidelines on related topics.

46. Unilateral, bilateral, and multilateral APAs are available in Canada, and pre-filing meetings for the APA application must take place within 180 days after the end of the first taxation year that is to be covered by the APA. Depending on the relevant facts and circumstances, the APA term is usually three to five years. Rollbacks may be negotiated

40. Refer DLA Piper – APA and MAP Country Guide 2019 https://www.dlapiper.com/en/us/insights/publications/2019/03/apa-and-map-country-guide-2019/ accessed on 11 August 2020.
41. Refer IC 94-4R dated 16 March 2001 https://www.canada.ca/en/revenue-agency/services/forms-publications/publications/ic94-4/international-transfer-pricing-advance-pricing.html accessed on 9 February 2021.

where the facts and circumstances of open prior years are similar to those on which the APA was concluded. Requests to retroactively apply an APA are separate and distinct from an APA request. A levy (filing fee) tailored to each case applies. Filing fee is charged on each accepted APA request or renewal request and the amount is included in an acceptance letter. The levy is a non-refundable user charge for each accepted APA request or renewal to cover anticipated 'out-of-pocket' costs, such as travel and accommodation expenses. Currently there is no charge for staff time. User charges for APAs are:

- outlined in an APA acceptance letter between the taxpayer and the CCRA; and
- payable upon taxpayer's reply to the CCRA's APA acceptance letter.

3.3.1 Rollback

47. There are provisions to apply the terms and conditions of an APA retroactively to non-statute-barred taxation years. Rollback of APA can only occur when the facts and circumstances of the open prior years were similar to those on which the APA was concluded. A request to retroactively apply the terms and conditions of an APA is separate and distinct from an APA request. It is to be ensured that the taxation years relating to the request for retroactive application do not become statute-barred in Canada and in the relevant foreign jurisdiction.

48. The Canadian tax authorities have issued a Transfer Pricing Memorandum, TPM-11 dated 28 October 2008[42] on rollback of APAs. The purpose of this transfer pricing memorandum is to convey the policy regarding an APA request to cover prior taxation years. The CCRA usually agrees to consider a request to expand the period of an APA to cover transactions in open taxation years where:

- a request for contemporaneous documentation has not been issued by a tax services office (TSO);
- the facts and circumstances are the same;
- the foreign tax administration and the relevant TSO have both agreed to accept the APA rollback request; and
- appropriate waivers, in the form outlined in subparagraph 152(4)(a)(ii) of the Act, have been filed.

49. A TSO will not issue a request for contemporaneous documentation for the transactions occurring in a taxation year that is proposed to be covered by an APA rollback where a taxpayer has requested an APA rollback. A taxpayer is considered to have requested an APA rollback once a pre-filing meeting has taken place between the taxpayer and the CASD officials regarding a potential APA rollback. Taxpayers are also

42. Refer TPM-11 dated 28 October 2008 https://www.canada.ca/en/revenue-agency/services/tax/international-non-residents/information-been-moved/transfer-pricing/11.html accessed on 10 February 2021.

expected to clearly indicate in their pre-filing package their intent to request an APA rollback should they decide to pursue an APA. If a taxpayer's request for an APA rollback is not accepted by the CCRA, a request for contemporaneous documentation may be issued by the TSO for the transactions formerly proposed to be covered in the APA rollback period.

50. A unilateral APA is only effective for Canadian income tax purposes and does not eliminate the potential for double taxation. Therefore, a foreign tax administration may decide during an audit to select a different TPM, a different PLI, or use different comparables resulting in double taxation. Consequently, the CCRA does not entertain an APA rollback when a taxpayer requests a unilateral APA.

3.3.2 APA Team

51. In pursuance of acceptance of an APA request, whereby the taxpayer having signed and returned the APA acceptance letter and paid the required user charge, a multidisciplinary team is assigned to the particular case. A team led by a case officer usually comprises an accountant/auditor, an economist, TSO of the CCRA audit personnel, other CCRA specialists, and legal counsel. The case officer contacts the taxpayer usually within thirty days after receiving the signed acceptance letter to discuss any concerns it may have about preparing the APA submission. The case officer coordinates further work and information requirements regarding the APA request with the taxpayer, the non-resident entities, the team, and, in the case of a BAPA or MAPA, with the relevant CAs. Although the case officer is responsible for the APA, all team members generally participate in various stages of the APA process. They help develop and resolve the case based on their background, knowledge, and experience. For example, in most instances, the TSO representative has extensive knowledge of the taxpayer's business and operations and significant exposure to the related industry. However, the TSO representative usually does not participate in BAPA or MAPA negotiations, as those take place between CAs. In exceptional or complex cases, a taxpayer may suggest in its APA request that an expert is needed or the APA team may determine that an independent expert is required to help evaluate the APA submissions. If the opinion of an independent expert is necessary, taxpayers are required to provide, usually at their own expense, an independent expert to review the proposed TPMs or other issues. The independent expert is required to analyse the APA submissions and provide a written opinion and the basis for the opinion and conclusions reached. If an independent expert is necessary, the APA team requests the taxpayer to give a written authorization to examine and discuss the APA request and submissions, and other relevant information, with the expert. The independent expert's opinion is not binding on any of the relevant participants in the APA process. The participating tax administrations also have full access to the expert's report and supporting documentation.

3.3.3 Purpose and Scope of APAs

52. The purpose of the APA programme is to provide a cooperative process for resolving transfer pricing issues prospectively. The APA process is designed to produce an APA specifying the following:

- taxpayer and the non-resident entities;
- nature and scope of transactions to be covered;
- appropriate TPMs to be employed;
- period for which an APA is to be effective; and
- other terms and conditions.

53. APA requests are accepted for current transactions and specified future transactions that are not hypothetical. An APA applies only to the taxpayer who is party to it and to the participants, transactions, and time periods specified in it. Each APA is unique and based solely on the facts and circumstances of the case. Issues similar or related to transfer pricing, such as the proper attribution of income between a permanent establishment (PE) and other parts of the same entity, may also be taken up under the APA.

3.3.4 APA Process

54. The APA process includes the following stages:

- pre-filing meeting(s);
- the APA request;
- the acceptance letter;
- the APA submission;
- preliminary review of the APA submission and establishment of a case plan;
- review, analysis, and evaluation;
- negotiations;
- agreements;
- the post-settlement meeting; and
- APA compliance.

3.3.5 Pre-filing Meeting

55. The pre-filing meetings are held within 180 days after the end of the first taxation year that is to be covered by the APA. If they are not completed by that date, the APA will usually not cover transactions of that first taxation year. Pre-filing meetings are attended by the taxpayer, its representatives, and CCRA officials to explore the suitability of an APA and to informally discuss the APA process and the matters set out in the IC. If requested by the taxpayer, CCRA conducts discussions on an anonymous basis also. Taxpayers are required to provide an APA request information package at least two weeks before the pre-filing meeting. A written authorization must be included for each of the taxpayer's representatives throughout the APA process. This allows the CCRA officials to release confidential taxpayer information related to the APA process to the designated representative(s), and examine and discuss that information with them. Pre-filing meetings also give an opportunity to discuss the types of information likely to be needed for the APA submission.

3.3.6 APA Application

56. Any taxpayer may apply for APA consideration, regardless of the size of the organization, the type or scope of its operations, or the nature of the transactions and proposed TPMs. The scope and complexity of a case and not the size of a company, as well as other factors (such as the extent of cooperation and quality of information), will determine the time needed to process an APA request. The APA process is flexible enough to adapt to the facts and circumstances of any particular case. There is no legal requirement to enter into APAs. The CCRA provides them as an administrative service. Merely filing an APA request or submission will not prevent or defer an audit of the years prior to the proposed APA years. The APA Program and the audit programmes of the CCRA are separate and distinct.

3.3.7 Processing an APA Request

57. The Canadian APA programme considers requests for BAPAs, MAPAs, and unilateral APAs. The CCRA officials confirm the commitment to accept a request for a BAPA, MAPA, or unilateral APA, by sending an acceptance letter usually within forty-five days after receiving the APA request. The acceptance letter sets out the user charge to be paid, and other terms and conditions under which the tax authorities pursue the APA request. The Canadian APA programme prefers to enter into BAPAs or MAPAs. If taxpayers request for a unilateral APA, they must state why they are not requesting a BAPA or MAPA if the proposed transactions involve countries with which Canada has income tax treaties. The APA process does not limit the CCRA from notifying a treaty partner in accordance with the relevant treaty that it has accepted a unilateral APA request. If the CA later needs to resolve potential double taxation arising from applying a unilateral APA, the provisions of Part VI 'Competent Authority Consideration' will apply.

58. In some circumstances, it may not be appropriate for the CCRA officials to accept or pursue an APA request. In that case, they may exercise their discretion and decline to consider such a request. After accepting a request, they decline to pursue or conclude an APA only in extraordinary circumstances. If the tax authorities propose to decline an APA request, or propose not to pursue an APA, reasons thereof are explained to the taxpayer who is also provided an opportunity to make further representations. For example, the tax authorities may decline an APA request when the central issue involves a matter that is before the courts. Applicants are permitted to withdraw their APA request at any time.

3.3.8 APA Reporting (Compliance Reports)

59. The APA applicants are required to file APA reports (compliance reports) according to the terms of the APA. An APA report describes the actual operations for the period and demonstrates the compliance with the terms and conditions of the APA. An APA report has to address all items called for by the APA, and any requests to revise or cancel the related APA. Each APA is unique, and each sets out the particular requirements of its APA report, such as content, scope, filing date and joint APA reports in the case of a BAPA or MAPA. APA applicants are required to file the original and two copies of each APA report with the Director General, within the time period specified in the APA. The Canadian tax authorities review the APA report for any items requiring a specific response, such as a request to revise the APA, and contact the applicant if needed to clarify or complete information in the APA report. The reviews of the APA report are then coordinated among the relevant TSO and representatives of the Canadian CASD. They review and evaluate the results of applying the agreed TPM and the information and explanations provided in the APA report. The Canadian tax authorities may confer with the applicant and the other participating tax administrations as necessary. The results of the review and consultation determine what action, if any, would be appropriate in the circumstances, i.e., whether there is a need to propose adjustments to the reported results, or to revise, cancel, or revoke the APA. If applicants do not file an APA report as required, the Canadian tax authorities may cancel the APA.

3.3.9 Auditing an APA

60. The APA applicant and non-resident entities are required to maintain books and records that allow the Canadian tax authorities to determine compliance with the APA. TSOs audit APAs as part of the regular audit cycle. They do not re-evaluate the TPMs or other terms and conditions agreed to in an APA. Their audit of the APA is limited to establishing taxpayer's compliance with the terms and conditions of the APA and whether:

- material representations in the APA request, the related submissions, and the periodic APA reports remain valid and accurately describe taxpayer's operations and those of non-resident entities;
- taxpayer has applied the agreed-upon TPMs consistently in accordance with the terms and conditions of the APA;
- supporting data and calculations used in applying the agreed-upon TPMs are correct in all material respects; and
- critical assumptions underlying the APA remain valid and relevant.

3.3.10 Renewal of APA

61. Requests to renew an APA follow the same form and procedures in effect at the time the request for renewal is made that applies to initial APA requests. The applicant is required to submit appropriate updated supporting documentation, similar to that required for the initial APA request and submission, with the renewal request. The applicant is required to file a request to renew an APA, except as otherwise provided for under the terms of an APA, within a reasonable time, but usually no later than nine months before the current APA expires. When determining the request date for any particular APA renewal request, the applicant is required to consider the specific facts and circumstances associated with the request, and the scope and complexity of the material contained in the renewal submission, including the degree to which facts, critical assumptions, or underlying circumstances of the previous APA have changed.

62. The CCRA may renew the APA under similar terms and conditions on request when both the applicant and the CCRA are satisfied that the TPMs in the previous APA continue to be appropriate and that:

- there have been no material changes in the facts and circumstances underlying the APA and the critical assumptions remain valid and relevant; and
- the applicant has complied with the terms and conditions of the previous APA.

63. Proposed amendments to the APA, in addition to updated studies, analyses, and supporting documentation, have to accompany the applicant's request to renew the APA when:

- material changes have occurred in the facts, circumstances, or critical assumptions underlying the APA; or
- the previous APA did not adequately consider subsequent economic, technical, product, or industry developments.

64. Accordingly, the CCRA may evaluate the renewal request, taking into account the amendments to the previous APA needed in light of changed facts and circumstances. The renewal process focuses on updating the critical assumptions and facts agreed to in the initial APA and amending related calculations. The Canadian tax authorities then proceed to obtain agreement on renewing the related BAPA or MAPA with the CA of the relevant treaty partners.

3.3.11 Revising an APA

65. An APA may be revised if it is established that:

- there has been a failure to meet a critical assumption;
- there has been a change in law, including a treaty provision, that modifies the Canadian federal income tax treatment of any matter covered by the APA;

- there has been a material change in circumstances; or
- the participating foreign tax administration's APA is not consistent with the applicant's APA or has been revised, cancelled, or revoked.

3.3.12 Cancelling an APA

66. The CCRA may cancel an APA if it is established that:

- the applicant or the non-resident entities made any material misrepresentation, mistake, or omission in the APA request, APA submission, related APA reports, or subsequent APA renewal submissions, or in supplying, or failing to supply, any relevant information under the IC;
- the applicant or the non-resident entities failed to comply with any material term or condition of the APA;
- there has been a failure to meet a critical assumption;
- there has been a change in law, including a treaty provision, that modifies the Canadian federal income tax treatment of any matter covered by the APA;
- the participating foreign tax administration's APA is not consistent with the applicant's APA or has been revised, cancelled, or revoked; or
- there has been a failure to conclude or sign a revised APA, BAPA or MAPA.

3.3.13 Revoking an APA

67. The CCRA may revoke an APA if it is established that the:

- applicant or the non-resident entities made any material misrepresentation attributable to neglect, carelessness, or wilful default in the APA request, APA submission, related APA reports, or subsequent APA renewal submissions, or in supplying, or failing to supply, any relevant information under the IC;
- applicant or the non-resident entities failed to comply with any material term or condition of the APA; or
- participating foreign tax administration's APA is not consistent with the applicant's APA or has been revised, cancelled, or revoked.

3.3.14 Statistics

68. A summary[43] of the key findings presented in APA – Program report – 2019 is provided below:

43. Refer Advance Pricing Arrangement – Program report – 2019 by Canada https://www.canada.ca/en/revenue-agency/services/tax/international-non-residents/competent-authority-services/advance-pricing-arrangements/2019-apa-program-report.html accessed on 10 February 2021.

- Based on the number of pre-filing meetings held with taxpayers in 2019, the CCRA had fifteen applicants to the programme.
- The year 2019 opened with an active case inventory of seventy-one APAs. Seven new cases were accepted into the programme, no cases were withdrawn, and twelve cases were completed. This resulted in a closing inventory of sixty-six cases for 2019.
- The vast majority of cases (89.4%) since 2015-2016 involve taxpayers seeking an APA on a bilateral or multilateral basis, as opposed to 10.6% of taxpayers seeking an APA on a unilateral basis.
- In 2019, the average time to complete a bilateral APA was 51.1 months. This increased from 2018 as a number of older APAs were closed during the year. In particular, 3 APAs took more than 80 months to complete.
- Cases involving transfers of tangible property made up the largest percentage of APAs in process (47%). Cases involving intangible property represented 27%, intra-group services represented 23% and financing arrangements represented 3%.
- In 2019, the CCRA's open APA cases involved taxpayers with operations in more than fifteen different industrial sectors.
- The CCRA is currently engaged in bilateral or multilateral APA processes involving taxpayers from sixteen different jurisdictions: Australia, Chile, China, France, Germany, India, Ireland, Japan, Korea, the Netherlands, New Zealand, Singapore, Sweden, Switzerland, the UK and the US.

69. Statistics on the number of APA requests received and resolved in various years in Canada are provided in Table 3.

Table 3 Number of APA Requests Received and Resolved in Various Years in Canada

Period	*Pre-filing Meetings*	*Applications Withdrawals*	*Applications Pending*	*Opening APA Balance*	*APAs Accepted*	*APAs Completed*	*APAs Unresolved*	*APAs Withdrawals*	*Closing APA Balance*
2019	15	0	16	71	7	12	0	0	66
2018	31	3	19	67	32	25	0	3	71
2017	24	2	23	90	16	36	0	3	67
2016	23	2	17	107	12	26	0	3	90
2015	24	2	8	109	23	21	1	3	107
2015-2016	24	3	10	94	25	24	0	0	95

Source: Advance Pricing Arrangement – Program report – 2019 by Canada https://www.canada.ca/en/revenue-agency/services/tax/international-non-residents/competent-authority-services/advance-pricing-arrangements/2019-apa-program-report.html.

3.3.15 Ready Reckoner on Availability of Article 9(2), BAPA and Rollback Provisions

70. Canada allows unilateral, bilateral and multilateral APAs, as well as rollback of APAs for BAPA and MAPA. A ready reckoner on existence of Article 9(2) to relieve economic double taxation in DTAAs between Canada and various countries and the presence of BAPA and rollback provisions in the legislation of Canada's treaty partners is provided in Table 4 by analysing the following database:

- status of Article 9(2) as provided under OECD MTC, 2017 in the DTAA[44] between Canada and respective treaty partner;
- if not already present, whether Article 9(2) shall get introduced through the MLI[45] in such DTAAs;
- the country MAP/Dispute Resolution profiles[46] of the respective treaty partners available on the OECD website.

Table 4 Ready Reckoner on Availability of Article 9(2), BAPA and Rollback Between Canada and Treaty Partners

S. N.	*Treaty Partner*	*Date of Signature of DTAA*	*Does Article 9(2) Already Exist?*	*If No, Will It Come Through MLI?*	*Does the Treaty Partner Have BAPA?*	*Does the Treaty Partner Have Rollback?*
1	Argentina	29.04.1993	Yes	–	No	No
2	Australia	21.05.1980	Yes *	–	Yes	Yes
3	Austria	09.12.1976	No	No	Yes	Yes
4	Belgium	23.05.2002	Yes	–	Yes	Yes
5	Bulgaria	03.03.1999	Yes	–	No	No
6	Chile	21.01.1998	Yes	–	Yes	Chilean tax legislation does not expressly provide for rollback of APAs
7	China	12.05.1986	No	No	Yes	Yes

44. Refer IBFD Tax Research Platform https://research.ibfd.org accessed on 10 February 2021.
45. Refer OECD – Signatories and Parties to the MLI http://www.oecd.org/tax/treaties/beps-mli-signatories-and-parties.pdf accessed on 10 February 2021.
46. Refer MAP profiles on www.oecd.org https://www.oecd.org/tax/dispute/country-map-profiles.htm accessed on 10 February 2021.

S. N.	*Treaty Partner*	*Date of Signature of DTAA*	*Does Article 9(2) Already Exist?*	*If No, Will It Come Through MLI?*	*Does the Treaty Partner Have BAPA?*	*Does the Treaty Partner Have Rollback?*
8	Colombia	21.11.2008	Yes	-	Yes	Yes
9	Croatia	09.12.1997	No	No	Yes	No
10	The Czech Republic	25.05.2001	Yes	-	Yes	No
11	Denmark	17.09.1997	Yes	-	Yes	Yes
12	Egypt	30.05.1983	Yes	-	No	No
13	Estonia	02.06.1995	Yes	-	Yes	Yes
14	Finland	20.07.2006	Yes	-	No formal programme. But can be considered based on MAP article	Can be considered
15	France	02.05.1975	No	No	Yes	No
16	Germany	19.04.2001	No	No	Yes	Yes
17	Greece	29.06.2009	Yes	-	Yes	No
18	Hong Kong	11.11.2012	Yes	-	Yes	Yes
19	Hungary	15.04.1992	Yes	-	Yes	Yes
20	Iceland	19.06.1997	Yes	-	No	No
21	India	11.01.1996	Yes	-	Yes	Yes
22	Indonesia	16.01.1979	No	No	Yes	Yes @
23	Ireland	08.10.2003	Yes	-	Yes	Yes
24	Israel	21.09.2016	Yes	-	No formal programme. But can be considered based on MAP article	No
25	Italy	03.06.2002	Yes	-	Yes	No
26	Japan	07.05.1986	Yes	-	Yes	Yes
27	Kazakhstan	25.09.1996	Yes	-	Yes	No
28	Kenya	27.04.1983	Yes	-	No	No
29	Korea	05.09.2006	Yes	-	Yes	Yes
30	Malaysia	15.10.1976	No	No	Yes	Yes
31	Mexico	12.09.2006	Yes	-	Yes	Yes

S. N.	*Treaty Partner*	*Date of Signature of DTAA*	*Does Article 9(2) Already Exist?*	*If No, Will It Come Through MLI?*	*Does the Treaty Partner Have BAPA?*	*Does the Treaty Partner Have Rollback?*
32	Morocco	22.12.1975	No	No	Yes	Yes
33	The Netherlands	27.05.1986	Yes	–	Yes	Yes
34	New Zealand	03.05.2012	Yes	–	Yes	Yes
35	Norway	12.07.2002	No	No	Yes	Yes
36	Oman	30.06.2004	Yes	–	No	No
37	Poland	14.05.2012	Yes	–	Yes	No
38	Portugal	14.06.1999	Yes	–	Yes	No
39	Romania	08.04.2004	Yes	–	Yes	No
40	Russia	05.10.1995	Yes	–	Yes	No
41	Serbia	27.04.2012	Yes	–	No	No
42	Singapore	06.03.1976	No	No	Yes	Yes
43	The Slovak Republic	22.05.2001	Yes	–	Yes	Yes
44	Slovenia	15.09.2000	Yes	–	Yes	Yes
45	South Africa	27.11.1995	Yes	–	No	No
46	Spain	23.11.1976	Yes	–	Yes	Yes
47	Sweden	27.08.1996	Yes	–	Yes	Yes
48	The Swiss Confederation	05.05.1997	Yes	–	Yes	Yes
49	Thailand	11.04.1984	Yes	–	Yes	Yes #
50	Turkey	14.07.2009	Yes	–	Yes	Yes
51	The United Arab Emirates	09.06.2002	Yes	–	No	No
52	United Kingdom	08.09.1978	Yes	–	Yes	Yes
53	US	26.09.1980	Yes *	–	Yes	Yes
54	Vietnam	14.11.1997	Yes	–	Yes	No

* Such provisions are in Article 9(3) of the DTAA.

@ Indonesia's Dispute Resolution Profile (last updated on 1 September 2016) states that rollback of APA is not permissible under the Indonesian APA programme. However, under the revised Ministry of Finance Regulation No. 22/PMK.03/2020, rollback is available in Indonesia.

On perusal of Thailand's Dispute Resolution Profile (last updated on 1 June 2020), it is mentioned that rollback of APAs is provided for in the bilateral APA programme. However, Guidance on APA process issued by the Revenue Department of Thailand is silent on this issue.

3.4 APA REGIME IN CHINA

71. China[47] has put in place a MAP mechanism to eliminate double taxation resulting from transfer pricing audits and a bilateral APA programme to provide certainty for cross-border taxpayers. Relevant information[48] in regard to the APA programme is contained in Public Notice on Matters Regarding Enhancing the Administration of Advance Pricing Arrangements (Public Notice of the SAT [2016] 64).[49] The CA in charge of the APA programme in China is the State Administration of Taxation (SAT) and the relevant local tax authority.

72. There are three types of APAs that are available: unilateral APAs, bilateral APAs and multilateral APAs. An APA generally covers related party transactions for three to five consecutive years in the future. The general threshold which a taxpayer needs to meet in order to apply for an APA is that the amount of annual related party transactions should be no less than RMB 40 million for the past three years prior to the application year.

3.4.1 Rollback

73. In accordance with stipulations and as per the taxpayer's application, the APA can be retrospectively applied to prior years for up to ten years.

3.4.2 APA Process

74. The APA process[50] involves the following six stages:

(1) a pre-filing meeting;
(2) submission of intent;
(3) analysis and evaluation;
(4) formal application;
(5) negotiation and signing; and
(6) implementation and monitoring.

75. An APA will commence from the year during which the tax authorities issue a Notice of Tax Related Issues informing the taxpayer that it may submit a letter of intent. The taxpayer may submit a formal APA application upon receiving a Notice of Tax Related Issues from the tax authorities that indicates their consent to receiving such a

47. Refer para. D.2.2.16 of the United Nations Practical Manual on Transfer Pricing for Developing Countries (2017).
48. Refer DLA Piper – APA and MAP Country Guide 2019 https://www.dlapiper.com/en/us/insights/publications/2019/03/apa-and-map-country-guide-2019/ accessed on 11 August 2020.
49. Refer Public Notice of the SAT [2016] 64 http://www.chinatax.gov.cn/n810341/n810755/c2292979/content.html accessed on 10 February 2021.
50. Refer section D.2.3.7 of the United Nations Practical Manual on Transfer Pricing for Developing Countries (2017).

submission. The Chinese SAT prioritizes the acceptance of the application from a taxpayer if it falls into one of the following categories:

- the taxpayer's annual reporting forms for related party dealings and contemporaneous transfer pricing documentation are well completed with adequate disclosures;
- the taxpayer has a level-A tax credit rating;
- a special tax investigation on the taxpayer has been conducted and closed;
- a renewal application was submitted by the taxpayer upon expiration of the existing APA with no substantial change to the facts and circumstances specified in the existing APA;
- information and documents submitted by the taxpayer are complete and adequate; value chain analysis and supply chain analysis are clear and thorough; location-specific factors including location savings and market premium have been given adequate consideration; and the proposed TPM and the calculation method are appropriate;
- the taxpayer shall actively cooperate with the tax authorities during the APA process;
- for a taxpayer applying for a bilateral APA, the CA of the relevant treaty partner has displayed a strong intention to move forward with the APA negotiation and attaches importance to the case; or
- there are any other factors present that benefit the negotiation and signing of the APA requested by the taxpayer.

3.4.3 Pre-filing Meeting

76. The taxpayer is required to make a written request to the tax authorities for a pre-filing meeting. Anonymous pre-filing is not available. The pre-filing meeting will require the following information and documentation:

- duration of the proposed APA;
- related parties involved and related party transaction to be covered;
- organizational and management structure of the enterprise and the group it belongs to;
- business operations and transfer pricing documentation of the enterprise for the most recent three to five years;
- allocation of functions and risks among related parties covered under the APA, including the parties involved, personnel, expenses and assets;
- market conditions, including industry development trends and competitive environment;
- any location-specific advantages (LSAs), including location savings and market premiums;
- whether the proposed APA is intended to be retrospective in application;

- in the case of a bilateral or multilateral APAs, copies of applications for APAs submitted with relevant foreign tax authorities;
- in the case of bilateral or multilateral APAs, business operations and intercompany transaction of the related party involved for the most recent three to five years; and
- in the case of bilateral or multilateral APAs, any international double taxation issues and relevant explanations.

3.4.4 APA Application

77. If an agreement is reached during the pre-filing meeting, the taxpayer is required to submit a Letter of Intent for negotiation and signing of an APA to the tax authorities and submit the APA application proposal, including the following documentation:

- the proposed TP method and calculation method, functional and risk analysis, comparability analysis and assumptions used for supporting such methods;
- value chain or supply chain analysis;
- annual information on business scale, result forecasts and plans for the proposed term of APA; and
- relevant domestic or international laws and rules in the industry that have an impact on the APA.

78. In addition, the applicants are required to submit a declaration that none of the following circumstances exist:

- the taxpayer has been under any tax-related investigation;
- the taxpayer has been non-compliant with related party dealings disclosure and contemporaneous transfer pricing documentation requirements; and
- the taxpayer and tax authorities were not able to reach an agreement during pre-filing meeting in relation to the APA application.

79. If the tax authorities determine that the APA application conforms to the arm's-length principle, a Notice of Tax Related Issues consenting to the taxpayer's submission of a formal APA application is issued. Subsequently, the taxpayer is required to submit a formal Application Letter for an APA. Taxpayers applying for a unilateral APA must submit all of the above-mentioned information and documentation to their local tax authority. Taxpayers applying for bilateral or multilateral APAs must submit all of the above-mentioned information and documentation to both the State Administration of Taxation and the relevant local tax authority. For APAs involving two or more provinces, autonomous regions, municipalities or cities with independent planning, or involving both the state and local tax bureau, the SAT shall be the designated tax authority.

80. In any of the following circumstances, the tax authority may refuse the taxpayer to submit a formal application:

- The pricing principles and calculation methods to be adopted in the draft application for APAs are unreasonable, and the taxpayer refuses to negotiate adjustments.
- The taxpayer refuses to provide relevant information. The material provided does not meet the requirements of the tax authority.
- The taxpayer refuses to cooperate with the tax authority to conduct functional and risk analysis or on-site interviews.
- Other situations that are not suitable for negotiating and signing APAs.

3.4.5 Advance Pricing Arrangement

81. After the competent tax authority and the taxpayer have reached an agreement on the unilateral APA text, the legal representatives of both parties sign the unilateral APA.

82. After the SAT and the tax authority of the other party to the tax treaty have reached an agreement on the text of a bilateral or multilateral APA, the representatives authorized by the two or more tax authorities sign the bilateral or multilateral APA.

83. The text of an APA may include the following:

(a) Basic information such as the name and address of the enterprise and its related parties.
(b) Related party transactions involved in the APA and applicable years.
(c) Pricing principles and calculations used in the APA methods, as well as comparable prices or comparable profit levels.
(d) Definitions of terms related to the application.
(e) Assumptions and notification obligations in case there are changes in assumptions.
(f) Annual reporting obligations of the enterprise.
(g) APA's validity.
(h) Renewal of APAs.
(i) Effectiveness, amendment and termination of APAs.
(j) Settlement of disputes.
(k) Obligation to keep confidential documents and other information.
(l) Information exchange of UAPAs.
(m) By-laws.

3.4.6 Annual Compliance Report

84. An ACR is required to be filed with the tax authorities within six months following each tax year end. The ACR must include:

- documentation of the relevant business operations and implementation of the APA;
- any need to amend or terminate the APA; and
- any unsettled issues or adverse issues expected to occur.

85. The tax authorities then proceed to monitor the taxpayer's implementation of the APA on an annual basis, with major areas of monitoring to include compliance with the provisions and requirements of the APA; whether the information provided in the ACR reflects the actual operations of the taxpayer; and whether the assumptions in the APA are still valid.

3.4.7 Renewal of APA

86. Applications for the renewal of APAs are required to be lodged within ninety days prior to the expiration of the existing APA. The taxpayer must submit an Advance Pricing Arrangement Renewal Application; a report specifying the implementation status of the existing APA; an explanation of any substantial changes to the facts or operational environment in the existing APA; and a forecast for the years covered by the renewal.

87. An enterprise that has submitted the 'APA Letter of Intent' to apply for APA with rollback after reaching agreement with the tax authorities in pre-filing meetings or that has submitted the 'APA Renewal Application' can be temporarily exempt from special tax investigation to the extent of the years and the related party transactions covered by the APA.[51]

3.4.8 Confidentiality of Information

88. All information and materials obtained during the negotiation and signing of APAs between the tax authority and the enterprise shall be kept confidential. Except in cases where information should be provided to relevant departments in accordance with the law, tax authorities shall not disclose information related to APAs in any way without the consent of taxpayers. If the tax authority and the enterprise are unable to reach an APA, the non-factual information about the applicant's proposals, reasoning, ideas, and judgments obtained by the tax authority during the negotiation process from the applicant shall not be used for special taxation of related party transactions.

3.4.9 Statistics

89. China has been negotiating APAs since the mid-1990s, with the first unilateral and bilateral APAs signed in 1998 and 2005, respectively. China's first bilateral APA was

51. Refer Article 5 of Public Notice of the SAT [2017] No. 6 http://www.chinatax.gov.cn/download/pdf/20171122.pdf accessed on 10 February 2021.

signed with Japan in 2005. By the end of 2015, China had signed fifty-one BAPAs. There were 203 APA applications at the application or signing stage at the end of 2017. Eight APAs were signed during 2017.

90. The Chinese tax authorities signed a total of 21 APAs in 2019, including 12 unilateral APAs and 9 bilateral APAs, with both achieving a historical record high since 2009. Of the total APAs signed between 2005 and 2019, 141 APAs relate to the manufacturing industry, accounting for 80 % of the total number. While the manufacturing industry forms a big chunk of the APA tally, it has been observed that in the past two years, there has been an increasing number of enterprises signing the APAs in the wholesale and retail industry (nineteen such entities have signed APAs, which accounts for 10 % of the signed APAs between 2005 and 2019). Generally, the Chinese tax authorities aim to conclude unilateral and bilateral APAs within twelve to twenty-four months of the submission of formal applications, respectively. Most unilateral APAs (89 %) and bilateral APAs (62 %) signed between 2005 and 2019 were concluded within two years of formal application. In 2019, most of the newly signed APAs were also concluded within two years of formal application. Five of the nine newly signed bilateral APAs in 2019 were concluded within only one year of formal application.[52] Statistics on the number of APA requests received and resolved in various years in China are provided in Table 5.

Table 5 Number of APA Requests Received and Resolved in Various Years in China

Phase	*Unilateral APA*		*Bilateral APA*		*Total*	
	By 2018 Year End	*By 2019 Year End*	*By 2018 Year End*	*By 2019 Year End*	*By 2018 Year End*	*By 2019 Year End*
Intent submitted	7	8	32	69	39	77
In application	9	15	56	42	65	57
Signed (cumulative)	89	101	67	76	156	177

Source: Advance Pricing Arrangement – Annual Report – 2019 by SAT https://www.pwc.com/gx/en/tax/newsletters/pricing-knowledge-network/assets/pwc-tp-china-2019-apa-stats.pdf.

3.4.10 Ready Reckoner on Availability of Article 9(2), BAPA and Rollback Provisions

91. China allows unilateral, bilateral and multilateral APAs, as well as rollback of APAs. A ready reckoner on existence of Article 9(2) to relieve economic double

52. Refer China's APA Annual Report, 2019 https://home.kpmg/us/en/home/insights/2020/11/tnf-china-annual-apa-report-statistics-2019-future-considerations.html accessed on 10 February 2021.

taxation in DTAAs between China and various countries and the presence of BAPA and rollback provisions in the legislation of China's treaty partners is provided in Table 6 by analysing the following database:

- status of Article 9(2) as provided under OECD MTC, 2017 in the DTAA[53] between China and respective treaty partner;
- if not already present, whether Article 9(2) shall get introduced through the MLI[54] in such DTAAs;
- the country MAP/Dispute Resolution profiles[55] of the respective treaty partners available on the OECD website.

Table 6 Ready Reckoner on Availability of Article 9(2), BAPA and Rollback Between China and Treaty Partners

S. N.	*Treaty Partner*	*Date of Signature of DTAA*	*Does Article 9(2) Already Exist?*	*If No, Will It Come Through MLI?*	*Does the Treaty Partner Have BAPA?*	*Does the Treaty Partner Have Rollback?*
1	Australia	17.11.1988	Yes *	–	Yes	Yes
2	Austria	10.04.1991	No	Yes	Yes	Yes
3	Belgium	07.10.2009	Yes **	Yes **	Yes	Yes
4	Bulgaria	06.11.1989	Yes ***	–	No	No
5	Canada	12.05.1986	No	No	Yes	Yes
6	Chile	25.05.2015	Yes	–	Yes	Chilean tax legislation does not expressly provide for rollback of APAs
7	Croatia	09.01.1995	Yes	–	Yes	No
8	The Czech Republic	28.08.2009	Yes	–	Yes	No
9	Denmark	16.06.2012	Yes	–	Yes	Yes
10	Egypt	13.08.1997	Yes	–	No	No
11	Estonia	12.05.1998	Yes	–	Yes	Yes

53. Refer IBFD Tax Research Platform https://research.ibfd.org accessed on 10 February 2021.
54. Refer OECD – Signatories and Parties to the MLI http://www.oecd.org/tax/treaties/beps-mli-signatories-and-parties.pdf accessed on 10 February 2021.
55. Refer MAP profiles on www.oecd.org https://www.oecd.org/tax/dispute/country-map-profiles.htm accessed on 10 February 2021.

S. N.	*Treaty Partner*	*Date of Signature of DTAA*	*Does Article 9(2) Already Exist?*	*If No, Will It Come Through MLI?*	*Does the Treaty Partner Have BAPA?*	*Does the Treaty Partner Have Rollback?*
12	Finland	25.05.2010	Yes	–	No formal programme. But can be considered based on MAP article	Can be considered
13	France	26.11.2013	Yes **	Yes **	Yes	No
14	Germany	28.03.2014	Yes	–	Yes	Yes
15	Greece	03.06.2002	Yes	–	Yes	No
16	Hungary	17.06.1992	No	Yes	Yes	Yes
17	Iceland	03.06.1996	Yes	–	No	No
18	India	18.07.1994	Yes	–	Yes	Yes
19	Indonesia	07.11.2001	Yes **	Yes **	Yes	Yes @
20	Ireland	19.04.2000	Yes	–	Yes	Yes
21	Israel	08.04.1995	Yes **	Yes **	No formal programme. But can be considered based on MAP article	No
22	Japan	06.09.1983	No	Yes	Yes	Yes
23	Kazakhstan	12.09.2001	Yes **	Yes **	Yes	No
24	Korea	28.03.1994	No	Yes	Yes	Yes
25	Malaysia	23.11.1985	No	Yes	Yes	Yes
26	Mexico	12.09.2005	Yes **	Yes **	Yes	Yes
27	Morocco	27.08.2002	Yes	–	Yes	Yes
28	The Netherlands	31.05.2013	Yes **	Yes **	Yes	Yes
29	New Zealand	16.09.1986	Yes **	Yes **	Yes	Yes
30	Norway	25.02.1986	No	Yes	Yes	Yes
31	Oman	25.03.2002	Yes	–	No	No
32	Poland	07.06.1988	No	Yes	Yes	No
33	Portugal	21.04.1998	Yes **	Yes **	Yes	No
34	Romania	04.07.2016	Yes **	Yes **	Yes	No
35	Russia	13.10.2014	Yes	–	Yes	No
36	Serbia	21.03.1997	Yes	–	No	No

S. N.	*Treaty Partner*	*Date of Signature of DTAA*	*Does Article 9(2) Already Exist?*	*If No, Will It Come Through MLI?*	*Does the Treaty Partner Have BAPA?*	*Does the Treaty Partner Have Rollback?*
37	Singapore	11.07.2007	Yes **	Yes **	Yes	Yes
38	The Slovak Republic	11.06.1987	Yes	–	Yes	Yes
39	Slovenia	13.02.1995	No	Yes	Yes	Yes
40	South Africa	25.04.2000	Yes **	Yes **	No	No
41	Spain	28.11.2018	Yes	–	Yes	Yes
42	Sweden	16.05.1986	Yes	–	Yes	Yes
43	The Swiss Confederation	25.09.2013	Yes	–	Yes	Yes
44	Thailand	27.10.1986	No	No ****	Yes	Yes #
45	Turkey	23.05.1995	Yes	–	Yes	Yes
46	The United Arab Emirates	01.07.1993	Yes **	Yes **	No	No
47	United Kingdom	27.06.2011	Yes **	Yes **	Yes	Yes
48	US	30.04.1984	Yes *****	–	Yes	Yes
49	Vietnam	17.05.1995	Yes	–	Yes	No

* Such provisions are in Article 9(3) of the DTAA.

** Such provisions are not as per Article 9(2) of the OECD MTC, 2017 in entirety; hence, appropriate notification under Article 17 of MLI has been made by China and the respective treaty partner.

*** Such provisions are in Article 7a of the DTAA.

**** Thailand is not a signatory to the MLI as of now.

***** Such provisions are in Article 8(2) of the DTAA.

@ Indonesia's Dispute Resolution Profile (last updated on 1 September 2016) states that rollback of APA is not permissible under the Indonesian APA programme. However, under the revised Ministry of Finance Regulation No. 22/PMK.03/2020, rollback is available in Indonesia.

On perusal of Thailand's Dispute Resolution Profile (last updated on 1 June 2020), it is mentioned that rollback of APAs is provided for in the bilateral APA programme. However, Guidance on APA process issued by the Revenue Department of Thailand is silent on this issue.

3.5 APA REGIME IN FRANCE

92. France was one of the first member countries of the OECD to introduce transfer pricing regulations, as early as 1933. Multinational companies with French operations must ensure that the pricing of intercompany transactions meets the arm's-length standard.[56]

93. France has had an APA (called prior agreement on transfer pricing) programme since 1999. The CA in charge of the APA programme in France is Direction Générale des Finances Publiques (tax authority).[57] The relevant provisions in regard to the implementation of the APA programme in France are contained in Article L.80 B 7° of the French Tax Procedure Code and supplemented by Administrative Guidelines BOI-SJ-RES-20-10-20180718.[58]

94. Unilateral, bilateral, and multilateral APAs are available in France. There is a five-year maximum term for an APA and a minimum term of three years. There is no filing fee. In accordance with the Administrative Guidelines, the agreements between tax authorities defining the rules for distributing the tax base are concluded, with the primary aim of avoiding double taxation, on the basis of Article 25(3) of the OECD MTC. As a result, BAPA/MAPA can only be concluded with States with which France has signed a DTAA including a provision of the type of Article 25(3) of the OECD MTC.

95. Unilateral APAs, which until the rectifying Finance Bill of 2004 were not authorized in France, are since being accepted by the French administration. However, in a regulation issued on 24 June 2005, the French Tax Administration (FTA) made it clear that it would still favour the conclusion of bilateral APAs.[59] Unilateral APAs may be available:

- where the relevant DTAA does not provide for a MAP and bilateral APAs are accordingly not possible;
- where the transactions involve a significant number of countries;
- for simple but frequent issues; and
- for small and medium enterprises (SMEs).

96. Under the regulations, ongoing tax audits do not prevent the taxpayer from initiating an APA for future financial years. An APA request will also not suspend any ongoing audits. If the taxpayer and the tax authority have reached a compromise in respect of a tax audit, or if after litigation a position has been taken by the courts, the taxpayer may attempt to extend the corresponding solutions to future financial years through an APA.

56. Refer Article by Cyril Maucour, Emmanuel du Douët and Jérôme Granotier, Bignon Lebray titled 'Transfer pricing in France: overview' https://uk.practicallaw.thomsonreuters.com/w-007-3859?transitionType = Default&contextData = (sc.Default)&firstPage = true accessed on 21 February 2021.
57. Refer DLA Piper – APA and MAP Country Guide 2019 https://www.dlapiper.com/en/us/insights/publications/2019/03/apa-and-map-country-guide-2019/ accessed on 11 August 2020.
58. Refer Administrative Guidelines https://bofip.impots.gouv.fr/bofip/1053-PGP.html/identifiant = BOI-SJ-RES-20-10-20180718 accessed on 11 August 2020.
59. Refer Note issued by PwC on Transfer Pricing in France https://www.pwc.com/gx/en/international-transfer-pricing/assets/france.pdf accessed on 9 February 2021.

3.5.1 Rollback

97. APAs are available for future years only and no rollback is available; i.e., the prior agreement cannot be retroactive.

3.5.2 APA Team

98. Since the prior agreement mechanism is essentially intended to eliminate the risk of double taxation by means of an agreement concluded with another contracting State, the negotiation of agreements therefore falls within the competence of the central administration. The Mission of International Legal and Economic Expertise (MEJEI), attached to the Legal Tax Department of the General Directorate of Public Finances, is responsible for examining requests, drafting and concluding agreements. All requests or information transmitted by the taxpayer must be addressed to that authority, including a copy of the Annual Report to be filed after the conclusion of the agreement. In order to assess the conditions of exercise of the taxpayer's activity and the specificities of the market, the Mission may call upon the opening of the investigation procedure, and an agent with a good knowledge of the sector. As part of the examination of the agreements, the Mission may also call on specialists and experts from the Ministry in charge of the economy, as necessary.

3.5.3 Pre-filing Meeting

99. Prior to filing of a formal APA application, there is a provision for an informal meeting with the tax authority to discuss:

- the appropriateness of an APA in the circumstances;
- the type of information required in the application;
- the timeline of the application procedure; and
- any other questions relating to the application.

100. This preliminary meeting before the formulation of an official request will make it possible to discuss the advisability of an agreement, the type and scope of the information necessary for the analysis of the company's transfer pricing policy, the provisional timetable of work involved as well as all questions relating to the methods of examining the request.

3.5.4 APA Application

101. The APA procedure must be initiated by the taxpayer at least six months before the beginning of the first financial year it is anticipated to cover. In respect of BAPA, at the same time as the request is made in France, applicants must formulate their request for an agreement in the other State concerned. The following information is required to be submitted by the applicant when filing its application:

(1) organization chart of the entire group and list of entities covered by the request for prior agreement; corporate name, address, tax identification number of the 'parties' to the agreement;
(2) description of:
  - the industrial or commercial operations of the group;
  - its global organization;
  - its capital structure (chains of participation, percentage of participation, composition of the capital of foreign entities, shareholder agreements, type of securities held, voting rights, etc.);
  - its capitalization;
  - financial agreements;
  - main activities and the place(s) where these activities are carried out as well as the main flows of transactions between the parties.
(3) representative financial and fiscal data concerning the parties covering the last three fiscal years, as well as any other data or document likely to support the proposed TPM;
(4) indication, for the operations covered by the agreement, of the functional currency of each party as well as the currency of settlement of transactions between the parties;
(5) indication of prior agreements concluded by other entities in the group or relating to transactions other than those covered by the request for agreement presented to the French administration;
(6) duration of the fiscal year of each party;
(7) description of the main financial accounting methods used by entities established abroad and which have a direct impact on the proposed TPM;
(8) regime applicable to the transactions concerned;
(9) study of statutory provisions, tax treaties, court rulings, regulations, rulings or procedures regarding income relating to the proposed TPM;
(10) description of any question relating to the TPM, which has been examined or is still under study, indicating the position of the taxpayer and that of the administration concerned and the solution eventually adopted. It may be a case of ongoing or terminated legal proceedings, proceedings pending before the CAs, both in France and in other countries.

102. The applicant may not refuse to provide the information requested by tax authorities on the grounds that it is confidential.

3.5.5 Evaluation of APA Application

103. The prior agreement on transfer pricing requires cooperation between the company and the administration. The study of the TPM and of the transactions submitted for examination by the administration is the subject of discussions between the parties. Technical meetings are organized to allow the taxpayer to present the documents necessary for the expertise of the transactions concerned and to justify the method applicant intends to use. The examination of this request leads to the study of the method presented by the applicant as part of a joint examination carried out by the FTA as part of a parallel negotiation between the French administration and the CA of the State concerned. With the agreement of the applicant, the agents of the tax administration responsible for processing the request can visit its site. The applicant or its advisers provide the administration with the information enabling the method presented to be analysed by all appropriate means (documentation, site visits, presentations of industrial and commercial techniques, etc.). While the request is being examined, the company keeps the French administration informed of the progress of the procedures initiated with the other CAs and provides it with the same documents as those it submits to the latter.

104. In order to justify the method proposed by the applicant for determining its transfer prices, the taxpayer must, as far as possible:

- collect the relevant data on the prices charged in comparable transactions in the free market;
- in the absence of being able to have this information, identify all the transactions likely to be comparable but for which reliable data is not available;
- unable to identify such transactions, gather relevant data on the prices applied in similar transactions, even if these are not closely comparable, carried out in the free market and propose the necessary adjustments for their application to its own operations.

105. In the absence of comparable data, the applicant will have to demonstrate that the method proposed makes it possible to determine the ALPs.

3.5.6 Advance Pricing Agreement

106. The agreement between the tax authority and the applicant shall *inter alia* contain the following information:

- companies and transactions covered by the agreement;
- description of the TPM used;
- description of the basic assumptions and modalities for revising or cancelling the agreement (compensatory or automatic adjustment mechanisms);
- date of entry into force of the agreement;
- duration of the agreement or years covered by the agreement;
- information to be included in the 'annual report' and monitoring mechanism as determined during the agreement;
- conditions for renewal of the agreement.

3.5.7 Annual Report

107. The taxpayer is required to lodge an annual report providing evidence of the proper application of the APA. The monitoring system is determined under the terms of the APA. The taxpayer is required to produce, under conditions determined within the framework of the agreement, an annual report in order to verify the conformity of the methods practised under the terms of the agreement. In the absence of regularization within thirty days of a formal notice, failure to produce the Annual Report will result in the cancellation of the agreement as of the financial year for which the report was not presented to the tax administration. The taxpayer is required to keep and make available to the tax authorities all the documentation relating to the determination of its transfer prices. In the event that the application of the method would lead to results different from those provided for in the agreement, the latter may be revised in accordance with the adjustment mechanisms provided for in the agreement.

3.5.8 Renewal of APA

108. At the request of the applicant, the agreement can possibly be renewed. Applications for the renewal of APAs are required to be lodged at least six months before expiry. Negotiations on the renewal of an APA may be less onerous if there are no major changes to the terms of the existing APA. In the absence of a renewal request within the required time limits, the administration will expressly inform the taxpayer that the agreement is brought back to the end of its term.

3.5.9 Confidentiality of Information

109. The tax administration undertakes not to disclose to third parties the information transmitted and to respect the rules of confidentiality. The rules relating to tax secrecy apply to information transmitted under the agreement.

3.5.10 Statistics

110. There were twenty-two APA application requests filed and twelve completed applications in 2017. There were nineteen APA application requests filed and seven completed applications in 2018. The average time of completion of the APA negotiations was around twenty-seven months. Statistics on the number of APA requests received and resolved in 2017, 2018 in France are provided in Table 7.

Table 7 Number of APA Requests Received and Resolved in 2017, 2018 in France

Total Number of All APAs in Force at the End of 2017		*Total Number of Bilateral and Multilateral APAs in Force at the End of 2017*		*Total Number of Unilateral APAs in Force at the End of 2017*		*Number of APA Requests Received in 2017*		*Number of APAs Granted in 2017*		*Number of APA Applications Rejected in 2017*		*Number of APA Applications Where the Taxpayer Withdrew Its Request in 2017*		*Average Time (In Months) to Negotiate Bilateral or Multilateral APAs*	
EU	*Non-EU*	*EU*	*Non-EU*	*EU*	*Non-EU*	*EU*	*Non-EU*	*EU*	*Non-EU*	*EU*	*Non-EU*	*EU*	*Non-EU*	*EU*	*Non-EU*
17	30	10	19	7	11	9	13	5	7	1	1	–	2	28	27

Total Number of All APAs in Force at the End of 2018		*Total Number of Bilateral and Multilateral APAs in Force at the End of 2018*		*Total Number of Unilateral APAs in Force at the End of 2018*		*Number of APA Requests Received in 2018*		*Number of APAs Granted in 2018*		*Number of APA Applications Rejected in 2018*		*Number of APA Applications Where the Taxpayer Withdrew Its Request in 2018*		*Average Time (In Months) to Negotiate Bilateral or Multilateral APAs*	
EU	Non-EU	EU	Non-EU	EU	Non-EU	EU	Non-EU	EU	Non-EU	EU	Non-EU	EU	Non-EU	EU	Non-EU
14	26	10	17	4	9	12	7	2	5	2	–	1	–	31	24

Source: Statistics on APAs in the EU at the end of 2017 https://ec.europa.eu/taxation_customs/sites/taxation/files/statistics_on_advance_pricing_agreements_2017_en.pdf.
and
Statistics on APAs in the EU at the end of 2018 https://ec.europa.eu/taxation_customs/sites/taxation/files/apa-and-map-2019-3.pdf.

3.6 APA REGIME IN GERMANY

111. Germany has had an APA programme since 2000. The CA in charge of the APA programme in Germany is Bundeszentralamt für Steuern (Federal Central Tax Office or Tax Authority).[60] The relevant provisions in regard to the implementation of the APA programme in Germany are contained in the Ministry of Finance Ordinance of 5 October 2006 (BMF, IV B 4-S 1341-38/06).[61]

112. Bilateral and multilateral APAs are available in Germany. Unilateral binding statements from the tax authority in Germany can be obtained in the form of advance tax rulings which are available only under exceptional circumstances. The Federal Ministry of Finance is typically not prepared to grant unilateral APAs in transfer pricing issues because unilateral APAs have no binding effect on the other country concerned. Therefore, the German tax authorities are instructed to grant APAs on a bilateral or multilateral basis only. This necessitates the respective other country to participate in the APA procedure and effecting APA proceedings on the legal basis of Article 25 of OECD MTC through MAP. Where no DTAA exists, the competent regional tax authority may, by arrangement with the Federal Central Tax Office, issue the taxpayer (on its request) with a unilateral decision on transfer pricing with future effect, provided the specific case is appropriate.

113. If the taxpayer reaches a unilateral APA with another country in accordance with the latter's laws without the involvement of the German tax authorities, then the German tax authorities shall not be bound by it. If the taxpayer files a request for the competent regional tax authority to be unilaterally bound by this APA, then this request will only be granted in consultation with the Federal Central Tax Office provided it can be easily ascertained that the APA with the other country does not impair German tax interests.

114. There is a five-year maximum term for an APA and a minimum term of three years. The APA generally commences from the beginning of the fiscal year in which the formal request is filed. Earlier commencement dates are allowed if the APA is filed before a tax return has been submitted for an earlier fiscal year and the statutory deadline for submission has not yet expired. Earlier commencement dates may be negotiated with the consent of the other relevant foreign tax authorities. A formal (written) request to the tax authority signed by the applicant or an authorized representative is required, in which the applicant must express an interest in conducting such procedure. The request has to include all relevant information, and the taxpayer must be eligible under the respective DTAA. An ongoing audit does not preclude an APA request.

60. Refer DLA Piper – APA and MAP Country Guide 2019 https://www.dlapiper.com/en/us/insights/publications/2019/03/apa-and-map-country-guide-2019/ accessed on 11 August 2020.
61. Refer Ministry of Finance Ordinance of 5 October 2006 – Information on bi or multilateral mutual agreement procedures under double taxation agreements for reaching Advance Pricing Agreements ('APA') in Germany https://www.oecd.org/ctp/dispute/47655669.pdf accessed on 11 August 2020.

115. Filing fee is required to be paid under the APA programme of Germany, as below:

- APA application fee - EUR 20,000 (approx. USD 22,680).
- APA renewals - EUR 15,000 (approx. USD 17,000).
- Modification of application - EUR 10,000 (approx. USD 11,350).

116. There is a 50% reduction in fees for small taxpayers. The following categories of taxpayers comprise small taxpayers:

- taxpayers with intercompany tangible goods transactions below EUR 5 million (approx. USD 5.7 million); and
- other intercompany transactions below EUR 500,000 (approx. USD 567,000).

117. No filing fee[62] is charged in case of hardship and specific interest of tax administration in APA.

3.6.1 Rollback

118. Rollback is available where the foreign tax authorities involved consents, and the applicant can provide proof that the circumstances brought about in the relevant preceding years match the circumstances during the years covered by the APA. If a rollback is desired, the applicant must provide all information requested within the APA process for the preceding years intended to be covered which matches the documentation for the period covered by the APA.

119. In Germany, in formal terms, the preceding years cannot be covered by the APA. Rollback is possible under MAP pursuant to Article 25(1) of the OECD MTC, which has to be initiated separately but may be conducted alongside the APA, though; the conclusion of such rollback procedure is legally independent.

120. As part of rollback of APA process in Germany, the tax authorities are free to check whether the results would have had to be determined in accordance with the method agreed in the APA procedure. In this respect, tax authorities take into account whether transfer prices comply with the arm's-length principle, which may be done in different ways and with different results (which is acceptable to all participants), even if circumstances in the rollback and APA periods are the same. Thus, in a way, under rollback, the tax authorities in Germany only make a correction for preceding years if these preceding years were wrongly or incorrectly treated during the audit process.

62. Refer Germany Dispute Resolution Profile https://www.oecd.org/tax/dispute/Germany-Dispute-Resolution-Profile.pdf accessed on 11 August 2020.

3.6.2 APA Team[63]

121. Within the Federal Ministry of Finance, the competence for APA applications and for granting an APA has been centralized in one department and is not allocated over several state-specific departments. This centralized department is located within the Federal Tax Office in Bonn. In addition to the Federal Ministry of Finance, the local tax office (including the tax auditor) is regularly involved in an APA procedure. In addition, expert auditors for international tax issues from the Federal Tax Office may be involved in the proceedings.

3.6.3 Principles Adopted in APA Process

122. The APA process in Germany follows the principles stated hereunder:

- the applicant must submit to the tax authorities all the known relevant facts for an objective review of transfer prices and give them unlimited assistance in their efforts to clarify the matter. The applicant should be involved more than in a normal MAP; in particular, the TPM proposed by the applicant has to be thoroughly discussed with it;
- the tax authorities have to consider all the circumstances to the taxpayer's advantage and disadvantage that emerge during the APA procedure, even if the APA ultimately fails. By means of international administrative assistance, the tax authorities may exchange information obtained with other countries involved under the regulations laid down in the General Tax Code, in EU laws on mutual assistance, and in respective DTAAs. The rules on tax secrecy remain unaffected;
- an APA request has no direct impact on other proceedings in or out of court. Furthermore, an APA request does not prevent a tax audit being conducted or continued, particularly since a tax audit generally involves other assessment periods; in some cases, it may be wise to arrange to prolong the audit until an agreement is reached in the APA procedure. The German tax authorities conclude an APA provided the taxpayer waives its right to appeal against tax notices implementing the outcome of the agreement during the period covered by it.

3.6.4 Pre-filing Meeting

123. Any administrative or tax issues that are relevant to and may affect the outcome of the APA are to be addressed and resolved at the pre-filing stage with the Federal Central Tax Office. Taxpayers should request from the tax authority a pre-filing meeting to discuss the procedure, agree on the content of the APA request and

63. Refer Note issued by PwC on Transfer Pricing in Germany https://www.pwc.com/gx/en/international-transfer-pricing/assets/germany.pdf accessed on 9 February 2021.

documents that are required. Pre-filing is also available on an anonymous basis. During the pre-filing meeting, taxpayers are required to do the following:

- explain why an APA is suitable in its circumstances;
- outline the proposed TP method;
- introduce all relevant parties of the proposed APA;
- discuss with the tax authority the documentation required for formal filing;
- agree with the tax authority on a filing date and timetable; and
- gauge whether any of the relevant foreign tax authorities foresee major roadblocks that could prevent the APA application from reaching successful completion.

3.6.5 APA Application

124. In Germany, only persons covered under Article 1 of the OECD MTC are entitled to file an APA request with the CA (Federal Central Tax Office), in accordance with Article 25(1) of the OECD MTC. Taxpayers must file the formal APA application with the tax authority, enclosing four copies of each document required. APA applications must include:

(1) details of the companies involved:
  - name, address;
  - information on potential restructurings in the past.

(2) years for which the APA should be applicable;

(3) shareholding structure between the domestic and the foreign company/companies;

(4) a description of the company structure and the role of the involved domestic and foreign company within the group;

(5) economic situation of the company/the PE in Germany:
  - expected win/loss situation prior to the APA period (five years);
  - expected win/loss situation within the APA period (five years);
  - tax implications of the APA (additional taxes/tax refunds, reduction/increase of loss carry forwards).

(6) a description of the industry in which the relevant parties operate;

(7) presentation of business relationships with related parties covered by the APA;

(8) presentation of business relationships with related parties not covered by the APA;

(9) short description of TP problem;

(10) details on the proposed TP methodology:
  - description of the functions, risks as well as the assets used;
  - description of the TP method used prior to the envisioned APA period;
  - reasons for maintaining or changing this TP method;

- information on comparable reference values used by comparable companies or other sources of applied comparative data.

(11) annexes:
- respective contracts;
- balance sheets and profit and loss statement from the last audited period prior to the APA period;
- documents supporting the proposed TP method.

125. The application and position of the applicant are scrutinized by Federal Central Tax Office, by coordinating closely with local tax auditors and by undertaking negotiations with the relevant foreign tax authorities. The applicant does not attend the actual APA procedure. The Federal Central Tax Office keeps the applicant informed at regular intervals about the stage the procedure has reached. As the 'CA', it decides together with the other country whether the applicant or the applicant's representative may attend some of the negotiations in person. The APA process is accelerated on giving the applicant the possibility of presenting its position to both countries at these negotiations and discussing it with them. Apart from this opportunity, in all other respects, the applicant is required to cooperate, provide information, and submit documents and records in support of its application to the tax authority in Germany, which may also entail allowing investigations on its own business premises (site visit). After reaching an agreement, taxpayers are formally asked for approval. Once approved, a ruling is granted. Until the APA is concluded with legal effect, the request may be altered by the applicant at any time. However, substantial alterations by the applicant will be regarded as an entirely new request.

3.6.6 Remedy When There Are Adjustments Made by a Third Country after Conclusion of an APA

126. On conclusion of an APA, it may happen that an applicant liable to resident taxation in Germany is subjected to double taxation involving a third country not party to the APA. This may arise if the said third country does not recognize the outcome of the APA and carries out initial adjustments in the case of the applicant. In such a situation, the Federal Central Tax Office either institutes or takes part in a MAP with this third country, aiming to get it to eliminate the double taxation by amending the relevant foreign tax assessment notes/orders. The country with which the APA was originally concluded is informed without delay, and if necessary, included in the MAP with the third country. If the double taxation cannot be eliminated by way of such MAP, then various possibilities can be considered depending on the circumstances of the specific case, aiming on the one hand to uphold the APA and on the other hand to eliminate double taxation. The Federal Central Tax Office decides on such procedure to be adopted by the German tax authorities in each specific case. The taxpayer is given an opportunity to present its case while arriving at an amicable and acceptable solution/decision.

3.6.7 Annual Report

127. An annual report (Compliance Report) must be submitted to the tax authority in Germany and relevant foreign tax authorities demonstrating that the critical assumptions have been satisfied, and including any deviations or adjustments made. The Compliance Report must be delivered by the earlier of the following:

- the same time as delivered to the foreign tax authorities; or
- filed with the tax return for the relevant assessment period.

128. The Federal Central Tax Office takes charge of reviewing whether according to the Annual Report the critical assumptions have been satisfied. Any doubts arising have to be jointly clarified with the competent local tax authority. If applicable, the latter points out to the Federal Central Tax Office any inconsistencies between the Annual Report and the tax return that has been filed. In tax audit, it has to be established whether the taxpayer has complied with the APA, and in particular whether the decisive circumstances have actually been brought about and the critical assumptions have been satisfied. If indicators which are contrary to the APA are reported, the Federal Central Tax Office shall decide whether it is necessary to take any measures regarding the APA, e.g., to terminate the APA, or to take up negotiations with the treaty partner country.

3.6.8 Renewal of APA

129. An APA may be renewed if the renewal request is duly filed, there is consent from the relevant foreign tax authorities, and it can be proved that the underlying facts in the future will continue to match those on which the existing APA is based. An abbreviated procedure without submission of the documents required in an initial request is possible in such circumstances.

3.6.9 Failure to Satisfy the Critical Assumptions

130. If critical assumptions fail to be satisfied in substantial respects, then the basis for the APA ceases to exist; the APA may be revoked with effect as from the date when the critical assumptions are not (or are no longer) satisfied. The Federal Central Tax Office shall inform the other country immediately about any such circumstance. In case of immaterial deviations, the Federal Central Tax Office may allow the APA to continue, or it may adjust it accordingly through agreement with the taxpayer after holding (written) consultations with the other country. The Federal Central Tax Office shall inform the other country without delay on establishing any deviation from the position taken in the APA. The Federal Central Tax Office may take up negotiations with the other country in order to adjust the APA to the altered circumstances. For this, a request (change request) from the taxpayer is required enclosing all the necessary documents. If the request is not filed or if an adjustment by mutual agreement with the other country is not possible, then the APA loses effect as from the date when the critical assumptions are not (or are no longer) satisfied; the APA may be revoked accordingly.

3.6.10 Statistics

131. There were thirty-six APA application requests filed and twenty-eight completed applications in 2017. There were fifty-six APA application requests filed and thirty-four completed applications in 2018. The average time of completion of the APA negotiations was around fifty months. Statistics on the number of APA requests received and resolved in 2017, 2018 in Germany are provided in Table 8.

Table 8 Number of APA Requests Received and Resolved in 2017, 2018 in Germany

Total Number of All APAs in Force at the End of 2017		*Total Number of Bilateral and Multilateral APAs in Force at the End of 2017*		*Total Number of Unilateral APAs in Force at the End of 2017*		*Number of APA Requests Received in 2017*		*Number of APAs Granted in 2017*		*Number of APA Applications Rejected in 2017*		*Number of APA Applications Where the Taxpayer Withdrew Its Request in 2017*		*Average Time (In Months) to Negotiate Bilateral or Multilateral APAs*	
EU	*Non-EU*	*EU*	*Non-EU*	*EU*	*Non-EU*	*EU*	*Non-EU*	*EU*	*Non-EU*	*EU*	*Non-EU*	*EU*	*Non-EU*	*EU*	*Non-EU*
16	23	16	23	–	–	16	20	11	17	1	–	1	4	36 (average for APAs granted in 2017)/38 (overall average for APAs granted in 2015, 2016 and 2017)	47 (average for APAs granted in 2017)/51 (overall average for APAs granted in 2015, 2016 and 2017)

Total Number of All APAs in Force at the End of 2018		*Total Number of Bilateral and Multilateral APAs in Force at the End of 2018*		*Total Number of Unilateral APAs in Force at the End of 2018*		*Number of APA Requests Received in 2018*		*Number of APAs Granted in 2018*		*Number of APA Applications Rejected in 2018*		*Number of APA Applications Where the Taxpayer Withdrew Its Request in 2018*		*Average Time (In Months) to Negotiate Bilateral or Multilateral APAs*	
EU	Non-EU	EU	Non-EU	EU	Non-EU	EU	Non-EU	EU	Non-EU	EU	Non-EU	EU	Non-EU	EU	Non-EU
19	24	19	24	–	–	32	24	17	17	1	–	3	1	52 (average for APAs granted in 2018)/43 (overall average for APAs granted in 2016, 2017 and 2018)	45 (average for APAs granted in 2018)/49 (overall average for APAs granted in 2016, 2017 and 2018)

Source: Statistics on APAs in the EU at the end of 2017 https://ec.europa.eu/taxation_customs/sites/taxation/files/statistics_on_advance_pricing_agreements_2017_en.pdf.
and
Statistics on APAs in the EU at the end of 2018 https://ec.europa.eu/taxation_customs/sites/taxation/files/apa-and-map-2019-3.pdf.

3.7 APA REGIME IN INDIA

3.7.1 Introduction of TP Regulations

132. In India, a separate code on transfer pricing under sections 92-92F of the Income Tax Act, 1961[64] covering intra-group cross-border transactions became applicable from 1 April 2001 through section 49[65] of the Finance Act, 2001. The regulations are based on the arm's-length principle and provide for determination of ALP of international transactions between AEs. Rules 10A-10E of the Income Tax Rules, 1962[66] deal with procedural aspects regarding the implementation of transfer pricing law. The Central Board of Direct Taxes (CBDT) effective from 1 April 2012 had prescribed the sixth method called 'Other Method' for computation of ALP under section 92C of the Income Tax Act, 1961 and Rule 10B of the Income Tax Rules, 1962 (other five conventional methods are: Comparable Uncontrolled Price Method, Resale Price Method, Cost-Plus Method, Profit-Split Method, and Transactional Net Margin Method (TNMM)). The 'Other Method' is not a method prescribed in the OECD TP Guidelines. This method is increasingly being used in the concluded APAs in India for cases in which application of five established methods becomes difficult for various reasons, for example, cases involving complex transactions, or transactions for which comparable data is not available, or financial information concerning third-party independent enterprises is not available.

3.7.2 Introduction of APA Programme in India

133. In India, the APA provisions were introduced from 1 July 2012 vide Finance Act, 2012. In this regard, the memorandum to the Finance Bill, 2012[67] states that APA is an agreement between a taxpayer and a taxing authority on an appropriate TPM for a set of transactions over a fixed period of time in future. The APAs offer better assurance on TPMs and are conducive in providing certainty and unanimity of approach. Accordingly, new sections 92CC and 92CD were inserted in the Act to provide a framework for APA under the Act. These sections provide the following:

- It empowers Board, to enter into an advance pricing agreement with any person undertaking an international transaction.
- Such APAs shall include determination of the arm's length price or specify the manner in which arm's length price shall be determined, in relation to an international transaction which the person undertake.

64. Refer sections 92-92F of the Income Tax Act, 1961 https://www.incometaxindia.gov.in/Pages/acts/income-tax-act.aspx.
65. Refer Finance Act of India, 2001 https://www.incometaxindia.gov.in/Pages/acts/finance-acts.aspx accessed on 10 August 2019.
66. Refer Rules 10A-10E of the Income Tax Rules, 1962 https://www.incometaxindia.gov.in/Pages/rules/income-tax-rules-1962.aspx.
67. Refer Finance Bill, 2012 https://www.incometaxindia.gov.in/Pages/budget-and-bills/finance-bill.aspx.

- The manner of determination of arm's length price in such cases shall be any method including those provided in sub-section (1) of section 92C, with necessary adjustments or variations.
- The arm's length price of any international transaction, which is covered under such APA, shall be determined in accordance with the APA so entered and the provisions of section 92C or section 92CA which normally apply for determination of arm's length price would be modified to this extent and arm's length price shall be determined in accordance with APA.
- The APA shall be valid for such previous years as specified in the agreement which in no case shall exceed five consecutive previous years.
- The APA shall be binding only on the person and the Commissioner (including income-tax authorities subordinate to him) in respect of the transaction in relation to which the agreement has been entered into. The APA shall not be binding if there is any change in law or facts having bearing on such APA.
- The Board is empowered to declare, with the approval of Central Government, any such agreement to be void ab initio; if it finds that the agreement has been obtained by the person by fraud or misrepresentation of facts. Once an agreement is declared void ab initio, all the provisions of the Act shall apply to the person as if such APA had never been entered into.
- For the purpose of computing any period of limitation under the Act, the period beginning with the date of such APA and ending on the date of order declaring the agreement void ab-initio shall be excluded. However, if after the exclusion of the aforesaid period, the period of limitation referred to in any provision of the Act is less than sixty days, such remaining period shall be extended to sixty days.
- The Board is empowered to prescribe a Scheme providing for the manner, form, procedure and any other matter generally in respect of the advance pricing agreement.
- Where an application is made by a person for entering into such an APA, proceedings shall be deemed to be pending in the case of the person for the purposes of the Act like for making enquiries under section 133(6) of the Act.
- The person entering into such APA shall necessarily have to furnish a modified return within a period of three months from the end of the month in which the said APA was entered in respect of the return of income already filed for a previous year to which the APA applies. The modified return has to reflect modification to the income only in respect of the issues arising from the APA and in accordance with it.
- Where the assessment or reassessment proceedings for an assessment year relevant to the previous year to which the agreement applies are pending on the date of filing of modified return, the Assessing Officer shall proceed to complete the assessment or reassessment proceedings in accordance with the agreement taking into consideration the modified return so filed and normal period of limitation of completion of proceedings shall be extended by one year.
- If the assessment or reassessment proceedings for an assessment year relevant to a previous year to which the agreement applies has been completed before the expiry of period allowed for furnishing of modified return, the Assessing Officer shall, in a case where modified return is filed, proceed to assess or reassess or recompute the total income of the relevant assessment year having regard to and in accordance with the APA and to such assessment, all the provisions relating to assessment shall apply as if the modified return is a return furnished under section 139 of the Act. The period of limitation for completion of such assessment or reassessment is one year from the end of the financial year in which the modified return is furnished.

- All the other provisions of this Act shall apply accordingly as if the modified return is a return furnished under section 139.

134. At the time of introduction of India's APA programme in 2012, it did not have rollback of APA provisions. The provisions concerning rollback of APA (for four years) were introduced in the Income Tax Act, 1961 with effect from 1 October 2014 through subsection (9A) inserted in section 92CC by section 33 of Finance (No. 2) Act, 2014. In this regard, the memorandum to the Finance (No. 2) Bill, 2014[68] states as below:

- Section 92CC of the Act provides for Advance Pricing Agreement (APA). It empowers the Central Board of Direct Taxes, with the approval of the Central Government, to enter into an APA with any person for determining the Arm's Length Price (ALP) or specifying the manner in which ALP is to be determined in relation to an international transaction which is to be entered into by the person. The agreement entered into is valid for a period, not exceeding 5 previous years, as may be mentioned in the agreement. Once the agreement is entered into, the ALP of the international transaction, which is subject matter of the APA, would be determined in accordance with such an APA.
- In many countries the APA scheme provides for 'roll back' mechanism for dealing with ALP issues relating to transactions entered into during the period prior to APA. The 'roll back' provisions refer to the applicability of the methodology of determination of ALP, or the ALP, to be applied to the international transactions which had already been entered into in a period prior to the period covered under an APA. However, the 'roll back' relief is provided on case-to-case basis subject to certain conditions. Providing such a mechanism in Indian legislation would also lead to reduction in large scale litigation which is currently pending or may arise in future in respect of the transfer pricing matters.
- Therefore, it is proposed to amend the Act to provide roll back mechanism in the APA scheme. The APA may, subject to such prescribed conditions, procedure and manner, provide for determining the arm's length price or for specifying the manner in which arm's length price is to be determined in relation to an international transaction entered into by a person during any period not exceeding four previous years preceding the first of the previous years for which the advance pricing agreement applies in respect of the international transaction to be undertaken in future.

135. *APA defined*: In accordance with the extant provisions of the Income Tax Act, 1961, an APA is an agreement between the CBDT and any person, which determines in advance the ALP or specifies the determination of ALP in relation to an international transaction. Once an APA has been entered into, the ALP is determined in accordance with the APA itself for the tenure of the agreement. The APA process is voluntary and supplements appellate proceedings and other dispute resolution mechanisms. Presently, any taxpayer having international transactions can request an APA. There are no restrictions of any type like minimum threshold on the annual value of related party

68. Refer Finance (No. 2) Bill, 2014 https://www.incometaxindia.gov.in/Pages/budget-and-bills/finance-bill.aspx.

transactions or nature of transactions for taxpayers seeking an APA. The international transactions under transfer pricing audit or international transactions that are pending for decision with any judicial authority can also be covered in the APA. APAs can be unilateral (between the taxpayer and the CBDT), bilateral (between CBDT; the other country's government; and the respective taxpayer/applicant of the two countries involved) or multilateral (between CBDT; other countries' governments; and the respective taxpayers/applicants of the countries involved).

136. *Objective of APA*: The primary objective of an APA is to provide certainty and comfort to taxpayers so that predictable and foreseeable conditions and outcomes can be expected regarding transfer pricing practices. The benefits of an APA are many. The risk of double taxation is eliminated in the bilateral APA. The APA also provides for an agreement on maintenance of documentation, so that the burden of record-keeping is reduced. Further, there is no full-scale transfer pricing audit and only a compliance audit to check the adherence to the terms and conditions agreed in APA. A taxpayer would be able to have certainty in matters of transfer pricing for a maximum period of nine years (prospective five years and four rollback years) by applying for an APA along with an application for the rollback of the APA.

3.7.3 Statutory Provisions Governing the APA Programme

137. As mentioned above, in India, the APA provisions were introduced in the form of sections 92CC and 92CD of the Income Tax Act, 1961[69] through section 40[70] of Finance Act, 2012. Section 92CC of the Income Tax Act, 1961 is the primary section providing the statutory powers for entering into an APA, the manner of determination of ALP under an APA, period of APA and other regulations for implementation of the APA programme in India. Section 92CC, *inter alia*, provides as below:

> (1) The Board, with the approval of the Central Government, may enter into an advance pricing agreement with any person, determining the –
> (a) arm's length price or specifying the manner in which the arm's length price is to be determined, in relation to an international transaction to be entered into by that person;
> (b) income referred to in clause (i) of sub-section (1) of section 9, or specifying the manner in which said income is to be determined, as is reasonably attributable to the operations carried out in India by or on behalf of that person, being a non-resident.
>
> (2) The manner of determination of the arm's length price referred to in clause (a) or the income referred to in clause (b) of sub-section (1) may include the methods referred to in sub-section (1) of section 92C or the methods provided by rules made under this Act, respectively, with such adjustments or variations, as may be necessary or expedient so to do.

69. Refer sections 92CC and 92CD of the Income Tax Act, 1961 https://www.incometaxindia.gov.in/Pages/acts/income-tax-act.aspx.
70. Refer Finance Act, 2012 https://www.incometaxindia.gov.in/Pages/acts/finance-acts.aspx accessed on 10 August 2019.

(3) Notwithstanding anything contained in section 92C or section 92CA or the methods provided by rules made under this Act, the arm's length price of any international transaction or the income referred to in clause (b) of sub-section (1), in respect of which the advance pricing agreement has been entered into, shall be determined in accordance with the advance pricing agreement so entered.

(4) The agreement referred to in sub-section (1) shall be valid for such period not exceeding five consecutive previous years as may be specified in the agreement.

(5) The advance pricing agreement entered into shall be binding –

  (a) on the person in whose case, and in respect of the transaction in relation to which, the agreement has been entered into; and

  (b) on the Principal Commissioner or Commissioner, and the income-tax authorities subordinate to him, in respect of the said person and the said transaction.

(6) The agreement referred to in sub-section (1) shall not be binding if there is a change in law or facts having bearing on the agreement so entered.

(7) The Board may, with the approval of the Central Government, by an order, declare an agreement to be void ab initio; if it finds that the agreement has been obtained by the person by fraud or misrepresentation of facts.

(8) Upon declaring the agreement void ab initio,

  (a) all the provisions of the Act shall apply to the person as if such agreement had never been entered into; and

  (b) notwithstanding anything contained in the Act, for the purpose of computing any period of limitation under this Act, the period beginning with the date of such agreement and ending on the date of order under sub-section (7) shall be excluded:

    Provided that where immediately after the exclusion of the aforesaid period, the period of limitation, referred to in any provision of this Act, is less than sixty days, such remaining period shall be extended to sixty days and the aforesaid period of limitation shall be deemed to be extended accordingly.

138. Section 92CD of the Income Tax Act, 1961 provides the mechanism for giving effect to an APA, i.e., furnishing of modified return, its status under the Act and further action in respect thereof to be taken by the tax authorities. Section 92CD, *inter alia*, provides as below:

(1) Notwithstanding anything to the contrary contained in section 139, where any person has entered into an agreement and prior to the date of entering into the agreement, any return of income has been furnished under the provisions of section 139 for any assessment year relevant to a previous year to which such agreement applies, such person shall furnish, within a period of three months from the end of the month in which the said agreement was entered into, a modified return in accordance with and limited to the agreement.

(2) Save as otherwise provided in this section, all other provisions of this Act shall apply accordingly as if the modified return is a return furnished under section 139.

(3) If the assessment or reassessment proceedings for an assessment year relevant to a previous year to which the agreement applies have been completed before

the expiry of period allowed for furnishing of modified return under sub-section (1), the Assessing Officer shall, in a case where modified return is filed in accordance with the provisions of sub-section (1), pass an order modifying the total income of the relevant assessment year determined in such assessment or reassessment, as the case may be, having regard to and in accordance with the agreement.

(4) Where the assessment or reassessment proceedings for an assessment year relevant to the previous year to which the agreement applies are pending on the date of filing of modified return in accordance with the provisions of sub-section (1), the Assessing Officer shall proceed to complete the assessment or reassessment proceedings in accordance with the agreement taking into consideration the modified return so furnished.

(5) Notwithstanding anything contained in section 153 or section 153B or section 144C,
  (a) the order under sub-section (3) shall be passed within a period of one year from the end of the financial year in which the modified return under sub-section (1) is furnished;
  (b) the period of limitation as provided in section 153 or section 153B or section 144C for completion of pending assessment or reassessment proceedings referred to in sub-section (4) shall be extended by a period of twelve months.

(6) For the purposes of this section,
  (i) 'agreement' means an agreement referred to in sub-section (1) of section 92CC;
  (ii) the assessment or reassessment proceedings for an assessment year shall be deemed to have been completed where –
    (a) an assessment or reassessment order has been passed; or
    (b) no notice has been issued under sub-section (2) of section 143 till the expiry of the limitation period provided under the said section.

139. Thereafter, Rules 10F-10T and 44GA under Income Tax Rules, 1962[71] were notified on 30 August 2012, providing the mechanism to implement the APA scheme in India. These rules are discussed in detail hereunder.

140. Rule 10F provides meaning of expressions used in matters of APA. For the purposes of Rules 10F-10T, the said rule provides as below:

(a) 'agreement' means an advance pricing agreement entered into between the Board and the applicant, with the approval of the Central Government, as referred to in sub-section (1) of section 92CC of the Act;
(b) 'application' means an application for advance pricing agreement made under rule 10-I;
(ba) 'applicant' means a person who has made an application;
(c) 'bilateral agreement' means an agreement between the Board and the applicant, subsequent to, and based on, any agreement referred to in rule 44GA between the competent authority in India with the competent authority in the other country regarding the most appropriate transfer pricing method or the arms' length price;

71. Refer Rules 10F-10T and 44GA under Income Tax Rules, 1962 https://www.incometaxindia.gov.in/Pages/rules/income-tax-rules-1962.aspx.

(d) 'competent authority in India' means an officer authorised by the Central Government for the purpose of discharging the functions as such for matters in respect of any agreement entered into under section 90 or 90A of the Act;
(e) 'covered transaction' means the international transaction or transactions for which agreement has been entered into;
(f) 'critical assumptions' means the factors and assumptions that are so critical and significant that neither party entering into an agreement will continue to be bound by the agreement, if any of the factors or assumptions are changed;
(g) 'most appropriate transfer pricing method' means any of the transfer pricing method, referred to in sub-section (1) of section 92C of the Act, being the most appropriate method, having regard to the nature of transaction or class of transaction or class of associated persons or function performed by such persons or such other relevant factors prescribed by the Board under rules 10B and 10C;
(h) 'multilateral agreement' means an agreement between the Board and the applicant, subsequent to, and based on, any agreement referred to in rule 44GA between the competent authority in India with the competent authorities in the other countries regarding the most appropriate transfer pricing method or the arms' length price;
(ha) 'rollback year' means any previous year, falling within the period not exceeding four previous years, preceding the first of the previous years referred to in sub-section (4) of section 92CC;
(i) 'tax treaty' means an agreement under section 90, or section 90A of the Act for the avoidance of double taxation;
(j) 'team' means advance pricing agreement team consisting of income-tax authorities as constituted by the Board and including such number of experts in economics, statistics, law or any other field as may be nominated by the Director General of Income-tax (International Taxation);
(k) 'unilateral agreement' means an agreement between the Board and the applicant which is neither a bilateral nor multilateral agreement.

141. Rule 10G provides eligibility of persons who can apply for APAs. It states that any person who has undertaken an international transaction or is contemplating to undertake an international transaction shall be eligible to enter into an agreement under these rules. The term 'person' is defined in subsection (31) of section 2 of the Income Tax Act, 1961 as below:

'person' includes –

(i) an individual,
(ii) a Hindu undivided family,
(iii) a company,
(iv) a firm,
(v) an association of persons or a body of individuals, whether incorporated or not,
(vi) a local authority, and
(vii) every artificial juridical person, not falling within any of the preceding sub-clauses.

Explanation – For the purposes of this clause, an association of persons or a body of individuals or a local authority or an artificial juridical person shall be deemed to be a person, whether or not such person or body or authority or juridical person was formed or established or incorporated with the object of deriving income, profits or gains.

142. Rule 10H provides the procedure for pre-filing consultation process, which is optional and at the discretion of applicants, in India's APA programme. The said rule provides the procedure of pre-filing consultation process as below:

(1) Any person proposing to enter into an agreement under these rules may, by an application in writing, make a request for a pre-filing consultation.
(2) The request for pre-filing consultation shall be made in Form No. 3CEC to the Chief Commissioner of Income-tax (International Taxation).
(3) On receipt of the request in Form No. 3CEC, the team shall hold pre-filing consultation with the person referred to in rule 10G.
(4) The competent authority in India or his representative shall be associated in pre-filing consultation involving bilateral or multilateral agreement.
(5) The pre-filing consultation shall, among other things,
    (i) determine the scope of the agreement;
    (ii) identify transfer pricing issues;
    (iii) determine the suitability of international transaction for the agreement;
    (iv) discuss broad terms of the agreement.
(6) The pre-filing consultation shall –
    (i) not bind the Board or the person to enter into an agreement or initiate the agreement process;
    (ii) not be deemed to mean that the person has applied for entering into an agreement.

143. Rule 10I provides the procedure for filing of APA application in Form No. 3CED, fee payable alongside and time of filing of the APA application in respect of the proposed international transactions to be covered under the APA. The said rule provides as below:

(1) Any person, referred to in rule 10G may, if desires to enter into an agreement, furnish an application in Form No. 3CED, along with the requisite fee.
(2) The application shall be furnished to Chief Commissioner of Income-tax (International Taxation) in case of unilateral agreement and to the competent authority in India in case of bilateral or multilateral agreement.
(3) Application in Form No. 3CED may be filed by the person referred to in rule 10G at any time –
    (i) before the first day of the previous year relevant to the first assessment year for which the application is made, in respect of transactions which are of a continuing nature from dealings that are already occurring; or
    (ii) before undertaking the transaction in respect of remaining transactions.
(4) Every application in Form No. 3CED shall be accompanied by the proof of payment of fees as specified in sub-rule (5).
(5) The fees payable shall be in accordance with the following table based on the amount of international transaction entered into or proposed to be undertaken in respect of which the agreement is proposed:

Amount of international transaction entered into or proposed to be undertaken in respect of which agreement is proposed during the proposed period of agreement	**Fee (In Rs)**
Amount up to Rs 100 crores	Rs 10 lakhs
Amount exceeding Rs. 100 crores and up to Rs 200 crores	Rs 15 lakhs
Amount exceeding Rs 200 crores	Rs 20 lakhs

144. Rule 10J provides the procedure for withdrawal of the APA application filed in Form No. 3CED at any time prior to entering into an APA. The said rule provides that the application for withdrawal shall be submitted in Form No. 3CEE and the fee paid shall not be refunded on withdrawal of application by the applicant, in case the processing of application filed in Form No. 3CED has commenced. However, if an application is not allowed to be proceeded with in accordance with Rule 10K, the fee paid by the applicant shall be refunded.

145. Rule 10K provides the procedure for preliminary processing of the APA application filed in Form No. 3CED as below:

(1) Every application filed in Form No. 3CED shall be complete in all respects and accompanied by requisite documents.
(2) If any defect is noticed in the application in Form No. 3CED or if any relevant document is not attached thereto or the application is not in accordance with understanding reached in any pre-filing consultation referred to in rule 10H, the Chief Commissioner of Income-tax (International Taxation) (for unilateral agreement) and competent authority in India (for bilateral or multilateral agreement) shall serve a deficiency letter on the applicant before the expiry of one month from the date of receipt of the application.
(3) The applicant shall remove the deficiency or modify the application within a period of fifteen days from the date of service of the deficiency letter or within such further period which, on an application made in this behalf, may be extended, so however, that the total period of removal of deficiency or modification does not exceed thirty days.
(4) The Chief Commissioner of Income-tax (International Taxation) or the competent authority in India, as the case may be, on being satisfied, may pass an order providing that application shall not be allowed to be proceeded with if the application is defective and defect is not removed by applicant in accordance with sub-rule (3).
(5) No order under sub-rule (4) shall be passed without providing an opportunity of being heard to the applicant and if an application is not allowed to be proceeded with, the fee paid by the applicant shall be refunded.

146. Rule 10L provides the procedure for processing of the APA application filed in Form No. 3CED (which is allowed to be processed under Rule 10K) for the purposes of reaching an agreement, as below:

(1) If the application referred to in rule 10K has been allowed to be proceeded with, the team or the competent authority in India or his representative shall process the same in consultation and discussion with the applicant in accordance with provisions of this rule.

(2) For the purpose of sub-rule (1), it shall be competent for the team or the competent authority in India or its representative to –
  - (i) hold meetings with the applicant on such time and date as it deems fit;
  - (ii) call for additional document or information or material from the applicant;
  - (iii) visit the applicant's business premises; or
  - (iv) make such inquiries as it deems fit in the circumstances of the case.

(3) For the purpose of sub-rule (1), the applicant may, if he considers it necessary, provide further document and information for consideration of the team or the competent authority in India or his representative.

(4) For bilateral or multilateral agreement, the competent authority shall forward the application to Chief Commissioner of Income-tax (International Taxation) who shall assign it to one of the teams.

(5) The team, to whom the application has been assigned under sub-rule (4), shall carry out the enquiry and prepare a draft report which shall be forwarded by the Chief Commissioner of Income-tax (International Taxation) to the competent authority in India.

(6) If the applicant makes a request for bilateral or multilateral agreement in its application, the competent authority in India shall in addition to the procedure provided in this rule invoke the procedure provided in rule 44GA.

(7) The Chief Commissioner of Income-tax (International Taxation) (for unilateral agreement) or the competent authority in India (for bilateral or multilateral agreement) and the applicant shall prepare a proposed mutually agreed draft agreement enumerating the result of the process referred to in sub-rule (1) including the effect of the arrangement referred to in sub-rule (5) of rule 44GA which has been accepted by the applicant in accordance with sub-rule (8) of the said rule.

(8) The agreement shall be entered into by the Board with the applicant after its approval by the Central Government.

(9) Once an agreement has been entered into the Chief Commissioner of Income-tax (International Taxation) or the competent authority in India, as the case may be, shall cause a copy of the agreement to be sent to the Commissioner of Income-tax having jurisdiction over the assessee.

147. Rule 10M provides the terms to be specified in the agreement, *inter alia*, also providing the importance of continued satisfaction of critical assumptions for the agreement to subsist, as below:

(1) An agreement may among other things, include –
  - (i) the international transactions covered by the agreement;
  - (ii) the agreed transfer pricing methodology, if any;
  - (iii) determination of arm's length price, if any;
  - (iv) definition of any relevant term to be used in item (ii) or (iii);
  - (v) critical assumptions;

(va) rollback provision referred to in rule 10MA;
(vi) the conditions if any other than provided in the Act or these rules.

(2) The agreement shall not be binding on the Board or the assessee if there is a change in any of critical assumptions or failure to meet conditions subject to which the agreement has been entered into.
(3) The binding effect of agreement shall cease only if any party has given due notice of the concerned other party or parties.
(4) In case there is a change in any of the critical assumptions or failure to meet the conditions subject to which the agreement has been entered into, the agreement can be revised or cancelled, as the case may be.
(5) The assessee which has entered into an agreement shall give a notice in writing of such change in any of the critical assumptions or failure to meet conditions to the Chief Commissioner of Income-tax (International Taxation) as soon as it is practicable to do so.
(6) The Board shall give a notice in writing of such change in critical assumptions or failure to meet conditions to the assessee, as soon as it comes to the knowledge of the Board.
(7) The revision or the cancellation of the agreement shall be in accordance with rules 10Q and 10R respectively.

148. Rule 10N provides the procedure for amendment of the APA application filed in Form No. 3CED at any stage prior to finalization of the terms of the agreement. The said rule provides that the Chief Commissioner of Income Tax (International Taxation) (for unilateral agreement) or the CA in India (for bilateral or multilateral agreement) may allow the amendment to the application if such an amendment does not have the effect of altering the nature of the application as originally filed. The amendment shall be given effect only if it is accompanied by the additional fee, if any, necessitated by such amendment in accordance with Rule 10-I.

149. Rule 10O provides the procedure for furnishing of ACR by the taxpayer and subsequent action thereon, as below:

(1) The assessee shall furnish an annual compliance report to Chief Commissioner of Income-tax (International Taxation) for each year covered in the agreement.
(2) The annual compliance report shall be in Form 3CEF.
(3) The annual compliance report shall be furnished in quadruplicate, for each of the years covered in the agreement, within thirty days of the due date of filing the income-tax return for that year, or within ninety days of entering into an agreement, whichever is later.
(4) The Chief Commissioner of Income-tax (International Taxation) shall send one copy of annual compliance report to the competent authority in India, one copy to the Commissioner of Income-tax who has the jurisdiction over the income-tax assessment of the assessee and one copy to the Transfer Pricing Officer having the jurisdiction over the assessee.

150. In order to ensure that the terms and conditions of the APA have been complied with by the taxpayer, Rule 10P provides for compliance audit of the agreement by the TPO, as below:

(1) The Transfer Pricing Officer having the jurisdiction over the assessee shall carry out the compliance audit of the agreement for each of the year covered in the agreement.
(2) For the purposes of sub-rule (1), the Transfer Pricing Officer may require –
   (i) the assessee to substantiate compliance with the terms of the agreement, including satisfaction of the critical assumptions, correctness of the supporting data or information and consistency of the application of the transfer pricing method;
   (ii) the assessee to submit any information, or document, to establish that the terms of the agreement have been complied with.
(3) The Transfer Pricing Officer shall submit the compliance audit report, for each year covered in the agreement, to the Chief Commissioner of Income-tax (International Taxation) in case of unilateral agreement and to the competent authority in India, in case of bilateral or multilateral agreement, mentioning therein his findings as regards compliance by the assessee with terms of the agreement.
(4) The Chief Commissioner of Income-tax (International Taxation) shall forward the report to the Board in a case where there is finding of failure on part of assessee to comply with terms of agreement and cancellation of the agreement is required.
(5) The compliance audit report shall be furnished by the Transfer Pricing Officer within six months from the end of the month in which the Annual Compliance Report referred to in rule 10-O is received by the Transfer Pricing Officer.
(6) The regular audit of the covered transactions shall not be undertaken by the Transfer Pricing Officer if an agreement has been entered into under rule 10L except where the agreement has been cancelled under rule 10R.

151. Rule 10Q provides the procedure and conditions for revision of an APA, as below:

(1) An agreement, subsequent to it having been entered into, may be revised by the Board, if,
   (a) there is a change in critical assumptions or failure to meet a condition subject to which the agreement has been entered into;
   (b) there is a change in law that modifies any matter covered by the agreement but is not of the nature which renders the agreement to be non-binding; or
   (c) there is a request from competent authority in the other country requesting revision of agreement, in case of bilateral or multilateral agreement.
(2) An agreement may be revised by the Board either suo motu or on request of the assessee or the competent authority in India or the Chief Commissioner of Income-tax (International Taxation).
(3) Except when the agreement is proposed to be revised on the request of the assessee, the agreement shall not be revised unless an opportunity of being heard has been provided to the assessee and the assessee is in agreement with the proposed revision.
(4) In case the assessee is not in agreement with the proposed revision the agreement may be cancelled in accordance with rule 10R.
(5) In case the Board is not in agreement with the request of the assessee for revision of the agreement, the Board shall reject the request in writing giving reason for such rejection.
(6) For the purpose of arriving at the agreement for the proposed revision, the procedure provided in rule 10L may be followed so far as they apply.

(7) The revised agreement shall include the date till which the original agreement is to apply and the date from which the revised agreement is to apply.

152. Rule 10R provides the procedure and conditions for cancellation of an APA, as below:

(1) An agreement shall be cancelled by the Board for any of the following reasons:
  (i) the compliance audit referred to in rule 10P has resulted in the finding of failure on the part of the assessee to comply with the terms of the agreement;
  (ii) the assessee has failed to file the annual compliance report in time;
  (iii) the annual compliance report furnished by the assessee contains material errors; or
  (iv) the agreement is to be cancelled under sub-rule (4) of rule 10Q or sub-rule (7) of rule 10RA.

(2) The Board shall give an opportunity of being heard to the assessee, before proceeding to cancel an application.

(3) The competent authority in India shall communicate with the competent authority in the other country or countries and provide reason for the proposed cancellation of the agreement in case of bilateral or multilateral agreement.

(4) The order of cancellation of the agreement shall be in writing and shall provide reasons for cancellation and for non-acceptance of assessee's submission, if any.

(5) The order of cancellation shall also specify the effective date of cancellation of the agreement, where applicable.

(6) The order under the Act, declaring the agreement as void ab initio, on account of fraud or misrepresentation of facts, shall be in writing and shall provide reason for such declaration and for non-acceptance of assessee's submission, if any.

(7) The order of cancellation shall be intimated to the Assessing Officer and the Transfer Pricing Officer, having jurisdiction over the assessee.

153. Rule 10S provides the procedure for renewing an agreement for which request is to be made by the applicant as a new application for APA, using the same procedure as outlined in the relevant rules mentioned above, except pre-filing consultation, as referred to in Rule 10H.

154. Rule 10T provides certain miscellaneous provisions in respect of the APA programme, as below:

(1) Mere filing of an application for an agreement under these rules shall not prevent the operation of Chapter X of the Act for determination of arms' length price under that Chapter till the agreement is entered into.

(2) The negotiation between the competent authority in India and the competent authority in the other country or countries, in case of bilateral or multilateral agreement, shall be carried out in accordance with the provisions of the tax treaty between India and the other country or countries.

155. Rule 44GA outlines the procedure to be adopted by the CA in India to deal with requests for bilateral or multilateral APAs, as below:

(1) Where a person has made request for a bilateral or multilateral advance pricing agreement in an application filed in Form No. 3CED in accordance with rule 10-I, the request shall be dealt with subject to provisions of this rule.
(2) The process for bilateral or multilateral advance pricing agreement shall not be initiated unless the associated enterprise situated outside India has initiated process of advance pricing agreement with the competent authority in the other country.
(3) The competent authority in India shall, on intimation of request of the applicant for a bilateral or multilateral agreement, consult and ascertain willingness of the competent authority in other country or countries, as the case may be, for initiation of negotiation for this purpose.
(4) In case of willingness of the competent authority in other country or countries, as the case may be, the competent authority in India shall enter into negotiation in this behalf and endeavour to reach a set of terms which are acceptable to the competent authority in India and the competent authority in the other country or countries, as the case may be.
(5) In case of an agreement after consultation, the competent authority in India shall formalise a mutual agreement procedure arrangement with the competent authority in other country or countries, as the case may be, and intimate the same to the applicant.
(6) In case of failure to reach agreement on such terms as are mutually acceptable to parties mentioned in sub-rule (4), the applicant shall be informed of the failure to reach an agreement with the competent authority in other country or countries.
(7) The applicant shall not be entitled to be part of discussion between competent authority in India and the competent authority in the other country or countries, as the case may be; however, the applicant can communicate or meet the competent authority in India for the purpose of entering into an advance pricing agreement.
(8) The applicant shall convey acceptance or otherwise of the agreement within thirty days of it being communicated.
(9) The applicant, in case the agreement is not acceptable may at its option continue with process of entering into an advance pricing agreement without benefit of mutual agreement process or withdraw application in accordance with rule 10J.

156. In order to provide adequate information concerning the APA programme in India, a booklet[72] was released by the CBDT encapsulating the salient provisions of the scheme and clarifications on technical aspects of the scheme in the form of Frequently Asked Questions (FAQs).

3.7.4 Statutory Provisions Governing Rollback of APA

157. As mentioned above, at the time of the introduction of the Scheme, the APA provisions provided for an agreement for a period not exceeding five consecutive financial years going forward and there was no provision for rollback of APA. The provisions concerning rollback of the APA (four years) were introduced in the Income

72. Refer Tax Payers Information Series – 43 www.incometaxindia.gov.in.

Tax Act, 1961 through subsection (9A) inserted in section 92CC by section 33[73] of Finance (No. 2) Act, 2014 and the relevant rules, namely, Rules 10MA and 10RA under Income Tax Rules, 1962, were notified.

158. Subsection (9A) of section 92CC provides for rollback of the APA and states as below:

> (9A) The agreement referred to in sub-section (1), may, subject to such conditions, procedure and manner as may be prescribed, provide for determining the –
>
> (a) arm's length price or specify the manner in which the arm's length price shall be determined in relation to the international transaction entered into by the person;
> (b) income referred to in clause (i) of sub-section (1) of section 9, or specifying the manner in which the said income is to be determined, as is reasonably attributable to the operations carried out in India by or on behalf of that person, being a non-resident,
>
> during any period not exceeding four previous years preceding the first of the previous years referred to in sub-section (4), and the arm's length price of such international transaction or the income of such person shall be determined in accordance with the said agreement.

159. Rule 10MA *inter alia* provides that the applicant is required to seek Rollback of the APA in Form No. 3CEDA, subject to payment of fee and satisfaction of various conditions as below:

> (1) Subject to the provisions of this rule, the agreement may provide for determining the arm's length price or specify the manner in which arm's length price shall be determined in relation to the international transaction entered into by the person during the rollback year (hereinafter referred to as 'rollback provision').
> (2) The agreement shall contain rollback provision in respect of an international transaction subject to the following, namely:
>   (i) the international transaction is the same as the international transaction to which the agreement (other than the rollback provision) applies;
>   (ii) the return of income for the relevant rollback year has been or is furnished by the applicant before the due date specified in Explanation 2 to sub-section (1) of section 139;
>   (iii) the report in respect of the international transaction had been furnished in accordance with section 92E;
>   (iv) the applicability of rollback provision, in respect of an international transaction, has been requested by the applicant for all the rollback years in which the said international transaction has been undertaken by the applicant; and
>   (v) the applicant has made an application seeking rollback in Form 3CEDA in accordance with sub-rule (5);

73. Refer Finance (No. 2) Act, 2014 https://www.incometaxindia.gov.in/Pages/acts/finance-acts.aspx.

(3) Notwithstanding anything contained in sub-rule (2), rollback provision shall not be provided in respect of an international transaction for a rollback year, if,

(i) the determination of arm's length price of the said international transaction for the said year has been subject matter of an appeal before the Appellate Tribunal and the Appellate Tribunal has passed an order disposing of such appeal at any time before signing of the agreement; or

(ii) the application of rollback provision has the effect of reducing the total income or increasing the loss, as the case may be, of the applicant as declared in the return of income of the said year.

(4) Where the rollback provision specifies the manner in which arm's length price shall be determined in relation to an international transaction undertaken in any rollback year then such manner shall be the same as the manner which has been agreed to be provided for determination of arm's length price of the same international transaction to be undertaken in any previous year to which the agreement applies, not being a rollback year.

(5) The applicant may, if he desires to enter into an agreement with rollback provision, furnish along with the application the request for the same in Form No. 3 CEDA with proof of payment of an additional fee of five lakh rupees:

Provided that in a case where an application has been filed on or before the 31st day of March 2015, Form No.3CEDA along with proof of payment of additional fee may be filed at any time on or before the 30th day of June 2015 or the date of entering into the agreement whichever is earlier.

Provided further that in a case where an agreement has been entered into on or before the 31st day of March 2015, Form No.3CEDA along with proof of payment of additional fee may be filed at any time on or before the 30th day of June 2015 and, notwithstanding anything contained in rule 10Q, the agreement may be revised to provide for rollback provision in the said agreement in accordance with this rule.

160. Rule 10RA provides the procedure for giving effect to rollback of an APA as below:

(1) The effect to the rollback provisions of an agreement shall be given in accordance with this rule.

(2) The applicant shall furnish modified return of income referred to in section 92CD in respect of a rollback year to which the agreement applies along with the proof of payment of any additional tax arising as a consequence of and computed in accordance with the rollback provision.

(3) The modified return referred to in sub-rule (2) shall be furnished along with the modified return to be furnished in respect of first of the previous years for which the agreement has been requested for in the application.

(4) If any appeal filed by the applicant is pending before the Commissioner (Appeals), Appellate Tribunal or the High Court for a rollback year, on the issue which is the subject matter of the rollback provision for that year, the said appeal to the extent of the subject covered under the agreement shall be withdrawn by the applicant before furnishing the modified return for the said year.

(5) If any appeal filed by the Assessing Officer or the Principal Commissioner or Commissioner is pending before the Appellate Tribunal or the High Court for a rollback year, on the issue which is subject matter of the rollback provision for that year, the said appeal to the extent of the subject covered under the

agreement shall be withdrawn by the Assessing Officer or the Principal Commissioner or the Commissioner, as the case may be, within three months of filing of modified return by the applicant.

(6) The applicant, the Assessing Officer or the Principal Commissioner or the Commissioner, shall inform the Dispute Resolution Panel or the Commissioner (Appeals) or the Appellate Tribunal or the High Court, as the case may be, the fact of an agreement containing rollback provision having been entered into along with a copy of the same as soon as it is practicable to do so.

(7) In case effect cannot be given to the rollback provision of an agreement in accordance with this rule, for any rollback year to which it applies, on account of failure on the part of applicant, the agreement shall be cancelled.

161. For the ease of stakeholders, in order to clarify the finer nuances of the rollback of the APA provisions, FAQs[74] were issued. The primary condition for the rollback of the APA is that the international transaction in the rollback period shall be the same as in the APA period. The functions performed, assets utilized and risks assumed (FAR) analysis of the rollback year shall not differ materially from the FAR analysis validated for the APA years. The rollback provisions are applicable for four years prior to the first year of the APA period, and the applicant does not have the option to pick and choose the years for which it wants to apply for rollback. The applicant must apply the rollback of the APA for all four years or not apply at all. For example, if the applicant's transfer price is accepted to be at arm's length in the transfer pricing audit for any of the four previous years or a year is not in the transfer pricing audit, these years cannot be left out, and rollback of the APA would apply to these years also.

3.7.5 Structure of APA Teams at CBDT Level and Field Level

162. *BAPA authorities*: The CA in charge of the APA programme in India is the CBDT. Applications for bilateral/multilateral APAs are to be filed in the office of the CA of India, having its office in New Delhi. There is a team in the office of Joint Secretary, Foreign Tax and Tax Research-I Division (FT&TR-I), CBDT that deals with applications where the AE of the applicant is resident of US, other countries of North America, UK and other countries in Europe. The second team is the office of the Joint Secretary FT&TR-II, CBDT (CA of India) which deals with applications where the AE of the applicant is resident of Japan, Australia, Asia, South America, i.e., countries other than those handled by the office of Joint Secretary FT&TR-I, CBDT. In the case of bilateral/multilateral APA, the AE must initiate the procedure for entering into APA with the CA of other country and evidence of the same shall be furnished to the CA in India. Negotiations are held by the CA in bilateral/multilateral APAs with their counterparts prior to entering into an APA. The provisions of MAP (Article 25 or equivalent) and associated enterprises (Article 9 or equivalent) of relevant tax treaty are used to negotiate and agree at the bilateral and multilateral APAs with the tax authority of other countries. The applicant must accept the terms of an agreement before a bilateral or multilateral APA is entered with other CAs.

74. Refer Circular No. 10/2015 dated 10 June 2015 www.incometaxindia.gov.in.

163. *UAPA authorities*: All unilateral APA applications and pre-filing applications are to be filed in the office of the Pr. Chief Commissioner of Income Tax (International Taxation), New Delhi, who, in turn, assigns them to the APA teams, located in the field at New Delhi, Mumbai and Bengaluru, for examination and analysis thereof. At present, each APA team is headed by an officer of the rank of Commissioner of Income Tax and is assisted by an officer of the rank of Additional/Joint Commissioner of Income Tax and the latter is assisted by two officers of the rank of Deputy/Assistant Commissioner of Income Tax and other support staff.

3.7.6 Conditions for Entering into BAPA/MAPA

164. A bilateral/multilateral APA can be entered into by the CBDT in light of the following circumstances:

- A tax treaty exists between India and the other country(ies) containing an article on 'Mutual Agreement Procedure'.
- In the case of international transactions leading to economic double taxation arising out of TP adjustments, the said treaty contains provisions similar to paragraph 2 of Article 9 as provided in the OECD MTC on 'Associated Enterprises'.
- The corresponding APA Program exists in the other country(ies).

3.7.7 Salient Processes/Steps Involved in India's APA Programme

165. The steps involved in processing of unilateral and bilateral/multilateral applications by the APA teams are similar. The APA scheme in India involves the following salient processes/steps:

(a) Rule 10H of Income Tax Rules, 1962[75] allows pre-filing consultation, which is optional/discretionary, for the applicants to decide. Applicants desirous of undertaking pre-filing consultation are required to apply in Form No. 3CEC[76] in the office of Chief Commissioner of Income Tax (International Taxation), New Delhi, following which discussions are held by the APA team with such filers. The minutes of the meeting are recorded by the APA team for its internal record and a broad understanding is conveyed to the applicant comprising the following:
  (i) determine the scope of the agreement;
  (ii) identify transfer pricing issues;
  (iii) determine the suitability of international transaction for the agreement;
  (iv) discuss broad terms of the agreement.

75. Refer Rule 10H of Income Tax Rules, 1962 www.incometax india.gov.in.
76. Refer Form No. 3CEC https://www.incometaxindia.gov.in/Pages/downloads/forms.aspx.

Pre-filing consultation can also be sought on an anonymous basis. The pre-filing consultation process is non-binding on both the parties.

(b) On successful completion of pre-filing consultations, if opted, the applicants are required to furnish an APA application in Form No. 3CED and/or rollback application in Form No. 3CEDA. The formal application in Form No. 3CED must contain the specified information. The application needs to state the multinational group structure, organization arrangement, mention covered transactions explicitly, provide FAR analysis of the applicant and all relevant entities for the covered transactions, economic analysis, a copy of intercompany agreements for all covered transactions, audited accounts, and the proposed terms and conditions. A taxpayer is free to cover all or select only some international transactions for the APA. The application can be made for continuing transactions and proposed (new) transactions. Every APA application in Form No. 3CED shall be accompanied by a fee, computed as below:

Cumulative Amounts of International Transactions Entered into or Proposed to Be Undertaken in Respect of Which Agreement Is Proposed	*Fee (In INR and USD) (INR 70 = 1 USD)*
Amount up to INR 100 crores (USD 14.286 million)	INR 10 lakhs (USD 14,286)
Amount exceeding INR 100 crores and up to INR 200 crores (USD 14.286 million to USD 28.572 million)	INR 15 lakhs (USD 21,429)
Amount exceeding INR 200 crores (USD 28.572 million)	INR 20 lakhs (USD 28,572)

(c) Similarly, every rollback application in Form No. 3CEDA is to be accompanied by a fixed fee of INR 5 lakhs (USD 7,143).

(d) The APA and rollback applications are subjected to preliminary verification under Rule 10K of Income Tax Rules, 1962 to ensure completeness and applicants are called upon to remove deficiencies, if any. Upon removal of deficiencies, the applications are accepted and proceeded with. In case deficiencies are not removed, within the time stipulated in Rule 10K of Income Tax Rules, 1962, the applications may get rejected and fee paid by the applicant is refunded.

(e) Rule 10N of Income Tax Rules, 1962 provides for amendment to an APA application, if the applicant so desires, so as to include/exclude any international transaction, AE, etc. post-filing of the application.

(f) *Processing of APA application*: Site visit by the APA team at the premises of the applicant is an important aspect of examination, wherein the APA team interacts with the top management of the applicant so as to verify FAR analysis as declared in the APA application. A visit to the applicant's business premises, taking into account the convenience of the taxpayer, provides the APA Team with first-hand information on the underlying business activities concerning the covered transactions and helps it to better understand the facts of the transactions, business model and business realities of the taxpayer. The visit to the business premises also helps the taxpayer and the APA Team to understand each other's perspectives, concerns and agree on a time frame for completion of the APA process. The visit allows discussion of the issues directly with the responsible officials of the applicant. The focus of the office visit depends on the nature of the business and business model adopted by the applicant. In the case of taxpayers applying bilateral APA, a joint site visit along with the representatives of the other CA is also possible. The applicant is expected to give full cooperation for this purpose. During analysis and detailed evaluation of the application, additional information or documentation may be requested. The APA Team is required to do detailed functional analysis and examines the APA application in a reasonable and fair manner taking into consideration all the pieces of evidence and information furnished by the applicant or collected by it. On completion of the examination of the APA application, the APA team prepares a position paper which is submitted to the CBDT for internal approval. In the position paper, the APA team outlines its impression of the case, proposing the range of margin at which agreement may be executed with the applicant along with critical assumptions (other terms and conditions) which need to be satisfied by the applicant during the tenure of the agreement. After obtaining the internal approval from CBDT, in UAPA cases, the APA team negotiates the margin, other terms and conditions of the agreement, including critical assumptions with the applicant and on successful completion of this process, the unilateral agreement is signed by the CBDT and the applicant. In case of applications for bilateral/multilateral APAs, the CA of India carries out negotiations with the CAs of other countries. It would be expedient to state here that the APA finalized includes a section on critical assumptions,[77] which are those factors and assumptions that are critical and significant to the agreement, including operational, legal, tax, financial, accounting and economic conditions or assumptions. These may also include those factors which are not within the taxpayer's control.

(g) *Entering into an APA*: The procedure of negotiations, approval, and signing of the APA is different for unilateral and bilateral APA. The negotiations with the applicant in case of unilateral APA are carried out by the APA Team. These negotiations are focussed on the appropriate TPM, the basis of arriving at ALP or arm's-length results, terms and conditions, critical assumptions, nature of documents to be maintained by the applicant and to

77. Refer Rule 10F(f) of Income Tax Rules, 1962 www.incometax india.gov.in.

be filed along with the ACR. After completion of the negotiations, a mutually agreed draft agreement is sent to the CBDT by the APA Team for seeking approval of the Central Government. The CBDT signs the agreement with the applicant after obtaining approval of the Central Government. In the case of a bilateral APA, the negotiations are carried out by the CA with the other CA and the applicant is not a part of the negotiation between two CAs, but it may be consulted for this purpose by the Indian CA. The provisions of MAP apply regarding the bilateral/multilateral APA process.

(h) APA provisions in India allow conversion of an already filed unilateral APA to bilateral/multilateral APA.

(i) Till the time an APA is signed, proceedings before the Assessing Officer (AO) and/or the TPO continue without taking cognizance of the separate APA proceedings in progress.

(j) *Taxpayer's obligations after the signing of the agreement*: The applicant is obliged to file a modified return of income, based on the terms and conditions of the agreement, for the completed years of the APA period including rollback years and pay additional tax and interest as per provisions of the Income Tax Act, 1961. The applicant is also required to withdraw an appeal pending with the administrative or judicial authorities concerning the covered transactions and for the period covered in the APA. Rule 10O of Income Tax Rules, 1962 provides for filing of ACR by the taxpayer/applicant, which are subjected to compliance audit by the TPO under Rule 10P of Income Tax Rules, 1962. In pursuance of compliance audit, if the TPO finds that the taxpayer has failed to comply with the terms of the agreement, the CBDT in accordance with provisions contained in Rule 10Q of Income Tax Rules, 1962 may revise the agreement or may cancel the agreement altogether in accordance with provisions contained in Rule 10R of Income Tax Rules, 1962.

(k) *Tax Administration's obligations after the signing of the agreement*: The modified return of income filed by the taxpayer is deemed to be a regular return of income filed under section 139 of Income Tax Act, 1961 and all provisions of the Income Tax Act, 1961 apply accordingly. The APA years including rollback years covered in the agreement are not subject to the regular transfer pricing audit. However, there is no protection from the regular transfer pricing audit of international transactions which are not included in the agreement. After the APA is signed, the ongoing transfer pricing audit will be stopped. The Revenue will withdraw all appeals filed by it before the Income Tax Appellate Tribunal (ITAT), High Court and Supreme Court.

(l) Rule 10S of Income Tax Rules, 1962 provides for renewal of an APA, at the option of the applicant. Request for renewal of an agreement may be made as a new application for agreement, using the same procedure as outlined in the rules except pre-filing consultation as referred to in Rule 10H.

(m) The taxpayer/applicant can withdraw[78] the APA application by filing a request in Form No. 3CEE at any time before the finalization of the terms of the agreement. The fee paid shall not be refunded on withdrawal of the Application.

(n) *Cancellation of an agreement*: The CBDT can cancel an existing agreement unilaterally after providing an opportunity of being heard to the taxpayer in the following circumstances:
   - the taxpayer has failed to comply with the terms of the agreement;
   - the taxpayer has failed to file the ACR in time;
   - the ACR furnished by the taxpayer contains a material error; or
   - the taxpayer does not agree with the revision of the existing agreement proposed by the CBDT.

   The cancellation order must be a reasoned order in writing and must specify the effective date of cancellation of the agreement. The agreement can also be cancelled from the very beginning of the effective date for the reason of fraud or misrepresentation of facts by the taxpayer, and the order of cancellation must be in writing detailing appropriate reasons for the same. As of now, no occasion has ever arisen in India's APA programme calling for cancellation of the APA. However, there are chances of litigation if the agreement is rendered void or cancelled without proper reasoning or by arbitrary use of powers by an authority. To support this view, the US case of *Eaton Corp.*[79] *v. Commissioner*[80] is critically examined. Eaton Corp. and the Inland Revenue Service (IRS) entered into two APAs, first in the year 2004 covering the 2001-2005 tax years and second in 2006 for renewing the agreement. The IRS determined that Eaton Corp. did not comply with the terms of the APAs and cancelled the APAs. They asserted that the taxpayer owed taxes on over USD 360 million in additional income and levied USD 51 million in penalties. Eaton and the IRS approached the court to determine the legal standards that are to apply if the IRS unilaterally cancels an APA retroactively. Eaton argued that APAs were enforceable contracts, and that the IRS must show that they are entitled to revoke the APAs. They claimed to have complied with the terms and conditions of the APAs and that the IRS had abused its discretion in cancelling them. The IRS countered that it cancelled the APAs under revenue procedures and these were administrative determinations. The IRS may revoke an APA due to malfeasance, fraud or lack of good faith with respect to compliance with the APA's terms and conditions. The Eaton case tests the flaws of the APA programme as to whether a tax jurisdiction can dismiss it at will. Tax

78. Refer Rule 10J of the Income Tax Rules, 1962 www.incometax india.gov.in.
79. Excerpts taken from K. Spencer & M. Kelleher, Are Advance Pricing Agreements Binding Commitments? 20 International Transfer Pricing Journal 2 (2013), Journals IBFD.
80. 140 T.C. No. 18 (26 June 2013), US.

authorities should therefore refrain from taking arbitrary decisions of cancelling APAs.[81]

(o) In order to make actual allocation of funds consistent with that of the primary transfer pricing adjustment, Finance Act 2017 inserted section 92CE in the Income Tax Act 1961 with effect from 01.04.2018 and Rule 10CB of Income Tax Rules, 1962 on computation of interest income pursuant to secondary adjustment by attributing income[82] to the excess money lying in the hands of the AE.

3.7.8 Statistics[83] on India's APA Programme

166. Over the last seven years, more than 1,150 applications have been filed in India. A majority of these applications (about 82%) are for unilateral APAs between the Indian taxpayer and the CBDT. Till 31 March 2019, 271 agreements have been entered into (240 unilateral and 31 bilateral). As at 30 September 2019,[84] 300 agreements have been signed. The total number of applications filed on an annual basis (till 31 March 2019) is as below:

FY	*Unilateral APA Applications*	*Bilateral APA Applications*	*Total*
2012-2013	117	29	146
2013-2014	206	26	232
2014-2015	192	14	206
2015-2016	113	19	132
2016-2017	78	23	101
2017-2018	115	53	168
2018-2019	123	47	170
Total	**944**	**211**	**1155**

167. The number of agreements that have been entered into, year-wise, till 31 March 2019 is as below:

81. Refer Article by Anurag Soan and Shreya Ganju titled 'India – Advance Pricing Agreements' https://research.ibfd.org/#/doc?url=/collections/aptb/html/aptb_2014_01_in_1.html#d18e337 accessed on 2 September 2020.
82. Refer Explanatory Memorandum vide Notification No. 52/2017 dated 15 June 2017 (www.incometaxindia.gov.in) in respect of insertion of Rule 10CB of Income Tax Rules, 1962 on computation of interest income pursuant to secondary adjustments.
83. Refer Annual Report (2018-2019) by Central Board of Direct Taxes on Advance Pricing Agreement (APA) Programme of India, November 2019 https://www.irsofficersonline.gov.in/Documents/OfficalCommunique/129112019165648.pdf accessed on 13 December 2019.
84. Refer Press Release by Press Information Bureau, Government of India dated 1 October 2019 https://pib.gov.in/newsite/PrintRelease.aspx?relid=193539 accessed on 13 December 2019.

FY	*Unilateral*	*Bilateral*	*Total*
2013-2014	5	0	5
2014-2015	3	1	4
2015-2016	53	2	55
2016-2017	80	8	88
2017-2018	58	9	67
2018-2019	41	11	52
Total	**240**	**31**	**271**

168. In 2018-2019, the average time taken by the CBDT to conclude the 41 unilateral agreements was 45.22 months. This is more than the average time taken in any of the previous 5 years. As a result, the average time taken to conclude unilateral APAs in India has increased from 31.75 months (as at 31 March 2018) to 32.50 months (as at 31 March 2019). The table below shows the status of bilateral APA applications as at 31 March 2019:

FY	*(A) No. of Applications Filed*	*(B) No. of Agreements Signed Out of (A)*	*(C) No. of Applications Disposed of Out of (A) Due to Other Reasons*	*(D) No. of Applications under Processing Out of (A)*
2012-2013	35	18	7	10
2013-2014	36	6	9	21
2014-2015	33	6	0	27
2015-2016	26	0	0	26
2016-2017	23	1	0	22
2017-2018	53	0	0	53
2018-2019	47	0	0	47
Total	**253**	**31**	**16**	**206**

169. In 2018-2019, the average time taken to conclude bilateral APAs has gone up to 51.82 months. This has increased the average time taken for all bilateral APAs concluded till 31 March 2019 from 42.10 months (as at 31 March 2018) to 44.32 months. However, it is interesting to note that while India has entered into 271 APAs in 6 years, China has entered into 156 APAs in 14 years between 2005 and 2018. Statistics on the number of APA requests received and resolved in various years in India are provided in Figure 7.

Figure 7 Number of APA Requests Received and Resolved in Various Years in India

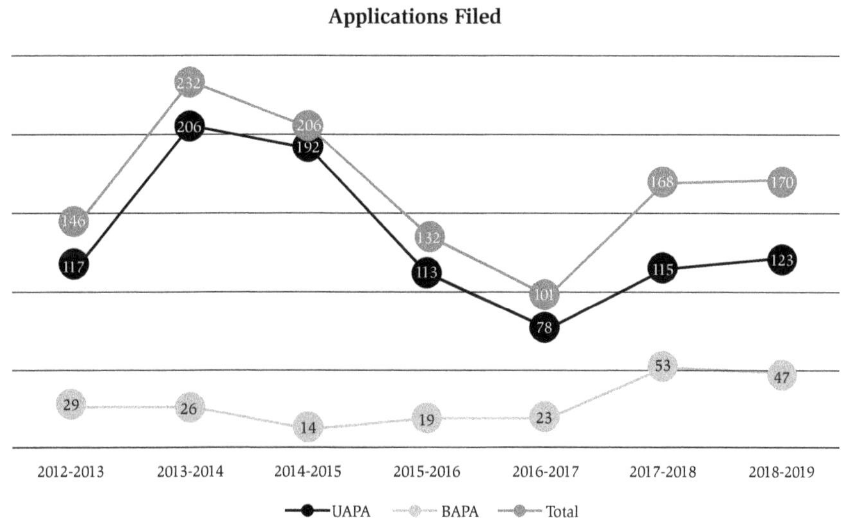

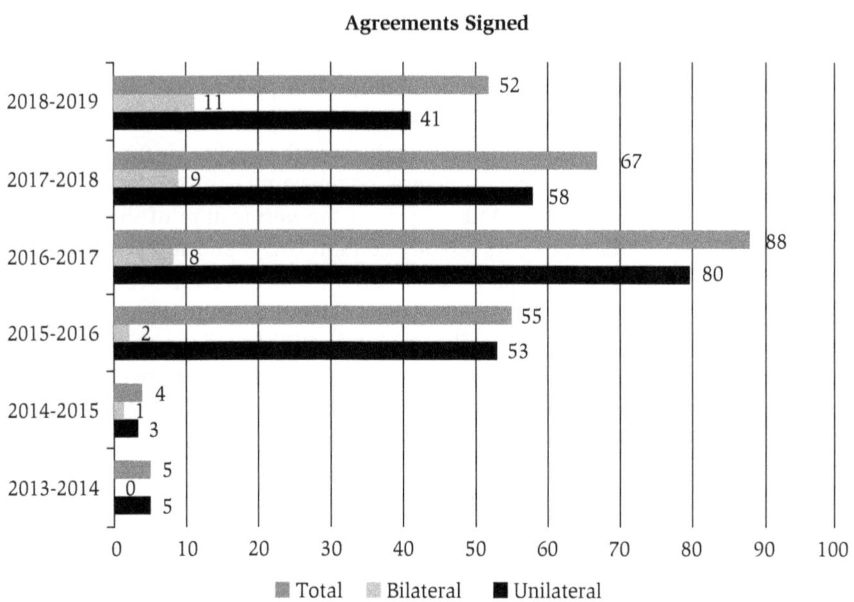

Source: Annual Report (2018-19) by Central Board of Direct Taxes on Advance Pricing Agreement (APA) Programme of India, November 2019 https://www.irsofficersonline.gov.in/Documents/OfficalCommunique/12911201916 5648.pdf.

3.7.9 Ready Reckoner on Availability of Article 9(2), BAPA and Rollback Provisions

170. BEPS Action 14[85] is one of the four minimum standards articulated in the OECD/G20 BEPS Project. The measures developed under Action 14 of the BEPS Action Plan aim to strengthen the effectiveness and efficiency of the MAP process. They aim to minimize the risks of uncertainty and unintended double taxation by ensuring the consistent and proper implementation of tax treaties, including the effective and timely resolution of disputes regarding their interpretation or application through the MAP. These measures are underpinned by a strong political commitment to the effective and timely resolution of disputes through the MAP and make further progress to rapidly resolve disputes. Minimum Standard under BEPS Action 14 is being speedily implemented through BEPS Action 15, under which, MLI[86] has been formulated.

171. BEPS Action 14 *inter alia* provides for Best Practice 1, which states that countries should include paragraph 2 of Article 9 in their tax treaties. The above has been taken care by India and most of the other countries which are signatory to the MLI through Article 17 of MLI. BEPS Action 14 through Element 2.1 provides that countries should publish rules, guidelines and procedures to access and use the MAP and take appropriate measures to make such information available to taxpayers. Countries should ensure that their MAP guidance is clear and easily accessible to the public. Further, BEPS Action 14 through Element 2.2 provides that countries should publish their country MAP profiles on a shared public platform. Best Practice 4 under Action 14 provides that countries should implement bilateral APA programme. BEPS Action 14 through Element 2.7 provides that countries with BAPA programmes should provide for the rollback of APAs in appropriate cases, subject to the applicable time limits (such as statutes of limitation for assessment) where the relevant facts and circumstances in the earlier tax years are the same and subject to the verification of these facts and circumstances. Since Indian tax laws already contain BAPA and rollback provisions, the country MAP/Dispute Resolution profiles[87] on the OECD website were seen, and it was observed that India can have BAPA and rollback of APA with a number of countries. A ready reckoner on availability of Article 9(2) to relieve economic double taxation in DTAAs between India and various countries and the presence of BAPA and rollback provisions in the legislation of India's treaty partners is provided in Table 9.

---

85. Refer BEPS Action 14 – www.oecd.org http://www.oecd.org/tax/beps/beps-actions/action14/ accessed on 4 August 2019.
86. Refer MLI – www.oecd.org https://www.oecd.org/tax/treaties/multilateral-convention-to-implement-tax-treaty-related-measures-to-prevent-BEPS.pdf accessed on 4 August 2019.
87. MAP profiles on www.oecd.org https://www.oecd.org/tax/dispute/country-map-profiles.htm accessed on 4 August 2019.

Table 9 Ready Reckoner on Availability of Article 9(2), BAPA and Rollback Between India and Treaty Partners

S. N.	*Treaty Partner*	*Date of Signature of DTAA*	*Does Article 9(2) Already Exist?*	*If No, Will It Come Through MLI?*	*Does the Treaty Partner Have BAPA?*	*Does the Treaty Partner Have Rollback?*
1	Australia	25.07.1991	Yes *	–	Yes	Yes
2	Austria	08.11.1999	Yes	–	Yes	Yes
3	Belgium	26.04.1993	No	Yes	Yes	Yes
4	Bulgaria	26.05.1994	No	Yes	No	No
5	Canada	11.01.1996	Yes	–	Yes	Yes
6	China	18.07.1994	Yes	–	Yes	Yes
7	Colombia	13.05.2011	Yes	–	Yes	Yes
8	Croatia	12.02.2014	Yes	–	Yes	No
9	The Czech Republic	01.10.1998	No	No	Yes	No
10	Denmark	08.03.1989	Yes **	–	Yes	Yes
11	Egypt	20.02.1969	No	No	No	No
12	Finland	15.01.2010	Yes	–	No formal programme. But can be considered based on MAP article	Can be considered
13	France	29.09.1992	No	Yes	Yes	No
14	Georgia	24.08.2011	Yes	–	No	No
15	Germany	19.06.1995	No	No *****	Yes	Yes
16	Greece	11.02.1965	No	Yes	Yes	No
17	Hong Kong	19.03.2018	Yes	–	Yes	Yes
18	Hungary	03.11.2003	Yes	–	Yes	Yes
19	Iceland	23.11.2007	Yes	–	No	No
20	Indonesia	27.07.2012	Yes	–	Yes	Yes @
21	Ireland	06.11.2000	Yes	–	Yes	Yes
22	Israel	29.01.1996	Yes	–	No formal programme. But can be considered based on MAP article	No

S. N.	*Treaty Partner*	*Date of Signature of DTAA*	*Does Article 9(2) Already Exist?*	*If No, Will It Come Through MLI?*	*Does the Treaty Partner Have BAPA?*	*Does the Treaty Partner Have Rollback?*
23	Italy	19.02.1993	No	Yes	Yes	No
24	Japan	07.03.1989	Yes ***	Yes ***	Yes	Yes
25	Kazakhstan	09.12.1996	Yes	–	Yes	No
26	Kenya	11.07.2016	Yes	–	No	No
27	Korea	18.05.2015	Yes	–	Yes	Yes
28	Malaysia	09.05.2012	Yes	–	Yes	Yes
29	Mauritius	24.08.1982	No	No *****	No	No
30	Mexico	10.09.2007	Yes	–	Yes	Yes
31	The Netherlands	30.07.1988	Yes	–	Yes	Yes
32	New Zealand	17.10.1986	Yes	–	Yes	Yes
33	Norway	02.02.2011	Yes	–	Yes	Yes
34	Poland	21.06.1989	Yes	–	Yes	No
35	Portugal	11.09.1998	Yes	–	Yes	No
36	Romania	08.03.2013	Yes	–	Yes	No
37	Russia	25.03.1997	No	Yes	Yes	No
38	Serbia	08.02.2006	Yes	–	No	No
39	Singapore	24.01.1994	Yes	–	Yes	Yes
40	The Slovak Republic	27.01.1986	No	Yes	Yes	Yes
41	Slovenia	13.01.2003	Yes	–	Yes	Yes
42	South Africa	04.12.1996	Yes	–	No	No
43	Spain	08.02.1993	Yes **	–	Yes	Yes
44	Sweden	24.06.1997	No ****	Yes	Yes	Yes
45	The Swiss Confederation	02.11.1994	Yes	–	Yes	Yes
46	Thailand	29.06.2015	Yes	–	Yes	Yes #
47	Turkey	31.01.1995	Yes	–	Yes	Yes
48	The United Arab Emirates	29.04.1992	No	Yes	No	No
49	United Kingdom	25.01.1993	Yes **	–	Yes	Yes
50	Uruguay	08.09.2011	Yes	–	No	No

S. N.	Treaty Partner	Date of Signature of DTAA	Does Article 9(2) Already Exist?	If No, Will It Come Through MLI?	Does the Treaty Partner Have BAPA?	Does the Treaty Partner Have Rollback?
51	US	12.09.1989	Yes	–	Yes	Yes
52	Vietnam	07.09.1994	No	******	Yes	No

* Such provisions are in Article 9(3) of the DTAA.
** Such provisions are in Article 10(2) of the DTAA.
*** Such provisions are not as per Article 9(2) of the OECD MTC, 2017 in entirety; hence, appropriate notification under Article 17 of MLI has been made by India and the respective treaty partner.
**** Such provisions are partly embedded in Article 9 of the DTAA allowing resolution under MAP.
***** India not included as a Covered Tax Agreement (CTA) in treaty partner's MLI position.
****** Vietnam has not signed the MLI as of now.
@ Indonesia's Dispute Resolution Profile (last updated on 1 September 2016) states that rollback of APA is not permissible under the Indonesian APA programme. However, under the revised Ministry of Finance Regulation No. 22/PMK.03/2020, rollback is available in Indonesia.
# On perusal of Thailand's Dispute Resolution Profile (last updated on 1 June 2020), it is mentioned that rollback of APAs is provided for in the bilateral APA programme. However, Guidance on APA process issued by the Revenue Department of Thailand is silent on this issue.

172. Further, for the convenience of the taxpayers, India has issued a Press Release dated 27 November 2017[88] to provide accessibility to BAPA regardless of the presence or otherwise of paragraph 2 of Article 9 (or its relevant equivalent) in the DTAAs. The CBDT accepts a request for bilateral or multilateral APA only when the other country also has a corresponding APA programme.

3.7.10 Survey of Corporates on APAs in India

173. It would be interesting to mention here the findings and suggestions of a survey conducted on the impression about India's APA programme among 150 Indian corporates surveyed, belonging to manufacturing and service sectors, published in the *International Journal of Economics, Commerce and Research* (IJECR).[89] The survey conveyed the following findings:

- a majority of the respondents (60%) are 'Satisfied' and 19.33% are 'Highly Satisfied' with the APA documentation procedure;

88. Issued by CBDT through Press Information Bureau titled 'Clarification of India's position on the acceptance of MAP and bilateral APA in cases of countries where Article 9(2) of OECD Model Tax Commentary is absent' (27 November 2017) http://pib.nic.in/newsite/PrintRelease.aspx?relid=173885, accessed on 6 August 2019.
89. Refer Article by Jabiulla titled 'Advance Pricing Agreement in India: Empirical evidence from corporate respondents' http://www.tjprc.org/publishpapers/2-41-1472021079-2.%20IJECR%20-%20ADVANCE%20PRICING%20AGREEMENT%20IN%20INDIA.pdf accessed on 16 February 2021.

- a majority of the respondents are 'Satisfied' with APA procedure adopted in unilateral APAs;
- in regard to the procedure adopted in bilateral and multilateral APAs, a majority of the respondents (64.67%) are 'Neither Satisfied nor Dissatisfied' and 'Dissatisfied'. However, 33.33% of the respondents are 'Highly Satisfied' and 'Satisfied';
- in regard to the fee structure under APAs, 58.00% of the respondents are 'Dissatisfied' or 'Highly Dissatisfied';
- 66% of the respondents are not 'Satisfied' with the procedure adopted in renewal of APAs;
- in regard to the time consumed in finalizing the APAs, 46.66% of the total respondents were 'Highly Satisfied' or 'Satisfied' and 36.67% of the respondents were 'Neither Satisfied nor Dissatisfied';
- in regard to cooperation of tax authorities in APA process, majority (51.34%) of the respondents were 'Dissatisfied' or 'Highly Dissatisfied', though a significant 32% of the respondents were satisfied with the cooperation of the authorities in APA process;
- in regard to rollback of APAs, 68.67% of the respondents were 'Highly Satisfied' or 'Satisfied', whereas 12% of the respondents were 'Dissatisfied' or 'Highly Dissatisfied'.

174. On the basis of the above findings of the research paper, the following measures were suggested for the improvement of the APAs in India:

- The implementation of APA regime should be made efficient as India's performance in signing bilateral APAs and multilateral APAs is extremely poor. It is suggested that the roadblocks involved in signing of APAs should be removed and the process should be made easier to provide the benefits of APAs to deserving assessees.
- The renewal of APAs should be made simple. The department has to use the existing relation and credibility of the assessee positively in renewing the APAs and to that extent fresh investigation should not be attempted. The continuity of APAs by way of renewal should be a simple process.
- The time taken for processing of APAs needs to be reduced by rationalizing the steps involved in completing the process, so that more assessees are attracted.

3.8 APA REGIME IN INDONESIA

175. In Indonesia, for income tax purposes, the legislation[90] dealing with transfer pricing is found in Article 18 of the 1983 Income Tax Law, as revised by the 1991, 1994 and 2000 Income Tax Laws, and further in September 2008, Parliament passed Income

90. Refer Note issued by PwC on Transfer Pricing in Indonesia https://www.pwc.com/gx/en/international-transfer-pricing/assets/indonesia.pdf accessed on 9 February 2021.

Tax Law No. 36/2008, which came into effect from 1 January 2009. Article 18(3) of the Income Tax Law provides that the five arm's-length pricing methodologies from the OECD Guidelines should be used to set or review transfer prices. Article 18 states that the tax authorities may adjust a taxpayer's taxable income for related party transactions that were not carried out on an arm's-length basis. Related parties are deemed to exist in the following circumstances:

- ownership or participation of capital;
- control; or
- familial relationship by blood relatives or marriage.

176. Indonesia has had an APA programme since 2010. On 31 December 2010, the Director General of Taxation (DGT) released APA Regulation No. 69/PJ/2010 (PER 69). The CA in charge of the APA programme in Indonesia is the DGT.[91] Under Article 18(3a) of Indonesian Income Tax Law Number 36 Year 2008, DGT is authorized to conclude agreement with a taxpayer and with tax authority from other countries on TP method between related taxpayer. The other relevant regulations in regard to the implementation of the APA programme in Indonesia are contained in Ministry of Finance Regulation No. 7/PMK.03/2015[92] and subsequently, Ministry of Finance Regulation No. 22/PMK.03/2020[93] has been issued which has revised the implementation of the APA programme in Indonesia so as to fully conform to the minimum standards in Action Plan 14 of the OECD/G20 BEPS Project and to improve the effectiveness of the provision and to provide legal certainty, primarily regarding the determination of transfer price, procedures, periods, and the implementation of an APA.

177. Unilateral, bilateral and multilateral APAs are available in Indonesia. Indonesia basically does not have a multilateral APA programme. However, if the covered transactions and covered entities are from more than two countries, the APA can be conducted by applying multiple BAPAs with the countries concerned.[94] Earlier, there was a three-year maximum term for unilateral APAs and a four-year maximum term for bilateral and multilateral APAs. This period has now been enhanced to up to five years by Ministry of Finance Regulation No. 22/PMK.03/2020. There is no filing fee in the APA programme of Indonesia.

91. Refer DLA Piper - APA and MAP Country Guide 2019 https://www.dlapiper.com/en/us/insights/publications/2019/03/apa-and-map-country-guide-2019/ accessed on 11 August 2020.
92. Refer Ministry of Finance Regulation No. 7/PMK.03/2015 in Indonesia https://www.pajak.go.id/sites/default/files/2019-03/PMK-7-2015%20%28EN%29.pdf accessed on 11 August 2020.
93. Refer Ministry of Finance Regulation No. 22/PMK.03/2020 in Indonesia https://pajak.go.id/sites/default/files/2020-08/REGULATION%20OF%20THE%20MINISTER%20OF%20FINANCE%20NUMBER%2022PMK.032020.pdf accessed on 28 February 2021.
94. Refer Snapshot: advance pricing agreements in Indonesia https://www.lexology.com/library/detail.aspx?g=b4d63ed8-373b-4632-8f16-3a0b647b70da#:~:text=Indonesia%20basically%20does%20not%20have,BAPAs%20with%20the%20countries%20concerned. accessed on 3 March 2021.

178. APAs will not be declined solely by reference to the size of the transactions giving rise to the transfer pricing issues. Domestic taxpayer may submit APA applications insofar as the following conditions are fulfilled:

- it has fulfilled the obligation to submit the annual corporate income tax return based on the tax provisions for three fiscal years prior to the fiscal year when APA application is submitted;
- it has been required and has fulfilled the obligation to produce and keep transfer price documentation in the form of master file and local file based on tax provisions for three fiscal years prior to the fiscal year when APA application is submitted;
- it is not currently under investigation for tax crime or currently under penalty for tax crime;
- the related party and related party transactions proposed to be included in the APA application are the same that have been reported by the taxpayer in the annual corporate income tax return; and
- the proposed transfer pricing in the APA application is based on the arm's-length principle and does not result in the taxpayer's operating profit smaller than the operating profits as reported in the annual corporate income tax return.

3.8.1 Rollback

179. Under the revised Ministry of Finance Regulation No. 22/PMK.03/2020, roll-back[95] is available as long as in the taxable year the following conditions are met:

- the facts and conditions of the related party transaction do not differ materially from the facts and conditions of the related party in the APA;
- the statute of limitation transaction agreed for tax assessment has not been surpassed;
- no corporate income tax assessment notice has been issued; and
- no criminal investigation is being conducted or criminal punishment is being served.

3.8.2 APA Team

180. Based on APA request, DGT shall form an APA assessment team under Ministry of Finance Regulation No. 7/PMK.03/2015, which shall consist of civil servants in DGT

95. Note: Indonesia's Dispute Resolution Profile (last updated on 1 September 2016), accessed on 3 March 2021, states that rollback of APA is not permissible under the Indonesian APA programme. However, in view of the revised Ministry of Finance Regulation No. 22/PMK.03/2020, rollback of APA is now available in Indonesia.

and/or experts who are appointed by the DGT. The APA team shall perform the following tasks:

- analyse and evaluate APA application including economic analysis for tax years covered in APA;
- request taxpayer to furnish other required data or information and visit the business premises of taxpayer and/or parties in affiliation if necessary;
- request for necessary information from other relevant parties if necessary;
- conduct APA discussion with taxpayer;
- conduct discussions with related units in DGT;
- prepare recommendation proposal for APA; and
- make documentation regarding activities related to APA.

181. In addition, under Ministry of Finance Regulation No. 7/PMK.03/2015, a QA team is established by the DGT for discussing APA recommendations of the APA assessment team. In the event that it is necessary during APA formation process, DGT may involve experts from outside the DGT.

3.8.3 APA Process

182. The process involved in the course of reaching an agreement is broadly as under:

- APA proposal submission from taxpayer to DGT.
- Analysis and evaluation and APA submission assessment between APA assessment team and taxpayer.
- APA discussion through MAP in the event that APA is involving tax authority of partner country or partner jurisdiction.
- Formulation of APA.

3.8.4 Pre-filing Meeting (Also Referred to as Prelodgement) under the Erstwhile Ministry of Finance Regulation No. 7/PMK.03/2015

183. Under the Erstwhile Ministry of Finance Regulation No. 7/PMK.03/2015, requests for a preliminary meeting were required to be submitted at least six months prior to the start of the tax year that is intended to be covered by the APA. Provisions for Anonymous pre-filing were not available. Upon request of the pre-filing meeting (also referred to as prelodgement), the taxpayer was required to disclose the following to the APA authorities:

- a description of the taxpayer's reasons for applying for an APA;
- a full overview of the taxpayer's business plan and its business activities;
- the taxpayer's corporate structure, including group, ownership and organizational structures;

- the shareholders of the taxpayer and the nature of their related party transactions;
- other related parties and the nature of their related party transactions;
- the transactions covered under the proposed APA;
- the TP method and relevant documentation;
- changes of the business conditions that may materially affect the appropriateness of the taxpayer's TP method;
- accounting system, production process and decision-making process;
- a list of competitors including information in relation to the competitors' characteristics and market share;
- a copy of the taxpayer's articles of association; and
- a copy of the taxpayer's corporate income tax return and financial statements for the last three years.

184. During the pre-filing meeting between taxpayer and the DGT under the Ministry of Finance Regulation No. 7/PMK.03/2015, the following issues need to be discussed:

- the factors that make it a necessity to implement the APA;
- the scope of APA proposed by the taxpayer;
- the proposed TP method;
- any other existing APAs involving foreign CA(s);
- the taxpayer's documentation and analysis;
- a time frame for the conclusion of the APA; and
- other matters relating to the conclusion and implementation of the APA.

185. For prelodgement purposes, DGT could visit the taxpayer's business premises in order to supplement the required data or information. Prelodgement can be used for further consideration of APA and is not intended to bind either the DGT or taxpayer to form an APA.

3.8.5 Pre-filing Meeting Requirement Discontinued under the Current Ministry of Finance Regulation No. 22/PMK.03/2020

186. The pre-filing meeting (prelodgement) requirement has been discontinued under the latest Ministry of Finance Regulation No. 22/PMK.03/2020.

187. For the prelodgement request which had been accepted by DGT since the implementation of Regulation of the Minister of Finance No. 7/PMK.03/2015 until the implementation of the latest Minister of Finance Regulation No. 22/PMK.03/2020, the DGT shall issue notification to the taxpayer to submit the APA request which shall be in accordance with the provisions as regulated in the latest Ministerial Regulation of 2020.

3.8.6 APA Application

188. The formal request for an APA and its supporting documentation must be received by the DGT by the end of the financial year preceding the start of the year that would be covered by the proposed APA. APA application can be submitted by:

- Indonesian taxpayer and foreign taxpayer who conducts business or performs activities in the form of PE in Indonesia; or
- domestic taxpayer from partner country or partner jurisdiction.

189. A formal APA request form is required to be addressed to the DGT and *inter alia* consist of the following:

(1) name of taxpayer, tax identification number, and address;
(2) identity of related parties;
(3) the scope of transactions and fiscal years covered by the proposed APA;
(4) the TP method proposed by the taxpayer and documentation that support the selection of this method;
(5) the conditions that are used as the basis for determination of the TP method;
(6) explanation and documentation that the proposed TP method is consistent with the arm's-length principle; and
(7) critical assumptions, taking into account the following:
    - amendments to tax laws and regulations;
    - changes in tariff and import duties;
    - amendment to industry regulations;
    - force majeure events;
    - new competitors who have significant impact on market price structure;
    - new government regulations that have significant impact on the taxpayer's business activities;
    - economic conditions that have significant impact on sales volume, production units or market share;
    - changes of taxpayer's business activities such as company restructuring; and
    - significant changes in relevant foreign exchanges rates.

190. In the case of a bilateral APA, the taxpayer is expected to ensure that all information provided in the application to one administration is made available at the same time to the other administration involved.

3.8.7 Evaluation of APA Application (Material Assessment of the Completion of APA Application)

191. In the material assessment (conducted by applying arm's-length principle), the DGT is authorized to:

- carry out a review with the taxpayer concerning the taxpayer's APA application;
- visit the place of business of the taxpayer and/or taxpayer's related party;
- interview the management and/or employee of the taxpayer;
- ask for the taxpayer to provide additional data and/or information in the form of evidence, whether in the form of document or statement;
- ask for the related party or other parties concerned to provide data and/or information in the form of evidence, whether in the form of document or statement.

192. DGT shall carry out APA negotiation with tax resident of Indonesia, in the event of unilateral APA. Unilateral APA negotiation must be started no later than six months since tax resident of Indonesia submitted the requirements of the APA request and concluded within twelve months period since the starting of the APA negotiation. The result of the APA negotiation is deemed to be a disagreement in the event that the APA negotiation does not result in any agreement until the end of the period of the APA negotiation as referred above.

193. In the event of involvement of tax authority of partner country or partner jurisdiction during APA discussion, APA discussion shall be carried out in accordance with MAP provisions. In the event that bilateral APA involving tax authority of partner country or partner jurisdiction cannot result in mutual agreement, following is the follow-up for APA discussion:

- the tax resident of Indonesia may file a request for unilateral APA negotiation to the DGT through Director of International Taxation, following which, unilateral APA discussion shall be held between DGT and the taxpayer; or
- termination of APA discussion.

194. The matter which shall be agreed on and regulated in APA among others are:

- parties in affiliation;
- transaction which is considered as part of APA scope;
- TPM;
- comparables;
- APA period;
- critical assumptions; and
- transfer pricing adjustment.

195. The DGT may disagree on the APA in the event of the following:

- the affiliated transaction is not based on the economic purpose;
- the economic substance of the affiliated transaction is different with its formal form;
- the affiliated transaction is conducted with one of its purposes is to minimalize the tax expense;
- the information and/or evidence or statement submitted by the tax resident of Indonesia is not true or not in accordance with the actual condition;
- the additional information and/or evidence or statement cannot be obtained from the taxpayer by DGT within the period of fourteen days since the date of written request; and/or
- the taxable year contained within the APA period or the rollback has been issued notice of tax assessment of corporate income tax thereof.

196. In the event it is discovered that the taxpayer is being investigated for a tax crime, or undergoing punishment related with tax crime, DGT shall terminate the negotiation and issue written notification to:

- the taxpayer; and
- the CA of treaty partner, in the event of a bilateral APA.

3.8.8 Withdrawal of APA Request

197. Tax resident of Indonesia can submit a request for withdrawal of its APA request. The withdrawal of the APA request must meet the following requirements:

- the withdrawal is written in Bahasa Indonesia by stating the reason of the withdrawal;
- the withdrawal is submitted prior to any agreements;
- the withdrawal is signed by director whose name is written in the deed of incorporation or its amendment, in the event that the board of directors was amended; and
- the withdrawal of the APA request is prepared by using the format as attached in the revised Ministerial Regulation.

198. Upon the submitted withdrawal of the APA request, DGT examines the fulfilment of the requirements of the withdrawal of the APA request and issues written notification of the termination of the APA process to:

- the tax resident of Indonesia; and
- the CA of the treaty partner, in the event of a bilateral APA, within the period of ten working days since the withdrawal of the APA request is received by DGT.

3.8.9 Advance Pricing Agreement

199. APA discussion which may result in an agreement between DGT and taxpayer shall be followed up by formulation of APA script/report. APA Transcript means a document that contains the agreement between DGT and tax resident of Indonesia concerning transfer pricing criteria and determination of advance transfer pricing in accordance with the arm's-length principle throughout the APA period and rollback. APA script/report should include at least the following:

- company's name, ID Tax Number, address, and the identity of parties in affiliation with taxpayer related to APA;
- the scope of covered transaction;
- covered tax years;
- general provisions which are used under APA;
- agreed TPM;
- factors which influence critical assumption in implementing TPM;
- ALP or arm's-length profit for each type of covered transaction;
- obligation which has to be met during APA implementation and reporting obligation;
- legal consequence;
- confidentiality;
- review and cancellation;
- settlement mechanism for issues which may occur during implementation;
- conditions which may lead DGT to review or cancel APA; and
- other supporting information.

200. In the event of bilateral APA, the result of the APA negotiation is a mutual agreement in accordance with the provision of the regulation on MAP.

201. Upon conclusion of the APA negotiation, the DGT follows up:

- the APA script/report by issuing the decision for the implementation of the APA within a period of no longer than one month since the APA script/report is signed; or
- the mutual agreement by issuing the decision of the implementation of the APA in accordance with the provision of the regulations on MAP.

202. Government Regulation-74 of 2011[96] stipulates that any documents used during the negotiation of an APA should be returned to the taxpayer if no agreement is reached and the documents cannot be used by the Indonesian Tax Office as the basis to conduct a tax audit or audit for preliminary evidence. It also provides that provisions regarding the procedures of the exchange of APA shall be stipulated or based on the Minister of

96. Refer Government Regulation-74 of 2011 https://www.pajak.go.id/sites/default/files/2019-03/PP-74-2011%20%28EN%29.pdf accessed on 3 March 2021.

Finance Regulation and DGT shall not make adjustment during audit on the matters already agreed in the APA.

3.8.10 Procedure of Implementation of the APA

203. As per the Minister of Finance Regulation No. 22/PMK.03/2020, ACR is not necessarily to be submitted as a separate document. Tax resident of Indonesia must implement the agreement in the APA in accordance with the provisions of legislation on taxation. The agreements contained in the APA must be reflected in the transfer pricing policy of the tax resident of Indonesia, and its implementation must be stated in the transfer pricing documentation for the APA period. In the event that in respect of the APA period and/or rollback:

- it has already filed corporate income tax return;
- DGT has not conducted any tax audit yet; and
- there is an underpaid income tax due calculated based on the agreement in the APA,

the tax resident of Indonesia must amend the filed corporate income tax return in accordance with the agreements of the APA no later than one month after the issuance of the decision of the implementation of the APA.

204. The difference between the value of related party transaction which is not in accordance with arm's-length principle and the value of related party transaction which is in accordance with arm's-length principle shall be deemed as dividend which shall be taxed in accordance with the provisions of legislations on income taxation.

3.8.11 Monitoring/Evaluation of Agreement

205. In monitoring the agreement, the DGT carries out evaluation in respect of agreements made in the APA. In evaluation, DGT is authorized to:

- carry out a review with the taxpayer concerning the implementation of agreements made in APA;
- ask for the taxpayer to provide information and/or evidence or statement necessary;
- visit the place of business of the taxpayer and/or taxpayer's related party;
- interview the management and/or employee of the taxpayer; and/or
- ask for information and/or evidence or statement from the related party or other parties concerned.

206. Based on the result of evaluation, the DGT is authorized to carry out:

- review of APA, to the extent that there is a material change on facts and conditions of the related party transactions which are covered in the APA with critical assumptions agreed in the APA; or

- cancellation of the APA, before the APA period ends.

3.8.12 Renewal of APA

207. The APA renewal request which has been accepted by DGT after the issuance of Regulation of the Minister of Finance No. 7/PMK.03/2015 until the latest Ministerial Regulation has come into force shall be processed based on the provisions as referred to in Article 21 of the latest Ministry of Finance Regulation No. 22/PMK.03/2020. Request for APA renewal is required to be submitted by the applicant directly and within a period of twelve months up to six months before the last taxable year in the previous APA period. Renewal of APA can be granted in the event that:

- the taxpayer has implemented all agreements in the previous APA;
- there is no material change to the facts and/or conditions of related party transactions covered in the previous APA with critical assumptions agreed in the previous APA; and
- entities and the related party transaction proposed to be included in the APA renewal are the same vis-à-vis the previous APA.

3.8.13 Review of APA

208. Apart from review of APA by the DGT, it can also be carried out based on request for APA review submitted by the taxpayer. The results of the APA review negotiations shall be set forth in the amendments to the APA text or to the mutual agreement. During the review, relevant/appropriate procedures prescribed to process the UAPA or MAP shall be adopted/implemented. Upon the amendments to the APA Text or the amendments to the mutual agreement, DGT shall issue a decision regarding the amendment of APA by indicating the tax year in the APA period which is reviewed.

3.8.14 Cancellation of APA

209. DGT may cancel the APA if based on the result of evaluation it is found that:

(1) taxpayer provided information and/or evidence or statement that is not true or not in accordance with the actual conditions; and/or
(2) taxpayer does not provide information and/or evidence or statement to the DGT which:
   - is known or should be known by taxpayer; and
   - may affect the outcome of the agreement in APA.

210. Upon reaching the decision to cancel the APA, the DGT shall issue:

- cancellation decision to the taxpayer; and
- notification of APA cancellation to the CA of treaty partner, in the event of bilateral APA.

211. In the event of cancellation of APA by the DGT, the taxpayer may have to face the following implications:

- taxpayer cannot resubmit APA application for APA and/or rollback periods covered in the cancelled APA; and
- DGT may carry out audits, preliminary investigation, and /or investigation in accordance with the provisions of legislation on taxation.

3.8.15 Statistics

212. Statistics on the number of APA requests received and closed/resolved in various years in Indonesia are provided in Table 10.

Table 10 Number of APA Requests Received and Closed/Resolved in Various Years in Indonesia

Year	*Item*	*UAPA*	*BAPA*
Pre-2016	Requested	3	10
	Closed	0	0
	Ending Balance	3	10
2016	Beginning Balance	3	10
	Requested	11	13
	Closed	0	3
	Ending Balance	14	20
2017	Beginning Balance	14	20
	Requested	2	2
	Closed	1	2
	Ending Balance	15	20
2018	Beginning Balance	15	20
	Requested	0	10
	Closed	11	3
	Ending Balance	4	27
2019	Beginning Balance	4	27
	Requested	3	11
	Closed	4	9
	Ending Balance	3	29

Source: Guidance regarding Advance Pricing Agreement (APA) and Mutual Agreement Procedure in Indonesia https://pajak.go.id/id/apa-map#APA.

3.9 APA REGIME IN IRELAND

213. In the APA programme of Ireland, an Advance Pricing Agreement (also commonly referred to as Advance Pricing Arrangement) is an arrangement that determines, in advance of controlled transactions, an appropriate set of criteria (e.g., method, comparables and appropriate adjustments thereto, critical assumptions as to future events) for the determination of the transfer pricing for those transactions over a fixed period of time. The CA in charge of the APA programme in Ireland is Transfer Pricing Branch of the Revenue (hereinafter 'Revenue'). In Ireland, the relevant provisions in regard to the implementation of the APA programme are contained in BAPA Guidelines 2016 (hereinafter 'Guidelines'), available on the Revenue's website.[97]

214. Recognizing the BEPS Action 14 recommendation, as well as the need for greater certainty in relation to the taxation of cross-border transactions entered into by MNEs, Ireland decided to introduce a formal bilateral APA programme. Prior to the introduction of the formal programme, Ireland accepted requests for bilateral APAs on an ad hoc basis in situations where a double tax treaty partner agreed to enter into a bilateral APA negotiation. The introduction of a formal programme provided certainty to taxpayers with respect to the process involved in applying for a bilateral APA and the ongoing reporting and administrative requirements once an APA had been entered into. Ireland's bilateral APA programme is effective from 1 July 2016 and applies to bilateral APA applications made to Revenue on or after this date. Accordingly, the Guidelines do not apply with respect to: (i) bilateral APAs which have been signed prior to 1 July 2016 and (ii) formal bilateral APA applications which have been submitted to Revenue before 1 July 2016 (but in respect of which an APA has not been concluded as of 1 July 2016).[98]

215. There are two types of APAs available in Ireland: bilateral (under treaties) and multilateral (to the extent that they consist of a series of bilateral agreements). Revenue does not enter into unilateral APAs, i.e., an agreement solely between the taxpayer and Revenue and not involving another CA. The bilateral and multilateral APA programme is a voluntary programme. Taxpayers can choose whether or not to enter into it. There is a five-year maximum term for an APA. There is no APA filing fee in Ireland's APA programme. Ireland's bilateral APA programme is conducted within the legal framework of the double tax treaty which Ireland has entered into with the other jurisdiction concerned; i.e., there must be a double tax treaty in place in order for a bilateral APA application to be considered. APAs are conducted under the MAP article of the relevant treaty where the relevant enabling provision is present in the treaty. APAs may be sought for transfer pricing issues, including the attribution of profits to a PE.

97. Refer DLA Piper – APA and MAP Country Guide 2019 https://www.dlapiper.com/en/us/insights/publications/2019/03/apa-and-map-country-guide-2019/ accessed on 11 August 2020.
98. Refer Ireland's Bilateral Advance Pricing Agreement Guidelines 2016, Part 35-02-07 https://www.revenue.ie/en/tax-professionals/tdm/income-tax-capital-gains-tax-corporation-tax/part-35/35-02-07.pdf accessed on 19 March 2021.

3.9.1 BAPA Guidelines 2016[99]

216. The relevant provisions in regard to the implementation of the APA programme in Ireland are contained in the Guidelines. The intent, purpose and principles under the Irish APA programme as expressed in these Guidelines are as below:

- Revenue is committed to operating the programme on the basis of trust and mutual cooperation with the taxpayer and the other tax administration in order to ensure the efficient and fair processing of requests for an APA. Revenue expects that taxpayers considering a bilateral APA request will adopt a similar approach to the programme and regards taxpayer cooperation as critical to the success of the programme.
- Transparency is a fundamental aspect of the bilateral APA programme. Throughout the APA process, the taxpayers are expected to ensure that both tax administrations are provided with the same information at the same time. This applies to any information submitted by the taxpayers to either tax administration as part of the APA process.
- In negotiating bilateral APAs, Revenue considers that each case is unique and is based on a specific set of facts and circumstances. The APA terms agreed between Revenue and the foreign tax administration do not create a precedent for transactions involving the same taxpayers for any years other than those years included in the APA period (including any rollback period) or for transactions involving taxpayers other than those specified in the APA.

3.9.2 Rollback of APA

217. Rollbacks are available subject to the applicable time limits of the jurisdictions involved in the APA; the relevant facts and circumstances; and whether there are any ongoing audits, examinations, appeals or judicial proceedings in respect of the periods or transactions which are to be covered by the rollback. In determining whether to grant a rollback, the Transfer Pricing Branch will consult with the Revenue office which is responsible for dealing with the tax affairs of the taxpayer.

3.9.3 APA Team

218. The bilateral APA programme is administered by the Transfer Pricing Branch of Revenue's International Tax Division. Certain officers within this Branch are specifically authorized by Revenue to be an authorized representative for the purposes of being a CA under the terms of Ireland's double taxation agreements and conventions; i.e., the officers concerned have the authority to conclude bilateral APAs with Ireland's

99. *Id.*

double tax treaty partners. The Transfer Pricing Branch also deals with requests from taxpayers for MAP assistance to resolve transfer pricing disputes with treaty partners.

3.9.4 APA Process

219. The APA process is made up of a number of distinct stages as follows:

(i) pre-filing;
(ii) formal APA application;
(iii) evaluation of APA application and negotiation of APA;
(iv) formal agreement; and
(v) annual reporting.

3.9.5 Pre-filing Meeting

220. Taxpayers are encouraged to contact the Revenue to discuss the APA application in a pre-filing meeting on an informal basis. Anonymous pre-filing is available; however, the Revenue strongly recommends pre-filing meetings are conducted on a named basis. In any case, Revenue will not admit a taxpayer into the APA programme until the identity of the taxpayer is known. The purpose of the pre-filing meeting is to enable parties to establish whether an APA is appropriate. Since Revenue does not accept all applications, pre-filing meeting enables them to identify issues at an early stage. The meeting includes a discussion of the following:

- a high-level overview of the business and corporate structure of the taxpayer and MNE;
- the parties to the APA and the jurisdictions involved;
- the nature of the transactions to be covered under the APA, years to be covered and the amounts involved;
- the proposed TP method (if decided upon);
- a high-level overview of any transfer pricing audits related to the transaction that is subject of the APA discussions; and
- any other information which the taxpayer considers important and relevant to the APA application.

221. The pre-filing meeting gives Revenue the opportunity to explain to the taxpayer how the APA process works, to identify any problems with the APA proposal at an early stage and to deal with any queries which the taxpayer may have. Following a pre-filing meeting, Revenue normally gives an indication of whether it is likely to accept an application from a taxpayer for an APA. Where Revenue believes that a case is not suitable for an APA, it discusses the same with the taxpayer. In the event that Revenue continues to believe that the case is not suitable for an APA, it issues a letter to the taxpayer outlining the reasons. The taxpayer is at liberty to have the matter reviewed in accordance with Revenue's Complaint and Review Procedures if it still wishes to be admitted into the programme.

3.9.6 APA Application

222. Taxpayers are required to submit an APA application before the beginning of the first accounting period to be covered by the APA. Taxpayers must submit two hard copies of the APA application to the Director of the Transfer Pricing Branch. In addition, an electronic copy of the APA application should be submitted using the secure Revenue File Transfer System. The application is required to *inter alia* include the following details/documents:

- an executive summary;
- details on the company background;
- an industry analysis;
- relevant financial information (including statements and projections);
- an economic analysis (covering the proposed TP method, search for comparables and any adjustments); and
- details of any related audits.

223. Factors which are more likely to result in a request for an APA being accepted by the Revenue include the following:

- significant doubt over the TP method;
- a high likelihood of double taxation arising if no APA is in place;
- taxpayer is applying a bespoke TPM to the transaction(s);
- the application of the TP method is complex and/or requires complex calculations;
- reliable comparables are not readily available and/or significant and complex adjustments are required; and
- the transactions which are to be covered by the APA have already been entered into or are about to be entered into and are not expected to change throughout the APA period.

224. On receipt of the application, the Revenue consults the foreign tax authorities involved prior to acceptance into the programme. Once satisfied that the transaction is suitable for an APA, the Revenue issues an acceptance letter to the taxpayer. Similar to the pre-filing stage, in cases where Revenue denies entry into the APA programme, it issues a letter to the taxpayer outlining the reasons why the case is not considered suitable for an APA. The taxpayer may seek to have the matter reviewed in accordance with Revenue's Complaint and Review Procedures if it still wishes to be admitted into the programme.

3.9.7 Evaluation of APA Application

225. This stage of the APA process has two distinct phases. The first phase involves the evaluation by Revenue of the application submitted by the taxpayer. The second phase involves Revenue negotiating the terms and conditions of the APA with the CA of the foreign tax administration.

226. Revenue performs a detailed evaluation of the application and, if necessary, may seek clarifications from the taxpayer on the information submitted or may request additional information. The taxpayer is required to respond to such requests for additional information in a timely manner, generally within sixty days of the request. Revenue may extend the time in certain circumstances where it may take longer for the taxpayer to prepare the information requested, e.g., for additional benchmarking analysis.

227. Revenue may request a site visit and interviews with appropriate personnel from the taxpayer's organization during the processing of the application. Where a taxpayer wishes to have joint meetings with representatives of both tax administrations in order to share relevant information, Revenue is generally receptive and prepared to participate in such meetings.

228. Revenue endeavours to conclude bilateral APA cases within twenty-four months of receipt of the formal bilateral APA application from the taxpayer. This is dependent on a number of factors such as the complexity of the case, the cooperation of the taxpayer and the number of rounds of negotiations required. To the extent that there are significant repeated delays by the taxpayer in providing the relevant information to Revenue, this may lead to Revenue even terminating the APA process itself.

229. The evaluation phase allows Revenue to formulate its view of the TPM, comparables, APA term (including any rollback), critical assumptions and ultimately the appropriate arm's-length pricing for the transaction(s). This may take the form of a position paper that is prepared and shared by Revenue with the other tax administration. The position paper is subject to the confidentiality restrictions of the relevant double tax treaty.

230. Following evaluation of the APA application, Revenue enters into negotiations with the CA of the foreign tax administration. The negotiation phase allows both CAs to resolve any differences which may arise between the CAs with the objective that one agreed set of terms and conditions can be provided to the taxpayer. The taxpayer is not a party to these negotiations. Revenue keeps the taxpayer informed of upcoming negotiations with the other CA and of the outcome of such negotiations. In the event that Revenue is unable to reach agreement with the CA of the foreign tax administration, Revenue will notify the taxpayer within thirty days of the CA meeting, setting out the reasons why agreement could not be reached. Revenue is not obliged to engage in further discussions with the other CA where Revenue or the other CA believes that agreement cannot be reached.

3.9.8 Withdrawal of APA

231. The taxpayer can withdraw from the APA programme at any time prior to the conclusion of the APA. It may be the case that the terms of the APA agreed between Revenue and the other CA differ from what the taxpayer requested. Where the taxpayer does not agree with the APA terms agreed between both CAs, Revenue consults with the taxpayer and the other CA to see whether any modification can be made to the terms and conditions so that a final set of terms and conditions can be achieved which are agreeable to the taxpayer, Revenue and the other CA. In the event that no agreement is reached, the taxpayer is not obliged to accept the terms and may withdraw from the APA process. In this case, the taxpayer is required to confirm in writing to Revenue that it is withdrawing from the APA process.

3.9.9 Denial of APA

232. If a taxpayer is involved in a case with the tax appeals commission or in court proceedings in respect of a matter which is related to the transactions covered by the proposed APA, the APA application may be rejected. The Revenue expects that any such involvement in appeals or court proceedings should be disclosed at the pre-filing meeting stage itself.

233. Other factors which are more likely to result in a request for an APA being rejected by the Revenue are as below:

- The transactions are routine, and there is unlikely to be significant doubt over the application of the appropriate TPM in determining the ALP.
- The transactions to be covered by the APA represent a small portion of the Irish entity's overall cross-border transactions.
- The transactions which are the subject of the APA appear to be part of a scheme or arrangement, the purpose of which or one of the purposes of which is the avoidance of tax or, alternatively, Revenue is of the view that the transaction may facilitate the avoidance of tax by a third party.
- Where the APA request is rejected by the relevant double tax treaty partner, Revenue will also reject the request as a bilateral agreement will not be possible.

If the taxpayer is dissatisfied with Revenue's decision to withdraw, it may seek a review of a decision made by Revenue in relation to its request for an APA, its APA application or any aspect of the APA. In such circumstances, it is entitled to have Revenue's decision reviewed in accordance with Revenue's Complaint and Review Procedures.

3.9.10 Advance Pricing Agreement

234. Where agreement is reached between Revenue and the CA of the foreign tax administration on the terms and conditions of an APA, Revenue notifies the taxpayer in writing of the agreed terms and conditions within thirty days of the CA meeting with an expectation that the taxpayer shall respond in writing within thirty days of receipt of the letter from Revenue to confirm whether they accept these terms. The terms that are typically agreed between the two CAs are *inter alia* as below:

(1) nature of the covered transaction(s);
(2) term for which the APA will be effective (including any rollback period);
(3) TPM used;
(4) compensating adjustments;
(5) critical assumptions; and
(6) taxpayer annual reporting requirements.

3.9.11 Annual Report

235. Taxpayers are required to file an annual report by the due date of filing of their annual corporate income tax return. The Annual Report is required to include the following:

- a statement of compliance with the APA, including critical assumptions;
- a statement as to whether critical assumptions underlying the TPM remained valid throughout the period of the APA;
- financial data for the period comparing the actual results for the covered transaction with the targeted arm's-length result agreed in the APA;
- details of any compensating adjustments made to stay within the targeted arm's-length range agreed in the APA;
- details of any pending requests to modify, renew or cancel the APA; and
- identification and correction of any incorrect or incomplete information which has been submitted to Revenue which comes to the taxpayer's attention prior to submission of the Annual Report which may have a material impact on the APA.

236. Additional information may be requested by the Revenue so as to satisfy itself that compliance to the APA has been adequate. In addition, where the taxpayer provides additional information to the foreign tax administration as part of its APA annual reporting in that jurisdiction, the taxpayer is required to notify the Director of the Transfer Pricing Branch that such additional information is being provided.

237. For those transactions which are covered under the terms of the APA, the extent of any audit would be limited, under normal circumstances, to determining: (i) the taxpayer's compliance with the terms and conditions of the APA and (ii) whether the circumstances and critical assumptions necessary for the continued application of the chosen TPM continue to exist. All other transactions not covered by the APA may be audited by Revenue in the normal manner in accordance with the provisions of the Taxes Consolidation Act 1997 and Revenue's Code of Practice for Revenue Audit and other Compliance Interventions.

3.9.12 Renewal of APA

238. Taxpayers are encouraged to make early contact with the Revenue to request the renewal of an APA. The taxpayer may be required to outline any changes to the material facts and circumstances and critical assumptions from the original APA, and address the continued appropriateness of the TP method employed. The renewal of an APA is not automatic. It is dependent on a number of factors including the consent of both CAs and on the taxpayer demonstrating that the critical assumptions contained in the original APA continue to apply. Where transfer pricing issues differ significantly from the original APA, the Revenue may require the taxpayer to submit an application for a new APA.

3.9.13 Revision of APA

239. Revenue, with the agreement of the other CA, may seek to revise an APA in the following circumstances:

- there has been a change in any of the critical assumptions or in the terms and conditions of the APA; or
- there has been a change in law and/or a change in a double tax treaty that impacts the Irish tax treatment of transactions covered by the APA.

240. Where a taxpayer believes that a revision may be required to an APA, it is required to notify the Director of Revenue's Transfer Pricing Branch within thirty days of becoming aware of the need for such revision and specify the reasons for the proposed revision. Revenue then liaises with the taxpayer and the other CA.

241. Where agreement cannot be reached between the two CAs on a revised APA, or the taxpayer does not accept the terms of a revised APA negotiated between the two CAs, Revenue cancels the existing APA. Where agreement is reached between the two CAs on a revision to an APA and this revision is accepted by the taxpayer, the revised APA shall indicate the date from which the revision is effective and from which date the terms of the original APA are no longer effective.

3.9.14 Revoking or Cancelling the APA

242. Revoking an APA means that the terms of an APA are no longer effective for any part of the period specified in the APA. Where Revenue revokes an APA, the taxpayer's position is the same as if the APA had never been agreed. Revocation is retroactive to the first day of the period covered by the APA. Cancelling an APA means that the terms of an APA are no longer effective for a period commencing after the start of the period covered by the APA. Where Revenue cancels an APA, the effective date of cancellation is determined by reference to the event that led to the cancellation. The taxpayer's position, for the period from the effective date of cancellation, is the same as if the APA had never been agreed.

243. Before Revenue revokes or cancels an APA, it first consults with the CA of the foreign tax administration and also discusses the case with the taxpayer. The taxpayer is given an opportunity to respond before Revenue takes a final decision on revoking or cancelling the APA. In the event that Revenue revokes or cancels an APA, Revenue notifies the taxpayer and the CA of the foreign tax administration, specifying the reason(s) for the revocation or cancellation. Revenue may revoke or cancel an APA where it is established that any of the following situations have arisen:

- there has been a misrepresentation, mistake or omission in the information submitted by the taxpayer, whether as part of the formal APA application, any further information submitted as part of the APA application or negotiation process, the annual reports or any other related information;
- for the full period or part of the period of the APA, the participating taxpayer(s) failed to comply with a material term or condition of the APA; or
- the tax administration in the foreign jurisdiction has revoked or cancelled the APA.

244. Additionally, an APA can be cancelled if:

- one or more of the critical assumptions proved to be materially incorrect;
- there was a material departure from one or more of the critical assumptions;
- there has been a change in tax law or in a provision of a double tax treaty that is materially relevant to the APA and it has not been possible to revise the APA to take account of the changed circumstances; or
- there has been a failure to conclude a revised APA in a situation where matters have arisen which would otherwise require the revision of an APA.

245. Under the APA programme of Ireland, Revenue may waive cancellation of the APA if the taxpayer can show reasonable cause, to the satisfaction of Revenue, and if the taxpayer agrees to make any adjustment proposed by Revenue to correct the misrepresentation, mistake, omission or non-compliance, or take into account the changes in critical assumptions, tax law or treaty provisions relevant to the APA.

3.9.15 Confidentiality and Protection of Information

246. The information submitted to Revenue as part of the APA process, e.g., the APA application, the annual reports confirming the taxpayer's compliance with the APA terms and any other information submitted to Revenue by the taxpayer in connection with the APA application or the APA, is treated as confidential in accordance with the provisions of the Taxes Consolidation Act 1997. The exchange of information between Revenue and the CA of the treaty partner country in relation to an APA is carried out in accordance with the provisions of the relevant double tax treaty. Information exchanged under Ireland's double tax treaties is confidential and can only be used and disclosed in accordance with the provisions of the treaty.

3.9.16 Statistics

247. There were eight APA application requests in 2017 and two granted applications. In 2018, there were nine APA application requests and three granted applications. The statistics on Irish APA programme for the years 2017 and 2018 are provided in Table 11.

Table 11 Number of APA Requests Received and Resolved in 2017, 2018 in Ireland

Total Number of All APAs in Force at the End of 2017		*Total Number of Bilateral and Multilateral APAs in Force at the End of 2017*		*Total Number of Unilateral APAs in Force at the End of 2017*		*Number of APA Requests Received in 2017*		*Number of APAs Granted in 2017*		*Number of APA Applications Rejected in 2017*		*Number of APA applications Where the Taxpayer Withdrew Its Request in 2017*		*Average Time (In Months) to Negotiate Bilateral or Multilateral APAs*	
EU	Non-EU	EU	Non-EU	EU	Non-EU	EU	Non-EU	EU	Non-EU	EU	Non-EU	EU	Non-EU	EU	Non-EU
2	2	2	2	–	–	4	4	–	2	–	–	–	1		44

Total Number of All APAs in Force at the End of 2018		*Total Number of Bilateral and Multilateral APAs in Force at the End of 2018*		*Total Number of Unilateral APAs in Force at the End of 2018*		*Number of APA Requests Received in 2018*		*Number of APAs Granted in 2018*		*Number of APA Applications Rejected in 2018*		*Number of APA applications Where the Taxpayer Withdrew Its Request in 2018*		*Average Time (In Months) to Negotiate Bilateral or Multilateral APAs*	
EU	Non-EU	EU	Non-EU	EU	Non-EU	EU	Non-EU	EU	Non-EU	EU	Non-EU	EU	Non-EU	EU	Non-EU
1	3	1	3	–	–	6	3	2	1	–	–	–	–	18	17

Source: Statistics on APAs in the EU at the end of 2017 https://ec.europa.eu/taxation_customs/sites/taxation/files/statistics_on_advance_pricing_agreements_2017_en.pdf.
and
Statistics on APAs in the EU at the end of 2018 https://ec.europa.eu/taxation_customs/sites/taxation/files/apa-and-map-2019-3.pdf.

3.10 APA REGIME IN JAPAN

248. The CA in charge of the APA programme in Japan is National Tax Agency (NTA) and relevant regional tax bureau. The relevant provisions governing the APA regime in Japan are contained in Commissioner's Directive on the Operation of Transfer Pricing (Administrative Guidelines) issued by the NTA on 1 June 2001, amended on 16 February 2018[100] with the latest amendment on 28 June 2019.[101]

249. All the three types of APAs, i.e., unilateral, bilateral, and multilateral APAs, are available in Japan. There is a five-year maximum term for an APA. Under the Japanese APA programme, there is no filing fee.

3.10.1 Rollback

250. Rollback of the APA is available for bilateral APAs for up to six prior tax years where the TP method is regarded by the competent tax authorities as appropriate for those prior years. Rollback is not available for unilateral APAs.

3.10.2 Pre-filing Meeting

251. Before filing APA requests, taxpayers are encouraged to have pre-filing consultations with the office responsible for the APA in the NTA and the Regional Taxation Bureau (RTB). The consultation is intended to help taxpayers with conducting APA procedures smoothly. Anonymous pre-filing is also available. During pre-filing, the following information is discussed:

- necessary items for formal filing of an APA application;
- information necessary for the taxpayer to decide whether to file the APA and what kind of APA filing is appropriate;
- whether the competent tax authorities can accept the APA application; and
- timeline of the application.

3.10.3 APA Application

252. If a mutual consent is reached during the pre-filing meeting, the taxpayer is required to file the formal APA application which must include the following:

- an outline of the transaction covered by the proposed APA and organization(s) conducting those transactions;

100. Refer DLA Piper – APA and MAP Country Guide 2019 https://www.dlapiper.com/en/us/insights/publications/2019/03/apa-and-map-country-guide-2019/ accessed on 11 August 2020.
101. Refer Japan Dispute Resolution Profile (Last updated: 1 August 2019) https://www.oecd.org/tax/dispute/Japan-Dispute-Resolution-Profile.pdf accessed on 11 August 2020.

- the ALP computation method and explanation of why the proposed method is the most appropriate;
- critical assumptions;
- transaction flows, money flows and currencies used;
- description of the capital relationships and 'control in substance' relationships between the foreign related parties and the taxpayer;
- analysis on functions, risks and assets of the taxpayer and related parties;
- description of the business operations, accounting and circumstances of the applicant and foreign related parties for the past three business years;
- outline of the issues concerned in any audit, administrative appeal, or lawsuit pertaining to transfer pricing of which the related party is subject in its jurisdiction;
- documentation that proves, based on TP methods applied to the three business years prior to the years covered by the proposed APA, that the TP method is the most rational; and
- overview of the ultimate parent company of the MNE to which the taxpayer belongs (for unilateral APA application only).

253. Any APA request needs to be filed on or before the commencing date of the first taxable year of the APA term requested by the applicant. If a bilateral or multilateral APA with a request for rollback is filed before a TP examination commences, the tax authorities will not commence an examination of the rollback years. However, if an examination has already commenced, the examination will not be stopped due to filing of an APA application. A taxpayer filing a formal APA application having paid-in capital of JPY 100 million (approx. USD 910,000) or more must be submitted to the Commissioner of the taxpayer's regional tax bureau. Taxpayers filing applications with paid-in capital of lower amount are required to submit applications to the director of the taxpayer's district tax office.

254. An applicant for a BAPA is also required to submit an 'Application for the Mutual Agreement Procedure' based on the 'Commissioner's Directive on the Mutual Agreement Procedure (Administrative Guidelines)' issued on 25 June 2001 (latest amendment on 7 May 2019). The APA request shall be filed in duplicate (in triplicate when a MAP is requested) in cases of a corporation handled by the RTB Large Enterprise Examination Division, or in triplicate (in quadruplicate when a MAP is requested) in cases of all other corporations.

3.10.4 Processing of APA Application

255. The RTB division in charge shall review the APA request in the following manner:

- The RTB division in charge shall commence the APA review promptly upon receipt of an APA request, and shall conduct the review in a balanced manner appropriate to the complexity and difficulty of the case while endeavouring to process the request correctly and swiftly. The NTA division in charge shall additionally be involved in APA review as necessary. As the cooperation of the applicant is essential to process an APA review swiftly, a better understanding of the applicant on the importance of such cooperation is promoted.

- The RTB division in charge shall in principle perform APA reviews in accordance with the relevant provisions of Commissioner's Directive on the Operation of Transfer Pricing (Administrative Guidelines) dated 1 June 2001 (as amended from time to time).
- In cases where more documents, other than those prescribed, are found to be required for an APA review, the RTB division in charge shall explain this to the applicant and request that the applicant submits such documents. In order to expedite the APA review process, the RTB division in charge shall set a deadline for the submission of such documents that is deemed reasonable in view of the circumstances of the applicant in light of the period ordinarily required to prepare such documents.
- The RTB division in charge may request the applicants to amend their requests in the case where the division concludes that the TPM requested is not the most appropriate.
- The NTA division in charge shall request the RTB division in charge to report on the status of the APA review process as necessary.

3.10.5 Amendment to APA Request

256. In cases where an applicant for APA submits documents pertaining to amendments to the filed request, the Examination Group (Corporation) of the Tax Office or the RTB Large Enterprise Examination Division shall process the request.

3.10.6 Withdrawal of APA Request

257. In cases where an applicant for APA submits statements pertaining to the withdrawal of the APA request, the Examination Group (Corporation) of the Tax Office or the RTB Large Enterprise Examination Division shall process such statements.

3.10.7 Compliance Report

258. The taxpayer is required to submit to the competent tax authorities a report demonstrating compliance with the APA. The submission is to be made prior to the deadline for filing the final tax return and must include:

- evidence that the taxpayer has filed its return for the covered years in compliance with the APA;
- income statements of the applicant and foreign related parties (where deemed necessary);
- critical assumptions that were the premise for the APA;

- where results of the confirmed transaction do not comply with the APA, an explanation of the adjustments to prices that the taxpayer has carried out; and
- financial circumstances of both the taxpayer and the foreign related parties during the covered years.

259. The regional tax bureau may also conduct audit of taxpayer's compliance with APAs, involving a site visit and request for additional information to verify the taxpayer's statements in the ACRs.

3.10.8 Renewal of APA

260. An APA renewal request goes through the same stages as the initial APA request.

3.10.9 Revision of APA

261. In cases where a request for revision is filed by the applicant owing to a situation having arisen that causes material differences to business and economic conditions essential to the continuation of the APA in each of the confirmed taxable years, the District Director shall receive and process it.

3.10.10 Cancellation of APA

262. Under the following conditions, an APA shall be cancelled:

- The taxpayer does not submit the request for revision even when material differences arise.
- The taxpayer fails to comply with the contents of the APA in its tax returns.
- The taxpayer fails to submit the report prescribed, or the report contains material errors.
- Any of the facts based on which the APA was given are revealed to be false, or the APA request contains material errors.

3.10.11 Statistics

263. Japan's APA programme was introduced in 1987. In Japan, APAs are one of the popular options used to avoid potential TP risk and to enhance the predictability and transparency of taxation. Also, tax audits in Japan are carried out periodically, and include a high level of detail. There has been an increase in the number of taxpayers who consider filing an APA in order to minimize the burden of a tax audit in relation to TP aspects, to avoid TP risk, and to strengthen their compliance with regulations. APAs provide much benefit to taxpayers, and thus the number of APA cases is increasing. The NTA also recommends applying a bilateral APA as an effective way to improve predictability. Additionally, the coverage of countries taking part in bilateral

APAs has increased and has been diversified, which is a recent characteristic of APAs/MAPs in Japan. Although the US is the major counterparty country, followed by European countries such as the UK, the number of APAs with Asia-Pacific countries such as Australia, China, South Korea, Thailand, India, Indonesia, Singapore, and Hong Kong has recently increased. Considering these increases in APAs, the Japanese tax authorities have enhanced their internal resources (e.g., the number of employees) and expanded their network with foreign countries.[102] There were 166 active bilateral APA applications during NTA's operation year 2017 (as at 30 June 2018) and 122 completed applications.[103]

264. During the 2018 operation year (from July 2018 to June 2019), the NTA received 219 MAP requests (BAPA were 163 (74%); transfer pricing adjustment, etc., were 56 (26%)). The number of MAP requests resolved during the 2018 operation year amounted to 187 (BAPA were 146 (78%); Transfer pricing adjustment, etc., were 41 (22%)).[104]

265. Statistics on the number of BAPA requests received and resolved in various years in Japan are provided in Figure 8.

102. Refer Japanese transfer pricing 2018 dated 23 August 2018 – Update https://www.tpweek.com/articles/update-on-japanese-transfer-pricing-2018/arkkxtkp accessed on 4 August 2019.
103. Refer DLA Piper – APA and MAP Country Guide 2019 https://www.dlapiper.com/en/us/insights/publications/2019/03/apa-and-map-country-guide-2019/ accessed on 11 August 2020.
104. Refer Mutual Agreement Procedures Report 2019 by NTA https://www.nta.go.jp/english/MAP-Report/2019.pdf accessed on 12 February 2021.

Figure 8 Number of BAPA Requests Received and Resolved in Various Years in Japan

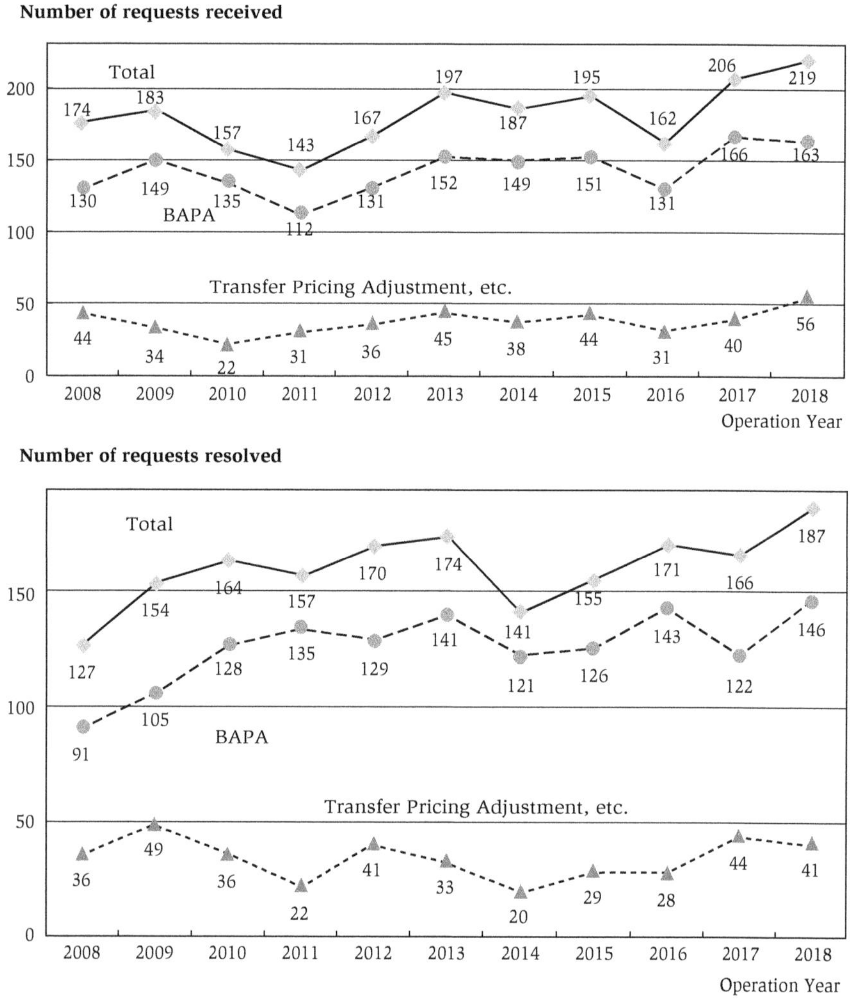

Source: Mutual Agreement Procedures Report 2019 by NTA https://www.nta.go.jp/english/MAP-Report/2019.pdf.

3.10.12 Ready Reckoner on Availability of Article 9(2), BAPA and Rollback Provisions

266. Japan allows unilateral, bilateral and multilateral APAs, as well as rollback of APAs for BAPA and MAPA. A ready reckoner on existence of Article 9(2) to relieve economic double taxation in DTAAs between Japan and various countries and the presence of BAPA and rollback provisions in the legislation of Japan's treaty partners is provided in Table 12 by analysing the following database:

- status of Article 9(2) as provided under OECD MTC, 2017 in the DTAA[105] between Japan and respective treaty partner;
- if not already present, whether Article 9(2) shall get introduced through the MLI[106] in such DTAAs;
- the country MAP/Dispute Resolution profiles[107] of the respective treaty partners available on the OECD website.

Table 12 Ready Reckoner on Availability of Article 9(2), BAPA and Rollback Between Japan and Treaty Partners

S. N.	*Treaty Partner*	*Date of Signature of DTAA*	*Does Article 9(2) Already Exist?*	*If No, Will It Come Through MLI?*	*Does the Treaty Partner Have BAPA?*	*Does the Treaty Partner Have Rollback?*
1	Australia	31.01.2008	Yes *	–	Yes	Yes
2	Austria	30.01.2017	Yes	–	Yes	Yes
3	Belgium	12.10.2016	Yes	–	Yes	Yes
4	Bulgaria	07.03.1991	Yes **	Yes **	No	No
5	Canada	07.05.1986	Yes	–	Yes	Yes
6	China	06.09.1983	No	Yes	Yes	Yes
7	Colombia	19.12.2018	Yes	–	Yes	Yes
8	Croatia	19.10.2018	Yes	–	Yes	No
9	The Czech Republic	11.10.1977	No	No	Yes	No
10	Denmark	11.10.2017	Yes	–	Yes	Yes
11	Egypt	03.09.1968	No	No	No	No
12	Finland	29.02.1972	No	Yes	No formal programme. But can be considered based on MAP article	Can be considered
13	France	03.03.1995	Yes **	Yes **	Yes	No
14	Germany	17.12.2015	Yes	–	Yes	Yes
15	Hong Kong	09.11.2010	Yes	–	Yes	Yes

105. Refer IBFD Tax Research Platform https://research.ibfd.org accessed on 13 February 2021.
106. Refer OECD – Signatories and Parties to the MLI http://www.oecd.org/tax/treaties/beps-mli-signatories-and-parties.pdf accessed on 13 February 2021.
107. Refer MAP profiles on www.oecd.org https://www.oecd.org/tax/dispute/country-map-profiles.htm accessed on 13 February 2021.

S. N.	*Treaty Partner*	*Date of Signature of DTAA*	*Does Article 9(2) Already Exist?*	*If No, Will It Come Through MLI?*	*Does the Treaty Partner Have BAPA?*	*Does the Treaty Partner Have Rollback?*
16	Hungary	13.02.1980	No	Yes	Yes	Yes
17	Iceland	15.01.2018	Yes	–	No	No
18	India	07.03.1989	Yes **	Yes **	Yes	Yes
19	Indonesia	03.03.1982	No	Yes	Yes	Yes @
20	Ireland	18.01.1974	No	Yes ***	Yes	Yes
21	Israel	08.03.1993	Yes **	Yes **	No formal programme. But can be considered based on MAP article	No
22	Italy	20.03.1969	No	Yes	Yes	No
23	Kazakhstan	19.12.2008	Yes **	Yes **	Yes	No
24	Korea	08.10.1998	Yes **	Yes **	Yes	Yes
25	Malaysia	19.02.1999	Yes	–	Yes	Yes
26	Mexico	09.04.1996	Yes	–	Yes	Yes
27	The Netherlands	25.08.2010	Yes **	Yes **	Yes	Yes
28	New Zealand	10.12.2012	Yes **	Yes **	Yes	Yes
29	Norway	04.03.1992	Yes	–	Yes	Yes
30	Poland	20.02.1980	No	Yes	Yes	No
31	Portugal	19.12.2011	Yes **	Yes **	Yes	No
32	Romania	12.02.1976	No	Yes	Yes	No
33	Russia	07.09.2017	Yes	–	Yes	No
34	Singapore	09.04.1994	Yes **	Yes **	Yes	Yes
35	The Slovak Republic	11.10.1977	No	Yes	Yes	Yes
36	Slovenia	30.09.2016	Yes	–	Yes	Yes
37	South Africa	07.03.1997	Yes **	Yes **	No	No
38	Spain	16.10.2018	Yes	–	Yes	Yes
39	Sweden	21.01.1983	Yes	–	Yes	Yes
40	The Swiss Confederation	19.01.1971	Yes	–	Yes	Yes
41	Thailand	07.04.1990	Yes	–	Yes	Yes #
42	Turkey	08.03.1993	Yes	–	Yes	Yes
43	The United Arab Emirates	02.05.2013	Yes **	Yes **	No	No

S. N.	*Treaty Partner*	*Date of Signature of DTAA*	*Does Article 9(2) Already Exist?*	*If No, Will It Come Through MLI?*	*Does the Treaty Partner Have BAPA?*	*Does the Treaty Partner Have Rollback?*
44	United Kingdom	02.02.2006	Yes **	Yes **	Yes	Yes
45	US	06.11.2003	Yes	–	Yes	Yes
46	Vietnam	24.10.1995	Yes	–	Yes	No

* Such provisions are in Article 9(3) of the DTAA.
** Such provisions are not as per Article 9(2) of the OECD MTC, 2017 in entirety; hence, appropriate notification under Article 17 of MLI has been made by Japan and the respective treaty partner.
*** Such provisions are in Article 10 of the DTAA.
@ Indonesia's Dispute Resolution Profile (last updated on 1 September 2016) states that rollback of APA is not permissible under the Indonesian APA programme. However, under the revised Ministry of Finance Regulation No. 22/PMK.03/2020, rollback is available in Indonesia.
# On perusal of Thailand's Dispute Resolution Profile (last updated on 1 June 2020), it is mentioned that rollback of APAs is provided for in the bilateral APA programme. However, Guidance on APA process issued by the Revenue Department of Thailand is silent on this issue.

3.11 APA REGIME IN KOREA (SOUTH)

267. The CA in charge of the APA programme in Korea is National Tax Service (NTS). In Korea, Transfer Pricing and APAs are governed by the Law for the Coordination of International Tax Affairs (LCITA).[108] The LCITA[109] authorizes the tax authorities to adjust the transfer price based on an ALP and to determine or recalculate a resident's taxable income when the transfer price of a Korean company and its foreign counterpart is either below or above an ALP. Korea's Dispute Resolution Profile[110] states that paragraphs 1 and 2 of Article 6 of Adjustment of International Taxes Act (AITA)[111] provide for implementation of APA programme as below:

(1) A resident may, where he/she intends to apply the arm's length price computation method to the taxable years for a specific period, file an

108. Refer DLA Piper – APA and MAP Country Guide 2019 https://www.dlapiper.com/en/us/insights/publications/2019/03/apa-and-map-country-guide-2019/ accessed on 11 August 2020.
109. Refer Law for the Coordination of International Tax Affairs https://transferpricing.com/pdf/Korea_LCITA.pdf accessed on 13 February 2021.
110. Refer Korea's Dispute Resolution Profile https://www.oecd.org/tax/dispute/Korea-Dispute-Resolution-Profile.pdf accessed on 13 February 2021.
111. Refer Adjustment of International Taxes Act (AITA) https://www.global-regulation.com/law/korea/643987/adjustment-of-international-taxes-act.html.

application for approval with the Commissioner of the National Tax Service not later than the end of the first taxable year for a specific period in which he/she intends to apply the arm's length price computation method, as prescribed by Presidential Decree.

(2) The Commissioner of the National Tax Service may, where a resident applies for approval for the arm's length price computation method under paragraph (1), grant approval for such method, if agreed with the competent authority of the Contracting State through mutual agreement procedures as prescribed by Presidential Decree: Provided, That in such cases as prescribed by Presidential Decree, he/she may grant prior approval (hereinafter referred to as 'unilateral prior approval' in this Article) for the arm's length price computation method without going through the mutual agreement procedures.

268. APAs can be unilateral, bilateral or multilateral, and can be sought for a three-year to five-year period. There is no filing fee. The unilateral APAs are mandated by the LCITA to be completed within two years from the application date which makes the unilateral APA process to be more streamlined compared to the bilateral or multilateral APAs.[112] Additionally, the approval process is handled by the International Co-operations Office, which is in charge of all APA negotiations, which allows the taxpayer to deal with the tax examiners who are specialized in transfer pricing. Accordingly, when dealing with transfer pricing issues, unilateral APAs provide more flexibility and benefits to the taxpayers than going through the general corporate tax audits which are generally conducted by tax examiners with limited transfer pricing understanding or experience. Having said that, taxpayers with moderate to high transfer pricing risks are encouraged in Korea to manage their transfer pricing risks through unilateral APAs.

3.11.1 Rollback of APA

269. Rollback is available in Korea. The period covered under rollback is up to five years for BAPA, MAPA and up to three years for UAPA. Paragraph 3 of Article 6 of AITA *inter alia* provides for implementation of rollback of APA as below:

> (3) The Commissioner of the National Tax Service may, when a resident files an application for the retroactive application of the arm's length price computation method to the taxable year before the period subject to the application for approval, grant approval for the retroactive application to no longer than five years preceding the period subject to the application for approval: Provided, That approval for the retroactive application to within three years preceding the period subject to the application for approval may be granted in cases where a unilateral prior approval has been given.

112. Refer Article by Gil Won Kang, Dong Kwan Kim and Pius Tae Hyun Park titled 'Korea: Navigating transfer pricing issues: Korean perspectives' (14 March 2014) https://www.internationaltaxreview.com/Article/3319660/Korea-Navigating-transfer-pricing-issues-Korean-perspectives.html?ArticleId=3319660 accessed on 3 August 2019.

270. TP-related amendments[113] in tax legislation were included and approved by the National Assembly of Korea in December 2020, whereby there is an extension of the retroactive application period for APAs. These are effective for APAs submitted on or after 1 January 2021. For bilateral APAs, the extension is increased to seven years (from five years). For unilateral APAs, the extension is increased to five years (from three years).

3.11.2 Pre-filing Meeting

271. Taxpayers are encouraged to request a pre-filing meeting with the NTS to discuss the APA process, wherein key points of the application, required information and documentation to be submitted are discussed. Anonymous pre-filing is also available. Key points discussed in a pre-filing meeting include:

- background of the APA request;
- records of tax returns, such as operating margins that are filed prior to the tax years covered by the APA;
- eligibility of the taxpayer to apply for an APA;
- eligibility of the transaction to be covered; and
- appropriateness of the proposed TP method.

3.11.3 APA Application

272. The application for an APA must be submitted to the NTS by the end of the first taxable year to be covered by the APA (unilateral APA). Taxpayers are required to submit the APA application form (Form No. 3 of Article 3, section 1 of the Ministerial Enforcement Decree of the LCITA) containing information such as the covered APA term, covered transactions, involved parties and the TP method, as well as the following documentation:

- business profile, organization, and investment relationship;
- financial statements for the past three years, a copy of tax returns, a copy of contracts for international transactions, and any other relevant documents;
- documents detailing suggested TP method;
- method used to adjust the difference between actual transaction prices and ALP;
- where the taxpayer requests a MAP, the MAP application form as designated by the Ministry of Strategy and Finance; and
- other documentation supporting the appropriateness of the TP method suggested for an APA.

113. Refer Report dt 17 February 2021 by KPMG titled 'Korea: Transfer pricing-related amendments in tax legislation' https://home.kpmg/us/en/home/insights/2021/02/tnf-korea-transfer-pricing-related-amendments-tax-legislation.html accessed on 29 March 2021.

3.11.4 Withdrawal from APA

273. The taxpayer has the right to withdraw the APA application without consequences. Once the terms of the APA have been finalized, the results are legally binding on the NTS and on the taxpayer.

3.11.5 Compliance Report

274. When an APA approval is obtained, taxpayers are required to file an annual APA report which shows that the transfer prices have been determined by the method agreed upon under the APA. Taxpayers must submit four copies of an annual report within six months from the following day of corporate tax return period for the covered years. The NTS may cancel an APA if an annual report is not filed, or contains false information on material matters. The Annual Report must include:

- critical assumptions and their realization as a prerequisite of the approved TP method;
- ALP calculated by the approved TP method and its calculating process;
- where applicable, the method used to adjust the difference between actual transaction prices and ALP; and
- other information agreed to be included in the Annual Report.

275. In addition, having obtained an APA, a taxpayer is required to file an amended tax return that reflects the change from its prior intercompany price with a related party and the price determined under the APA.

3.11.6 Renewal of APA

276. Under the Korean APA programme, taxpayers may request for renewal of an APA when it expires.

3.11.7 Confidentiality of Information

277. Any data submitted with the application for an APA is used to only determine whether or not to grant an APA. If an application for an APA is refused or withdrawn, such data will be returned to the applicant in order to safeguard the confidentiality right of the taxpayer.

3.11.8 Statistics

278. The APA programme was first introduced on 1 January 1997 in Korea, and the number of APA applications per year has been increasing every year as taxpayers try to avoid unexpected tax issues from their operations and mitigate potential risks. In 2012, more than half of the concluded APAs were bilateral APAs requested by foreign multinationals. Unilateral APAs are usually concluded within eighteen months, while bilateral/multilateral APAs are generally completed within two to three years.[114] There were 158 active APA applications during the income year 2015 (as at 31 December 2015) and 42 completed applications. The average completion time in this period was twenty-nine months for bilateral APAs and twenty-one months for unilateral APAs.[115] The average time taken to conclude APAs in 2019 was twenty-two months for UAPA and thirty-five months for BAPA. The NTS has received a total of 726 APA requests and has completed 508 cases as of the end of 2019. The NTS concluded its first APA with the US in May 1997.[116]

279. Statistics on the number of APA requests received and resolved in various years in Korea are provided in Table 13.

Table 13 Number of APA Requests Received and Resolved in Various Years in Korea

Year	*Total*		
	Received	*Concluded*	*Ongoing*
~ 2014	456	298	158
2015	43	42	159
2016	53	39	173
2017	45	39	179
2018	70	45	204
2019	59	45	218
Total	726	508	218

Source: APA Annual Report, 2019 published by NTS https://www.bdo.global/en-gb/microsites/tax-newsletters/corporate-tax-news/issue-57-january-2021/korea-transfer-pricing-advance-pricing-agreement-updates.

114. Refer Article by Gil Won Kang, Dong Kwan Kim and Pius Tae Hyun Park titled 'Korea: Navigating transfer pricing issues: Korean perspectives' (14 March 2014) https://www.internationaltaxreview.com/Article/3319660/Korea-Navigating-transfer-pricing-issues-Korean-perspectives.html?ArticleId=3319660 accessed on 3 August 2019.
115. Refer DLA Piper – APA and MAP Country Guide 2019 https://www.dlapiper.com/en/us/insights/publications/2019/03/apa-and-map-country-guide-2019/ accessed on 11 August 2020.
116. Refer APA Annual Report, 2019 published by NTS https://www.bdo.global/en-gb/microsites/tax-newsletters/corporate-tax-news/issue-57-january-2021/korea-transfer-pricing-advance-pricing-agreement-updates accessed on 13 February 2021.

3.11.9 Ready Reckoner on Availability of Article 9(2), BAPA and Rollback Provisions

280. Korea allows unilateral, bilateral and multilateral APAs, as well as rollback of APAs. A ready reckoner on existence of Article 9(2) to relieve economic double taxation in DTAAs between Korea and various countries and the presence of BAPA and rollback provisions in the legislation of Korea's treaty partners is provided in Table 14 by analysing the following database:

- status of Article 9(2) as provided under OECD MTC, 2017 in the DTAA[117] between Korea and respective treaty partner;
- if not already present, whether Article 9(2) shall get introduced through the MLI[118] in such DTAAs;
- the country MAP/Dispute Resolution profiles[119] of the respective treaty partners available on the OECD website.

Table 14 Ready Reckoner on Availability of Article 9(2), BAPA and Rollback Between Korea and Treaty Partners

S. N.	*Treaty Partner*	*Date of Signature of DTAA*	*Does Article 9(2) Already Exist?*	*If No, Will It Come Through MLI?*	*Does the Treaty Partner Have BAPA?*	*Does the Treaty Partner Have Rollback?*
1	Australia	12.07.1982	Yes *	–	Yes	Yes
2	Austria	08.10.1985	No	No	Yes	Yes
3	Belgium	29.08.1977	No	Yes	Yes	Yes
4	Bulgaria	11.03.1994	Yes	–	No	No
5	Canada	05.09.2006	Yes	–	Yes	Yes
6	China	28.03.1994	No	Yes	Yes	Yes
7	Colombia	27.07.2010	Yes	–	Yes	Yes
8	Croatia	13.11.2002	Yes	–	Yes	No
9	The Czech Republic	12.01.2018	Yes	–	Yes	No
10	Denmark	11.10.1977	No	Yes	Yes	Yes
11	Egypt	09.12.1992	No	No	No	No

117. Refer IBFD Tax Research Platform https://research.ibfd.org accessed on 13 February 2021.
118. Refer OECD – Signatories and Parties to the MLI http://www.oecd.org/tax/treaties/beps-mli-signatories-and-parties.pdf accessed on 13 February 2021.
119. Refer MAP profiles on www.oecd.org https://www.oecd.org/tax/dispute/country-map-profiles.htm accessed on 13 February 2021.

S. N.	*Treaty Partner*	*Date of Signature of DTAA*	*Does Article 9(2) Already Exist?*	*If No, Will It Come Through MLI?*	*Does the Treaty Partner Have BAPA?*	*Does the Treaty Partner Have Rollback?*
12	Finland	08.02.1979	No	Yes	No formal programme. But can be considered based on MAP article	Can be considered
13	France	19.06.1979	No	Yes	Yes	No
14	Georgia	31.03.2016	Yes	–	No	No
15	Germany	10.03.2000	Yes	–	Yes	Yes
16	Greece	20.03.1995	Yes	–	Yes	No
17	Hong Kong	08.07.2014	Yes	–	Yes	Yes
18	Hungary	29.03.1989	No	Yes	Yes	Yes
19	Iceland	15.05.2008	Yes	–	No	No
20	India	18.05.2015	Yes	–	Yes	Yes
21	Indonesia	10.11.1988	Yes	–	Yes	Yes @
22	Ireland	18.07.1990	No	Yes	Yes	Yes
23	Israel	18.03.1997	Yes	–	No formal programme. But can be considered based on MAP article	No
24	Italy	10.01.1989	No	Yes	Yes	No
25	Japan	08.10.1998	Yes **	Yes **	Yes	Yes
26	Kazakhstan	18.10.1997	Yes	–	Yes	No
27	Kenya	08.07.2014	Yes	–	No	No
28	Malaysia	20.04.1982	No	Yes	Yes	Yes
29	Mexico	06.10.1994	No	Yes	Yes	Yes
30	The Netherlands	25.10.1978	No	Yes	Yes	Yes
31	New Zealand	06.10.1981	No	Yes	Yes	Yes
32	Norway	05.10.1982	No	No	Yes	Yes
33	Poland	21.06.1991	Yes	–	Yes	No
34	Portugal	26.01.1996	No	Yes	Yes	No
35	Romania	11.10.1993	Yes	–	Yes	No
36	Russia	19.11.1992	No	Yes	Yes	No
37	Serbia	22.01.2016	Yes	–	No	No
38	Singapore	13.05.2019	Yes	–	Yes	Yes

S. N.	*Treaty Partner*	*Date of Signature of DTAA*	*Does Article 9(2) Already Exist?*	*If No, Will It Come Through MLI?*	*Does the Treaty Partner Have BAPA?*	*Does the Treaty Partner Have Rollback?*
39	The Slovak Republic	27.08.2001	No	Yes	Yes	Yes
40	Slovenia	25.04.2005	Yes	-	Yes	Yes
41	South Africa	07.07.1995	Yes	-	No	No
42	Spain	17.01.1994	No	Yes	Yes	Yes
43	Sweden	27.05.1981	No	Yes	Yes	Yes
44	The Swiss Confederation	12.02.1980	Yes	-	Yes	Yes
45	Thailand	16.11.2006	Yes	-	Yes	Yes #
46	Turkey	24.12.1983	No	No	Yes	Yes
47	The United Arab Emirates	27.02.2019	Yes	-	No	No
48	United Kingdom	25.10.1996	Yes	-	Yes	Yes
49	Uruguay	29.11.2011	Yes	-	No	No
50	US	04.06.1976	Yes ***	-	Yes	Yes
51	Vietnam	20.05.1994	Yes	-	Yes	No

* Such provisions are in Article 9(5) of the DTAA.

** Such provisions are not as per Article 9(2) of the OECD MTC, 2017 in entirety; hence, appropriate notification under Article 17 of MLI has been made by Korea and the respective treaty partner.

*** Such provisions are embedded in Article 11(1) of the DTAA.

@ Indonesia's Dispute Resolution Profile (last updated on 1 September 2016) states that rollback of APA is not permissible under the Indonesian APA programme. However, under the revised Ministry of Finance Regulation No. 22/PMK.03/2020, rollback is available in Indonesia.

On perusal of Thailand's Dispute Resolution Profile (last updated on 1 June 2020), it is mentioned that rollback of APAs is provided for in the bilateral APA programme. However, Guidance on APA process issued by the Revenue Department of Thailand is silent on this issue.

3.12 APA REGIME IN MEXICO

281. The CA in charge of the APA programme in Mexico is Central Administrator for Transfer Pricing Audits, State Administration of Tax (SAT). Article 34-A of the Federal

Tax Code[120] enables Mexican taxpayers to submit APA requests to the Mexican Tax Administration regarding transfer pricing. Article 34-A of the Federal Fiscal Code *inter alia* states as below:

> Rulings issued in accordance with this Article may be valid regarding the fiscal year in which they are requested, the immediately preceding year, and for up to three fiscal years following that in which they are requested. Rulings may be valid regarding a longer period when they stem from a mutual agreement procedure in accordance with an international convention to which Mexico is a party.

282. In Mexico, unilateral, bilateral or multilateral APAs can be applied.[121] There is a five-year maximum term for an APA; however, this validity period may be extended for bilateral and multilateral APAs negotiated under the MAP provisions of a DTAA, and at the discretion of the relevant CAs involved. The period of validity may cover the year of submission, the preceding year and the following three years.

3.12.1 Rollback

283. The years to be covered in Rollback of the APA are either subject to the terms of the treaty or the domestic statute of limitations.[122]

3.12.2 Pre-filing Meeting

284. Although there is no explicit procedure for a pre-filing conference, in practice taxpayers may, in conjunction with the Central Administration of International Fiscal Audit branch of the General Administration of Large Taxpayers within the SAT, analyse the information and TP method expected to be submitted for consideration. Anonymous pre-filing is also available. There is no specific guidance on submission of APAs; however, in practice requests are more likely to be successful if:

- the transfer pricing issues are complex and uncertainty exists as to how the arm's-length standard should be applied;
- a significant number of APAs relate to maquiladora (a maquiladora is a Mexican subsidiary company, usually 100% foreign owned, whose primary role is assembly. Maquiladoras are defined in the Presidential Decree (Decrees for the Fostering and Operation of the Maquiladora Industry for Export) as assembly plants undertaking maquiladora activities under permit by the Ministry of Economy. Maquiladoras are usually structured as cost centres, with marginal profits. Their activities include the maintenance of assets and

120. Refer para. D.4.7.1 of the United Nations Practical Manual on Transfer Pricing for Developing Countries (2017).
121. Refer DLA Piper – APA and MAP Country Guide 2019 https://www.dlapiper.com/en/us/insights/publications/2019/03/apa-and-map-country-guide-2019/ accessed on 11 August 2020.
122. Refer Mexico's Dispute Resolution Profile https://www.oecd.org/tax/dispute/Mexico-Dispute-Resolution-Profile.pdf accessed on 13 February 2021.

inventories provided by foreign residents for their transformation (production, sub-assembly and assembly) by maquiladoras into semi-finished and finished goods destined for export (mainly for the US market). Typically, foreign parent companies own inventories, equipment and machinery, provide the maquiladora with all the input, technology and know-how to carry out the manufacturing process, and allow the maquiladora the use of patents and technical assistance free of charge. Maquiladoras usually own or lease some assets, including a physical facility in Mexico; they hire and manage the labour pool required, and use capital free-loaned from the parent company to transform inputs into products for export to the parent company or another related party. Many maquiladoras actually perform additional functions for the parent company. However, maquiladoras are generally treated as 'contract' companies in the sense that they are assumed to perform functions requiring no valuable intangibles and very few routine intangibles);[123] and
- there is a high probability of double taxation without an APA.

3.12.3 APA Application

285. APA applicants are required to pay a fee in accordance with Article 53-G of the Federal Fees Law in force and, for each annual review, they are required to pay a fee in accordance with Article 53-H of the Federal Fees Law. The filing fee for an APA is MXN 216,309 (approx. USD 10,500). The fee for an annual review is MXN 43,262 (approx. USD 3,000). Documentation indicating that the fee for the APA application has been paid is required to be submitted. All documentation is required to be submitted electronically. In accordance with the administrative Rule 2.12.8., taxpayers that submit a consultation related to the TPM used in their transactions with related parties should provide the information and Form No. 102/CFF 'Consultation Related to the Transfer Pricing' included in Annex 1-A of the administrative rules. The application for an APA must be submitted with the following documentation:

(1) the taxpayer's tax identification number and country of tax residency, indicating whether it has branches in Mexico;
(2) the name or corporate business name, tax identification number, and address of all related parties in Mexico or abroad that have direct or indirect ownership in the equity of the Mexican taxpayer; indicating direct shareholders, as well as the ultimate parent company of the holding company in line with the International Financial Reporting Standards;
(3) the name or corporate business name, tax identification number, and address of all related parties in Mexico that have a business relationship with the Mexican taxpayer; as well as any establishment, branches, warehouses, platforms, vessels, or areas where exploration or extraction of

123. Refer paras D.4.8.3 and D.4.8.4 of the United Nations Practical Manual on Transfer Pricing for Developing Countries (2017).

hydrocarbons that may be relevant regarding the TP method that is selected in the application;

(4) the name or corporate business name, tax identification number, and address of the foreign related parties that have a business relationship with the Mexican taxpayer;
(5) the name or corporate business name, tax identification number, and address of all related parties in Mexico or abroad that may be involved in dealing with the response to the APA application request;
(6) the tax years intended to be covered under the proposed APA;
(7) the currency under which the transactions to be covered were agreed between the Mexican taxpayer and its related parties in Mexico or abroad;
(8) a description of the business activities of the group of which the taxpayer is part of, specifying the following:
    - the background of the group of which the taxpayer is part;
    - a description of the relevant factors that generate profits for the group;
    - detail of transfer pricing policies implemented by the group;
    - a description of the main business activities carried out by the entities that are part of the group;
    - consolidated financial statements of the tax year for the group;
    - industry analysis of which the taxpayer belongs in Mexico and abroad, describing current behaviour and forecast, size, main competitors, its market position, access to substitute goods and services, competitors' purchase power, and government regulations; and
    - international financial structures used by the group.
(9) a description of intangibles that belong to the group, including:
    - the name and country of residence of the legal owner of the intangibles that belong to the group, and documentation supporting such ownership;
    - the name, country of residence and financial information of the companies that have recorded the ownership of the intangibles for accounting purposes; and
    - the name and country of residence of the entities that carry out development activities, improvement, maintenance, protection and exploitation of intangibles that are owned by the group.
(10) the name and country of residence of the entities that belong to the group that generate income, or have expenses with third parties, related to the business of the group, segregating them by income and expenses;
(11) a detailed description of the taxpayer's activities, including:
    - a description of the activities carried out, assets used and risks assumed by the taxpayer;
    - register of nominal shares as provided by Article 128 of the General Corporate Law;
    - financial profits and loss statements of the taxpayer for the three previous tax years, with a cost and expense breakdown, and of the local and foreign related parties that have a business relationship;

- a statement verifying that annual and amended corporate tax returns were filed in the tax year for which the APA application is made, and the three previous tax years;
- a copy of the dictamen fiscal (tax report), as well as audited financial statements and corresponding exhibits for the last three years;
- contracts and agreements entered into between the taxpayer and its Mexican or foreign related parties;
- an operational chart through which names and roles can be identified in the corporate group of the taxpayer and its Mexican and foreign related parties, as well as the geographical place where the activities are carried out;
- a description of business strategies, specifying whether it has been or will carry out a restructure, through which functions, assets or activities would be migrated; changing its business operations; and
- a list of main competitors.

(12) for the transactions or operations for which the taxpayer is requesting an APA:
- a detailed description of the functions and activities carried out by the taxpayer and the Mexican or non-resident related parties that maintain a contractual or business relationship with the taxpayer, including a description of the assets held and the risks borne by each of the parties;
- the TP method proposed by the taxpayer to determine the transfer price, including the criteria and other objective elements used to demonstrate that the method is appropriate for the covered transaction(s) for which the taxpayer is requesting an APA;
- financial information corresponding to the fiscal years to be covered and an application of the proposed TP method to its intercompany transactions;
- information on comparable transactions or companies, indicating the reasonable adjustments made to eliminate differences;
- a statement indicating whether the taxpayer's non-resident related parties have been subjected to a transfer pricing audit by any tax authority and, if so, a description of the status of the audit; and
- information on whether the non-resident related parties are disputing a tax controversy related to the transfer pricing before the tax authorities of a court and, if so, a description of the status of that dispute.

3.12.4 Evaluation of APA Application

286. As part of the APA process, SAT may request site visits for verification of the functional analysis, business purpose, and other relevant information.

3.12.5 Annual Report

287. In terms of Article 34A of the Federal Tax Code, the authority can condition the validity of APA rulings on the taxpayer fulfilling some requirements demonstrating that the transactions to which such rulings refer are conducted at prices or consideration amounts that would have been used by independent parties in comparable transactions. In this sense, it is not rare to find in the rulings a provision conditioning its validity to the taxpayer filing an annual report before the authority, which would allow them to verify that the business circumstances and other critical assumptions considered for the issuance of the ruling remain applicable.[124]

3.12.6 Renewal of APA

288. There is no specific guidance for the renewal procedure.

3.12.7 Statistics

289. There are no statistics publicly available on APAs in respect of Mexico.[125]

3.12.8 Ready Reckoner on Availability of Article 9(2), BAPA and Rollback Provisions

290. Mexico allows unilateral, bilateral and multilateral APAs, as well as rollback of APAs. A ready reckoner on existence of Article 9(2) to relieve economic double taxation in DTAAs between Mexico and various countries and the presence of BAPA and rollback provisions in the legislation of Mexico's treaty partners is provided in Table 15 by analysing the following database:

- status of Article 9(2) as provided under OECD MTC, 2017 in the DTAA[126] between Mexico and respective treaty partner;
- if not already present, whether Article 9(2) shall get introduced through the MLI[127] in such DTAAs;
- the country MAP/Dispute Resolution profiles[128] of the respective treaty partners available on the OECD website.

124. Refer Article by Christian R. Natera titled 'Getting an APA in Mexico' https://www.natera.com.mx/euromoney/Transfer_Pricing_2011-12.pdf accessed on 13 February 2021.
125. Refer DLA Piper – APA and MAP Country Guide 2019 https://www.dlapiper.com/en/us/insights/publications/2019/03/apa-and-map-country-guide-2019/ accessed on 11 August 2020.
126. Refer IBFD Tax Research Platform https://research.ibfd.org accessed on 13 February 2021.
127. Refer OECD – Signatories and Parties to the MLI http://www.oecd.org/tax/treaties/beps-mli-signatories-and-parties.pdf accessed on 13 February 2021.
128. Refer MAP profiles on www.oecd.org https://www.oecd.org/tax/dispute/country-map-profiles.htm accessed on 13 February 2021.

Table 15 Ready Reckoner on Availability of Article 9(2), BAPA and Rollback Between Mexico and Treaty Partners

S. N.	*Treaty Partner*	*Date of Signature of DTAA*	*Does Article 9(2) Already Exist?*	*If No, Will It Come Through MLI?*	*Does the Treaty Partner Have BAPA?*	*Does the Treaty Partner Have Rollback?*
1	Australia	09.09.2002	Yes	–	Yes	Yes
2	Austria	13.04.2004	Yes	–	Yes	Yes
3	Belgium	24.11.1992	No	Yes	Yes	Yes
4	Canada	12.09.2006	Yes	–	Yes	Yes
5	China	12.09.2005	Yes *	Yes *	Yes	Yes
6	Colombia	13.08.2009	Yes	–	Yes	Yes
7	The Czech Republic	04.04.2002	No	No	Yes	No
8	Finland	12.02.1997	Yes	–	No formal programme. But can be considered based on MAP article	Can be considered
9	France	07.11.1991	No	Yes	Yes	No
10	Germany	09.07.2008	Yes	–	Yes	Yes
11	Greece	13.04.2004	Yes	–	Yes	No
12	Hong Kong	18.06.2012	Yes	–	Yes	Yes
13	Hungary	24.06.2011	Yes	–	Yes	Yes
14	Iceland	11.03.2008	Yes	–	No	No
15	India	10.09.2007	Yes	–	Yes	Yes
16	Indonesia	06.09.2002	Yes *	Yes *	Yes	Yes @
17	Ireland	22.10.1998	Yes	–	Yes	Yes
18	Israel	20.07.1999	Yes	–	No formal programme. But can be considered based on MAP article	No
19	Italy	08.07.1991	No	Yes	Yes	No
20	Japan	09.04.1996	Yes	–	Yes	Yes
21	The Netherlands	27.09.1993	Yes	–	Yes	Yes
22	New Zealand	16.11.2006	Yes	–	Yes	Yes
23	Poland	30.11.1998	Yes *	Yes *	Yes	No
24	Portugal	11.11.1999	Yes	–	Yes	No

S. N.	*Treaty Partner*	*Date of Signature of DTAA*	*Does Article 9(2) Already Exist?*	*If No, Will It Come Through MLI?*	*Does the Treaty Partner Have BAPA?*	*Does the Treaty Partner Have Rollback?*
25	Romania	20.07.2000	Yes	–	Yes	No
26	Russia	07.06.2004	Yes	–	Yes	No
27	Singapore	09.11.1994	No	Yes	Yes	Yes
28	The Slovak Republic	13.05.2006	Yes	–	Yes	Yes
29	South Africa	19.02.2009	Yes	–	No	No
30	Spain	24.07.1992	Yes	–	Yes	Yes
31	Sweden	21.09.1992	Yes	–	Yes	Yes
32	The Swiss Confederation	03.08.1993	Yes *	Yes *	Yes	Yes
33	Turkey	17.12.2013	Yes	–	Yes	Yes
34	The United Arab Emirates	20.11.2012	Yes	–	No	No
35	United Kingdom	02.06.1994	Yes	–	Yes	Yes
36	Uruguay	14.08.2009	Yes	–	No	No
37	US	18.09.1992	Yes	–	Yes	Yes

* Such provisions are not as per Article 9(2) of the OECD MTC, 2017 in entirety; hence, appropriate notification under Article 17 of MLI has been made by Mexico and the respective treaty partner.
@ Indonesia's Dispute Resolution Profile (last updated on 1 September 2016) states that rollback of APA is not permissible under the Indonesian APA programme. However, under the revised Ministry of Finance Regulation No. 22/PMK.03/2020, rollback is available in Indonesia.

3.13 APA REGIME IN THE NETHERLANDS

291. The Netherlands is a member of the OECD, and according to the transfer pricing decrees of 30 March 2001 and 21 August 2004, the OECD Guidelines are directly applicable in the Netherlands. Also, the explanatory memorandum to the October 2001 proposals on the transfer pricing legislation, effective from January 2002, reconfirms the adoption of the OECD Guidelines by the Dutch Tax Authorities (DTAs).[129] In 2013, the Dutch Ministry of Finance issued a transfer pricing decree, No. IFZ2013/184M or the '2013 transfer pricing decree', which combines and replaces two previous transfer

129. Refer Note issued by PwC on Transfer Pricing in The Netherlands https://www.pwc.com/gx/en/international-transfer-pricing/assets/netherlands.pdf accessed on 4 March 2021.

pricing decrees released in 2001 and 2004 (No. IFZ2001/295M and No. IFZ2004/689M, respectively). As in the past, the OECD Transfer Pricing Guidelines are incorporated in domestic law by reference in the said transfer pricing decree.[130] The basic features of the transfer pricing legislation in the Netherlands are as follows:

- Codification of the arm's-length principle.
- A widening of the scope of the transfer pricing legislation through a broader concept of 'control' between affiliated businesses that are directly or indirectly participating in the capital, management or supervision of another company, as long as there is sufficient influence on the prices charged between the companies involved. The level of control and influence is not quantified in the law. This legislation applies to transactions where one party controls the other or both parties are under common control.
- A requirement to maintain data in the administration that demonstrates the arm's-length nature of the transfer prices and how these prices have been derived.
- A strict interpretation of the documentation requirements implies that taxpayers should prepare the relevant documentary evidence when the intra-group transactions take place.

292. The CA in charge of the APA programme in the Netherlands is APA/Advance Tax Ruling (ATR) team of the DTA (APA/ATR team). The relevant provisions in regard to the implementation of the APA programme in the Netherlands are contained in Decree DGB 2014/3098 regarding the APA application procedure and Decree DGB 2014/296M regarding the organizational and competence aspects of the APA/ATR practices.[131]

293. Unilateral, bilateral, and multilateral APAs are available in the Netherlands. There is a five-year maximum term for an APA, although longer terms may be possible if the taxpayer's circumstances involve long-term contracts. There is no filing fee. BAPA/MAPA can only be concluded with States with which the Netherlands has signed a DTAA including a provision of the type of Article 25(3) of the OECD MTC. APAs may include TPMs covering different types of related party transactions or specific transactions, including transfers of tangible or intangible property, financing and licensing activities and the provision of services. APAs may cover all the taxpayer's transfer pricing issues or may be limited to one or more specific issues.

294. The Netherlands provide APAs only if either:

130. Refer 'Doing Business in The Netherlands 2020-2021' by Baker McKenzie https://www.bakermckenzie.com/-/media/files/insight/publications/2020/02/doing-business-in-the-netherlands-20202021_v2.pdf accessed on 4 March 2021.
131. Refer DLA Piper – APA and MAP Country Guide 2019 https://www.dlapiper.com/en/us/insights/publications/2019/03/apa-and-map-country-guide-2019/ accessed on 11 August 2020.

- the taxpayer or relevant parties conduct operational activities in the Netherlands, or can prove they have plans to do so; or
- the taxpayer meets specified minimum substance and real risk requirements for intermediary holding companies and intergroup financing, licensing, and leasing companies.

295. As of July 2019, rulings (APAs and ATRs) shall only be granted if the taxpayer has 'economic nexus' with the Netherlands. In practice, this means that operational activities in the Netherlands (or the plans to bring these to the Netherlands) will be required for a ruling. Meeting a list of substance requirements will no longer be enough. The tax authorities have developed the following minimum requirements of substance in the Netherlands for a Dutch financial services company (FSC):

- at least 50% of all authorized directors are tax residents of the Netherlands;
- the directors residing in the Netherlands have the relevant professional knowledge and skills to execute their obligations as directors;
- the FSC has qualified personnel to execute and administer its transactions;
- the (main) directorial decisions are taken in the Netherlands;
- the FSC's (main) bank account is maintained in the Netherlands;
- the FSC's books and accounts are kept in the Netherlands;
- the FSC is a tax resident of the Netherlands and is not deemed a resident of any other country;
- the FSC has a minimum of EUR 100,000 labour costs in relation to the licensing and/or financing activities; and
- the FSC has its own office space at its disposition (minimum twenty-four months lease).

This means that a business activity must be carried out by a sufficient number of relevant employees in the Netherlands. A ruling will not be granted if the purpose or one of the main purposes of the transaction is to avoid Dutch or foreign taxation, or if low-taxed (tax rate lower than 9%) or EU-blacklisted jurisdictions are involved in the transaction.[132]

296. Since 1 July 2019, the formal procedure in the Netherlands for granting a tax ruling in a cross-border situation requires a second review, approval, and signature by a newly composed team of specialists within the DTAs: the College International Tax Certainty. This team, consisting of seven experts in transfer pricing and international tax, could therefore be considered as a second assessment team. Alongside the tightened internal procedure, one of the other most significant changes is the introduction of eligibility requirements for entitlement to prior consultation with the Dutch tax ruling team to obtain a tax ruling with an international character. As a result of these

132. Refer 'Doing Business in The Netherlands 2020-2021' by Baker McKenzie https://www.bakermckenzie.com/-/media/files/insight/publications/2020/02/doing-business-in-the-netherlands-20202021_v2.pdf accessed on 4 March 2021.

changes, the requirements to be eligible to enter into prior consultation have become stricter and more extensive.[133]

297. On 22 June 2020, the Dutch State Secretary of Finance published a new decree relating to mutual agreement procedures (MAP Decree).[134] The MAP Decree also refers to the existing option allowing a taxpayer to request the Dutch CA to enter into BAPA or MAPA discussions with other jurisdictions as a means to prevent or solve (potential) tax disputes based on the applicable tax treaty. In this respect, a BAPA or MAPA can also cover transactions that have already been implemented and applied for rollback years as long as the facts and circumstances have remained comparable and the other jurisdiction(s) agrees to follow this procedure. The requirements for these types of APAs are the same as for unilateral APAs. Different from a unilateral APA, however, requests for BAPAs and MAPAs are handled by the Ministry of Finance (i.e., the Dutch CA), instead of the APA team of the Dutch tax administration.

3.13.1 Rollback of APA

298. Rollbacks are available if the facts and circumstances in prior years are comparable to those in the APA application, or if accurate adjustments can be made to the relevant prior years. For unilateral APA requests, rollback is available in case the rollback does not result in a decrease of taxable profits of still open years. For bilateral and multilateral APAs, the foreign tax authorities should agree with the rollback.

3.13.2 Pre-filing Meeting

299. The pre-filing meeting creates the potential to discuss the APA request with the APA team before it is actually filed. The benefit to the taxpayer is a clarification of the information that is likely to be required and specific elements likely to be pertinent to the formal APA request. Pre-filing meetings also provide the taxpayer with the opportunity to obtain clarity on the documentation requirements and essential elements for a successful APA application. A joint case management plan can be prepared in collaboration with the APA/ATR team, outlining the formal APA negotiation process and the anticipated timeline between formal filing and completion. The intention of this case management plan is to reduce uncertainty for the taxpayer with respect to the handling process of the application. The critical dates negotiated with the APA/ATR team at the pre-filing meeting will determine the date from which the APA will commence. Anonymous pre-filing is also available.

---

133. Refer 'An in-depth analysis of published anonymized APA and APA request summaries under the revised Dutch Tax Ruling Practice (Intertax, vol. 49, 2021, issue 3) by Koen Bolink (Houthoff)' http://kluwertaxblog.com/2021/02/18/an-in-depth-analysis-of-published-anonymized-apa-and-apa-request-summaries-under-the-revised-dutch-tax-ruling-practice-forthcoming-intertax-vol-49-2021-issue-3/ accessed on 5 March 2021.
134. Refer 'Netherlands issues new MAP decree' https://taxnews.ey.com/news/2020-1684-netherlands-issues-new-map-decree accessed on 5 March 2021.

3.13.3 APA Application

300. The APA request needs to be filed with the tax inspector or directly with the APA/ATR team of the DTAs (particularly in cases where the request concerns activities to be established in the Netherlands). In all cases, the inspector is obliged to present the request to the APA/ATR team of the DTAs for binding advice (in cases of new policy after consultation of the Transfer Pricing Co-ordination Group). In the case of a bilateral APA request, the Dutch Ministry of Finance initiates the bilateral agreement procedure with the other country involved. The APA/ATR team generally requires the following information to be submitted in an APA application:

- the names and addresses of the entities involved;
- the accounting period or fiscal years to be covered;
- the transactions, products, businesses or arrangements to be covered;
- a description of the enterprises and/or PEs involved in the transactions/agreements;
- the relevant foreign tax authorities involved;
- the global organizational structure, history, financial statement data, products, functions (including risks assumed) and assets (tangible and intangible) of the enterprises involved;
- a description of market conditions including industry trends and competitive environment;
- a description of the proposed TP method, including a comparability analysis; and
- critical assumptions underpinning the APA application and a discussion of the effect of changes in those assumptions or other events.

3.13.4 Compliance Requirements

301. Under the APA programme of the Netherlands, ACRs are not required. The taxpayer is required to indicate that it has obtained an APA in its tax return. Periodic audits by the APA/ATR team may take place to ensure compliance with critical assumptions included in the APA.

3.13.5 Renewal of APA

302. At the request of the taxpayer, the APA/ATR team can evaluate whether a new APA can be concluded under the same conditions as those of an existing APA.

3.13.6 Statistics

303. Statistics on the number of APA requests received and resolved in 2017, 2018 in the Netherlands are given in Table 16.

Table 16 Number of APA Requests Received and Resolved in 2017, 2018 in the Netherlands

FY	*Number of APA Requests Received*	*Number of APAs Granted*	*Number of APA Applications Rejected*	*Number of APA Applications Where the Taxpayer Withdrew Its Request*	*Average Time (In Months) to Negotiate Bilateral or Multilateral APAs*
2017	176	132	4	40	24
2018	148	118	–	45	24

Source: Statistics on APAs in the EU at the end of 2017 https://ec.europa.eu/taxation_customs/sites/taxation/files/statistics_on_advance_pricing_agreements_2017_en.pdf.
and
Statistics on APAs in the EU at the end of 2018 https://ec.europa.eu/taxation_customs/sites/taxation/files/apa-and-map-2019-3.pdf.

3.14 APA REGIME IN NEW ZEALAND

304. New Zealand's transfer pricing rules have been amended to ensure alignment with the new OECD guidance and remain effective at combatting BEPS. The following key amendments have been made:

- The economic substance and actual conduct of the parties, along with the legal contract, will determine the transfer pricing analysis. In certain circumstances, the economic substance and actual conduct will have priority over the terms of the legal contract. This is achieved by requiring the transfer pricing transaction to be 'accurately delineated' as depicted in Figure 9.

Figure 9 Accurate Delineation of International Transaction in New Zealand's Legislation

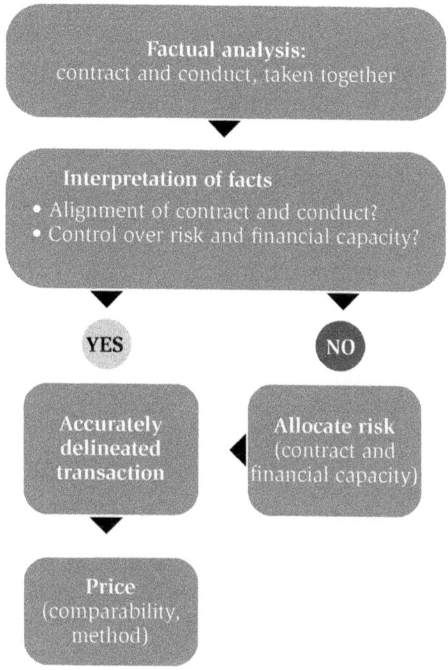

Source: New Zealand – Compliance Focus – 2019 https://www.ird.govt.nz/-/media/project/ir/home/documents/international/multinational-enterprises---compliance-focus-documents/compliance-focus---2019.pdf.

- Where a transfer pricing arrangement is not commercially rational because it includes unrealistic terms that unrelated parties would not be willing to agree to, the transaction may be disregarded and, if appropriate, replaced.

305. The CA in charge of the APA programme in New Zealand is Inland Revenue Department (IRD). The relevant provisions in regard to the implementation of the APA programme in New Zealand are contained in Part 5A of the Tax Administration Act (TAA), and general guidance is available on the IRD's website.[135]

306. Unilateral, bilateral, and multilateral APAs are available in New Zealand under the private binding rulings regime. There is no specific guidance for APA term limits. In practice there is usually a maximum term of five years. A flat fee of NZD 322 (approx. USD 226) is payable to the IRD. If any overseas travel is required for the

135. Refer DLA Piper – APA and MAP Country Guide 2019 https://www.dlapiper.com/en/us/insights/publications/2019/03/apa-and-map-country-guide-2019/ accessed on 11 August 2020.

completion of an APA, the IRD seeks to recover out of pocket expenses on an actual and reasonable basis from the taxpayer. An estimate of such costs is provided to the taxpayer prior to the travel being undertaken. Section 91E of the TAA allows a unilateral APA to be issued in the form of a binding ruling. BAPA/MAPA can only be concluded under MAP provisions with States with which New Zealand has signed a DTAA. Applications for entering into the APAs from taxpayers who are under investigation by the IRD for tax issues are not entertained.

3.14.1 Salient Legislative Provisions[136]

307. Section 91E of the TAA *inter alia* provides that the Commissioner is empowered to make private rulings on application, as below:

- the Commissioner must make a private ruling on how a taxation law applies, or would apply, to a person and to the arrangement, whether a single or a recurring arrangement, for which the ruling is sought.
- the Commissioner may make a private ruling on how a taxation law applies to the arrangement described in an application whether or not reference was made to that taxation law in the application.
- the Commissioner may decline to make a private ruling if –
  - the Commissioner considers that the correctness of the ruling would depend on which conditions were stipulated about a future event or other matter; or
  - the arrangement on which the ruling is sought, or a separately identifiable part of that arrangement, is substantially the same as an arrangement which is subject to an objection, challenge, or appeal, whether in relation to the applicant or any other person; or
  - the applicant has outstanding debts relating to earlier binding ruling applications.

308. Section 91EB of the TAA *inter alia* provides for circumstances of application of a private ruling, as below:

- A private ruling on a taxation law for a tax type applies to a person in relation to an arrangement –
  - only if the taxation law is expressly referred to in the ruling; and
  - only for the period or tax year for which the ruling applies.
- A private ruling does not apply to a person in relation to a tax type for an arrangement, to the extent to which, in relation to the tax type –
  - the arrangement is materially different from the arrangement identified in the ruling; or
  - the circumstances are materially different from the circumstances described in the ruling; or
  - there was a material omission or misrepresentation in, or in connection with, the application for the ruling; or

136. Refer Private Binding Rulings under Chapter 5A of the TAA https://www.legislation.govt.nz/act/public/1994/0166/latest/DLM348343.html accessed on 4 March 2021.

- the private ruling states an assumption that the Commissioner made about a future event or other matter, and the assumption subsequently proves to be materially incorrect; or
- the Commissioner stipulates a condition that is not satisfied.

309. Section 91ED of the TAA *inter alia* prescribes disclosure requirements of a private ruling on the part of the applicant, as below:

- An application for a private ruling must –
  - identify the applicant; and
  - disclose all relevant facts and documents relating to the arrangement for which the ruling is sought; and
  - state the taxation laws in respect of which the ruling is sought; and
  - state the propositions of law (if any) which are relevant to the issues raised in the application; and
  - provide a draft ruling.

310. Section 91EF of the TAA *inter alia* empowers the Commissioner to stipulate the conditions on which private ruling is based, as below:

- If the Commissioner considers that the correctness of a private ruling would depend on conditions being stipulated about a future event or other matter, the Commissioner may –
  - stipulate the conditions on which the Commissioner bases the ruling; or
  - decline to make the ruling.

3.14.2 Rollback

311. IRD is of the view that if the APA has been made pursuant to a treaty that contains a specific time limit override, then there is no restriction on rolling back the agreed TPM.[137]

3.14.3 APA Process

312. Under New Zealand's APA programme, the broad phases that are usually undertaken in completing APAs are as below:

- Pre-application.
- Formal application.
- Reviewing an application.
- Agreeing outcomes.
- ACR.

137. Refer New Zealand's Dispute Resolution Profile (updated on 19 July 2019) https://www.oecd.org/tax/dispute/New-Zealand-Dispute-Resolution-Profile.pdf accessed on 4 March 2021.

3.14.4 Pre-filing Meeting

313. Taxpayers intending to apply for an APA are required to contact for a pre-application meeting with a Principal Advisor (Transfer Pricing) to discuss the proposal informally. Anonymous pre-filing is not available.

314. The pre-application phase typically involves the following steps:

- submitting a completed APA pre-application meeting form, which contains brief details of the proposed application, including the business background, forecast financial information, the international associated party transactions in question and suggested TPM to be applied;
- a pre-application meeting shortly afterwards to discuss the proposal informally;
- depending on the complexity of issues being addressed, a series of targeted follow-up submissions and meetings.

315. During the meeting, the following issues are normally discussed and presented for consideration:

- an overview of the business operations;
- background information on the foreign entities involved in the transactions intended to be covered by the APA; and
- TP method intended to be applied.

3.14.5 APA Application

316. After a successful pre-filing meeting, the APA application is formalized and submitted by the taxpayer for consideration of IRD. The APA application is required to include the following:

- a full functional analysis;
- analysis of key profit drivers and value additions;
- identification of the tested party;
- the choice of methodology;
- a study of comparables;
- proposed application of methodology and comparables;
- copies of all intercompany agreements.

317. Unilateral APAs are issued in the form of a binding ruling. The application should be submitted along with a completed Application for Private Ruling - IR713 form and Application for Private Ruling on Transfer Pricing Arrangement - Additional Declaration - IR713A form. These forms are to be provided to the Team Manager, Technical Services, Tax Counsel Office, Wellington. Bilateral/multilateral APAs are entered into in accordance with New Zealand's double tax treaties. Applications are to be addressed to the Manager (International Revenue Strategy), International Revenue Strategy, Wellington.

3.14.6 Evaluation of APA Application

318. Site visits and interviews may be required during the application review stage to inspect the actual operations of the relevant associated parties, especially where valuable intangibles are an issue and a residual profit-split methodology is proposed. Once IRD is familiar with applicant's business, it checks whether the methodology is appropriate and carries out a review of the comparables. Frequently, IRD carries out its own search for comparables rather than simply accept the comparables offered in the application. IRD also does a cross-check using another methodology to see if the results are consistent and give an answer supportive of the proposed methodology.

319. When the review is completed, IRD engages with the officers of the other jurisdiction (bilateral APA) or with the taxpayer (unilateral APA) to discuss any differences of opinion and findings. There may be further exchanges of fact and opinion until an agreement is reached. In the case of bilateral APAs, IRD endeavours to keep in contact with the taxpayer throughout the process to ensure that the outcome agreed between the tax authorities will also satisfy the objectives of the taxpayer.

3.14.7 Advance Pricing Agreement

320. IRD has found unilateral APAs successful in both inbound and outbound transfer pricing scenarios. Although unilateral APAs are one-sided, should double taxation arise on transactions covered by a unilateral APA, IRD shall enter into CA negotiations with the other jurisdiction on the basis of the unilateral APA position. Unilateral APAs are especially viable where the amounts at stake are small and/or where most of the transfer pricing risk lies in New Zealand. IRD aims to complete unilateral APAs within six months of the date of acceptance of a formal application. Bilateral negotiations, especially beyond Australia, generally take considerably longer to conclude.

3.14.8 Compliance Report

321. Taxpayers are required to provide an ACR at the time of filing their annual returns and indicate whether or not they have adhered to the terms of the APA. The report's contents are based on the taxpayer's specific facts and circumstances and are an agreed term of the APA. This provides the taxpayer with compliance cost savings. Indicatively, the content may include items such as:

- financial statements;
- computations of the TPM reconciled to financial statements or underlying financial data, as appropriate;
- confirmation of adherence to the terms of the agreement;

- confirmation that no critical assumptions have been breached.

3.14.9 Renewal of APA

322. A taxpayer may request to renew an existing APA following the same process as it did to initiate the existing APA.

3.14.10 Statistics

323. The Inland Revenue concluded its first bilateral APA (with Australia) in 2001. Since then, the Inland Revenue has concluded several other bilateral APAs with Canada, Japan, Korea, Switzerland and the US.[138] As at 30 June 2017,[139] 170 APAs had been completed by the IRD, whereas it completed 23 APAs in 2019, 11 more than the number completed in 2018. As at 30 June 2019,[140] New Zealand had completed 205 APAs in total. Statistics on the number of APA requests resolved in New Zealand are provided in Table 17.

Table 17 Number of APA Requests Resolved in New Zealand

Applications	*Number*
Completed as at 30 June 2018	182
Completed in year ended 30 June 2019	23
Total	205

Source: APA requests resolved in New Zealand https://www.ird.govt.nz/international-tax/business/transfer-pricing/practice-issues/advance-pricing-agreements.

3.15 APA REGIME IN NIGERIA

324. Nigeria has worked to develop its own transfer pricing rules based on the Organisation for Economic Co-operation and Development Transfer Pricing Guidelines for Multinational Enterprises and Tax Administrations (OECD Guidelines) and the commentary surrounding the creation of the UN Transfer Pricing Manual (UN Manual) which was formally approved in October 2012. The Federal Inland Revenue Service (FIRS) released the draft transfer pricing rules in May 2012, and the final rules in

138. Refer Note issued by PwC on Transfer Pricing in New Zealand https://www.pwc.com/gx/en/international-transfer-pricing/assets/new-zealand.pdf accessed on 4 March 2021.
139. Refer DLA Piper – APA and MAP Country Guide 2019 https://www.dlapiper.com/en/us/insights/publications/2019/03/apa-and-map-country-guide-2019/ accessed on 11 August 2020.
140. Refer New Zealand – Compliance Focus – 2019 https://www.ird.govt.nz/-/media/project/ir/home/documents/international/multinational-enterprises---compliance-focus-documents/compliance-focus---2019.pdf accessed on 6 March 2021.

September 2012, as the Income Tax (Transfer Pricing) Regulations No. 1, 2012 (the Regulations).[141]

325. The CA in charge of the APA programme in Nigeria is the FIRS. The relevant provisions in regard to the implementation of the APA programme in Nigeria are contained in Regulation 9 of the Transfer Pricing Regulations of 2018 (the Regulations).[142] The new Regulations replace the Income Tax (Transfer Pricing) Regulations, 2012 (old Regulations) and shall apply to financial years beginning after 12 March 2018. The new Regulations were issued to reflect some of the main transfer pricing (TP) related changes introduced to the 2017 edition of the Organisation for Economic Co-operation and Development Transfer Pricing Guidelines for Multinational Enterprises and Tax Administrations (OECD TPG) and the United Nations Practical Manual on Transfer Pricing for Developing Countries (UN TP Manual).[143]

326. Unilateral, bilateral, and multilateral APAs are available in Nigeria. The APA term limit is restricted to a maximum of a three-year term. There is no filing fee. There are no deadlines for negotiating and approving an APA. Completion of the negotiation will determine the date from which the APA shall commence. There is no specific guidance on rollback of APA.

3.15.1 Salient Legislative Provisions[144]

327. Regulation 9 under Part II of the Nigerian Transfer Pricing Regulations of 2018 contains the relevant provisions in regard to the implementation of the APA programme in Nigeria.

328. Sub-regulation (1) of Regulation 9 provides that an applicant can enter into an APA with the FIRS, as below:

> (1) A connected person may request that the Service enters into an Advance Pricing Agreement (APA) to establish an appropriate set of criteria for determining whether the person has complied with the arm's length principle for certain future controlled transactions undertaken by the person over a fixed period of time provided that such agreement shall be consistent with the requirements established by this regulation.

141. Refer Article by Taiwo Oyedele, Anthony Curtis, Elizabeth Sweigart and Robert Smallwood titled 'The Impact of Nigeria's New Transfer Pricing Rules on Multinational Enterprises' https://pwcnigeria.typepad.com/files/nigeria-tp-article_lexisnexis.pdf accessed on 7 March 2021.
142. Refer DLA Piper – APA and MAP Country Guide 2019 https://www.dlapiper.com/en/us/insights/publications/2019/03/apa-and-map-country-guide-2019/ accessed on 11 August 2020.
143. Refer Executive summary by EY https://www.ey.com/en_gl/tax-alerts/nigeria-releases-new-transfer-pricing-regulations accessed on 7 March 2021.
144. Refer Nigerian Transfer Pricing Regulations of 2018 https://taxaide.com.ng/files/Income%20Tax%20(Transfer%20Pricing)%20Regulations%202018.pdf accessed on 7 March 2021.

329. Sub-regulation (2) of Regulation 9 provides description of the details/documents to be submitted by the applicant along with the APA application, as below:

> (2) A request under sub-regulation (1) of this regulation shall be accompanied by –
>
> (a) a description of the activities of the taxable person to be addressed by the Advance Pricing Agreement, including –
> (i) a detailed description of the controlled transactions to be included within the scope of the Advance Pricing Agreement,
> (ii) an analysis of functions to be performed, assets to be employed and risks to be assumed by the parties to the covered transactions, and
> (iii) the proposed duration of the Advance Pricing Agreement;
>
> (b) a proposal by the taxable person for the determination of the transfer prices for the transactions to be covered by the Advance Pricing Agreement, including the following information –
> (i) an analysis of the comparability factors,
> (ii) the selection of the most appropriate transfer pricing method to the circumstances of the controlled transactions, and
> (iii) the critical assumptions as to future events under which the determination is proposed;
>
> (c) the identification of any other country or countries that the person wishes to participate in the Advanced Pricing Agreement;
>
> (d) any other relevant information that the Service may require to complete its analysis of the Advance Pricing Agreement request.

330. Sub-regulation (3) of Regulation 9 provides for acceptance, modification or rejection of the APA application by the FIRS, as below:

> (3) The Service may accept, modify or reject a request made by a connected person under sub-regulation (1) of this regulation after taking into account matters specified in sub-regulation (2) of this regulation and the expected benefits from an Advance Pricing Agreement.

331. Sub-regulation (4) of Regulation 9 provides that FIRS may provide the basis for acceptance, modification or rejection of the APA application, as below:

> (4) The Service may in addition to the provisions of sub-regulation (3) of this regulation specify the basis for acceptance, modification or rejection of a request.

332. Sub-regulation (5) of Regulation 9 provides that FIRS may enter into a UAPA or BAPA or MAPA, as below:

> (5) The Service may enter into an Advance Pricing Agreement with a taxable person either alone or together with the competent authority of countries of the connected person.

333. Sub-regulation (6) of Regulation 9 provides that results/terms agreed in the APA shall not be subjected to any subsequent TP adjustment, where the transactions are consistent with the terms of the APA, as below:

(6) Where the Service approves or modifies a proposal under sub-regulation (3) of this regulation, it may enter into an Advance Pricing Agreement which shall provide, among other things, a confirmation to the connected person that no Transfer Pricing adjustment will be made to controlled transactions covered by the Agreement where the transactions are consistent with the terms of the Agreement.

334. Sub-regulation (7) of Regulation 9 provides for the APA term not exceeding three years, as below:

(7) An Advance Pricing Agreement entered into under this regulation shall apply to the controlled transactions for a period not exceeding three years.

335. Sub-regulation (8) of Regulation 9 provides for termination of the APA by FIRS and conditions leading to termination, as below:

(8) The Service may terminate an Advance Pricing Agreement by notice where –

(a) the connected person has failed to materially comply with fundamental terms of the Advance Pricing Agreement;
(b) there has been a material breach of one or more of the critical assumptions underlying the Advance Pricing Agreement;
(c) there is a change in the tax law that is materially relevant to the Advance Pricing Agreement; or
(d) the Advance Pricing Agreement was entered into based on a misrepresentation, mistake or omission by the connected person.

336. Sub-regulation (9) of Regulation 9 provides for request to FIRS by the taxpayer for termination of the APA and the circumstances necessitating such request, as below:

(9) A connected person may terminate an Advance Pricing Agreement by a notice given to the Service where –

(a) there is a material change in the premise upon which the advance pricing request was made;
(b) the Advance Pricing Agreement is no longer relevant based on significant changes to the structure of the controlled transaction; or
(c) there is a change in tax law applicable in the jurisdiction of the controlled transaction that is materially relevant to the Advance Pricing Agreement.

337. Sub-regulation (10) of Regulation 9 provides that information provided by the taxpayer during the course of APA proceedings is to be treated as confidential by FIRS, as below:

(10) The Service shall treat as confidential any trade secret or other commercially sensitive information or documentation provided to the Service in the course of negotiating or entering into an Advance Pricing Agreement.

3.15.2 Pre-filing Meeting

338. There is no specific guidance on pre-filing meetings in the Nigerian Regulations on APA. However, guidelines on MAP dated 21 February 2019[145] in Nigeria provide that a taxpayer seeking a MAP should first carry out a pre-filing consultation with FIRS, which could be in the form of a meeting or via written correspondence. A request for a meeting for such consultation or a written correspondence thereof should be accompanied by documents providing a summary of the taxation that is the subject of a MAP request, facts that led to such taxation and reason(s) for the MAP request. This procedure is expected to be followed in evaluation of BAPA or MAPA applications also.

3.15.3 APA Application

339. A request to FIRS for an APA is required to *inter alia* state the following:

- the proposed activities, controlled transactions, and the scope of the APA; and
- an analysis of the comparability factors and the critical assumptions in respect of future events under which a determination can be made as to whether the person has complied with the arm's-length principle for certain future controlled transactions.

340. The applicant is required to submit the following information at the time of filing the APA application:

- a detailed description of the controlled transactions to be included within the scope of the APA;
- an analysis of functions to be performed, assets to be employed, and risks to be assumed by the parties to the transactions in the APA; and
- the proposed duration of the APA.

341. Additionally, a proposal by the taxable entity for the determination of the transfer prices should set out the following information:

- an analysis of the comparability factors;
- the selection of the most appropriate TP method to the circumstances of the controlled transactions;
- the critical assumptions as to future events under which the determination is proposed;
- the identification of any other country or countries that the person wishes to participate/include in the APA; and
- any other information that the FIRS may require.

145. Refer Guidelines on Mutual Agreement Procedure (MAP) in Nigeria No. 2019/01 dated 21 February 2019 https://assets.kpmg/content/dam/kpmg/ng/pdf/tax/FIRS-guidelines-on-the-mutual-agreement-procedure-in-Nigeria.pdf accessed on 7 March 2021.

3.15.4 Evaluation of APA Application

342. There is no specific guidance on procedures involved in evaluation of APA application in the Nigerian Regulations. However, guidelines on MAP dated 21 February 2019[146] in Nigeria provide that MAP negotiations between the Nigerian CA and the CA of Treaty Partners are a government-to-government process in which there is generally no direct taxpayer involvement. Therefore, taxpayer involvement in the MAP is limited to presenting its views and assisting in the fact-finding without participating in the negotiation process. However, the taxpayer may be invited to make a presentation to the CAs, where appropriate, to ensure a common understanding of the facts of a particular case. This procedure is expected to be followed in evaluation of BAPA or MAPA applications also.

3.15.5 Compliance of APA

343. Apparently, there is no requirement to file an annual report by the taxpayer. The FIRS has the powers to monitor and investigate compliance with the provisions of the APA during tax reviews.

3.15.6 Renewal of APA

344. The Nigerian Regulation is silent on renewal of APA; however, it is expected that the APA will include a renewal provision and will be renewable provided there is no prior breach, or non-compliance with the APA, or any material change in the tax legislation in Nigeria. Where any of the above occurs, FIRS is authorized to terminate the APA itself.

3.15.7 Statistics

345. According to Regulation 7 of the TP regulations (2012), a taxpayer may approach the FIRS to enter into an APA to establish an appropriate set of criteria for determining whether the taxpayer has complied with the arm's-length principle for certain future controlled transactions undertaken by the taxpayer over a fixed period of three years. The revised TP regulations (2018) retain the general provisions of APAs as under the TP regulations (2012).[147] This implies that APAs have been in place in Nigeria since 2012. However, no APAs have been concluded so far in Nigeria.[148]

---

146. *Id.*
147. Refer Article by Victor Adegite titled 'Nigeria - Evaluation of Transfer Pricing in Nigeria (2012-2020)' paras 3.5 and 5.4, Published online on 10 June 2020 in Volume 27 of International Transfer Pricing Journal, 2020 (Volume 27), No. 4 https://research.ibfd.org/#/doc?url=/collections/itpj/html/itpj_2020_04_ng_1.html accessed on 26 March 2021.
148. Refer Nigeria - Transfer Pricing - Country Tax Guides - 17. Dispute Resolution (Last Reviewed: 18 October 2020) https://research.ibfd.org/#/doc?url=/linkresolver/static/tp_ng_s_17.&refresh=1616919768981#tp_ng_s_17. accessed on 26 March 2021.

3.16 APA REGIME IN POLAND

346. In January 2006, Poland introduced APA legislation which, from 1 January 2007, also applies to the allocation of profits to PEs.[149] The CA in charge of the APA programme in Poland is the Head of National Fiscal Administration (Tax Authority). The relevant provisions in regard to the implementation of the APA programme in Poland are contained in Unit IIa, Articles 20a-20r of the Tax Ordinance Act 1997.[150]

347. Unilateral, bilateral, and multilateral APAs are available in Poland. The APA term limit is restricted to a maximum of five years, with possibility of renewal for subsequent periods no longer than five years. The APA filing fee, as prescribed in Article 20m of the Tax Ordinance Act 1997, is 1 % of the transaction value and with the following thresholds:

- Domestic unilateral agreement PLN 5,000-PLN 50,000 (approx. USD 1,365-USD 13,650).
- Foreign unilateral agreement PLN 20,000-PLN 100,000 (approx. USD 5,460-USD 27,300).
- Bilateral/multilateral agreements PLN 50,000-PLN 200,000 (approx. USD 13,650-USD 54,600).
- Fee for renewal amounts to half the fee for the original APA application.

348. Article 20n of the Tax Ordinance Act 1997 provides that if, in the course of proceedings for concluding an agreement, the CA states that the value of the transaction that may be the object of the agreement was understated in the submitted application, the tax authority will fix the amount of the supplementary fee, to be calculated in accordance with Article 20m. The ruling on the supplementary fee can be contested by the taxpayer.

349. In Poland, unilateral APAs are expected to be concluded within six months; bilateral APAs are expected to be concluded within twelve months; and multilateral APAs are expected to be concluded within eighteen months, as prescribed in Article 20j of the Tax Ordinance Act 1997. The tax authority may extend the deadline in certain circumstances.

3.16.1 Salient Legislative Provisions[151]

350. Article 20a of the Tax Ordinance Act 1997 provides for entering into a unilateral agreement, as below:

149. Refer Note issued by PwC on Transfer Pricing in Poland https://www.pwc.com/gx/en/international-transfer-pricing/assets/poland.pdf accessed on 4 March 2021.
150. Refer DLA Piper – APA and MAP Country Guide 2019 https://www.dlapiper.com/en/us/insights/publications/2019/03/apa-and-map-country-guide-2019/ accessed on 11 August 2020.
151. Refer Unit IIa, Articles 20a-20r of the Tax Ordinance Act, Poland https://supertrans2014.files.wordpress.com/2014/06/the-tax-ordinance-act.pdf accessed on 4 March 2021.

> The minister responsible for public finances, hereinafter referred to as 'the authority competent for an agreement', at the request of a domestic entity, shall recognise the correctness of the selection and the application of the method for setting the transaction price between:
> 1) domestic entities affiliated with each other, or
> 2) a domestic entity affiliated with a foreign entity and that foreign entity, or
> 3) a domestic entity affiliated with a foreign entity and other domestic entities affiliated to the same foreign entity
>
> – hereinafter referred to as the 'unilateral agreement'.

351. Article 20b of the Tax Ordinance Act 1997 provides for entering into bilateral and multilateral agreements, as below:

> § 1. The tax authority competent for an agreement, at the request of a domestic entity, after obtaining the consent of the competent tax authority for a foreign entity affiliated with the requesting party, shall declare the correctness of the selection and the application of the method for setting the transaction price between the domestic entity affiliated with a foreign entity and that foreign entity (bilateral agreement).
> § 2. If an agreement refers to foreign entities coming from more than one state, concluding the agreement requires the approvals of the tax authorities of those states competent for the foreign entities with whom the transaction is to be concluded (multilateral agreement).

352. Article 20c of the Tax Ordinance Act 1997 prescribes the transactions covered by the APA, as below:

> The agreement shall cover transactions that are to be concluded after an application to conclude an agreement has been submitted, as well as transactions that started before the day of submitting the application. The agreement shall not be concluded within the scope of transactions that started before the day of submitting an application for the agreement, and which are covered by tax proceedings, a tax inspection, a tax investigation conducted by the tax inspection authority, or proceedings before the administrative court.

353. Article 20d of the Tax Ordinance Act 1997 prescribes the course of action in case the other CA(s) does not give consent to the APA, as below:

> § 1. If the tax authority competent for the foreign entity does not agree to conclude an agreement, or if there is a justified risk that consent shall not be given within six months from the day of filing the application, the authority competent for agreement shall notify the applicant thereof.
> § 2. In the case referred to in § 1, the applicant may, within 30 days from the day of receiving such notice:
> 1) withdraw the application to conclude the agreement – upon the refund of half of the fee paid;
> 2) modify the application to conclude a bilateral agreement into an application to conclude a unilateral agreement – upon the refund of one quarter of the fee paid;
> 3) modify the application to conclude a multilateral agreement into an application to conclude a bilateral agreement, if only the tax authority of

one State gives its consent to conclude an agreement – upon the refund of one quarter of the fee paid;
4) accept a bilateral or multilateral agreement without including these foreign affiliated entities posing the obstacles indicated in § 1- without a change in the amount of the fee.

354. Article 20e of the Tax Ordinance Act 1997 provides that the CA may address the doubts of the taxpayer (in a pre-filing meeting and prior to filing of the APA application), as below:

> Before submitting an application to conclude an agreement for setting transaction prices, the domestic entity interested in concluding an agreement may ask the authority competent for the agreement to explain any doubts concerning the conclusion of an agreement in that individual case, and, in particular, the purposefulness of concluding the agreement, the scope of necessary information, procedure and the probable time of concluding the agreement, as well as the expected conditions and validity thereof.

355. Article 20f of the Tax Ordinance Act 1997 provides that the applicant is required to submit documents and details along with its APA application in support of the proposed TPM and other information, as below:

The party applying to conclude the agreement shall be obliged to present:

1) a proposal for applying the method of setting transaction prices, and in particular, to indicate one of the methods referred to in the provisions of the corporate income tax or personal income tax;
2) a description of the manner of applying the proposed method in relation to the transaction that is to be the object of the agreement, in particular to indicate:
   a) principles for calculating the transaction price;
   b) financial forecasts projections on which the transaction price calculation is based;
   c) analysis of comparative data used for the transaction price calculation;
3) circumstances that may influence the correct setting of the transaction price, and in particular:
   a) the type, object and value of the transaction, including the subject of an agreement,
   b) a description of the course of the transaction, including the analysis of assets, functions and risks of the parties thereto, and descriptions of transaction-related costs expected by the parties, as well as a description of the economic strategies of the parties to the transaction and other circumstances, if the strategy or the circumstances influence the price of the transaction,
   c) data concerning the economic situation of the branch of the industry in which the applicant pursues its economic activity, including data relating to the business transaction made by non-affiliated entities that were used to calculate the transaction price,
   d) the organisational and capital structure of the applying party and entities affiliated thereto, being parties to the transaction, and a description of the financial accounting standards applied by the affiliated entities;

4) documents with a significant influence on the amount of the transaction price, and in particular the provisions of contracts, agreements and other documents indicating the intentions of the parties;
5) proposals for the validity period of the agreement;
6) a list of affiliated entities with whom the transaction is to be concluded, including their consent to submit to the competent authority all documents concerning such transactions and to provide the necessary explanations.

356. Article 20g of the Tax Ordinance Act 1997 provides that in the course of processing the APA application, the CA may request an explanation or the submission of supplementary documents by the applicant and also provides for organizing of meetings, as below:

> § 1. If there are doubts as to the method of setting the transaction price by the applicant and the principles for the application thereof, or contents of the documents enclosed to the application, the competent authority will request an explanation of the doubts or the submission of supplementary documents.
> § 2. In order to explain the doubts referred to in § 1, the competent authority may organise a reconciliatory meeting.
> § 3. Minutes from the reconciliatory meeting shall be drawn up. In addition, the course of the meeting may also be recorded by audio visual recording devices or on IT data carriers.

357. Article 20h of the Tax Ordinance Act 1997 provides that in the course of processing the APA application, amendment of the proposal in respect of selection and application of method for fixing transaction price can *inter alia* be made, as below:

> § 1. Subject to § 2, the applicant may amend the proposal of the selection and application of the method for fixing the transaction price until the decision is issued.
> § 2. Where, in the course of the proceedings, the competent authority establishes the existence of obstacles that do not allow the acceptance of the selection and the application of the method for setting the transaction price described in the application, the authority will notify the applicant of these obstacles and will also propose another transaction price setting method. The notice shall include a factual and legal justification. The applicant may change the application or submit additional explanations and documents within 30 days from the day of delivering the notice.

358. Article 20i of the Tax Ordinance Act 1997 provides that on conclusion of processing of the APA application, an agreement shall be reached. The said article also provides details of contents of the agreement and other conditions attached to the APA, as below:

> § 1. In matters of approving the correctness of the selection and the application of the method for setting the transaction price between affiliated entities, a decision shall be issued, hereinafter referred to as 'the decision on the agreement'.
> § 2. The decision on the agreement shall be delivered to affiliated entities (domestic and foreign) with which transactions are to be concluded and, in the case of bilateral or multilateral agreements – also to the tax authorities

> competent for foreign entities and also the head of the tax office and the director of the tax inspection office competent for the applicant and the domestic entities affiliated thereto, the subjects being parties to the transaction covered by the decision on the agreement.
> § 3. The decision on the agreement shall, in particular, include:
> 1) the designation of entities covered by the agreement;
> 2) an indication of the value of the transactions covered by the agreement;
> 3) an indication of the type, the object of the transaction covered by the agreement and the period to which it relates;
> 4) an indication of the method for setting the transaction price, the price calculation algorithm and other rules for applying this method;
> 5) determining the essential conditions of applying the method referred to in item 4, taking into account the risk sharing functions performed by the entities and the commission earned by the entities referred to in item 1;
> 6) validity period of the decision.
> § 4. The validity period of the decision on an agreement cannot be longer than five years.
> § 5. The validity period of the decision on an agreement may be prolonged at the application of affiliated entities, submitted no later than six months before the lapse of that period, if the criteria of the method recognised in this decision for setting the transaction price between affiliated entities have not changed.
> § 6. The validity period of the decision on an agreement shall be prolonged in a decision.

359. Article 20j of the Tax Ordinance Act 1997 provides the period within which the unilateral, bilateral and multilateral APA proceedings are to be completed, as below:

> § 1. Unilateral agreement proceedings shall be completed without unnecessary delay, but not later than within six months from the day of its initiation.
> § 2. Bilateral agreement proceedings shall be completed without unnecessary delay, but not later than one year from the day of its initiation.
> § 3. Multilateral agreement proceedings shall be completed without unnecessary delay, but not later than within 18 months from the day of its initiation.

360. Article 20k of the Tax Ordinance Act 1997 provides the procedure for amendment or revision of an APA, as below:

> § 1. In the event of a change in business relations causing a gross inadequacy of the selection and application of the method for setting transaction price that was recognised as correct, the decision on an agreement may be amended or reversed by the competent authority before the lapse of the fixed validity period of the decision. The decision shall be amended or reversed at the party's request or ex officio.
> § 2. Proceedings initiated at the request of the party:
> 1) on amending a decision, shall be completed without unnecessary delay, but not later than within two months from the day of its initiation;
> 2) on reversing a decision, shall be completed without unnecessary delay, but not later than one month from the day of its initiation.

3.16.2 Rollback

361. Rollback for prior years is not available under Poland's APA programme. APAs can only apply prospectively from the day of submission of the APA application.

3.16.3 Pre-filing Meeting

362. As prescribed in Article 20e of the Tax Ordinance Act 1997, the taxpayer may consult with the tax authority in relation to the expediency of concluding the APA, the information required to be included in the application, the procedure and expected time of concluding the APA, and the expected conditions and validity attached to it once the APA gets effective. Under the Polish APA programme, there is no specific guidance on anonymous pre-filing availability.

3.16.4 APA Application

363. Under the Polish APA programme, the APA applications must include the selected TP method for fixing the transaction price (or the selected method of the division of costs in the case of APA applications concerning the division of costs). Specifically, applications must include the following information, as prescribed in Article 20f of the Tax Ordinance Act 1997:

(1) description of the manner of application of the proposed method in relation to the subject (proposed international transaction) of the application, indicating in particular:
  - transaction price calculation algorithm;
  - financial forecasts on which the transaction price calculation is based; and
  - analysis of comparative data used to calculate the transaction price.

(2) circumstances which may affect the correct setting of the transaction price:
  - conditions set between parties and a description of the course of the relevant transaction between the related parties;
  - analyses of assets, functions and risks of parties, and descriptions of the transaction-related costs envisaged;
  - a description of an economic strategy or any other circumstances that may affect the transaction price;
  - data concerning the economic situation of the branch of the industry in which the applicant pursues its activity and data concerning business transactions made by unrelated entities used for calculating the transaction price; and
  - the organizational and capital structure of the applicant and affiliated entities, and financial accounting principles applied by them.

(3) documents exerting an important influence on the conditions of the transaction, in particular texts of agreements, arrangements and other documents indicating the intentions of parties to the covered transactions;
(4) the proposed duration of the APA with an indication as to whether the application is intended to commence on the day of submitting the APA application;
(5) a list of related entities with whom the APA will be concluded and their consent to submit required documents to the tax authority; and
(6) a description of critical assumptions backing the proposed TP method in accordance with the arm's-length principle.

3.16.5 Advance Pricing Agreement

364. Article 20i of the Tax Ordinance Act 1997 provides the legal mandate for the formation of an APA and the contents to be incorporated in the APA. Within the APA, an important constituent is the acceptance of the specified TP method. The APA is delivered in the form of an administrative decision by the Head of National Fiscal Administration.

3.16.6 Annual Report

365. The taxpayers are required to provide an annual report together with their tax returns for the duration of the APA.

3.16.7 Renewal of APA

366. Applications for the renewal of APA are required to be lodged six months before expiry as prescribed in Item 5 of Article 20i of the Tax Ordinance Act 1997. Renewals will be allowed if the elements set in the existing APA decision issued by the Head of National Fiscal Administration for setting the transaction price between affiliated entities have not materially changed.

3.16.8 Statistics

367. In 2020, the number of APAs finalized was eighteen, including eleven unilateral APAs and as many as seven bilateral APAs, the best record since launching the programme in 2006. The total number of pending APA cases was 429 in 2020.[152] Statistics on the number of APA requests received and resolved in 2017, 2018 in Poland are given in Table 18.

152. Refer Article by Dr Monika Laskowska titled 'Poland APA statistics reveal alarming trends' https://mnetax.com/poland-apa-statistics-reveal-alarming-trends-42382 accessed on 16 February 2021.

Table 18 Number of APA Requests Received and Resolved in 2017, 2018 in Poland

FY	*Number of APA Requests Received*	*Number of APAs Granted*	*Number of APA Applications Rejected*	*Number of APA Applications Where the Taxpayer Withdrew Its Request*
2017	12	8	–	–
2018	70	9	–	–

Source: Statistics on APAs in the EU at the end of 2017 https://ec.europa.eu/taxation_customs/sites/taxation/files/statistics_on_advance_pricing_agreements_2017_en.pdf.
and
Statistics on APAs in the EU at the end of 2018 https://ec.europa.eu/taxation_customs/sites/taxation/files/apa-and-map-2019-3.pdf.

3.17 APA REGIME IN PORTUGAL

368. Law No. 30-G/2000 of 29 December 2000, which entered into force on 1 January 2001, by amending Article 57 of the Portuguese Corporate Income Tax Code (IRC Code), introduced detailed transfer pricing rules. This article was subsequently changed into Article 58 by Decree-Law No. 198/2001, dated 3 July 2001 (Decree-Law No. 198/2001) and changed again into Article 63 by Decree-Law No. 159/2009, dated 13 July 2009 (Decree-Law No. 159/2009). The new transfer pricing documentation rules are applicable to tax years starting on or after 1 January 2002. Article 63, number 13 of the Code states that a Ministerial Order from the Minister of Finance will regulate, among others, the application of the TPMs, the type, nature and contents of the documentation and the procedures applicable to (corresponding) adjustments. Thereafter, the state budget for 2008 introduced APA rules by means of adding Article 128-A to the Code. This article was subsequently changed into Article 138 by Decree-Law No. 159/2009.[153]

369. The CA in charge of the APA programme in Portugal is Large Taxpayers Unit of the Portuguese Tax Authority (PTA). The relevant provisions in regard to the implementation of the APA programme in Portugal are contained in Article 138 of the IRC Code and Ministerial Order No. 620-A/2008 of 16 July 2008.[154] Subsequently, Portugal published Law No. 119/2019 on 18 September 2019, which revised several tax code articles and introduced changes to the Portuguese TP regime. Specifically, the new law amended Articles 63, 130 and 138 of the IRC Code.[155]

153. Refer Note issued by PwC on Transfer Pricing in Portugal https://www.pwc.com/gx/en/international-transfer-pricing/assets/portugal.pdf accessed on 22 March 2021.
154. Refer DLA Piper – APA and MAP Country Guide 2019 https://www.dlapiper.com/en/us/insights/publications/2019/03/apa-and-map-country-guide-2019/ accessed on 11 August 2020.
155. Refer Tax News Update by EY dated 10 October 2019 titled 'Portugal amends transfer pricing regulations' https://taxnews.ey.com/news/2019-1801-portugal-amends-transfer-pricing-regu

370. Unilateral, bilateral, and multilateral APAs (also referred to as prior transfer pricing agreement (APPT) under the Portuguese APA programme) are available in Portugal. The APA term limit is restricted to a maximum of four years (as per paragraph 6 of Article 138 of the IRC Code), with possibility of renewal. The APA proposal is required to be presented at least 180 days before the beginning of the applicable tax year. The PTA is required under Article 10 of Ruling 620-A/2008 to complete the APA process within 180 days for unilateral APA applications, and 360 days for bilateral and multilateral APA applications. In accordance with Article 16 of Ordinance No. 620-A/2008, the conclusion of a prior agreement is subject to the payment of fees. The APA filing fee is between EUR 3,150 (approx. USD 3,700) and EUR 35,000 (approx. USD 41,250), depending on the taxpayer's turnover. The amount is calculated by applying the set of rates established in Ruling 923/99 of 20 October 1999 to the mathematical average of the taxpayer's turnover for the three taxable years prior to the filing of the APA application or, failing that, the expected turnover for the next twelve months.

3.17.1 Salient Legislative Provisions

371. The relevant provisions in regard to the implementation of the APA programme in Portugal are contained in Article 138[156] of the IRC Code, as below:

> 1 – Taxable persons may request the Directorate-General for Taxes, for the purposes of the provisions of article 63 of the IRC Code, to conclude an agreement whose object is to establish, in advance, the method or methods likely to ensure the determination of the terms and conditions that would normally be agreed, accepted or practiced between independent entities in commercial and financial operations, including the provision of intra-group services and cost sharing agreements, made with entities with which they are in a special relationship or in operations carried out between headquarters and permanent establishments.
>
> 2 – Whenever the taxable person intends to include in the scope of the agreement transactions with entities with which there are special relations resident in a country with which a convention has been signed to avoid double taxation, and intends that the agreement be of a bilateral or multilateral nature, it must ensure that the request, referred to in the previous number, be submitted to the respective competent authorities in the framework of the friendly procedure to be instituted for this purpose.
>
> 3 – The request is addressed to the director-general of taxes and must:
>
> a) Submit a proposal on the transfer pricing methods duly substantiated and accompanied by the relevant documentation;
> b) Identify the operations covered and the duration period;
> c) Be subscribed by all entities involved in the operations to be included in the agreement;

lations#: ~ :text = 119%2F2019%20on%2018%20September,General%20Regime%20for%20Tax%20Infractions. accessed on 22 March 2021.

156. Refer Article 138 of the IRC Code https://info.portaldasfinancas.gov.pt/pt/informacao_fiscal/codigos_tributarios/CIRC_2R/Pages/irc138.aspx accessed on 22 March 2021.

d) Contain a declaration by the taxable person on the fulfillment of the duty to collaborate with the tax administration in the provision of information and the provision of the necessary documentation without any professional or commercial secrecy rule being opposed.

e) Provide the necessary elements, under the terms of paragraph 12 of article 6 of Decree-Law no. 61/2013, of 10 May, in its current wording, to, if this is the case, the Authority Tax and Customs to ensure the mandatory and automatic exchange of information under administrative cooperation between competent authorities of the Member States of the European Union or with other jurisdictions.

4 – The agreement reached between the Tax and Customs Authority and the competent authorities of other countries, when applicable, is reduced to writing and the respective terms are communicated to the taxpayer, for the purpose of expressing, in writing, their acceptance.

5 – The agreement is confidential and the information transmitted by the taxable person in the negotiation process is protected by the duty of fiscal secrecy, without prejudice to the obligations regarding the exchange of information for tax purposes to which the Portuguese State is bound.

6 – The agreement must contain, in particular, the method or methods adopted, the operations covered, the basic assumptions, the conditions for review, revocation and extension and the term, which cannot exceed four years.

7 – In the absence of changes in the applicable legislation or significant variations in the economic and operational circumstances and other basic assumptions on which the methods are based, the Directorate-General for Taxation is bound to act in accordance with the terms established in the agreement.

8 – Taxable persons may not complain or appeal the content of the agreement.

9 – Taxable persons who have requested the conclusion of prior agreements on transfer prices are obliged to communicate to the Tax and Customs Authority any changes to the elements transmitted in the initial request that are relevant for the purposes of the mandatory and automatic exchange of information under the terms of the cooperation administrative.

10 – The requirements and conditions for the formulation of the request, as well as the procedures, information and documentation related to the conclusion of the agreements, are regulated by order of the Minister of Finance.

372. The purpose of Ordinance No. 620-A/2008[157] is to regulate the appropriate procedures for each of the phases of the process of signing an APA and also, during the period of its validity, establishing the obligations imposed on taxable persons and the tax administration. Some of the prominent articles of the Ordinance are provided hereunder.

373. Article 1 of Ordinance No. 620-A/2008 provides for entering into an APA, as below:

157. Refer Ordinance No. 620-A/2008 https://dre.pt/pesquisa/-/search/394311/details/maximized accessed on 22 March 2021.

A prior agreement on transfer prices is intended to guarantee to an IRS and IRC taxpayer the acceptance by the tax administration of the method or methods for determining the transfer prices of the linked transactions, as defined in article 2 of Ordinance No. 1446-C / 2001, of 21 December, in accordance with the principle set out in paragraph 1 of article 58 of the IRC Code, for a specified period.

374. Article 2 of Ordinance No. 620-A/2008 provides for types of prior agreements, as below:

1 - Prior transfer pricing agreements may be:

a) Unilateral, when the parties to the agreement are the Directorate-General for Taxation, DGCI for short, and one or more IRS and IRC taxpayers referred to in Article 2 of Ordinance No. 1446-C / 2001, of December 21st;
b) Bilateral or multilateral, when in addition to the agreement established between the DGCI and IRS and IRC taxpayers, mentioned in the previous paragraph, an agreement is also signed with another or other tax administrations, within the scope of the amicable procedure provided for in a convention aimed at avoiding double taxation of income taxes.

2 - Multilateral agreements involve two or more tax administrations in the countries where the related entities that are involved in the operations that are the subject of the requested agreement are resident or established and their negotiation is dependent on the subscription of the order by these entities and their acceptance by the competent authorities of those administrations, which can only be concluded when there is a convention aimed at avoiding double taxation that contains a provision relating to the amicable procedure with a wording identical to that of § 3 of article 25 of the OECD model of tax convention.

375. Article 3 of Ordinance No. 620-A/2008 provides for scope and methodology for entering into prior agreements, as below:

The agreements may relate to all or part of the operations carried out by the taxpayers of IRS and IRC, among those covered by paragraph 1 of article 58 of the IRC Code and articles 1 and 2 of Ordinance no. 1446-C / 2001, of 21 December, without prejudice to the fact that, in the assessment of the proposal, the DGCI may take into account all the relevant facts and circumstances likely to affect the determination of the transfer prices of the operations, even if not included in that proposal.

376. Article 4 of Ordinance No. 620-A/2008 provides for pre-filing meeting and its procedure prior to filing of APA application, as below:

1 - Before formalizing the request, the interested taxpayers must request, in writing, to the head of the Tax Inspection Services Directorate, a preliminary assessment of the terms and conditions under which the agreement can be concluded and about its effects.

2 - The preliminary phase is aimed at:

a) Analyze the transfer pricing policy of the interested entity;

b) Assess whether, in view of the concrete facts and circumstances that affect the operations carried out by the interested party, the agreement is possible and constitutes the most appropriate solution for the treatment of transfer prices;
c) Define the scope of the information and documentation that, given the complexity of the operations and the size of the taxable persons, must accompany the proposal for an agreement and establish the predictable timetable for its conclusion;
d) Identify the specificities inherent in the negotiation with the competent authorities of other States.

3 - The taxable person must include in the application referred to in paragraph 1 the characterization of the activity carried out and the related operations that he intends to include in the agreement, the identification of the related entities intervening in the operations and the description of the proposed methodology that he intends to submit, as well as provide other information or documentation requested.

4 - The preliminary phase may also comprise:

a) Meetings between the taxable person and the competent services of the DGCI; and
b) An assessment by the competent services of the DGCI, of the information and documentation or analysis submitted by the taxable person.

5 - When 60 days have elapsed since the date of submission of the preliminary assessment request without the DGCI expressly expressing its opinion, the taxable person may submit the proposal under the terms of the following article.

377. Article 5 of Ordinance No. 620-A/2008 provides for filing of APA application and necessary process involved for its processing, as below:

1 - The proposal for a prior agreement is addressed to the Director-General for Taxes and must be signed by the entities involved in the operations covered.

2 - The proposal for a prior agreement is to be sent to the Directorate of Tax Inspection Services of the Central Services of the DGCI up to 180 days before the beginning of the first financial year covered by the agreement.

3 - In the case of a proposal for a bilateral or multilateral agreement, it must be delivered in duplicate, one of which should be sent to the Directorate of International Relations Services, as the competent authority for the establishment of the friendly procedure, under the conventions aimed at avoiding the double taxation which, for this purpose, must notify the competent authority of the other State.

4 - When the taxable person intends to conclude a bilateral or multilateral agreement, he must contact the entities intervening in the related operations resident in other States so that they can also submit the request to the respective competent authorities.

5 - The beginning of the process of negotiation and conclusion of a prior bilateral or multilateral agreement always depends on the prior acceptance of the competent authorities of other States.

6 - Upon receipt of the proposal, the competent services of the DGCI must notify the taxable person, in writing, within 60 days, of the acceptance or refusal of the proposal and, when necessary, request the provision of additional information or

> documents, if applicable, that the counting of that period is interrupted until the receipt of the requested elements.
>
> 7 – The refusal of the proposal must be based, namely, on the insufficiency of the elements presented, on the lack of cooperation of the taxable person to provide the requested information and documentation or on the non-payment of the fee provided for in article 16.

378. Article 6 of Ordinance No. 620-A/2008 prescribes the contents of the APA application, as below:

> 1 – The proposal to be submitted by the taxable person must contain the elements referred to in Annex I and be accompanied by the documents indicated in Annex II, approved by this decree and which form an integral part thereof.
>
> 2 – The confidential nature of the information cannot be opposed to the DGCI in order to refuse the delivery of a document, and the latter is obliged not to disclose the information transmitted to third parties and to respect all rules regarding fiscal and professional secrecy with regard to financial data, commercial, technical and fiscal information made available to it within the framework of the proposal and the respective instruction, with the exception of the competent authority that is a party to the agreement.
>
> 3 – Documents in a foreign language must be translated into Portuguese, at the request of the DGCI.

379. Article 7 of Ordinance No. 620-A/2008 provides the procedure for consideration of the APA application and organizing meetings with the applicant, as below:

> After the acceptance of the proposal referred to in paragraph 6 of article 5, the competent services of the DGCI proceed with the analysis of the elements provided by the taxable person, and, for this purpose, the organization of face-to-face meetings with the taxpayers may be promoted or representatives of the entities involved with the purpose of obtaining the clarifications deemed useful and necessary to provide a better knowledge and evaluation of the operations that are the subject of the agreement and for the justification of the intended method or methods.

380. Article 8 of Ordinance No. 620-A/2008 provides for access of relevant documentation to the APA team, as below:

> 1 – In the evaluation phase of the proposal, the taxable person must provide the DGCI with all documentation that allows an understanding of the transfer pricing policy adopted, make available any document that may contribute to the clarification of all issues raised during the procedure, as well as provide access to the databases used to support the studies of the comparable elements presented.
>
> 2 – Whenever the taxable person submits technical studies prepared by other entities, they must be accompanied by a declaration of responsibility for the information and techniques used in such studies, issued by those entities.
>
> 3 – In the case of a bilateral or multilateral agreement, taxable persons must provide the DGCI with the same documents and information that the other parties involved in the transactions deliver to the tax administrations of the other States involved.

381. Article 9 of Ordinance No. 620-A/2008 provides for negotiation process between the CAs and also allows an opportunity to the applicant to opt for UAPA in case the CAs involved fail to reach an agreement, as below:

> 1 - In the case of a proposal for a bilateral or multilateral agreement, the result of the first assessment of the method proposed by the taxable person must be sent to the Directorate of International Relations Services, so that it can be transmitted to the competent authorities of the other States involved and initiate discussion and joint examination within the framework of the friendly procedure.
>
> 2 - If, at the end of the consultation process, the competent authorities of the other States conclude that they are not in a position to give their agreement to the proposal submitted by the taxpayers, the amicable procedure is closed and the proposer is informed by the DGCI of the decision taken, and within 60 days from the notification of the decision, the latter may request for convolution, with a proposal for a unilateral prior agreement.
>
> 3 - In the event of submission of the request for convolution provided for in the preceding paragraph, the taxable person must waive any correlative adjustments determined by corrections to the transfer prices of the operations covered, carried out by the said tax administrations of other States, based on the application of the method or methods set out in the agreement.

382. Article 10 of Ordinance No. 620-A/2008 provides the time period for APA procedures to culminate, as below:

> 1 - In the unilateral agreements, a period of 180 days is established for the evaluation procedure, counted from the date of formal acceptance of the proposal by the DGCI, under the terms defined in article 5 or in article 9, not counting for this purpose the delays attributable to the taxable person in responding to requests for documentation.
>
> 2 - In bilateral and multilateral agreements, a period of 360 days is fixed for the evaluation procedure, counted from the date of formal acceptance of the proposal by the DGCI, not counting for this purpose the delays attributable to the taxable person in responding to requests for documentation.

383. Article 11 of Ordinance No. 620-A/2008 provides the procedures for concluding the agreement, as below:

> 1 - In the case of a unilateral agreement, as soon as the Directorate of Tax Inspection Services is in a position to accept the method proposed by the applicant taxpayer or other methodology that both parties may define as appropriate, they submit the draft text of the agreement, containing the elements referred to in Annex III, approved by this decree and which is an integral part thereof, to the top manager of the service and, in the event of a decision of agreement, it must be communicated by the latter to the taxpayer, so that a declaration is affixed to acceptance of the agreement.
>
> 2 - In the case of a bilateral or multilateral agreement, when an agreement is reached between the DGCI and each of the other competent authorities, formalized by an exchange of letters, the respective draft text must be submitted by the Directorate of Tax Inspection Services to sanction the top manager of the service,

being subsequently sent to the taxable person, under the terms provided for in the final part of the previous number.

3 – The text of the agreement is confidential and its content is unappealable, without prejudice to the possibility for the DGCI to disseminate statistical data relating, namely, to the number of agreements, typology, sectors of activities and methods agreed.

384. Article 12 of Ordinance No. 620-A/2008 provides the circumstances in which the agreement may be terminated by DGCI, as below:

a) Provision of erroneous data, omission, concealment or misrepresentation of relevant information and false statements attributable to the taxable person;
b) Failure to comply with the terms and conditions established in the agreement and other obligations arising therefrom.

385. Article 13 of Ordinance No. 620-A/2008 provides the procedure for verification by tax authorities of compliance by the taxpayer with the terms and conditions of the agreement, as below:

1 – As part of the inspection action affecting the tax periods covered by the agreement, the data and information provided by the taxable person in the formulation of the proposal and during the evaluation phase can be examined and confirmed, and compliance with the obligations can be verified, including his position in the framework of the agreement, the evolution of facts and assumptions qualified as critical hypotheses, with the aim of assessing whether the method or methods accepted in the agreement remain valid or there are reasons that justify the initiation of the review procedure or possibly the revocation of the agreement.

2 – Without prejudice to the provisions of the preceding paragraph, the tax administration may carry out specific audits, aimed at:

a) Verify compliance with the terms and conditions of the agreement;
b) Confirm the data and information contained in the annual reports;
c) Validate the maintenance of economic circumstances and the critical assumptions on which the agreed methodology is based;
d) Evaluate the calculations and the consistency of the application of the method or methods established in the agreement.

386. Article 14 of Ordinance No. 620-A/2008 provides the procedure for review/revision of the APA, as below:

1 – The agreement may be subject to review at the initiative of either party, in the event of an event that substantially changes the circumstances in which they based the acceptance of the methodology for determining transfer prices.

2 – Any amendment to the agreement resulting from the review provided for in the preceding paragraph shall be submitted to the processing and procedures established under the terms of articles 5 to 10.

> 3 – The taxable person is obliged to notify the DGCI of all significant changes verified in the context or other economic circumstances and in the critical hypotheses on which the agreement is based, which are likely to affect the continuity of the application of the method of determining transfer prices.

3.17.2 Rollback of APA

387. Under the APA programme of Portugal, there is no specific guidance on rollback of APAs.

3.17.3 Pre-filing Meeting

388. Submission of a written request to initiate a preliminary evaluation of the agreement's terms and conditions is a mandatory step in the APA application process. The request must include a description of the activities carried out by the entity, related party transactions, the related entities, the APA proposal description and other relevant documents. The preliminary phase may involve joint meetings with the PTA. Under the APA programme of Portugal, there is no specific guidance on anonymized pre-filing meeting. The preliminary evaluation involves the following process:

- an analysis of the taxpayer's transfer pricing policy;
- an analysis of whether an APA is available in the circumstances and the most appropriate solution; and
- a determination of the documentation and information required in the formal APA application.

3.17.4 APA Application

389. The content of the APA proposal is discussed between PTA and the applicant during the preliminary phase. The application must include the following contents as per Annex I mentioned in Article 6 of Ordinance No. 620-A/2008:

> a) Identification of the entities (corporate name, headquarters, tax identification number), assumptions that determine the existence of a special relationship under paragraph 4 of article 58 of the IRC Code or, in the case of a permanent establishment, characterization of the entity to which it belongs;
> b) Characterization of the activities carried out by the related entities that are involved in the operations covered by the proposal;
> c) Description of the operations covered by the proposal, from a technical, economic, financial and legal point of view;
> d) Presentation of the method, within the limits permitted by paragraph 3 of article 58 of the IRC Code, which is intended to be used in setting the transfer prices of the operations referred to in the preceding paragraph;

e) Reasons that justify the selection of the proposed method as the most appropriate method for the operations in question, including an explanation of the mechanism for adapting the chosen methods to changes in the operational and economic conditions that influence the operations;
f) Tests carried out that made it possible to conclude by considering the most appropriate method;
g) Identification of the commercial database or other sources of information used;
h) Indication of the value or range of values obtained with the application of the method;
i) Identification of internal and external comparables to be used and justification, both of the criteria used in the selection of comparables and of the comparability adjustments made;
j) Distribution of profit / loss among the entities involved in the operations resulting from the use of the proposed method;
k) Duration of the agreement;
l) Indication of unilateral or bilateral agreements in force or under negotiation with tax administrations in other States;
m) Identification of related operations not covered by the proposal, indicating the counterparties for these operations;
n) Identification of the tax administrations of the States of residence of foreign entities that are involved in the operations covered by the agreement (in the case of a bilateral or multilateral agreement);
o) Confirmation of the simultaneous presentation of the proposal for an agreement with the tax administrations mentioned in the previous paragraph;
p) Reasons that justify the presentation of the proposal for a unilateral agreement for the operations in question;
q) Other elements considered pertinent;
r) Declaration of commitment that the duty to collaborate with the tax administration will be fulfilled in the provision of information and in the provision of the necessary documentation, including authorization to consult the database used, if it is a database to which the DGCI do not have access.

390. The APA application must include the following documents as per Annex II mentioned in Article 6 of Ordinance No. 620-A/2008:

a) Organization chart of the group in which the entities covered by the proposal for a prior agreement are included, their worldwide organization, capital structure (chains of participation and percentage of participation).
b) Analysis of the sectorial and market trends that may affect the activity performed (if possible, joint financial and market studies / reports).
c) Description of the business strategy outlined for the period covered by the agreement and, if different, of the strategy adopted in previous years (include strategic plans, covering critical areas: supply, production, marketing, R&D, management budgets, reports on the competitive situation in the sector in question), identifying who has the power of decision and the responsibility to dictate the commercial strategy.
d) Functional analysis of the entities involved in the operations covered by the agreement.

e) Analysis of the comparability factors, referred to in article 5 of Ordinance No. 1446-C / 2001, of 21 December, including comparable data and adjustments that, eventually, must be made to enable the comparability.
f) Identification and characterization of the critical hypotheses on which the application of the proposed methodology is based.
g) Demonstration of the application of the proposed method.
h) Information about the operations, products, deals or contracts that are covered by the order (including, if applicable, a brief explanation of the reasons why not all related operations, products and contracts are covered).
i) Financial statements of the entities covered by the agreement for the last three years prior to the presentation of the proposal, as well as other data or documents that may justify the proposed transfer pricing method.
j) List of contracts established between the taxable person and related entities that may affect the operations covered by the agreement.
k) List of other similar existing contracts with independent entities and respective amendments.
l) Declaration of waiver of the correlative adjustments provided for in paragraph 3 of article 9.
m) Other documentation considered relevant.

3.17.5 Advance Pricing Agreement

391. The text of the agreement to be submitted to the taxpayer for acceptance by the APA authorities in Portugal must contain the following elements as per Annex III mentioned in Article 11 of Ordinance No. 620-A/2008:

a) Entities and operations covered by the agreement;
b) Description of the agreed method for determining transfer prices and other related elements, namely comparables and the range of expected results;
c) Description of the critical hypotheses on which the agreed methodology is based;
d) Facts and circumstances that may determine the revision, expiry and revocation of the agreement;
e) Definition of the obligations that fall on the taxable person, namely, the preparation of annual reports;
f) The relevant documentation to maintain and the deadline for the taxable person to communicate to the tax administration the verification of a significant change in any of the premises on which the agreement is based;
g) Waiver of the correlative adjustment, in the situation provided for in paragraph 3 of article 9;
h) Circumstances that can determine the revision and termination of the agreement;
i) Duration and date of entry into force of the agreement;
j) Stipulation of the binding nature of the agreement for the tax administration;
k) Confidentiality clause.

3.17.6 Annual Report

392. The taxpayer is required to file an annual report with its tax return demonstrating compliance with the terms and conditions for each taxable year covered by the APA. In this regard, Article 17 of Ordinance No. 620-A/2008 states as below:

> 1 – The taxable person is obliged to prepare an annual report on the application of the agreement, which makes it possible to verify the conformity of the methods used with the terms of the agreement, and to send it to the Directorate of Tax Inspection Services, within the delivery period of the periodic income statement referred to in article 112 of the IRC Code.
>
> 2 – The absence of the report determines the expiry of the agreement, which takes effect from the tax period to which it relates.
>
> 3 – The taxable person must maintain the necessary documentation to enable the tax administration to monitor the agreement.

3.17.7 Renewal of APA

393. In accordance with Article 15 of Ordinance No. 620-A/2008, applications for the renewal of APAs are required to be lodged six months before expiry. An APA renewal request is subjected to go through the same stages as the initial APA request. In accordance with paragraph 4 of Article 16 of Ordinance No. 620-A/2008, in the renewal of APA process, fee is reduced by 50%.

3.17.8 Statistics

394. The statistics on Portuguese APA programme for the years 2017 and 2018 are provided in Table 19.

Table 19 Number of APA Requests Received and Resolved in 2017, 2018 in Portugal

Total Number of All APAs in Force at the End of 2017		*Total Number of Bilateral and Multilateral APAs in Force at the End of 2017*		*Total Number of Unilateral APAs in Force at the End of 2017*		*Number of APA Requests Received in 2017*		*Number of APAs Granted in 2017*		*Number of APA Applications Rejected in 2017*		*Number of APA Applications Where the Taxpayer Withdrew Its Request in 2017*		*Average Time (In Months) to Negotiate Bilateral or Multilateral APAs*	
EU	Non-EU	EU	Non-EU	EU	Non-EU	EU	Non-EU	EU	Non-EU	EU	Non-EU	EU	Non-EU	EU	Non-EU
7	3	1	1	6	2	5	1	3	3						

Total Number of All APAs in Force at the End of 2018		*Total Number of Bilateral and Multilateral APAs in Force at the End of 2018*		*Total Number of Unilateral APAs in Force at the End of 2018*		*Number of APA Requests Received in 2018*		*Number of APAs Granted in 2018*		*Number of APA Applications Rejected in 2018*		*Number of APA Applications Where the Taxpayer Withdrew Its Request in 2018*		*Average Time (In Months) to Negotiate Bilateral or Multilateral APAs*	
EU	Non-EU	EU	Non-EU	EU	Non-EU	EU	Non-EU	EU	Non-EU	EU	Non-EU	EU	Non-EU	EU	Non-EU
10	3	1	–	9	3	2	–	7	3	–	–	–	–	–	–

Source: Statistics on APAs in the EU at the end of 2017 https://ec.europa.eu/taxation_customs/sites/taxation/files/statistics_on_advance_pricing_agreements_2017_en.pdf.
and
Statistics on APAs in the EU at the end of 2018 https://ec.europa.eu/taxation_customs/sites/taxation/files/apa-and-map-2019-3.pdf.

3.18 APA REGIME IN ROMANIA

395. The Romanian transfer pricing legislation follows the OECD Guidelines and requires that transactions between related parties be carried out at market value. In case transfer prices are not set at arm's length, the Romanian tax authorities have the right to adjust the taxpayers' revenue and expenses so as to reflect the market value. The arm's-length principle was first introduced in domestic tax law in 1994. An important milestone in the development of the transfer pricing legislative framework occurred in 2004, upon the introduction of the fiscal code, which sets out in a systematic manner the definition of related parties, the statement of the arm's-length principle and the methods for setting transfer prices at arm's length. The fiscal code provides details of the scope and the application of transfer pricing rules. Although Romania is not a member of the OECD, these norms expressly stipulate that in the application of transfer pricing rules, the Romanian tax authorities will also consider the OECD Guidelines.[158]

396. The CA in charge of the APA programme in Romania is National Agency for Tax Administration (NATA). In Romania, the relevant provisions in regard to the implementation of the APA programme are contained in Article 52 of Law 207/2015 of the Fiscal Procedural Code and Order 3735/2015 for the procedure on the issuance and modification of APAs and the amendment of APAs.[159]

397. Government Ordinance No. 35/2006[160] amended the Fiscal Procedure Code (entered into force on 6 September 2006), which gave NATA the authority to issue APAs. Thereafter, on 12 June 2007, Government Decision No. 529/2007[161] was published in the State Gazette whereby procedure for the issuance of APAs was established.

398. There are three types of APAs available in Romania: unilateral, bilateral and multilateral APAs. Bilateral or multilateral APAs are issued only for transactions with taxpayers, residents of the countries that have concluded double taxation agreements with Romania, under the provisions of the MAP article. There is a five-year maximum term for an APA. Also, NATA may approve longer validity periods of APAs in respect

158. Refer Note issued by PwC in respect of Transfer Pricing in Romania https://www.pwc.com/gx/en/international-transfer-pricing/assets/romania.pdf accessed on 16 March 2021.
159. Refer DLA Piper – APA and MAP Country Guide 2019 https://www.dlapiper.com/en/us/insights/publications/2019/03/apa-and-map-country-guide-2019/ accessed on 11 August 2020.
160. Refer Report from IBFD correspondent Mr Romulus Badea, Bucharest dated 28 August 2006 titled 'Romania – Amendments to transfer pricing legislation' https://research.ibfd.org/#/doc?url=/data/tns/docs/html/tns_2006-08-28_ro_1.html accessed on 16 March 2021.
161. Refer Report from IBFD correspondent Romulus Badea, Soter & Partners, Bucharest dated 23 August 2007 titled 'Romania – Procedure for APAs and individual tax rulings established' https://research.ibfd.org/#/doc?url=/data/tns/docs/html/tns_2007-08-23_ro_1.html accessed on 16 March 2021.

of long-term intra-group agreements. The APA filing fee as prescribed in paragraph (17) of Article 52 of Law No. 207/2015 on the Fiscal Procedure Code[162] is as below:

> (17) The issuance of a price agreement in advance is subject to an issue/modification fee, as follows:
>
> a) of 20,000 euros, at the exchange rate communicated by the National Bank of Romania on the day of payment, for large taxpayers. In case of modification of the agreement, the fee is 15,000 euros, at the exchange rate communicated by the National Bank of Romania on the day of payment;
>
> b) of 10,000 euros, at the exchange rate communicated by the National Bank of Romania on the day of payment, for the other categories of taxpayers / payers. If the consolidated value of the transactions included in the agreement exceeds the equivalent of 4,000,000 euros, at the exchange rate communicated by the National Bank of Romania on December 31 of the fiscal year for which the report on the implementation of the terms and conditions of the agreement is submitted, or the taxpayer / payer is included in the category 'large taxpayers' during the period of validity of the agreement, the issuance fee is the one provided in letter a). In case of modification of the agreement, the fee is 6,000 euros, at the exchange rate communicated by the National Bank of Romania on the day of payment. If the consolidated value of the transactions included in the agreement exceeds the equivalent of 4,000,000 euros, at the exchange rate communicated by the National Bank of Romania on December 31 of the fiscal year for which the report on the implementation of the terms and conditions of the agreement is submitted, or the taxpayer / payer is classified as 'large taxpayers' during the validity period of the agreement, the modification fee is the one provided in letter a).

3.18.1 Salient Legislative Provisions[163]

399. Paragraph (2) of Article 52 of Law No. 207/2015 on the Fiscal Procedure Code provides for entering into an APA, as below:

> (2) The advance price agreement is the administrative act issued by the central tax authority in order to resolve a request of the taxpayer / payer, regarding the establishment of the conditions and modalities in which the transfer prices will be determined, during a fixed period, in the case of transactions with affiliated persons, as defined in the Fiscal Code. Future transactions that are the subject of an advance price agreement are assessed according to the date of submission of the application. The taxpayer / payer will also be able to request a price agreement in advance to determine the tax result attributable to a permanent establishment.

---

162. Refer Article 52 of the Law No. 207/2015 on the Fiscal Procedure Code https://static.anaf.ro/static/10/Anaf/cod_procedura/Cod_Procedura_Fiscala_cu_norme_2016.htm#__RefHeading__3257_1651101228 accessed on 16 March 2021.

163. *Id.*

400. Paragraph (3) of Article 52 of Law No. 207/2015 on the Fiscal Procedure Code provides for filing a pre-filing application and having a pre-filing meeting with the APA authorities prior to filing the APA application, as below:

> (3) Prior to submitting the application for an individual advance tax solution or for issuing / amending an advance price agreement, the taxpayer / payer may request in writing to the competent tax authority a preliminary discussion in order to establish the existence of the future fact for issuing a tax solution, respectively for concluding an agreement or, as the case may be, the conditions for amending the agreement.

401. Paragraph (11) of Article 52 of Law No. 207/2015 on the Fiscal Procedure Code provides that the APA is binding on the tax authorities, provided its terms and conditions are complied with by the taxpayer, as below:

> (11) The anticipated individual tax solution and the advance price agreement are opposable and binding on the tax authority, only if their terms and conditions have been complied with by the taxpayer / payer.

402. Paragraph (12) of Article 52 of Law No. 207/2015 on the Fiscal Procedure Code provides the timelines for resolution of APAs, as below:

> (12) The deadline for resolving the request for an advance price agreement is 12 months in the case of a unilateral agreement and 18 months in the case of a bilateral or multilateral agreement, as appropriate.

403. Paragraph (13) of Article 52 of Law No. 207/2015 on the Fiscal Procedure Code provides for filing of ACR by the taxpayer, as below:

> (13) The taxpayer / payer, holder of a price agreement in advance, has the obligation to submit annually, to the fiscal body issuing the agreement, a report on the manner of fulfillment of the terms and conditions of the agreement in the reporting year. The report is to be submitted by the deadline provided by law for the submission of annual financial statements, annual accounting reports respectively.

404. Paragraph (14) of Article 52 of Law No. 207/2015 on the Fiscal Procedure Code provides for amendment, revision or renewal of APA, as below:

> (14) During the period of validity, the advance price agreement may be amended by extending its validity, extending or, where appropriate, revising it at the request of the holder of the agreement, by submitting a request to that effect. The extension of the validity of the price agreement in advance may take place when the taxpayer / payer so requests in the event of the existence of the same terms and conditions. The extension may take place in the event that the taxpayer / payer requests the inclusion in the price agreement concluded in advance of other transactions with related persons. The review may take place in the event of circumstances and facts which were not foreseen or were inaccurately foreseen at the time of the issuance of the price agreement in advance and which may influence the terms and conditions of the agreement. The request for amendment

> may be submitted at least 30 days before the expiry of the validity period, under penalty of forfeiture. If the request for amendment is approved after the expiry of the term of the price agreement in advance, it shall take effect for the past and for the period between the expiry of the period of validity and the date of notification of the decision approving the amendment.

405. Paragraph (15) of Article 52 of Law No. 207/2015 on the Fiscal Procedure Code provides for entering into unilateral, bilateral and multilateral APAs, as below:

> (15) The advance price agreement may be issued unilaterally, bilaterally or multilaterally. The unilateral advance price agreement is issued by the competent fiscal body in Romania. The bilateral or multilateral advance price agreement is issued jointly by the competent fiscal body in Romania and the competent fiscal authorities in the states in whose jurisdiction the persons affiliated to the applicant taxpayer / payer are located. The bilateral / multilateral advance price agreement can be issued only for transactions with taxpayers / payers coming from countries with which Romania has concluded agreements to avoid double taxation. In this case, the provisions relating to the 'amicable settlement' provided for in the conventions for the avoidance of double taxation shall apply.

406. Paragraph (20) of Article 52 of Law No. 207/2015 on the Fiscal Procedure Code provides that APAs shall not be valid if there is change in underlying legal provisions, as below:

> (20) The anticipated individual tax solution and the advance price agreement are no longer valid if the legal provisions of fiscal material law on the basis of which the decision was taken change.

407. Paragraph (21) of Article 52 of Law No. 207/2015 on the Fiscal Procedure Code provides that the President of National Agency for Fiscal Administration (ANAF), Romania has the authority to accept and reject APAs, as below:

> (21) The individual advance tax solution and the advance price agreement, as well as the rejection of the request for the issuance of the individual advance tax solution and the advance price agreement shall be approved by order of the President of ANAF.

3.18.2 Timelines under the APA Programme

408. NATA generally issues its decision on the APA application within twelve months for unilateral agreements and eighteen months for bilateral or multilateral APAs. Depending upon the facts of the case, if NATA requests additional information, this time period is extended with the period equivalent to the date of the request and the date when such information was provided to it (that should be no longer than sixty working days when the information is requested from the taxpayer and six months when information is requested from tax authorities from other jurisdictions). After analysing the request, NATA issues a draft APA for expressions of opinion and the taxpayer has sixty working days to respond. If the APA is issued and the taxpayer does not agree with the content, the taxpayer has the right to submit a notification to NATA within thirty days from the date the APA was issued. A synopsis of timelines, duration of APAs and filing fee under the Romanian APA programme is provided in Figure 10.

Figure 10 Timelines, Duration of APAs and Filing Fee under the APA Programme of Romania

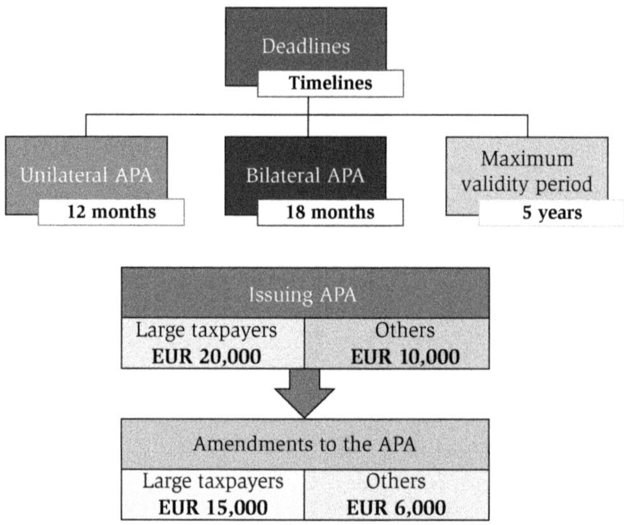

Source: Note by KPMG on Transfer Pricing Trends in Romania https://assets.kpmg/content/dam/kpmg/ro/pdf/2019/Transfer-Pricing-Trends-in-Romania-2019.pdf.

3.18.3 Rollback of APA

409. The general rule is for an APA to enter into force starting from the fiscal year following the one when the transaction was concluded. By way of exception, APAs may also apply starting from the fiscal year in which the application was submitted or the APA was issued, provided that certain conditions are met.

3.18.4 Pre-filing Meeting

410. The taxpayer may request a meeting with the representatives of NATA prior to submitting the APA request. This is recommended as it provides an opportunity to the taxpayer to present:

- the business currently carried out and anticipated to be carried out in Romania, as well as the overall activity of the taxpayer and intercompany transactions; and

- the transaction(s) covered by the APA, including the nature, pricing model, parties involved, and estimated financial results.

Subsequent to this pre-filing meeting, the NATA shall confirm if the transactions qualify for an APA. There is no obligation to submit or present any documentation to the NATA for the purpose of this meeting. Anonymous pre-filing is not available in Romania.

3.18.5 APA Application

411. Under the Romanian APA programme, the APA application must include the following information/documents:

- a description of the transaction to be covered under the proposed APA;
- details of the taxpayer and of the affiliated person(s)/PE involved in the transaction;
- an overview of the organizational, legal and operational structure of the group, a list of group entities and their geographical location, and shareholdings within the group;
- a general description of the activity of the group and of the taxpayer, business strategy, including any changes that have occurred prior to submitting the request;
- a description of the main functions performed, risks borne and assets used by each entity in the group that contribute significantly to defining and creating value;
- a description of intangible assets' owners within the group and of the relevant property rights, the arrangements for costs contributions, or any research and development activities;
- a description of any cost contribution arrangements concluded by the taxpayer with affiliated parties;
- a description of business restructurings which the taxpayer was involved in prior to submitting the APA application;
- a description of the transaction to be carried out between the taxpayer and an affiliated person/ PE that will be subject to the APA, highlighting the particulars of such transactions and including transactional flows, invoicing flows, and estimated value of the transaction;
- a general description of the transfer pricing policy applicable at the level of the taxpayer;
- a detailed presentation of the functional analysis and comparability analysis, including contractual terms of the transaction (copies of the draft agreement to be concluded between the parties should be included as an annex);
- description of the TP method chosen to set up pricing for the transaction covered under the proposed APA, together with details on how the tested party was established;
- the date from which the APA is to enter into force and its validity period;

- presentation of the critical presumptions that may influence the proposed APA;
- reference to the relevant foreign tax authorities involved in the APA;
- proof of payment of the APA filing fee;
- documentation of any APAs concluded with other foreign tax authorities that are related to the relevant transaction of the proposed APA, but to which NATA is not a party; and
- affidavits confirming the accuracy of the information included within the APA request, as well as any criminal or fiscal investigations over the transaction subject to the APA request.

3.18.6 Denial of APA

412. If the transaction(s) covered by the APA and/or the taxpayer is subject to any fiscal, administrative or criminal procedure, this will result in rejection of the APA application.

3.18.7 Annual Report

413. The taxpayer is required to submit annual reports regarding the manner in which the terms and conditions described and approved through the APA are fulfilled.

3.18.8 Renewal of APA

414. Under the Romanian APA programme, the taxpayer may request for an extension of an APA in writing at least thirty days prior to the end of the validity period of the existing APA, provided that the conditions covered by the existing APA remain unchanged.

3.18.9 Revision of APA

415. Under the Romanian APA programme, the taxpayer may request for amending an existing APA if the conditions of the transaction covered under the APA have changed.

3.18.10 Statistics

416. The statistics on Romanian APA programme for the years 2017 and 2018 are provided in Table 20.

Table 20 Number of APA Requests Received and Resolved in 2017, 2018 in Romania

Total Number of All APAs in Force at the End of 2017		*Total Number of Bilateral and Multilateral APAs in Force at the End of 2017*		*Total Number of Unilateral APAs in Force at the End of 2017*		*Number of APA Requests Received in 2017*		*Number of APAs Granted in 2017*		*Number of APA Applications Rejected in 2017*		*Number of APA Applications Where the Taxpayer Withdrew Its Request in 2017*		*Average Time (In Months) to Negotiate Bilateral or Multilateral APAs*	
EU	Non-EU	EU	Non-EU	EU	Non-EU	EU	Non-EU	EU	Non-EU	EU	Non-EU	EU	Non-EU	EU	Non-EU
10	3	–	3	10	–	6	1	5	–	–	–	–	–	18	18

Total Number of All APAs in Force at the End of 2018		*Total Number of Bilateral and Multilateral APAs in Force at the End of 2018*		*Total Number of Unilateral APAs in Force at the End of 2018*		*Number of APA Requests Received in 2018*		*Number of APAs Granted in 2018*		*Number of APA Applications Rejected in 2018*		*Number of APA Applications Where the Taxpayer Withdrew Its Request in 2018*		*Average Time (In Months) to Negotiate Bilateral or Multilateral APAs*	
EU	Non-EU	EU	Non-EU	EU	Non-EU	EU	Non-EU	EU	Non-EU	EU	Non-EU	EU	Non-EU	EU	Non-EU
12	3	–	3	12	–	10	–	3	–	–	–	–	–	–	26

Source: Statistics on APAs in the EU at the end of 2017 https://ec.europa.eu/taxation_customs/sites/taxation/files/statistics_on_advance_pricing_agreements_2017_en.pdf.
and
Statistics on APAs in the EU at the end of 2018 https://ec.europa.eu/taxation_customs/sites/taxation/files/apa-and-map-2019-3.pdf.

3.19 APA REGIME IN RUSSIA

417. Russian TP rules were first enacted on 1 January 1999 in Articles 20 and 40 of Russian Tax Code (RTC). From 1 January 2012, Russian TP rules aligned more closely with the OECD's TP guidelines. The TP documentation requirements and APAs were first introduced in 2012. Another notable event for the Russian TP system was in June 2018 when the Russian Ministry of Finance issued a procedure enabling Russian legal entities to conclude bilateral or multilateral APAs. Previously, only unilateral APAs were available in practice. As a result, there has been an increasing interest towards bilateral APAs among Russian taxpayers.[164]

418. The CA in charge of the APA programme in Russia is Federal Tax Service of Russia (FTS). In Russia, the relevant provisions in regard to the implementation of the APA programme are contained in Articles 105.19-105.25 of the RTC. On 29 March 2018, the Russian Ministry of Finance issued an 'Order' on the procedure for conclusion of bilateral APAs with the authorized bodies of foreign states (Order) (published on 3 May 2018).[165] According to the Order,[166] the procedure to enter into an APA contains the following specific features:

- an APA may only be concluded with countries with which Russia has a double taxation agreement (treaty);
- the FTS is the CA for the MAP and for information exchange;
- the FTS may ask the taxpayer to provide explanations related to issues that arise during negotiations with the component authority of a foreign state;
- only Russian companies classified as the largest taxpayers can apply to enter into an APA;
- the amount of stamp duty to be paid for filing the application to enter into an APA is set at RUB 2 million.

419. There are three types of APAs available in Russia: unilateral, bilateral and multilateral APAs. Requests are more likely to be successful if transfer pricing issues involve transactions that have various comparables recognized domestically and internationally. An APA will only come into force as of 1 January of the calendar year following the year in which it was signed. There is a three-year maximum term for an APA. The APA filing fee is RUB 2 million (approx. USD 32,100).

---

164. Refer Article by Evgenia Veter titled 'Russia's 20-year evolution of transfer pricing practices' https://www.internationaltaxreview.com/article/b1g76x4kthy1r0/russias-20-year-evolution-of-transfer-pricing-practices accessed on 18 March 2021.
165. Refer DLA Piper – APA and MAP Country Guide 2019 https://www.dlapiper.com/en/us/insights/publications/2019/03/apa-and-map-country-guide-2019/ accessed on 11 August 2020.
166. Refer Note by KPMG dated 6 May 2018 titled 'Russian Ministry of Finance publishes Order on advance pricing agreements involving Russian and foreign tax authorities' https://home.kpmg/ru/en/home/insights/2018/05/ru-eng-tax-tp-alert-order.html accessed on 18 March 2021.

3.19.1 Salient Legislative Provisions

420. Article 105.19.[167] of RTC provides general provisions on APAs, as below:

1. A Russian organization – a taxpayer, classified in accordance with Article 83 of this Code to the category of the largest taxpayers (hereinafter in this chapter – 'a taxpayer'), has the right to apply to the federal executive body authorized for control and supervision in the field of taxes and fees, with an application on concluding a pricing agreement for tax purposes (hereinafter also referred to as 'a pricing agreement').
2. A pricing agreement is an agreement between a taxpayer and the federal executive body authorized to control and supervise taxes and fees, on the procedure for determining prices and (or) applying pricing methods in controlled transactions for tax purposes during the period of its validity in order to ensure compliance with the provisions of paragraph 1 of Article 105.3 of this Code.
3. The subject of the pricing agreement is:
    1) types and (or) lists of controlled transactions and goods (works, services) in respect of which the agreement is concluded;
    2) the procedure for determining prices and (or) a description and procedure for applying the methods (formulas) of pricing for tax purposes;
    3) a list of sources of information used in determining the compliance of prices used in transactions with the terms of the agreement;
    4) the term of the agreement;
    5) the list, procedure and deadlines for the submission of documents confirming the fulfillment of the terms of the pricing agreement.
4. Other terms of the pricing agreement, in addition to those specified in paragraph 3 of this article, may be established by agreement of the parties.

421. Article 105.20.[168] of RTC provides details of parties to the APA, as below:

1. The parties to the pricing agreement are the taxpayer and the federal executive body authorized for control and supervision in the field of taxes and fees, represented by its head (deputy head), unless otherwise provided by paragraph 2 of this article.
2. If the conclusion of a pricing agreement is envisaged in relation to a foreign trade transaction, at least one party of which is a tax resident of a foreign state with which an agreement (agreement) on the avoidance of double taxation has been concluded, the taxpayer has the right to apply to the federal executive body authorized to control and supervision in the field of taxes and fees, with a statement on the conclusion of such an agreement on pricing with the participation of an authorized executive body of such a foreign state. The procedure for concluding such a pricing agreement is established by the Ministry of Finance of the Russian Federation.
   Under this paragraph an agreement on pricing is based on the mutual agreement of the federal executive body in charge of control and supervision

167. Refer Article 105.19. of Tax Code of the Russian Federation (Part One) dated 31 July 1998 N 146-FZ (as amended on 17 February 2021) http://www.consultant.ru/document/cons_doc_LAW_19671/a0c86ac1c3ab260f92c469dd683ec981bb527d8d/ accessed on 18 March 2021.
168. Refer Article 105.20. of Tax Code of the Russian Federation (Part One) dated 31 July 1998 N 146-FZ (as amended on 17 February 2021) http://www.consultant.ru/document/cons_doc_LAW_19671/0a4a5495b27af9f5435f41171b72cd7a51995712/ accessed on 18 March 2021.

in the field of taxes and fees, and authorized executive body of a foreign state, achieved as a result of carried out subject to the provisions of Chapter 20.3 of this Code mutual agreement procedure provided for in international the treaty of the Russian Federation on taxation issues.

3. In the event of similar controlled transactions between several Russian interdependent organizations (a group of taxpayers), a multilateral pricing agreement may be concluded with these organizations. Moreover, the terms of this agreement apply to the entire group of taxpayers who have entered into it. When concluding a pricing agreement, changing the conditions and checking the fulfillment of the terms of the pricing agreement in the manner prescribed by Articles 105.22, 105.23 of this Code, respectively, the common interests of a group of taxpayers may be represented by one organization from the group of taxpayers, whose powers are confirmed by powers of attorney issued in the manner prescribed the legislation of the Russian Federation.
4. A taxpayer who has entered into an agreement on pricing shall have the right to notify the persons with whom transactions are made about the fact of concluding such an agreement and about the procedure for determining the price used for tax purposes established therein.

422. Article 105.21.[169] of RTC provides details of duration of the APA, its extension and other details, as below:

1. An agreement on pricing may be concluded for one or several transactions (a group of similar transactions), having the same subject, for a period not exceeding three years.
   In this case, the effect of the pricing agreement may be extended to the period that has elapsed since the 1st day of the calendar year in which the taxpayer applied to the federal executive body authorized for control and supervision in the field of taxes and fees, with an application to conclude an agreement before the day of accession. by virtue of the said agreement, unless otherwise provided by this article.
   The effect of the pricing agreement, which is concluded in connection with the repeated application of the taxpayer with an application for concluding a pricing agreement on the basis of clause 8.1 of Article 105.22 of this Code, may be extended to the period that has expired from the 1st day of the calendar year in which the taxpayer applied to the federal an executive body authorized to control and supervise taxes and fees, with a statement on the conclusion of a pricing agreement, based on the results of its consideration, a decision was made to refuse to conclude a pricing agreement on the basis provided for by subparagraph 4 of paragraph 8 of Article 105.22 of this Code, until the date of entry into force of the said agreement.
2. A taxpayer, subject to his observance of all the terms of the pricing agreement, has the right to apply to the federal executive body authorized to control and supervise taxes and fees, with an application to extend the validity of the pricing agreement.
3. The pricing agreement may be extended by agreement of the parties for no more than two years in the manner prescribed by Article 105.22 of this Code.

169. Refer Article 105.21. of Tax Code of the Russian Federation (Part One) dated 31 July 1998 N 146-FZ (as amended on 17 February 2021) http://www.consultant.ru/document/cons_doc_LAW_19671/9aaeef7f31107ccf62dff8dd28d6908771fc1caf/ accessed on 18 March 2021.

4. The agreement on pricing shall enter into force on January 1 of the calendar year following the year in which it was signed, unless otherwise provided directly by the said agreement.

423. Article 105.22.[170] of RTC provides the procedure, documentation required and other details for concluding an APA, as below:

1. The taxpayer's application for concluding a pricing agreement, submitted by the taxpayer to the federal executive body authorized for control and supervision in the field of taxes and fees, shall be accompanied by:
   1) draft pricing agreement;
   2) documents on the taxpayer's activities related to controlled transactions, as well as on controlled transactions in respect of which the taxpayer is asked to conclude a pricing agreement;
   3) copies of the constituent documents of the taxpayer;
   4) – 5) are no longer valid. – *Federal Law of 17.02.2021 N 6-FZ*;
   6) accounting (financial) statements of the taxpayer for the last reporting period;
   7) a document confirming the payment by the applicant of the state fee for consideration by the federal executive body authorized for control and supervision in the field of taxes and fees, an application for concluding a pricing agreement;
   8) other documents containing information relevant to the conclusion of a pricing agreement.
2. The documents listed in paragraph 1 of this article shall be submitted to the federal executive body authorized for control and supervision in the field of taxes and fees, in any form, unless another form is established by the legislation of the Russian Federation.
3. The federal executive body authorized for control and supervision in the field of taxes and fees shall have the right to request from the taxpayer other documents not provided for by paragraph 1 of this article, which are necessary for the purposes of the pricing agreement.
   These documents must be submitted by the taxpayer to the federal executive body authorized for control and supervision in the field of taxes and fees, within 10 days from the date of receipt of the relevant request from the federal executive body authorized for control and supervision in the field of taxes and fees.
   If the requested documents cannot be submitted within the time period established by this paragraph, the federal executive body authorized for control and supervision in the field of taxes and fees, upon receipt from the taxpayer from whom the documents are requested, a notice of the impossibility of submitting documents within the established time limit and of the deadline (if necessary), during which these documents can be submitted, has the right to extend the deadline for the submission of these documents. This notification shall be submitted in the manner prescribed by paragraph 3 of Article 93 of this Code.

3.1. A taxpayer, together with an application for concluding a pricing agreement, submitted to the federal executive body authorized to control and supervise taxes and fees, in accordance with paragraph 2 of Article 105.20 of this Code,

170. Refer Article 105.22. of Tax Code of the Russian Federation (Part One) dated 31 July 1998 N 146-FZ (as amended on 17 February 2021) http://www.consultant.ru/document/cons_doc_LAW_19671/1c15cd7143ee3b88cf1e4fb4fc0ef2ae6bd6ff85/ accessed on 18 March 2021.

shall submit information on the submission by the counterparty of the taxpayer to the authorized executive body of a foreign of the state of which he is a tax resident, a similar statement for the purpose of concluding such an agreement, unless otherwise provided by this clause.
In the event that, as of the date of submission by the taxpayer to the federal executive body authorized for control and supervision in the field of taxes and fees, an application for the conclusion of a pricing agreement in accordance with paragraph 2 of Article 105.20 of this Code, a similar application has not been submitted to the authorized executive body of a foreign state, the tax resident of which is the taxpayer's counterparty, in order to conclude a pricing agreement; after the taxpayer's counterparty submits the said application, the taxpayer must inform the federal executive body authorized to control and supervision in the field of taxes and fees, on the submission of the specified application by the counterparty of the taxpayer. The relevant information shall be submitted by the taxpayer no later than six months from the date of submission by him of an application for concluding a pricing agreement in accordance with paragraph 2 of Article 105.20 of this Code.

4. The federal executive body authorized for control and supervision in the field of taxes and fees shall consider the application and other documents submitted by the taxpayer in accordance with paragraphs 1 – 3 of this article, within a period not exceeding six months from the date of receipt of the application, unless otherwise provided by this clause.
The application and other documents submitted by the taxpayer for the purpose of concluding a pricing agreement in accordance with paragraph 2 of Article 105.20 of this Code shall be considered by the federal executive body authorized for control and supervision in the field of taxes and fees, within a period not exceeding 24 months from the date of receipt of the application, and in the case provided for in clause 3.1 of this article – from the date of receipt from the taxpayer of information on the submission by his counterparty of an application to the authorized executive body of the foreign state of which he is a tax resident, in order to conclude such a pricing agreement.
The term for consideration of an application and other documents submitted by a taxpayer in accordance with paragraph 1 of this article in order to conclude a pricing agreement provided for in paragraph 2 of Article 105.20 of this Code shall be suspended for the period when the authorized executive body of a foreign state submits documents and (or) information in accordance with by a request sent by the federal executive body authorized for control and supervision in the field of taxes and fees, within the framework of the mutual agreement procedure provided for by the international treaty of the Russian Federation on taxation issues, taking into account the provisions of Chapter 20.3 of this Code.
The term for consideration of the documents submitted by the taxpayer may be extended up to nine months in the case specified in the first paragraph of this clause, and in the case provided for by the second paragraph of this clause – up to 27 months.
The grounds and procedure for extending the term for consideration of documents submitted by the taxpayer shall be established by the federal executive body authorized for control and supervision in the field of taxes and fees.
5. Based on the results of consideration of the documents submitted by the taxpayer in accordance with paragraphs 1 – 3 of this article, the federal executive body authorized for control and supervision in the field of taxes and fees, one of the following decisions is taken:

1) the decision to conclude a pricing agreement;
2) a reasoned decision to refuse to conclude such an agreement;
3) a decision on the need to finalize the draft agreement, in which the federal executive body authorized to control and supervise taxes and fees proposes the taxpayer to finalize in accordance with the requirements of this Code and resubmit the draft pricing agreement and the documents specified in subparagraph 2 paragraph 1 of this article.

6. The corresponding decision to conclude (to refuse to conclude, to revise the draft agreement) a pricing agreement (indicating the place, date and time of signing the pricing agreement in the event of a decision to conclude a pricing agreement) is sent to the taxpayer (authorized representative of the taxpayer) within five days from the date of such decision.

6.1. If the federal executive body authorized to control and supervise taxes and fees takes a decision provided for in subparagraph 3 of paragraph 5 of this article, the revised draft pricing agreement and the documents specified in subparagraph 2 of paragraph 1 of this article shall be submitted by the taxpayer on time no later than 30 days from the date of receipt by the taxpayer of the relevant decision.

7. When re-submitting the draft pricing agreement and documents on the basis of the decision provided for in subparagraph 3 of paragraph 5 of this article, or in accordance with paragraph 8.1 of this article:
   1) the state duty provided for by subparagraph 133 of paragraph 1 of Article 333.33 of this Code is not charged;
   2) by the federal executive body authorized for control and supervision in the field of taxes and fees, the decision is made within three months.

8. The grounds for making a decision to refuse to conclude a pricing agreement, in particular, are:
   1) failure to submit or submission not in full of the documents provided for in paragraph 1 of this article;
   2) non-payment or incomplete payment of the state duty;
   3) a reasoned conclusion that as a result of the application of the procedure for determining prices and (or) pricing methods proposed by the taxpayer in the draft agreement on pricing, the implementation of the provisions of paragraph 1 of Article 105.3 of this Code will not be ensured;
   4) failure to reach a mutual agreement with the authorized executive body of a foreign state in order to conclude a pricing agreement provided for in paragraph 2 of Article 105.20 of this Code;
   5) failure to submit the documents (information) provided for in paragraphs 3 and 3.1 of this article, in the manner and terms established by this article;
   6) the taxpayer's disagreement with the decision on the need to revise the draft pricing agreement (including in the form of failure to submit the revised draft pricing agreement within the time period established by clause 6.1 of this article);
   7) the taxpayer's disagreement with the decision to conclude a pricing agreement, which was expressed in the taxpayer's refusal to sign the pricing agreement (including in the form of the taxpayer's (his representative's) failure to appear to sign the pricing agreement with the federal executive body authorized for control and supervision in the field of taxes and fees).

8.1. If a decision is made to refuse to conclude an agreement on pricing on the grounds provided for in subparagraph 4 of paragraph 8 of this article, the taxpayer has the right, within three months from the date of receipt of the said decision, to re-submit to the federal executive body authorized for control and supervision in the field of taxes and fees, in the manner provided for in paragraph 7 of this article, a draft agreement on pricing in relation to a foreign trade transaction, at least one party of which is a tax resident of a foreign state with which an agreement (agreement) on avoidance of double taxation has been concluded, without the participation of an authorized executive body of such foreign state.

9. The decision to refuse to conclude a pricing agreement may be appealed to the court in accordance with the legislation of the Russian Federation.
10. A copy of the pricing agreement concluded with the taxpayer is sent by the federal executive body authorized for control and supervision in the field of taxes and fees, within three days from the date of signing this agreement to the tax authority at the place of registration of the taxpayer as the largest taxpayer.
11. A taxpayer's application for concluding a pricing agreement submitted by the taxpayer to the federal executive body authorized to control and supervise taxes and fees may be revoked by the said taxpayer. In this case, the paid amount of the state duty provided for by subparagraph 133 of paragraph 1 of Article 333.33 of this Code shall not be refunded.
12. The pricing agreement may be amended in the manner prescribed by this article.

424. Article 105.23.[171] of RTC provides for verification by tax authorities of execution and compliance to terms and conditions of an APA by the taxpayer, as below:

1. Verification of the execution by the taxpayer of the pricing agreement is carried out by the federal executive body authorized for control and supervision in the field of taxes and fees, in accordance with the procedure provided for in Chapter 14.5 of this Code.
2. If the taxpayer has complied with the terms of the pricing agreement (including when this circumstance is established following the results of the audit specified in paragraph 1 of this article), the federal executive body authorized to control and supervise taxes and fees does not has the right to make a decision on bringing (to refuse to bring) to responsibility for a tax offense, which provides for additional charging of taxes, penalties and fines or a reduction in the amount of loss, in respect of those controlled transactions, the prices for which (methods of their determination) were agreed in the pricing agreement.

425. Article 105.24.[172] of RTC provides the procedure for termination of an APA, as below:

1. The agreement on pricing shall be terminated upon the expiration of its validity period or may be terminated before the expiration of such term in the cases provided for by this article.

171. Refer Article 105.23. of Tax Code of the Russian Federation (Part One) dated 31 July 1998 N 146-FZ (as amended on 17 February 2021) http://www.consultant.ru/document/cons_doc_LAW_19671/88ba2afecdf8ef18d72de5ec3b144603d438307b/ accessed on 18 March 2021.
172. Refer Article 105.24. of Tax Code of the Russian Federation (Part One) dated 31 July 1998 N 146-FZ (as amended on 17 February 2021) http://www.consultant.ru/document/cons_doc_LAW_19671/365218d7ebf2ae01c908521ee759d0e314ceeef9/ accessed on 18 March 2021.

2. The pricing agreement is terminated ahead of schedule by the decision of the head (deputy head) of the federal executive body authorized to control and supervise taxes and fees, if the taxpayer violates the pricing agreement during its validity period, resulting in incomplete payment of taxes and identified during the inspection in the manner prescribed by Chapter 14.5 of this Code. The pricing agreement can also be terminated early by agreement of the parties or by a court decision.
3. The decision of the federal executive body authorized for control and supervision in the field of taxes and fees, on the termination of the pricing agreement, shall be handed to the taxpayer (his representative) against receipt or transmitted in another way, indicating the date of its receipt by the taxpayer (his representative), or sent to the taxpayer by registered mail within five days from the date of the relevant decision.
   The decision to terminate the pricing agreement sent to the taxpayer by registered mail shall be deemed to have been received six days after the date of sending such a registered letter.
   A copy of this decision within the same time frame is sent to the tax authority at the place of registration of this taxpayer as the largest taxpayer.
4. The decision of the federal executive body authorized for control and supervision in the field of taxes and fees to terminate the pricing agreement may be appealed by the taxpayer to the arbitration court in accordance with the procedure established by the arbitration procedural legislation of the Russian Federation.
5. Payment of the amount of tax, penalties and fines is carried out only if the termination of the pricing agreement due to non-fulfillment (violation) of its terms entailed an understatement of the tax amount.

426. Article 105.25.[173] of RTC provides for stability of the terms of an APA and right to amend the APA in view of changes in legislation, as below:

1. The terms of the pricing agreement remain unchanged in the event of changes in the legislation on taxes and fees in terms of regulating relations arising from the conclusion of a pricing agreement, amendments to it and its termination.
2. In the event of other changes to the legislation of the Russian Federation on taxes and fees and the legislation of the Russian Federation on customs affairs affecting the activities of the taxpayer, the parties to the agreement have the right to amend the text of the pricing agreement accordingly.

3.19.2 Rollback of APA

427. Under the APA programme of Russia, there is no specific guidance on rollback of APAs.

173. Refer Article 105.25. of Tax Code of the Russian Federation (Part One) dated 31 July 1998 N 146-FZ (as amended on 17 February 2021) http://www.consultant.ru/document/cons_doc_LAW_19671/6db5fd4c7ad795e2d227b23b7f3dedf7e73fa065/ accessed on 18 March 2021.

3.19.3 Pre-filing Meeting

428. There is no specific guidance on pre-filing meetings in the RTC. The Order introduces a pre-filing stage for the conclusion of bilateral APAs. Pre-filing is an optional (but advisable) stage, which allows the taxpayer and FTS to weigh up the prospects of a successful conclusion of an APA. The results of these preliminary negotiations are not legally binding. Anonymous pre-filing meeting is not permissible under the Russian APA programme. An application for a pre-filing negotiation must include the following information/documents:

(1) information relevant for conclusion of the APA:
   - the name and tax residence country of the parties involved;
   - the global group structure;
   - a description of cross-border transactions; and
   - the proposed TP method.

(2) issues to be considered:
   - the existence of the grounds for entering into an APA;
   - the procedure for determining prices and/or applying TP method suggested by the taxpayer;
   - the procedure and timeline for entering into the APA; and
   - the prospects for mutual agreement between the CAs and its implementation in the Russian Federation.

3.19.4 APA Application

429. The procedure for APAs is initiated by submitting a formal application in a prescribed form, together with all necessary documents. The application should contain the following information:

- the name and tax residence country of the parties involved;
- the global group structure;
- a description of the cross-border transaction(s) to be covered;
- actual conditions relevant to the cross-border transaction(s);
- arm's-length conditions relevant to the cross-border transaction(s);
- the proposed TP method and expected result of the proposed method;
- financial performance; and
- information on the outcome of the application of the proposed TP method, by providing an example from the most recent three years for which factual information is available.

430. The Order also provides a recommended APA application form and list of required documents, including:

- a draft APA;

- documents on all the activities involving controlled transactions and on those controlled transactions which are under an APA;
- copies of charter documents;
- financial performance for the last reporting period;
- document confirming payment of State duty; and
- other information and documentation as requested by the FTS.

3.19.5 Compliance of APA

431. The taxpayers are required to provide the FTS with a notification on controlled transactions under the APA. The FTS will check the taxpayer's compliance with the APA.

3.19.6 Renewal of APA

432. Applications for the renewal of an APA are required to be filed six months before the expiry date. APAs may be prolonged for a term not exceeding two years in accordance with the general procedure.

3.19.7 Statistics

433. On 20 November 2012, the first APA was concluded between federal tax authorities and a Russian oil company.[174] Since 2012, Russia has received eighty-two draft APAs and concluded twenty-five of those on a unilateral basis. Additionally, in the 2018 fiscal year, nine APAs have been concluded on a unilateral basis.

434. On 24 December 2020, Russia's federal tax authority announced the conclusion of its first bilateral APA with the Finnish tax administration.[175]

3.20 APA REGIME IN SINGAPORE

435. The CA in charge of the APA programme in Singapore is Inland Revenue Authority of Singapore (IRAS). In Singapore, APA is regarded as an arrangement between IRAS[176] and the taxpayer or the relevant foreign CA to agree in advance an appropriate set of criteria to ascertain the transfer pricing for a taxpayer's related party

174. Refer Note issued by PwC in respect of Transfer Pricing in Russia https://www.pwc.com/gx/en/international-transfer-pricing/assets/russia.pdf accessed on 18 March 2021.
175. Refer Report by KPMG dated 14 January 2021 titled 'Russia: First bilateral APA is concluded' https://home.kpmg/us/en/home/insights/2021/01/tnf-russia-first-bilateral-apa-concluded.html accessed on 29 March 2021.
176. IRAS e-Tax Guide: Transfer Pricing Guidelines (Fifth Edition) https://www.iras.gov.sg/irashome/uploadedFiles/IRASHome/e-Tax_Guides/etaxguide_Income%20Tax_Transfer%20Pricing%20Guidelines_5th.pdf accessed on 9 August 2019.

transactions for a specific period of time. Relevant provisions in regard to implementation of APAs in Singapore are *inter alia* contained in the IRAS e-Tax Guide: Transfer Pricing Guidelines (Fifth Edition). The IRAS has had an APA programme since 2003.[177]

436. There are three types of APAs available in Singapore: unilateral, bilateral and multilateral APAs. In unilateral APAs, involvement of the foreign CA is not required and exchange of documents, consultations happen between the taxpayer and IRAS. In bilateral and multilateral APAs, the APA negotiation is between the CAs, and so, taxpayers do not participate in or attend as observers at the negotiations unless they are called upon to make any clarification.

437. Section 8.10 of IRAS e-Tax Guide: Transfer Pricing Guidelines (Fifth Edition) states that UAPA is suitable for the following circumstances:

(a) Where the transfer pricing issue does not require the involvement of the foreign CA. For example, taxpayer seeks clarification on the domestic tax treatment in Singapore.
(b) Where the other related party to the transaction is resident in a jurisdiction with which Singapore does not have a DTAA.
(c) Where Singapore's DTAA partner has no APA programme or has prescribed a minimum transaction threshold for an APA application of which the taxpayer's transaction falls short.

438. A unilateral APA offers a lower level of assurance against double taxation on the same income than a bilateral or multilateral APA. This is because the APA terms are non-binding on the foreign CA which is not a party to the unilateral APA process. The information on cross-border UAPAs is exchanged by IRAS with:

(a) jurisdictions of residence of all related parties with which the taxpayer enters into transactions that are covered by the unilateral APAs; and
(b) jurisdictions of residence of the taxpayer's ultimate parent entity and immediate parent entity.

439. Section 8.14 of IRAS e-Tax Guide: Transfer Pricing Guidelines (Fifth Edition) states that BAPA is an agreement between IRAS and one of its DTAA partners. Where the agreed APA outcome between the IRAS and foreign CA is accepted by the relevant taxpayers, it is binding on the relevant parties.

440. Section 8.15 of IRAS e-Tax Guide: Transfer Pricing Guidelines (Fifth Edition) states that MAPA is an agreement between IRAS and two or more of its DTAA partners.

---

177. Refer DLA Piper – APA and MAP Country Guide 2019 https://www.dlapiper.com/en/us/insights/publications/2019/03/apa-and-map-country-guide-2019/ accessed on 11 August 2020.

Where the agreed APA outcome between the IRAS and foreign CAs is accepted by the relevant taxpayers, it is binding on all the relevant parties.

441. The acceptance of an APA application is at the discretion of the IRAS, which considers taxpayers' request for an APA based on the merits of each case. The IRAS is unlikely to deviate from determinations made by Singaporean tribunals or courts in the APA process. IRAS generally accepts an APA request to cover three to five future FYs (i.e., covered period). However, the duration of the covered period is based on the taxpayers' assessment that there will not be any significant changes during the covered period that may affect the validity of the APA. IRAS does not impose any fee for APAs except for unilateral APAs where the related party transactions involve a jurisdiction with which Singapore does not have a DTAA. Such unilateral APAs are processed under the Advance Ruling System with administrative fee/charges. Unilateral APAs are available to taxpayers regardless of whether they are Singapore tax residents or not. Bilateral APAs and multilateral APAs are available to taxpayers who:

(a) are Singapore tax residents; and
(b) are not Singapore tax residents but have a branch in Singapore. However, such applications are to be made by the taxpayers in the jurisdiction in which they are tax residents and with which Singapore has a DTAA.

442. Taxpayers are encouraged to apply for an APA in the following circumstances:

- there is a genuine motive to obtain certainty for the avoidance of double taxation;
- the request relates to specific current or future transactions that are not hypothetical;
- they are certain that the cross-border related party transactions will commence or continue to take place throughout the APA covered period;
- the incidence of double taxation is certain or highly probable for the fiscal years to be covered;
- the taxpayer has robust reasons and TP documentation to support the application; and
- the taxpayer has evaluated the suitability of an APA through an in-depth cost-benefit analysis of its tax situations.

3.20.1 Timelines

443. The APA process in Singapore follows strict timing deadlines, including:

- submission of pre-filing materials at least one month prior to the pre-filing meeting;
- the pre-filing meeting must take place at least nine months before the first day of the fiscal year the APA is intended to cover;

- the IRAS will indicate whether it is inclined to accept the APA request at least four months before the first day of the APA covered period; and
- APA application should be submitted within three months of the IRAS indicating that it will accept an APA application.

3.20.2 Rollback of APA

444. IRAS may consider taxpayers' request to extend the APA to two prior years (i.e., rollback years) for a bilateral or multilateral APA based on the merits of the request and when there is no significant difference in the facts and circumstances for the covered period and for the rollback years. Depending on the facts and circumstances of each request, IRAS may exercise its discretion to vary the number of rollback years. Relevant documents are required to be maintained to substantiate this aspect. IRAS does not accept request to extend the APA to prior years for a unilateral APA.

3.20.3 Pre-filing Meeting

445. Taxpayers are required to initiate a pre-filing meeting with IRAS either directly or through its tax agent. Anonymous pre-filing is not available in Singapore. Pre-filing materials to be submitted to IRAS include the following:

- the taxpayer's name, address, tax identification number and contact details;
- type of APA sought;
- any relevant foreign tax authorities;
- fiscal years intended to be covered under the proposed APA;
- a brief description of the transactions involved;
- the related parties to the transactions; and
- a letter of authorization (LOA) for the IRAS to discuss with appointed representatives of the taxpayer on the matters relating to the APA application.

446. The purpose of the pre-filing meeting is for:

- the taxpayer to explain its APA request and update IRAS on its meetings with the relevant foreign CAs;
- IRAS to ascertain the merits of the APA request before the taxpayer undertakes further work on the APA application;
- IRAS and the taxpayer to identify critical and relevant areas of focus and areas where additional information, documentation and analysis are required; and
- IRAS to ascertain the taxpayer's TP documentation.

447. The regulations in Singapore provide that the first pre-filing meeting should take place at least nine months before the first day of the APA covered period. IRAS will indicate if it is inclined to accept the APA request at least four months before the first day of the APA covered period. The taxpayer should submit its application to IRAS within three months of IRAS giving its indication that the application can be submitted. Late submission may cause the APA application to be rejected. Depending on the complexity of the APA application, it may be necessary to have more than one pre-filing meeting or site visit to the taxpayer's premises. For bilateral and multilateral APA, the taxpayer should submit the application simultaneously to IRAS and the relevant foreign CAs. Where the filing deadline imposed by a foreign CA is earlier than IRAS', the taxpayer is required to observe the earlier filing deadline, and this will not affect IRAS' consideration and observation of the timeline under its APA process.

3.20.4 APA Application

448. In case IRAS accepts the application, it will issue letters of acceptance to the taxpayer and the relevant foreign CA within one month of the receipt of the application. If IRAS rejects the application, it will notify the taxpayer in writing with reasons. The acceptance of an APA application does not necessarily mean that IRAS endorses all the proposals in the application. IRAS reserves the right to propose alternatives either on its own or in consultation with the relevant foreign CA. These may include a change in TPM or limiting/expanding the scope of the APA. The taxpayer is required to submit one electronic copy and a hard copy of the APA application within three months of the IRAS indicating that it will accept an APA application. The application must include the following information:

- the entities covered;
- the transactions covered;
- the period covered;
- the TP method;
- the agreed arm's-length remuneration for the covered transaction;
- compensating adjustment rules;
- critical assumptions; and
- any other documentation as agreed with the IRAS at the pre-filing stage.

449. The success of the APA process depends on cooperation from taxpayers. Taxpayers are therefore expected by IRAS to:

- act in good faith throughout the process;
- comply with all the requirements pertaining to pre-filing meetings and application processes;
- provide access to TP documentation;
- be forthcoming in providing complete and reliable information and good quality analysis relating to the APA application;
- adhere to all the stipulated timelines when providing any clarification, information and analysis that may be requested by IRAS and the relevant foreign CAs;
- update IRAS on all information that they have provided to or received from the relevant foreign CAs on a timely basis; and

- provide the same set of information to IRAS and the relevant foreign CAs.

450. Some instances where IRAS may discontinue the APA process are provided hereunder:

(a) When IRAS does not receive any information from the taxpayer regarding its application within six months from the date of the last pre-filing meeting.
(b) When the taxpayer fails to provide the information within three months after the agreed timeline. If the taxpayer fails to provide the information by the timeline and it remains outstanding for an extended period of time, IRAS will consider that the taxpayer has withdrawn from the MAP or APA process.
(c) If the taxpayer fails to provide any material information that could have affected the outcome of the APA, IRAS will consider discontinuing the APA process.

451. Upon accepting the application, IRAS will contact the relevant foreign CA to initiate APA discussion. IRAS will formulate its position concerning the APA application. IRAS may seek clarification or further information from the taxpayer (such as segmented financial data), hold discussions with the taxpayer or conduct site visits to the taxpayer's premises which include interviewing the taxpayer's key personnel. When an agreement is reached with the relevant foreign CA, IRAS will meet the taxpayer within one month of reaching agreement to discuss the details and implementation of the agreement. The taxpayer will have to decide whether the agreed outcome is acceptable.

3.20.5 Compliance Report

452. Once an APA becomes effective, the taxpayer is required to comply with the APA terms stipulated in the agreement. The taxpayer is required to file ACRs to demonstrate compliance with the terms and conditions of the APA together with its income tax returns. The taxpayer should keep relevant documents for the purpose of preparing the ACRs. There is no fixed/prescribed format for filing the report. However, IRAS has provided a guide on ACRs in its e-Tax Guide on Transfer Pricing Guidelines (Fifth Edition). The taxpayer is expected to notify IRAS and the relevant foreign CA of any breach of any of the conditions in the APA as early as possible. The taxpayer is also expected to provide an impact analysis and proposed course of action to facilitate the CAs' evaluation and discussion. As long as the taxpayer complies with the terms and conditions of the APA, IRAS does not audit the taxpayer's transfer prices for the covered period.

3.20.6 Renewal of APA

453. Taxpayers may request to renew an existing APA following the same process as it did to initiate the existing APA, wherein it is required to *inter alia* highlight any significant changes to the circumstances prevailing when the existing APA was made.

3.20.7 Revocation or Cancellation of an APA

454. IRAS may revoke or cancel an APA in the case of fraud or misrepresentation of information during the APA process, or when a taxpayer fails to comply with the terms and conditions of the APA. Before IRAS discontinues the APA process or cancels or revokes an APA, it will notify the relevant foreign CA of its intention and the reasons for such action.

3.20.8 Confidentiality of Information

455. All information obtained during the APA process in Singapore is protected by the confidentiality provisions in the Income Tax Act and the relevant DTAA.

3.20.9 Statistics

456. Statistics on the number of APA requests received and resolved in various years in Singapore are provided in Table 21.

Table 21 Number of APA Requests Received and Resolved in Various Years in Singapore

FY	*APAs Brought Forward*	*Received*	*Completed*	*Withdrawn/Rejected*	*Balance*
2013	29	26	13	2	40
2014	40	14	12	3	39
2015	39	20	16	2	41
2016	41	18	10	8	41
2017	41	17	10	6	42
2018	42	20	20	2	40
2019	40	21	15	0	46

Source: Data published by IRAS https://data.gov.sg/dataset/transfer-pricing-map-and-apa-cases-annual?view_id=e62e0ada-5b68-4558-b105-5b310ba09bf7&resource_id=765a764a-4283-4249-93e5-e5e819547812.

3.20.10 Ready Reckoner on Availability of Article 9(2), BAPA and Rollback Provisions

457. Singapore allows unilateral, bilateral and multilateral APAs, as well as rollback of APAs for BAPA and MAPA. A ready reckoner on existence of Article 9(2) to relieve economic double taxation in DTAAs between Singapore and various countries and the presence of BAPA and rollback provisions in the legislation of Singapore's treaty partners is provided in Table 22 by analysing the following database:

- status of Article 9(2) as provided under OECD MTC, 2017 in the DTAA[178] between Singapore and respective treaty partner;
- if not already present, whether Article 9(2) shall get introduced through the MLI[179] in such DTAAs;
- the country MAP/Dispute Resolution profiles[180] of the respective treaty partners available on the OECD website.

Table 22 Ready Reckoner on Availability of Article 9(2), BAPA and Rollback Between Singapore and Treaty Partners

S. N.	*Treaty Partner*	*Date of Signature of DTAA*	*Does Article 9(2) Already Exist?*	*If No, Will It Come Through MLI?*	*Does the Treaty Partner Have BAPA?*	*Does the Treaty Partner Have Rollback?*
1	Australia	11.02.1969	Yes *	–	Yes	Yes
2	Austria	30.11.2001	Yes **	Yes **	Yes	Yes
3	Belgium	06.11.2006	Yes **	Yes **	Yes	Yes
4	Bulgaria	13.12.1996	Yes **	Yes **	No	No
5	Canada	06.03.1976	No	No	Yes	Yes
6	China	11.07.2007	Yes **	Yes **	Yes	Yes
7	The Czech Republic	22.11.1997	Yes	–	Yes	No
8	Denmark	03.07.2000	Yes	–	Yes	Yes
9	Egypt	22.05.1996	No	No	No	No

178. Refer IBFD Tax Research Platform https://research.ibfd.org accessed on 15 February 2021.
179. Refer OECD – Signatories and Parties to the MLI http://www.oecd.org/tax/treaties/beps-mli-signatories-and-parties.pdf accessed on 15 February 2021.
180. Refer MAP profiles on www.oecd.org https://www.oecd.org/tax/dispute/country-map-profiles.htm accessed on 15 February 2021.

S. N.	*Treaty Partner*	*Date of Signature of DTAA*	*Does Article 9(2) Already Exist?*	*If No, Will It Come Through MLI?*	*Does the Treaty Partner Have BAPA?*	*Does the Treaty Partner Have Rollback?*
10	Finland	07.06.2002	Yes	–	No formal programme. But can be considered based on MAP article	Can be considered
11	France	15.01.2015	Yes **	Yes **	Yes	No
12	Georgia	17.11.2009	Yes	–	No	No
13	Germany	28.06.2004	Yes	–	Yes	Yes
14	Hungary	17.04.1997	No	Yes	Yes	Yes
15	India	24.01.1994	Yes	–	Yes	Yes
16	Indonesia	08.05.1990	No	Yes	Yes	Yes @
17	Ireland	28.10.2010	Yes **	Yes **	Yes	Yes
18	Israel	19.05.2005	Yes **	Yes **	No formal programme. But can be considered based on MAP article	No
19	Italy	29.01.1977	No	Yes	Yes	No
20	Japan	09.04.1994	Yes **	Yes **	Yes	Yes
21	Kazakhstan	19.09.2006	Yes **	Yes **	Yes	No
22	Malaysia	05.10.2004	Yes	–	Yes	Yes
23	Mexico	09.11.1994	No	Yes	Yes	Yes
24	The Netherlands	19.02.1971	No	Yes	Yes	Yes
25	New Zealand	21.08.2009	Yes **	Yes **	Yes	Yes
26	Norway	19.12.1997	No	No	Yes	Yes
27	Poland	04.11.2012	Yes	–	Yes	No
28	Portugal	06.09.1999	Yes **	Yes **	Yes	No
29	Romania	21.02.2002	Yes	–	Yes	No
30	Russia	09.09.2002	Yes	–	Yes	No
31	The Slovak Republic	09.05.2005	Yes	–	Yes	Yes
32	Slovenia	08.01.2010	Yes	–	Yes	Yes
33	South Africa	23.11.2015	Yes **	Yes **	No	No
34	Spain	13.04.2011	Yes	–	Yes	Yes
35	Sweden	17.06.1968	Yes ***	–	Yes	Yes

S. N.	Treaty Partner	Date of Signature of DTAA	Does Article 9(2) Already Exist?	If No, Will It Come Through MLI?	Does the Treaty Partner Have BAPA?	Does the Treaty Partner Have Rollback?
36	The Swiss Confederation	24.02.2011	Yes	–	Yes	Yes
37	Thailand	11.06.2015	Yes	–	Yes	Yes #
38	Turkey	09.07.1999	Yes	–	Yes	Yes
39	The United Arab Emirates	01.12.1995	Yes **	Yes **	No	No
40	United Kingdom	12.02.1997	Yes **	Yes **	Yes	Yes
41	Uruguay	15.01.2015	Yes	–	No	No
42	Vietnam	02.03.1994	Yes	–	Yes	No

* Such provisions are in Article 6(3) of the DTAA.
** Such provisions are not as per Article 9(2) of the OECD MTC, 2017 in entirety; hence, appropriate notification under Article 17 of MLI has been made by Singapore and the respective treaty partner.
*** Such provisions are in Article VI(2) of the DTAA.
@ Indonesia's Dispute Resolution Profile (last updated on 1 September 2016) states that rollback of APA is not permissible under the Indonesian APA programme. However, under the revised Ministry of Finance Regulation No. 22/PMK.03/2020, rollback is available in Indonesia.
# On perusal of Thailand's Dispute Resolution Profile (last updated on 1 June 2020), it is mentioned that rollback of APAs is provided for in the bilateral APA programme. However, Guidance on APA process issued by the Revenue Department of Thailand is silent on this issue.

3.21 APA REGIME IN SPAIN

458. The CA in charge of the APA programme in Spain is the Spanish Tax Agency. The relevant provisions in regard to the implementation of the APA programme in Spain are contained in Article 18(9) of the Corporate Income Tax Law.[181] The possibility to request for an APA was established on 27 December 1995, under Law 43/1995[182] on Corporations Tax under paragraph 6 of Article 16, as below:

> 6. Taxable persons may submit to the tax administration a proposal for the valuation of transactions carried out between persons or entities related to the performance of such transactions. This proposal will be based on the normal market value.

181. Refer DLA Piper – APA and MAP Country Guide 2019 https://www.dlapiper.com/en/us/insights/publications/2019/03/apa-and-map-country-guide-2019/ accessed on 11 August 2020.
182. Refer Law 43/1995 established on 27 December 1995 on Corporations Tax https://www.global-regulation.com/translation/spain/1461190/law-43-1995%252c-of-27-december%252c-the-corporate-income-tax.html accessed on 24 March 2021.

The proposal may also refer to the expenditure referred to in paragraphs 4 and 5.

The approval of the proposal shall have effect on the operations which are initiated after the date on which the said approval is carried out provided that they are carried out in accordance with the terms of the proposal approved, and will be valid for three tax periods.

In the event of significant variation of the economic circumstances existing at the time of the proposal's approval, the proposal may be modified to bring it into line with the new economic circumstances.

The tax administration may establish agreements with the Administrations of other States for the purposes of determining the normal market value.

The proposals referred to in this paragraph may be deemed to be rejected after the end of the resolution.

The procedure for the resolution of the related transactions valuation proposals will be established.

459. Unilateral, bilateral, and multilateral APAs (also referred to as related transaction valuation agreements under the APA programme of Spain) are available in Spain. The APA term limit is restricted to a maximum of four years (at the time of introduction of the programme in 1995, the tenure was three years), calculated from the date the agreement is reached. The is no filing fee under the APA programme of Spain. Both resident and non-resident taxpayers (PEs located in Spain) may submit APA applications with proposals regarding the valuation of future related transactions carried out with associated entities.

3.21.1 Salient Legislative Provisions

460. Elaborate details on the implementation of the APA programme are provided in Spain in the form of Article 18.9 of Corporate Income Tax Law (Law 27/2014 of 27 November)[183] and Chapter VII of Corporate Income Tax Regulations (CIT R), as drafted by Royal Decree 634/2015.[184]

461. Article 18.9 of the Corporate Income Tax Law provides as below:

9. Taxpayers may ask the tax authorities to determine the valuation of transactions carried out between persons or entities related to the performance of such persons or entities. Such a request shall be accompanied by a proposal based on the principle of free competition.

183. Refer Article 18.9 of Corporate Income Tax Law (Law 27/2014 of 27 November) https://www.global-regulation.com/translation/spain/1447828/law-27-2014-november-27%252c-from-corporate-income-tax.html accessed on 24 March 2021.

184. Refer Chapter VII of Corporate Income Tax Regulations (CIT R), as drafted by Royal Decree 634/2015 https://www.global-regulation.com/translation/spain/615992/royal-decree-634-2015%252c-july-10%252c-which-approves-the-regulation-of-tax.html accessed on 24 March 2021.

> The tax administration may conclude agreements with other administrations for the purpose of jointly determining the market value of the transactions.
>
> The valuation agreement shall have effect on the transactions carried out after the date on which it is approved, and shall be valid for the duration of the tax periods specified in the agreement itself, which may not exceed 4 tax periods following the date of the approval. In addition, it may be determined that their effects will be achieved in the operations of prior tax periods provided the domestic time limit has not expired and there has not been a firm tax assessment related to these years.
>
> In the event of significant variation of the economic circumstances existing at the time of the approval of the tax administration agreement, the tax administration may be modified to adapt it to the new economic circumstances.
>
> The proposals referred to in this paragraph may be deemed to be rejected after the time limit for resolution has elapsed.
>
> The procedure for the resolution of the related transaction valuation agreements, as well as that of their possible extensions, will be established.

3.21.2 Rollback of APA

462. The APA may also be applicable for previous periods, so long as these are not statute-barred and there is not a final assessment in place.

3.21.3 Pre-filing Meeting

463. Taxpayers are allowed to submit a preliminary application (prior request) under Article 21 of Chapter VII of CIT R, as drafted by Royal Decree 634/2015. Anonymous pre-filing is not available. During the pre-filing proceedings, the following information is required to be furnished by the taxpayer:

- identification of the parties;
- a brief description of the transaction(s) covered; and
- the basic elements of the intended pricing proposal.

464. The tax administration shall analyse the prior request, and may request for relevant clarifications from the interested parties and inform the interested parties of the feasibility or otherwise of the prior assessment agreement.

3.21.4 APA Application

465. The APA application must contain *inter alia* the following information and supporting documents:

- an arm's-length pricing proposal, including a description of the TP method and the analysis followed to determine the market value;
- a confirmation that the related parties know and accept the pricing proposal; and

- transfer pricing documentation that complies with Spanish regulations, as relevant to the APA.

466. In this regard, Article 22 of Chapter VII of CIT R, as drafted by Royal Decree 634/2015, states as below:

> 1. A person or a related entity may request the tax administration to provide a prior agreement for the valuation of transactions between persons or entities related to the conduct of such transactions, without prejudice to the provisions of Article 25.8 this Regulation.
>   Such an application may include the determination of the market value of the estimated income from transactions made by a taxpayer with a permanent establishment abroad, in those cases in which it is set out in a convention to avoid international double taxation resulting from it.
>   The application will be accompanied by a proposal that will be based on the principle of free competition, and will contain a description of the method and the analysis followed to determine the market value.
>   The application must be subscribed by the applicant persons or entities, who must prove to the Administration that the other persons or entities involved in the transactions whose valuation is requested know and accept the assessment request.
> 2. The application shall be accompanied by the documentation referred to in Articles 15 and 16 of this Regulation as soon as it is applicable to the assessment proposal and shall be adapted to the circumstances of the case.

3.21.5 Evaluation of APA Application

467. Article 24 of Chapter VII of CIT R, as drafted by Royal Decree 634/2015, provides that the tax administration will examine the proposal along with the submitted documentation. For this purpose, it may require the taxpayers to submit data, reports, background and supporting documents related to the proposal, as well as additional explanations or clarifications thereon.

468. The Spanish Tax Agency has a statutory six-month period to complete an APA application in accordance with paragraph 4 of Article 25 of Chapter VII of CIT R, as drafted by Royal Decree 634/2015.

469. The relevant provisions in regard to the procedure for the agreement on transactions linked to other tax administrations (involving BAPA or MAPA) are contained in Articles 31-36 of Chapter VII of CIT R, as drafted by Royal Decree 634/2015.

3.21.6 Advance Pricing Agreement

470. Article 25 of Chapter VII of CIT R, as drafted by Royal Decree 634/2015 *inter alia*, provides that the prior assessment agreement shall be formalized in a document which shall include at least the following:

(a) Place and date of its formalization.
(b) First and last name or social reason or full name and tax identification number of the contributors to whom the proposal relates.
(c) Conformity of the contributors to the content of the agreement.
(d) Description of the operations referred to in the proposal.
(e) Essential elements of the valuation method and value or range of values that are derived from it.
(f) Tax or settlement periods to which the agreement and date of entry into force of the agreement shall apply.
(g) Critical assumptions whose occurrence conditions the applicability of the agreement in terms of such agreement.

3.21.7 Annual Report/Statement

471. The taxpayer is required to report any significant changes in the circumstances on which the APA is based. Taxpayers must annually file together with their tax return a statement describing the following:

- related party transaction(s) carried out during the fiscal year applying the APA;
- prices agreed in the related party transaction(s);
- description of variations in the economic circumstances, if any;
- similar transactions to those described in the APA, prices and description of the differences between them; and
- other information as required by the Spanish Tax Agency.

3.21.8 Renewal of APA

472. An APA may be renewed through application of an extension six months before the expiry of the existing APA. In this regard, Article 30 of Chapter VII of CIT R, as drafted by Royal Decree 634/2015 *inter alia*, provides as below:

1. Taxpayers may request the tax administration to extend the validity of the valuation agreement that would have been approved. Such application must be submitted before the end of the six months preceding the end of the validity period and shall be accompanied by the documentation which it considers appropriate to justify the circumstances laid down in the application specifying that conditions of the original agreement have not varied.
2. The request for the extension of the prior assessment agreement shall be signed by the persons or entities that signed the prior agreement whose extension is requested, and must prove to the Administration that the other persons or entities linked to the operations they know and accept the request for an extension.
3. The tax administration shall have a period of six months to examine the documentation referred to in paragraph 1 above, and to notify the taxpayer

of the extension or not of the period of validity of the prior assessment agreement. For such purposes, the Administration may request any additional information and documentation.

4. After the period referred to in the previous paragraph has elapsed and taxpayer has not been notified of the extension of the period of validity of the prior assessment agreement, the application may be deemed to be rejected.

3.21.9 Revision of APA

473. Article 29 of Chapter VII of CIT R, as drafted by Royal Decree 634/2015, provides for modification of the prior assessment agreement. These provisions *inter alia* provide as below:

1. In the event of a significant change in the economic or technological circumstances existing at the time of the approval of the prior assessment agreement, it may be amended to bring it into line with the new economic circumstances. The amendment procedure may be initiated either on its own initiative by the Administration or at the request of the taxpayer.
2. The request for amendment must be signed by the applicant's persons or entities, who must prove to the Administration that the other persons or entities involved in the transactions whose valuation is requested, know and accept the modification request, and must contain the following information:
   a) Justification of significant variation of economic circumstances.
   b) Amendment which, in the light of that variation, is appropriate.

3.21.10 Statistics

474. There were fifty-four APA application requests in 2016 and fifty-three active APAs. The statistics on the Spanish APA programme for the years 2017 and 2018 are provided in Table 23.

Table 23 Number of APA Requests Received and Resolved in 2017, 2018 in Spain

Total Number of All APAs in Force at the End of 2017		*Total Number of Bilateral and Multilateral APAs in Force at the End of 2017*		*Total Number of Unilateral APAs in Force at the End of 2017*		*Number of APA Requests Received in 2017*		*Number of APAs Granted in 2017*		*Number of APA Applications Rejected in 2017*		*Number of APA Applications Where the Taxpayer Withdrew Its Request in 2017*		*Average Time (In Months) to Negotiate Bilateral or Multilateral APAs*	
EU	Non-EU	EU	Non-EU	EU	Non-EU	EU	Non-EU	EU	Non-EU	EU	Non-EU	EU	Non-EU	EU	Non-EU
46	14	6	2	40	12	19	9	10	3	1	1	3	2	24	26.5

Total Number of All APAs in Force at the End of 2018		*Total Number of Bilateral and Multilateral APAs in Force at the End of 2018*		*Total Number of Unilateral APAs in Force at the End of 2018*		*Number of APA Requests Received in 2018*		*Number of APAs Granted in 2018*		*Number of APA Applications Rejected in 2018*		*Number of APA Applications Where the Taxpayer Withdrew Its Request in 2018*		*Average Time (In Months) to Negotiate Bilateral or Multilateral APAs*	
EU	Non-EU	EU	Non-EU	EU	Non-EU	EU	Non-EU	EU	Non-EU	EU	Non-EU	EU	Non-EU	EU	Non-EU
65	14	10	2	55	12	62	8	17	2	5	–	9	5	14.42	

Source: Statistics on APAs in the EU at the end of 2017 https://ec.europa.eu/taxation_customs/sites/taxation/files/statistics_on_advance_pricing_agreements_2017_en.pdf.
and
Statistics on APAs in the EU at the end of 2018 https://ec.europa.eu/taxation_customs/sites/taxation/files/apa-and-map-2019-3.pdf.

3.22 APA REGIME IN SWEDEN

475. On 1 January 2007, the Swedish legislation dealing with transfer pricing was extended substantially. The statutory rule of the Swedish Income Tax Act (SITA) adopting the arm's-length principle for transactions between related enterprises was supplemented by formal documentation requirements. Besides the arm's-length rule, Chapter 19 section 2b of Law 2001:1227 introduced documentation requirements for all corporations registered in Sweden that conduct cross-border controlled transactions. It became compulsory to prepare written documentation on all cross-border transactions with associated companies. The statutory addendum came into effect as of 1 January 2007. In connection with the documentation requirement, Administrative Guidelines (SKVFS 2007:1) were issued by the Swedish Tax Agency (STA) on 14 February 2007.[185]

476. The CA in charge of the APA programme in Sweden is the STA. The relevant provisions in regard to the implementation of the APA programme in Sweden are contained in Act (2009:1289) on Advance Pricing Agreements Regarding International Transactions, supplemented by Ordinance (2009:1295) on Advance Pricing Agreements Regarding International Transactions; Bill (2009/10:17) on Advance Pricing Agreements Regarding International Transactions; and Guidance available on the STA website.[186]

477. Bilateral and multilateral APAs are available in Sweden. APA is also referred to as pricing notice in Sweden. An APA can only be issued in Sweden if the other involved country and Sweden have entered into a MAP article, which is part of a DTAA entered with that country, concerning the price setting of international transactions. Due to this, there is only a possibility to issue bilateral and multilateral APAs in Sweden. Therefore, if another country is unable to enter into a MAP with Sweden, then Sweden cannot issue an APA. Unilateral APAs shall not be issued since it does not help decrease the potential risks of economic double taxation.[187] Further, the Guidance[188] on Pricing Announcement (APA) issued by STA states in respect of UAPAs that this is not something that occurs in Sweden. A pricing notice can only be issued if there is a mutual agreement with one or more affected states with which Sweden has entered into a tax agreement. A unilateral pricing notice can thus not be submitted on the basis of Swedish law.

185. Refer Note issued by PwC in respect of Transfer Pricing in Sweden https://www.pwc.com/gx/en/international-transfer-pricing/assets/sweden.pdf accessed on 25 March 2021.
186. Refer DLA Piper – APA and MAP Country Guide 2019 https://www.dlapiper.com/en/us/insights/publications/2019/03/apa-and-map-country-guide-2019/ accessed on 11 August 2020.
187. Refer Degree Project – Business Administration by Maria Alm and Helena Ehrstedt titled 'Advance Pricing Agreements-The concept and its implementation in Swedish tax law' section 7.3.2.3 http://hj.diva-portal.org/smash/get/diva2:419020/FULLTEXT01 accessed on 25 March 2021.
188. Refer Guidance on Pricing Announcement (APA) https://www4.skatteverket.se/rattsligvagledning/edition/2021.5/339233.html?q=apa accessed on 25 March 2021.

478. The APA is valid for a predetermined period of three to five years. The filing fee for a new APA is SEK 150,000 (approx. USD 17,000). An APA application will only be accepted if the transaction(s) to be covered is considered by the STA to be of a sufficiently complex nature, and the arm's-length principle is applicable to the taxpayer's circumstances. The STA will make an assessment of the eligibility of the taxpayer on a case-by-case basis. The taxpayer is required to provide the information required for an APA to be concluded. The TP method chosen in the application, after any adjustments, is deemed to be able to provide a price that corresponds to what two independent parties would have applied.

3.22.1 Salient Legislative Provisions

479. Some of the prominent provisions on implementation of APAs are *inter alia* contained in Act (2009:1289) on Advance Pricing Agreements Regarding International Transactions[189] as below:

- *Section 7* The Swedish Tax Agency issues a pricing notice and makes other decisions in accordance with this Act.
- *Section 10* An application for a pricing notice shall be in writing and shall be submitted to the Swedish Tax Agency.
- *Section 11* An application for a pricing notice shall contain the information necessary for a pricing notice to be submitted.
- *Section 12* Pricing notice may be submitted
    1. the application for a pricing notice does not concern a matter of a simple nature or minor transactions;
    2. the transactions covered by the application may be considered independent of other transactions not covered by the application;
    3. the trader provides the information necessary for a mutual agreement to be concluded and a proper pricing notice to be provided;
    4. information necessary for the conclusion and verification of a reciprocal agreement may be obtained from the States covered by the reciprocal agreement; and
    5. the pricing method chosen in the application, after any adjustments, is deemed to be able to give a price that corresponds to what independent parties would have applied.
- *Section 13* Pricing notice may only be submitted if
    1. a mutual agreement on the pricing of international transactions has been entered into with a state specified in the application for a pricing notice and with which Sweden has entered into a tax agreement, and
    2. the mutual agreement is in accordance with the application for a pricing notice or has been accepted by the trader.
- *Section 14* A pricing notice states how the future pricing of certain international transactions shall take place and the assumptions, conditions and other conditions that shall apply to the applicability and validity of the notice.

    The pricing notice shall be in accordance with the mutual agreement referred to in section 13.

189. Refer Law (2009:1289) on Advance Pricing Agreements Regarding International Transactions https://www4.skatteverket.se/rattsligvagledning/321837.html accessed on 25 March 2021.

- *Section 15* The period of validity of a pricing notice shall be determined to be between three and five tax years if there are no special reasons to determine the period of validity for a longer or shorter period.
- *Section 16* A pricing notice is binding on the Swedish Tax Agency regarding the pricing of the transactions covered by the notice and in relation to the person to whom the notice relates, unless otherwise follows from section 18 or 19.
- *Section 17* The trader shall, without unreasonable delay, notify the Swedish Tax Agency of:
    1. a circumstance which entails or may result in the assumptions, conditions and other conditions specified in the pricing notice not being fulfilled, or
    2. the pricing notice does not apply.
- *Section 18* The Swedish Tax Agency may change a pricing notice, if the trader so requests or if:
  1. any of the assumptions and conditions or any of the other conditions specified in the notice in any material respect are not met, or
  2. a constitutional amendment in any material respect affects an issue to which the notice relates.

  An amendment pursuant to the first paragraph may only be made if such conditions as are referred to in sections 12 and 13 are met and the trader accepts the amendment.
- *Section 19* The Swedish Tax Agency may revoke a pricing notice in whole or in part if:
    1. the mutual agreement on which the notice is based has ceased to apply in whole or in part;
    2. the trader has notified the Swedish Tax Agency in accordance with section 17(2) that the notice is not applied,
    3. the trader has provided information that the notice has not been applied in accordance with Chapter Section 34 or Chapter 33 Section 6 of the Tax Procedure Act (2011: 1244), or
    4. the trader or partners in a trading company or another shareholder-taxed legal person has requested reconsideration of or appealed a decision on final tax in accordance with Chapter 66 or 67 of the Tax Procedure Act and has requested that the pricing notice not be applied to the issue to which the request for reconsideration or the appeal relates.
- *Section 23* In connection with an application for a pricing notice, the Swedish Tax Agency shall charge a fee to the trader for the examination that the application may give rise to.
- *Section 24* The Swedish Tax Agency may in an individual case decide on an exemption from all or part of the fee, if there are special reasons for it.
- *Section 25* Pricing notices and other decisions pursuant to this Act may not be appealed.

480. Some of the prominent provisions on implementation of APAs *inter alia* contained in Ordinance (2009:1295) on Advance Pricing Agreements Regarding International Transactions which supplement Act (2009:1289) are as below:

- *Section 3* The Swedish Tax Agency enters into a mutual agreement on pricing of international transactions in accordance with section 13 of the Act (2009:1289) on pricing notices for international transactions.
- *Section 4* If a matter concerning a pricing notice is of special importance or otherwise of such a nature that the negotiation of a mutual agreement should be

handled by the Government, the Tax Agency shall, with its own opinion, submit to the Government the part of the matter concerning the mutual agreement.

- *Section 6* An application for a pricing notice and other documents that have been submitted in a case in accordance with the Act (2009:1289) on pricing notices in international transactions or prepared or examined by the Tax Agency in such a case shall be stored in such a way that unauthorized persons cannot access them and if possible kept separate from other documents.
- *Section 7* A fee in accordance with section 23 of the Act (2009:1289) on pricing notices for international transactions shall be paid in the following amounts:

  Application for pricing notice SEK 150,000
  Application for renewal of pricing notice SEK 100,000
  Application for renewal (with changes) of pricing notice SEK 125,000

- *Section 8* If an application covers more than one foreign state, a fee in accordance with section 7 shall be paid as for an application per foreign state.
- *Section 9* The fee shall be paid to the Swedish Tax Agency when the application is submitted. If the fee is not paid then, the applicant must be ordered to pay the fee within a certain time. Such an injunction may be sent to the applicant in an ordinary letter or communicated in another suitable manner. If the injunction is not complied with within the prescribed time, the application must be rejected. The applicant shall be informed of this in the injunction.

3.22.2 Rollback of APA

481. There is no specific guidance on rollbacks; however, they may be available on a case-by-case basis at the discretion of the STA.

3.22.3 Pre-filing Meeting

482. A pre-filing meeting is generally conducted with the applicant and the STA unless special reasons imply that such a meeting should not be held. In practice, STA is open to allowing pre-filing meetings as per the Guidance[190] issued on Act (2009:1289). If the request for a pre-filing meeting is accepted, the meeting covers the conditions of a proposed APA, the timeline of the APA application process, and the information and documentation required to be included in the application. Anonymous pre-filing is not available in Sweden. Taxpayers are encouraged to address and resolve various administrative or tax issues that are relevant to and may affect the outcome of the APA at the pre-filing stage with the STA.

190. Refer Guidance issued on Act (2009:1289) https://www.skatteverket.se/foretagochorganisationer/skatter/internationellt/ansokanomprissattningsbesked.4.58d555751259e4d661680003946.html?q=apa accessed on 25 March 2021.

3.22.4 APA Application

483. An application for an APA is required to be submitted in four copies and should contain the following information/details in accordance with section 5 of Ordinance (2009:1295):

- the name, billing address, any organization numbers, personal identity number or any equivalent registration numbers, or equivalent foreign numbers for the relevant parties;
- information regarding which tax years the application concerns;
- information regarding which jurisdictions will be involved;
- information regarding any foreign APA that covers the entities in the applications and if this APA concerns similar transactions as the Swedish APA application;
- a description of the parties to the APA and their respective organization and business;
- information regarding the nature and scale of the transactions;
- a functional analysis;
- a comparative analysis;
- a description of the chosen TP method;
- justification for the chosen TP method and its feasibility; and
- information regarding the assumptions and conclusions that form the basis of the chosen TP method.

484. In accordance with the Guidance[191] issued on Act (2009:1289), it is important that an application contains all the information needed for the CA to be able to assess a pricing method or a transaction. Such information may, for example, be:

- an account of the trends and conditions prevailing in the market in which the company operates and which are expected to affect the company;
- the company's intended business strategy during the current period and also for previous years in cases where a change is intended to take place;
- accounts for the most recent financial years of the undertakings concerned;
- agreements concerning the transactions covered by the application;
- information on tax audits or mutual agreements that are relevant to the application; and
- other relevant information.

191. *Id.*

3.22.5 Compliance of APA

485. The taxpayer is required to notify the STA if any circumstances arise that the assumptions and conditions in the APA are no longer valid. Details regarding what should be included in the notification are settled on a case-by-case basis.

3.22.6 Renewal of APA

486. There is no specific regulation for renewal of an APA. It is at the discretion of the STA to adapt its procedure to take into consideration an application for an APA that is already in existence. The filing fee for a renewal application is SEK 100,000 (approx. USD 11,200).

3.22.7 Statistics

487. The STA has had an APA programme since 2010. The statistics on the Swedish APA programme for the years 2017 and 2018 are provided in Table 24.

Table 24 Number of APA Requests Received and Resolved in 2017, 2018 in Sweden

Total Number of All APAs in Force at the End of 2017		*Total Number of Bilateral and Multilateral APAs in Force at the End of 2017*		*Total Number of Unilateral APAs in Force at the End of 2017*		*Number of APA Requests Received in 2017*		*Number of APAs Granted in 2017*		*Number of APA Applications Rejected in 2017*		*Number of APA Applications Where the Taxpayer Withdrew Its Request in 2017*		*Average Time (In Months) to Negotiate Bilateral or Multilateral APAs*	
EU	Non-EU	EU	Non-EU	EU	Non-EU	EU	Non-EU	EU	Non-EU	EU	Non-EU	EU	Non-EU	EU	Non-EU
9	9	9	9	–	–	6	5	3	4	–	1	1	–	37	37

Total Number of All APAs in Force at the End of 2018		*Total Number of Bilateral and Multilateral APAs in Force at the End of 2018*		*Total Number of Unilateral APAs in Force at the End of 2018*		*Number of APA Requests Received in 2018*		*Number of APAs Granted in 2018*		*Number of APA Applications Rejected in 2018*		*Number of APA Applications Where the Taxpayer Withdrew Its Request in 2018*		*Average Time (In Months) to Negotiate Bilateral or Multilateral APAs*	
EU	Non-EU	EU	Non-EU	EU	Non-EU	EU	Non-EU	EU	Non-EU	EU	Non-EU	EU	Non-EU	EU	Non-EU
7	14	7	14	–	–	5	2	4	7	–	1	1	–	48	46

Source: Statistics on APAs in the EU at the end of 2017 https://ec.europa.eu/taxation_customs/sites/taxation/files/statistics_on_advance_pricing_agreements_2017_en.pdf.
and
Statistics on APAs in the EU at the end of 2018 https://ec.europa.eu/taxation_customs/sites/taxation/files/apa-and-map-2019-3.pdf.

3.23 APA REGIME IN THAILAND

488. In Thailand, APA is defined as an arrangement made between the taxpayer and the tax authority, providing transfer pricing certainty for intra-group transactions undertaken by affiliates for a certain period in advance with appropriate methodologies, terms, as well as conditions.

489. The CA in charge of the APA programme in Thailand is the Revenue Department (hereinafter 'Revenue'). The relevant provisions in regard to the implementation of the APA programme in Thailand are contained in Guidance on the APA process, available on the Revenue's website.[192]

490. Only bilateral APAs are available in Thailand. The APA is effective between three to five accounting periods. There is no filing fee for APAs in Thailand. Taxpayers must submit a written document of intent for a pre-filing meeting at least six months prior to the last day of the first accounting period that the APA aims to become effective. Furthermore, APA applications must be submitted to the Revenue within the last day of the first accounting period intended to be covered by the APA.

3.23.1 Salient Provisions of Guidance

491. Some of the prominent provisions on implementation of APAs contained in Guidance[193] on APA Process (hereinafter 'Guidance') issued by the Revenue *inter alia* are as below:

(a) In regard to filing of APA application for bilateral APAs, the Guidance states as below:

> A company or juristic partnership incorporated under Thai law, who enters into intra-group transactions with affiliates who are residents of Thailand's treaty partners, may submit a written document of intent (APA proposal) directly to the Director General of the Revenue Department. In this case, only Bilateral APA will be accepted.

(b) The Revenue shall notify the taxpayer of the result of the APA application within three months of filing of the application.

(c) In regard to taxpayer's cooperation to be rendered during the APA process, the Guidance states as below:

> During the APA process the Revenue Department needs to consider the documents as well as other related information. Taxpayers are required to give full cooperation to the Revenue Department, e.g., supplying additional

192. Refer DLA Piper – APA and MAP Country Guide 2019 https://www.dlapiper.com/en/us/insights/publications/2019/03/apa-and-map-country-guide-2019/ accessed on 11 August 2020.
193. Refer Guidance on APA process https://www.rd.go.th/publish/fileadmin/download/GUIDANCE-ON-APA-PROCESS-EN.pdf accessed on 26 March 2021.

information within a reasonable time, or attending meetings with the Revenue Department officials, during the period of APA process.
Any documents related to APA, which taxpayers provide to foreign tax authorities, shall also be required to be provided to the Revenue Department within 7 working days starting from the date documentation have been delivered to the foreign tax authority.

(d) The Guidance provides that the taxpayer has the option to withdraw its APA application by submitting a letter addressed to the Director General before the day an APA becomes effective.

(e) The Guidance provides that after conclusion of APA between the Revenue and the foreign tax authority, the Revenue shall inform the taxpayer with a written notice. The notice generally provides the following information:
   (1) Details of the taxpayer's information, i.e., name, address.
   (2) Details of APA's terms and conditions comprising the following:
      (i) Covered transaction.
      (ii) TPM.
      (iii) APA period.
      (iv) ALP/range.
      (v) Critical assumptions.
      (vi) Time frame for submitting APA annual report.
   (3) Other details, if any.

3.23.2 Rollback of APA

492. On perusal of Thailand's Dispute Resolution Profile (last updated on 1 June 2020),[194] it is mentioned that rollback of APAs is provided for in the bilateral APA programme. However, Guidance on APA Process issued by the Revenue is silent on this issue.

3.23.3 Pre-filing Meeting

493. Taxpayers are required to submit a written document of intent for a pre-filing meeting to the Director General of the Revenue at least six months prior to the last day of the first accounting period that the proposed APA is to become effective. Anonymous pre-filing is not available. The Guidance provides that pre-filing meeting is not legally binding on the APA parties. The objectives of the pre-filing meeting are the following:

- discuss the reason for the APA application;
- submit pre-filing documentation;
- discuss the documents required to be included in the APA application;
- discuss the filing date of the APA application; and

194. Refer Thailand's Dispute Resolution Profile https://www.oecd.org/ctp/dispute/thailand-dispute-resolution-profile.pdf accessed on 26 March 2021.

- discuss ways to minimize the time taken to process the APA application.

494. Pre-filing documents must be submitted at least fifteen days prior to the pre-filing meeting. Pre-filing documents include the following:

- name and address of the taxpayer seeking the APA;
- accounting period of the entity and the relevant transactions;
- structure and relationship of the related parties;
- details of business revenue account showing all transactions;
- detailed analysis of assets and risks of all transactions;
- detailed analysis of the structure of industries and their market share; and
- TP method chosen for the APA and explanation of the selection.

3.23.4 APA Application

495. Taxpayers are required to submit a written document of intent to the Revenue (five hard copies of each document and one electronic copy must be submitted to the Revenue) within the last day of the first accounting period intended to be covered by the APA. Required information and documents to be submitted include the following:

- the name and address of the taxpayer seeking the APA;
- the accounting period intended to be covered and the relevant transactions;
- the organizational structure and relationship of the related entities;
- details of business revenue accounts showing all transactions;
- a detailed analysis of assets and risks of all transactions;
- the TP method chosen for the APA and explanation of the selection;
- a benchmarking study of comparables;
- the critical assumptions;
- the history and status of any audits; and
- any other relevant documents requested by the Revenue.

3.23.5 Annual Report

496. There is no specific guidance on post-agreement filing procedures. The Guidance *inter alia* provides that after conclusion of APA between the Revenue and the foreign tax authority, the Revenue shall inform the taxpayer with a written notice. In that written notice, at the conclusion of the APA, the time frame for annual report submission is provided by the Revenue to the taxpayer for necessary compliance by the latter.

3.23.6 Renewal of APA

497. The Guidance is silent on this issue.

3.23.7 Revoking or Cancelling of APA

498. The Guidance provides that revoking or cancelling of APA proceedings shall commence under a written notice by the Revenue. In certain cases, the Revenue has the right to cancel or revoke an APA before its term ends, for example, in the following circumstances:

(1) the taxpayer gave incorrect or insufficient information;
(2) the taxpayer did not comply with regulation, process, and conditions of APA;
(3) the taxpayer refused to cooperate with the Revenue;
(4) the taxpayer, or the Revenue, may seek amendment, cancellation, or withdrawal of APA;
(5) any event that changes or affects the conditions or assumptions stated in the APA;
(6) any amendment of domestic laws and international agreements that are relevant to the APA.

In this regard, the Revenue shall notify the taxpayer with a written letter in advance, allowing it to submit additional information or objection, within a specified time period, before cancellation or revocation of APA is considered.

3.23.8 Statistics

499. As per Thailand's Dispute Resolution Profile,[195] statistics relating to bilateral APAs are not publicly available.

3.24 APA REGIME IN UK

500. The CA in charge of the APA programme in UK is HM Revenue and Customs (HMRC). HMRC has run an APA Programme since 1999 to assist businesses in determining the most appropriate methodology to derive the arm's-length outcome for complex transfer pricing issues and prevent disputes arising that may otherwise result in a MAP being necessary later. The legislation that relates to APAs appears at sections 218-230 of the Taxation (International and Other Provisions) Act 2010 (TIOPA).[196] In addition, HMRC has issued Policy Paper – Statement of Practice 2 (2010)[197] and

195. *Id.*
196. Refer DLA Piper – APA and MAP Country Guide 2019 https://www.dlapiper.com/en/us/insights/publications/2019/03/apa-and-map-country-guide-2019/ accessed on 11 August 2020.
197. Refer Policy paper issued by HM Revenue and Customs – Statement of Practice 2 (2010) – Updated 12 July 2019 https://www.gov.uk/government/publications/statement-of-practice-2-2010/statement-of-practice-2-2010 accessed on 4 August 2019.

Guidance[198] on APAs for the benefit of all stakeholders. The relevant Sections of TIOPA, Statement of Practice and Guidance issued by HMRC are discussed in detail hereunder.

3.24.1 Statutory Provisions Governing the APA Programme

501. Section 218 of TIOPA provides the meaning of an APA and the matters to which it relates, as below:

> (1) In this Part 'advance pricing agreement' means a written agreement that –
> (a) is made by the Commissioners with any person ('A') as a consequence of an application by A under section 223,
> (b) relates to one or more of the matters mentioned in subsection (2), and
> (c) declares that it is an agreement made for the purposes of this section.
>
> (2) Those matters are –
> (a) if A is not a company, the attribution of income to a branch or agency through which A has been carrying on a trade in the United Kingdom or is proposing to carry on a trade in the United Kingdom,
> (b) if A is a company, the attribution of income to a permanent establishment through which A has been carrying on a trade in the United Kingdom or is proposing to carry on a trade in the United Kingdom,
> (c) the attribution of income to any permanent establishment of A's, wherever situated, through which A has been carrying on, or is proposing to carry on, any business,
> (d) the extent to which income that has arisen or may arise to A is to be taken for any purpose to be income arising in a country or territory outside the United Kingdom,
> (e) the treatment for tax purposes of any provision made or imposed, whether before or after the date of the agreement, as between A and any associate (see section 219) of A's, and
> (f) the treatment for tax purposes of any provision made or imposed, whether before or after the date of the agreement, as between an oil-related ring-fence trade carried on by A (see section 206) and any other activities carried on by A.

502. Section 219 of TIOPA provides the meaning of 'associate' mentioned in section 218(2)(e), as below:

> (1) This section applies for the purposes of section 218(2)(e).
>
> (2) Two persons are associates in relation to provision made or imposed as between them if at the time of the making or imposition of the provision –
> (a) one of them is directly or indirectly participating in the management, control or capital of the other, or
> (b) the same person or persons is or are directly or indirectly participating in the management, control or capital of each of the two persons.
>
> (3) Two persons are also associates in relation to any provision if section 217(4) (which applies to provision made or imposed in connection with sales of oil)

198. Refer Guidance on APAs, published on 9 April 2016 by HMRC https://www.gov.uk/hmrc-internal-manuals/international-manual/intm422000 accessed on 17 February 2021.

requires the persons to be treated as controlled by the same person at the time of the making or imposition of that provision.

(4) For the interpretation of subsection (2), see sections 157(1), 158(4), 159(1) and 160(1) (which have the effect that references in subsection (2) to direct or indirect participation are to be read in accordance with provisions of Chapter 2 of Part 4).

503. Section 220 of TIOPA provides the effect of an APA on the party to it, as below:

(1) Subsection (2) applies if a chargeable period is one to which an advance pricing agreement relates.

(2) The Tax Acts have effect in relation to the chargeable period as if, in the case of the person with whom the Commissioners made the agreement, questions relating to the matters mentioned in section 218(2) are to be determined –

(a) in accordance with the agreement, and

(b) without reference to the provisions in accordance with which they would otherwise be determined.

(3) Subsection (2) is subject to –
subsections (4) and (5), and
section 221.

(4) A question is to be determined as mentioned in subsection (2) only so far as the agreement provides for the question to be determined in that way.

(5) In the case of so much of a question as –

(a) relates to any matter mentioned in paragraph (e) or (f) of section 218(2), and

(b) is not comprised in a question that relates to a matter within another paragraph of section 218(2),

reference to a provision is capable of being excluded under subsection (2) by an advance pricing agreement only if the provision is in Part 4.

504. Section 221 of TIOPA provides the effect of revocation of an APA or breach of its conditions, as below:

(1) An advance pricing agreement does not have effect in accordance with section 220(2) in relation to any determination of a question if any of conditions A, B and C is met.

(2) Condition A is that a time to which the question relates is after a time as from which an officer has revoked the agreement in accordance with the agreement's terms.

(3) Condition B is that the question relates to a time after, or in relation to which, there has been a failure by a party to the agreement to comply with a significant provision of the agreement.

(4) Condition C is that the question relates to a matter as respects which a key condition has not been met or is no longer met.

(5) A provision of the agreement is 'significant' for the purposes of subsection (3) if compliance with that provision is, under the terms of the agreement, to be a condition of the agreement's having effect.

(6) Any other condition that, under the terms of the agreement, is to be a condition of the agreement's having effect is a 'key condition' for the purposes of subsection (4).

505. Section 222 of TIOPA provides the effect and provisions to be determined in accordance with the agreement, as below:

(1) Subsections (2), (5) and (6) apply if –
  (a) an advance pricing agreement has effect in relation to any provision ('the actual provision') made or imposed as between any person ('A') and another ('B'), and
  (b) section 220(2) has the effect in A's case of requiring a question relating to the actual provision to be determined in accordance with the agreement rather than by reference to rules which would otherwise be applicable because of Part 4.
(2) The provisions mentioned in subsection (3) have effect in B's case on the assumption that any question within subsection (4) is to be determined, to the same extent as in A's case, by reference to the agreement.
(3) The provisions are –
  sections 174 to 178 (transfer pricing: claim by disadvantaged person), and sections 188 and 189 (transfer pricing: adjustment of double taxation relief if claim made).
(4) The questions are –
  (a) whether A is a person on whom a potential advantage in relation to United Kingdom taxation is conferred by the actual provision, and
  (b) what constitutes the arm's length provision in relation to the actual provision.
(5) Subsection (2) has effect subject to any advance pricing agreement made between the Commissioners and B.
(6) Any assumptions to be made because of the agreement are 'advance-pricing-agreement assumptions' for the purposes of paragraph (b) of the definition in section 185(5) of 'transfer-pricing determination'.

506. Section 223 of TIOPA provides for filing of an APA application, as below:

(1) For the purposes of section 218(1)(a), an application by a person ('A') is an application under this section if it complies with subsections (2) to (5).
(2) It must be an application to the Commissioners for the clarification by agreement of the effect in A's case of provisions by reference to which questions relating to any one or more of the matters mentioned in section 218(2) are to be, or might be, determined.
(3) It must set out A's understanding of what would in A's case be the effect, in the absence of any agreement, of the provisions in relation to which clarification is sought.
(4) It must set out the respects in which it appears to A that clarification is required in relation to those provisions.
(5) It must set out how A proposes that matters should be clarified in a manner consistent with the understanding mentioned in subsection (3).

507. Section 224 of TIOPA *inter alia* provides the period from which APAs in UK are to commence, periods corresponding to which APAs are to have effect and adjustments to be made for tax purposes in consequence to the agreement, as below:

(1) An advance pricing agreement may contain provision relating to chargeable periods ending before the agreement is made, subject to subsection (2).

(2) An advance pricing agreement may not contain provision relating to chargeable periods ending before 27 July 1999.
(3) If an advance pricing agreement –
    (a) relates to a chargeable period beginning or ending before the agreement is made, and
    (b) provides for the manner in which adjustments are to be made for tax purposes in consequence of the agreement,

the adjustments are to be made for those purposes in the manner provided for in the agreement.

508. Section 225 of TIOPA provides for modification and revocation of an APA, as below:

(1) Subsection (2) applies if an advance pricing agreement provides for the modification, or revocation, of the agreement –
    (a) by the Commissioners, or
    (b) by an officer.
(2) The agreement may provide for the modification or revocation to take effect as from such time as the Commissioners or officer may determine.
(3) A time determined under subsection (2) may be (but need not be) a time before the modification is made or the agreement is revoked.

509. Section 226 of TIOPA provides for annulment of an APA due to misrepresentation by the applicant or due to other factors, as below:

(1) Subsection (6) applies if each of conditions A to D is met.
(2) Condition A is that the Commissioners and any person ('A') have at any time purported to enter into an advance pricing agreement.
(3) Condition B is that, before that time, A fraudulently or negligently provided the Commissioners with information which was false or misleading.
(4) Condition C is that the information was so provided –
    (a) for or in connection with the application to the Commissioners for the making of the agreement, or
    (b) otherwise in connection with the preparation of the agreement.
(5) Condition D is that the Commissioners have notified A that the agreement is nullified by reason of the misrepresentation.
(6) The agreement is to be treated as never made.

510. Section 227 of TIOPA provides for levy of penalty on the applicant for making fraudulent, false or misleading statements in connection with an APA, as below:

A person is liable to a penalty of not more than £10,000 if the person fraudulently or negligently makes a false or misleading statement to the Commissioners or an officer –

(a) for or in connection with any application to the Commissioners for them to enter into an advance pricing agreement, or
(b) otherwise in connection with the preparation of an advance pricing agreement.

511. Section 228 of TIOPA makes it incumbent upon the applicant to provide reports and information required during the APA process, as below:

> A party to an advance pricing agreement must provide the Commissioners from time to time with all reports and other information that the party may be required to provide –
>
> (a) under the agreement, or
> (b) as a result of a request made by an officer in accordance with the agreement.

512. Section 229 of TIOPA provides for modifications of an APA for enabling effect to be given to the mutual agreement in relation to the subject matter of the APA, as below:

> (1) Subsection (2) applies if a mutual agreement made under and for the purposes of any double taxation arrangements is not consistent with the terms of an advance pricing agreement.
> (2) The Commissioners must ensure that the advance pricing agreement is modified so far as may be necessary for enabling effect to be given to the mutual agreement in relation to the subject-matter of the advance pricing agreement.
> (3) The Commissioners may comply with subsection (2) by exercising powers conferred on them by the advance pricing agreement or otherwise.
> (4) In this section 'double taxation arrangements' means arrangements that have effect under section 2(1) (double taxation relief by agreement with territories outside the United Kingdom).

513. Section 230 of TIOPA provides for meaning of 'Commissioners' and 'officer', as below:

> In this Part –
>
> 'the Commissioners' means the Commissioners for Her Majesty's Revenue and Customs, and
> 'officer' means an officer of Revenue and Customs.

3.24.2 APA Defined

514. An APA is a written agreement between a business and the Commissioners of HMRC which determines a method for resolving transfer pricing issues in advance of a return being made. When the terms of the agreement are complied with, it provides assurance to the business that the treatment of those transfer pricing issues will be accepted by HMRC for the period covered by the agreement. A bilateral APA provides a similar assurance in respect of the tax administration dealing with the entity at the other end of the transaction. Businesses operating in several countries may wish to seek APAs that involve all the relevant administrations affected by the transfer pricing issues. The term 'multilateral APA' has been used to describe such agreements, but there is no discrete mechanism for reaching multilateral agreements, and multilateral

APAs are strictly multiple and complementary bilateral APAs. As unilateral APAs are generally of less value to both HMRC and potential applicants and provide less transparency, applications for unilateral APAs are less likely to be accepted into the APA programme. Unilateral APAs are accepted where the other party to the transaction(s) is resident in a jurisdiction with which the UK has no DTAA, the treaty partner has no APA process, or HMRC considers there is little to be gained by seeking a bilateral agreement. However, each case is considered on the basis of its facts and features.

515. Typically, the APA term is from three to five years, and a longer term is considered in exceptional circumstances. There is no filing fee. Except where 'rollback' is being considered, the request for an APA in respect of future years will not in itself affect any transfer pricing enquiry into earlier years. However, to the extent such an approach is appropriate and feasible, HMRC coordinates the APA request in respect of future years with any transfer pricing enquiry in respect of prior years in order to improve overall efficiency and reduce duplication of enquiries.

3.24.3 Rollback of APA

516. The agreed TPM may be relevant for an earlier period, and to the resolution of any transfer pricing enquiries raised for earlier periods, if the particular facts and circumstances surrounding those years are substantially the same. Consequently, in such circumstances, the business may wish to consider requesting that the bilateral APA also covers this earlier period and is used as a basis for amending their self-assessment return for those years. This possibility is dependent on the ability and willingness of both administrations to 'rollback'. Rollback is available on a case-by-case basis after HMRC's consideration of the relevant facts and circumstances. In bilateral cases, the decision will also depend on the ability or willingness of the relevant foreign tax authorities.

3.24.4 APA Team

517. HMRC's Business, Assets and International Transfer Pricing Team are responsible for all the APA applications. The process involves such specialists and delegated CA officials as are necessary, and it is also ensured that the business' Customer Compliance Manager is duly involved.

3.24.5 Pre-filing (Expression of Interest) Meeting

518. At least one 'expression of interest meeting' with HMRC is recommended in order to discuss *inter alia* the following:

- the nature of the transfer pricing issues intended to be covered by an APA;
- details of the tax residence of the parties involved and importance to the wider business of the transactions covered;

- a description of the proposed TP method; and
- an indication of the nature of any current transfer pricing enquiries, CA claims, and any other relevant issues that the business is aware of in the context of the suggested APA, including the potential of Diverted Profits Tax (DPT) to apply to the covered transactions.

519. An APA may be requested by any one of the following:

- UK resident business, including a partnership, with transactions to which the provisions of Part 4 TIOPA 2010 apply.
- Any non-resident trading in the UK through a PE.
- Any UK resident trading through a PE outside the UK.

520. Anonymous pre-filing is not available. Negotiations between the taxpayer and HMRC during the pre-filing stage will determine the date from which the APA will commence. There is no requirement that the commencement of an APA should coincide with the commencement of the arrangements which it addresses, so it may apply to pre-existing issues. The HMRC is quite discrete in taking up an APA case. Every APA request is considered on the basis of its particular facts and features, but generally HMRC will be looking at the following factors taken together, whether:

- the transfer pricing issues are complex rather than straightforward. To HMRC, 'complex' means there is real doubt as to how the arm's-length standard should be applied. Conversely, where market comparables can be readily identified for the transaction(s) in point, in accordance with the OECD Transfer Pricing Guidelines, HMRC is likely to regard such a situation as 'straightforward'. HMRC will be willing to consider an innovative proposal providing that there is not a more appropriate and straightforward method, it is compliant with OECD Guidelines, and not one that HMRC considers it or its treaty partners would regard as being overtly tax aggressive;
- without an APA there is a high likelihood of double taxation.
- HMRC considers that it is a good use of taxpayer and governmental resources.

521. In UK, APAs are not declined solely by reference to the size of the transactions giving rise to the transfer pricing issues because HMRC recognizes that complex transfer pricing issues can be encountered by smaller businesses as well as large multinationals. However, many SMEs are exempt from the UK transfer pricing legislation by virtue of section 166 TIOPA 2010, and so there may be limited occasions where the APA process will be appropriate for smaller businesses.

522. The APA legislation does not provide for a determination that a PE does or does not exist. The determination of profits to be attributed to any PE will only be considered for inclusion in an APA once the existence of the PE through which a company has been, or is proposing to, carrying on a trade in the UK is established. Similarly, the APA legislation also does not provide for a determination of the potential impact of the DPT or other legislation on the covered transactions. The applicants are advised that these issues should be raised with HMRC at the pre-filing stage.

3.24.6 APA Application

523. Where, following HMRC's indication that it is willing to consider the APA proposal, the applicant wishes to proceed, it is required to submit a formal written application within six months or such longer period explicitly agreed at the pre-filing meeting. If there is a delay in submitting a written application, HMRC reserves the right to not accept it. The application should ideally be made before the start of the first chargeable period proposed to be covered by the APA, but HMRC may exercise discretion over this, for instance, when a bilateral APA is sought and the other administration is prepared to allow the business more time to lodge its application. The APA application is required to contain the following information:

(1) the applicant's understanding of the effect of the relevant legislation and DTTA(s) in relation to the relevant transfer pricing issues;
(2) the areas where clarification to that effect is required; and
(3) a proposal for clarifying the effect of the legislation in accordance with the applicant's understanding.
(4) all proposals are required to be supported by:
  - identification of the parties and accounts for previous three years;
  - description of the transfer pricing issues proposed, analysis of the functions and risks, and actual and projected financial data of the parties;
  - description of the global group structure, and major categories of transaction flows of the relevant parties;
  - description of records to be maintained in support of proposed TP method and information demonstrating that the taxpayer's tax returns will conform to the APA's terms;
  - description of any current tax enquiries or HMRC claims relevant to issues covered by the proposed APA;
  - chargeable periods to be covered by the APA;
  - identification of assumptions made in developing the proposed TP method critical to the reliability of its application under the arm's-length standard;
  - analysis of the DPT position in respect of the covered transactions and any transactions directly connected to them;
  - any current or expired rulings issued by a foreign tax authority; and
  - where appropriate, a request for HMRC assistance in reaching a bilateral or multilateral APA.

3.24.7 Evaluation of APA Application

524. On receipt of an application, HMRC evaluates its contents and seeks clarification and further information from the business as necessary. The examination of the application is a cooperative process in which the transfer pricing issues are discussed openly and access to relevant supporting information and documentation is made available. Lack of cooperation in these respects may result in HMRC declining to give any further consideration to the application. Where a bilateral APA is being sought, HMRC expects the business to continue to make relevant information available at the same time to each administration involved, and in turn itself keeps the treaty partner informed about the progress of its examination of the APA request, seeks to discuss with the treaty partner key issues arising at the earliest opportunity and keeps the business informed about the progress of the bilateral process. While the finalizing of a bilateral agreement with a treaty partner is a government-to-government process, HMRC is generally prepared to participate in, and encourages, joint meetings involving the business and the other administration(s) to assist in the exploration and evaluation of key factual issues.

525. HMRC aims to complete the APA process within eighteen to twenty-one months from the date of the formal submission. This objective is dependent on the complexity of the case and, in the case of bilateral or multilateral applications, may be dependent on the working practice of the administration(s) in the other country or countries. It is also, of course, dependent on cooperation from the applicant. HMRC may view significant delay on the part of the business as indicative of a lack of cooperation or a loss of interest in agreeing to an APA and may then terminate the APA process as a result. A business may withdraw an APA request at any time before final agreement is reached.

3.24.8 Advance Pricing Agreement

526. The agreement between HMRC and the business is made subject to its terms being observed. The terms *inter alia* include the following:

- A commitment from the business to demonstrate adherence to the agreed method for dealing with the transfer pricing issues during the term of the APA in the form of a regular compliance report (an 'Annual Report') as required by section 228 TIOPA 2010.
- The identification of Critical Assumptions bearing materially on the reliability of the method and which, if subject to change, may render the agreement invalid. This will generally include an assumption that the relevant transfer pricing law and OECD Guidelines remain materially the same.

527. It is possible that a chargeable period to which the APA relates may have ended before agreement is reached. Section 224, TIOPA 2010, allows the APA to be effective for that chargeable period, and the agreement may set out any adjustments to be made for tax purposes as a consequence of the agreement. HMRC and generally its treaty partners expect the actual pricing of the transactions covered by an APA to be consistent with the TPM and terms defined within it. Adjustments arising within the tax computation are expected to also be made in the accounts, thereby ensuring that the economic and tax position of the ALP is aligned.

3.24.9 Annual Report

528. The Annual Report will generally accompany the business' tax return. The particular requirements of each report will be set out in the finalized agreement and will focus narrowly on the issue covered by the APA. Thus, relevant details as to what should be included in the Annual Report are provided on a case-by-case basis. The broad intention is that annual reports should demonstrate, in a concise format, whether the business has complied with the terms and conditions of the APA.

3.24.10 Renewal of APA

529. Where the facts and circumstances have not changed, the business may request renewal of an APA for an additional fixed period. Applications for the renewal of APAs are required to be lodged six months before expiry. HMRC may consider interest in a renewal in light of current international thinking and HMRC's practice at the time. It may also consider whether the previous APA methodology and its monitoring requirements for all parties have functioned as well as intended. There is no expectation within the HMRC that a renewal will always be worthwhile and any renewal process is also dependent on the view and approach of the relevant treaty partners.

3.24.11 Revision of APA

530. In some cases, the APA may provide for modification of its terms in specific circumstances; for example, a particular agreement may provide that where there has been a change which makes the agreed methodology difficult to apply, but which does not go as far as to invalidate a critical assumption, the agreement may be modified with the consent of the parties to resolve that difficulty. In such cases, the APA may be revised in accordance with section 225, TIOPA 2010 after consultations between the business and HMRC and, in the case of bilateral agreements, the CA of the other country involved.

3.24.12 Revocation of APA

531. In accordance with section 225, TIOPA 2010, an APA may be revoked by HMRC in accordance with its terms, where the business does not comply with the terms and conditions of the agreement, or where the identified critical assumptions cease to be valid. In practice, when considering nullifying, revoking or cancelling a bilateral APA,

HMRC will consult with the business and with the CA of the treaty partner involved. Where false or misleading information is supplied fraudulently, or negligently, in connection with an application for or in the process of monitoring an APA, penalties may be applied and the APA might be nullified.

3.24.13 Confidentiality of Information

532. APA information is subject to the same rules of confidentiality as any other information about taxpayers. Information exchanged with treaty partners, for instance, in the course of BAPA process is also protected from disclosure by the terms of the Exchange of Information Article in the relevant DTAA.

3.24.14 Statistics

533. Statistics on the number of APA requests received and resolved in various years in UK are provided in Figure 11.

Figure 11 Number of APA Requests Received and Resolved in Various Years in United Kingdom

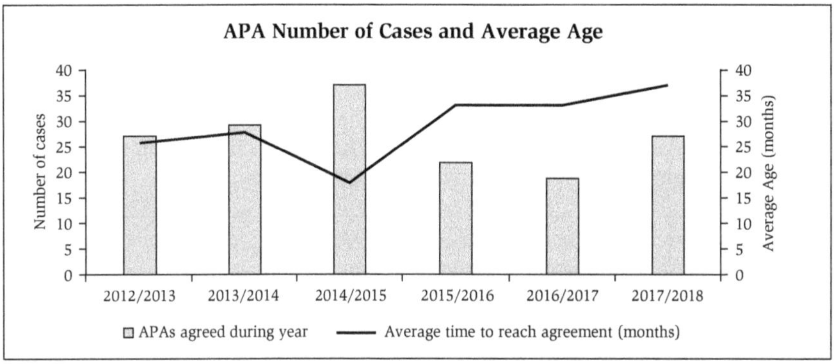

	2012/2013	*2013/2014*	*2014/2015*	*2015/2016*	*2016/2017*	*2017/2018*
Applications made during year	45	43	66	47	32	16
Applications turned down	0	0	2	3	5	6
APAs agreed during year	27	29	37	22	19	27
Average time to reach agreement (months)	26	27.8	18.00	33.00	32.8	37.1
50% agreed within (months)	15	19.7	15.6	32.3	34.7	35.1

Source: Data published by United Kingdom https://assets.publishing.service.gov.uk/government/uploads/system/uploads/attachment_data/file/729876/Transfer_Pricing_and_Diverted_Profits_Tax_statistics.pdf.

3.24.15 Ready Reckoner on Availability of Article 9(2), BAPA and Rollback Provisions

534. UK allows unilateral, bilateral and multilateral APAs, as well as rollback of APAs. A ready reckoner on existence of Article 9(2) to relieve economic double taxation in DTAAs between UK and various countries and the presence of BAPA and rollback provisions in the legislation of UK's treaty partners is provided in Table 25 by analysing the following database:

- status of Article 9(2) as provided under OECD MTC, 2017 in the DTAA[199] between UK and respective treaty partner;
- if not already present, whether Article 9(2) shall get introduced through the MLI[200] in such DTAAs;
- the country MAP/Dispute Resolution profiles[201] of the respective treaty partners available on the OECD website.

Table 25 Ready Reckoner on Availability of Article 9(2), BAPA and Rollback Between United Kingdom and Treaty Partners

S. N.	*Treaty Partner*	*Date of Signature of DTAA*	*Does Article 9(2) Already Exist?*	*If No, Will It Come Through MLI?*	*Does the Treaty Partner Have BAPA?*	*Does the Treaty Partner Have Rollback?*
1	Australia	21.08.2003	Yes *	–	Yes	Yes
2	Austria	23.10.2018	Yes	–	Yes	Yes
3	Belgium	01.06.1987	Yes **	Yes **	Yes	Yes
4	Bulgaria	26.03.2015	Yes **	Yes **	No	No
5	Canada	08.09.1978	Yes	–	Yes	Yes
6	China	27.06.2011	Yes **	Yes **	Yes	Yes
7	Colombia	02.11.2016	Yes	–	Yes	Yes
8	Croatia	15.01.2015	Yes	–	Yes	No
9	Denmark	11.11.1980	Yes **	Yes **	Yes	Yes
10	Finland	17.07.1969	Yes ***	–	No formal programme. But can be considered based on MAP article	Can be considered
11	France	19.06.2008	Yes ***	Yes **	Yes	No
12	Georgia	13.07.2004	Yes	–	No	No
13	Germany	30.03.2010	Yes	–	Yes	Yes
14	Greece	25.06.1953	No	Yes	Yes	No
15	Hong Kong	21.06.2010	Yes	–	Yes	Yes
16	Hungary	07.09.2011	Yes	–	Yes	Yes
17	Iceland	17.12.2013	Yes	–	No	No
18	India	25.01.1993	Yes ***	–	Yes	Yes

199. Refer IBFD Tax Research Platform https://research.ibfd.org accessed on 17 February 2021.
200. Refer OECD – Signatories and Parties to the MLI http://www.oecd.org/tax/treaties/beps-mli-signatories-and-parties.pdf accessed on 17 February 2021.
201. Refer MAP profiles on www.oecd.org https://www.oecd.org/tax/dispute/country-map-profiles.htm accessed on 17 February 2021.

S. N.	*Treaty Partner*	*Date of Signature of DTAA*	*Does Article 9(2) Already Exist?*	*If No, Will It Come Through MLI?*	*Does the Treaty Partner Have BAPA?*	*Does the Treaty Partner Have Rollback?*
19	Indonesia	05.04.1993	Yes ****	Yes **	Yes	Yes @
20	Ireland	02.06.1976	Yes *****	Yes **	Yes	Yes
21	Israel	26.09.1962	Yes ******	–	No formal programme. But can be considered based on MAP article	No
22	Italy	21.10.1988	No	Yes	Yes	No
23	Japan	02.02.2006	Yes **	Yes **	Yes	Yes
24	Kazakhstan	21.03.1994	Yes **	Yes **	Yes	No
25	Kenya	31.07.1973	No	Yes	No	No
26	Malaysia	10.12.1996	Yes	–	Yes	Yes
27	Mexico	02.06.1994	Yes	–	Yes	Yes
28	The Netherlands	26.09.2008	Yes **	Yes **	Yes	Yes
29	New Zealand	04.08.1983	Yes *******	Yes **	Yes	Yes
30	Norway	14.03.2013	Yes	–	Yes	Yes
31	Poland	20.07.2006	Yes	–	Yes	No
32	Portugal	27.03.1968	Yes *******	Yes **	Yes	No
33	Romania	18.09.1975	Yes ********	Yes **	Yes	No
34	Russia	15.02.1994	Yes	–	Yes	No
35	Serbia	06.11.1981	No	Yes	No	No
36	Singapore	12.02.1997	Yes **	Yes **	Yes	Yes
37	The Slovak Republic	05.11.1990	Yes *******	–	Yes	Yes
38	Slovenia	13.11.2007	Yes	–	Yes	Yes
39	South Africa	04.07.2002	Yes **	Yes **	No	No
40	Spain	14.03.2013	Yes	–	Yes	Yes
41	Sweden	26.03.2015	Yes	–	Yes	Yes
42	The Swiss Confederation	08.12.1977	Yes	–	Yes	Yes
43	Turkey	19.02.1986	Yes	–	Yes	Yes
44	UAE	12.04.2016	Yes **	Yes **	No	No
45	Uruguay	24.02.2016	Yes	–	No	No

S. N.	Treaty Partner	Date of Signature of DTAA	Does Article 9(2) Already Exist?	If No, Will It Come Through MLI?	Does the Treaty Partner Have BAPA?	Does the Treaty Partner Have Rollback?
46	US	24.07.2001	Yes	–	Yes	Yes
47	Vietnam	09.04.1994	Yes	–	Yes	No

* Such provisions are in Article 9(3) of the DTAA.
** Such provisions are not as per Article 9(2) of the OECD MTC, 2017 in entirety; hence, appropriate notification under Article 17 of MLI has been made by UK and the respective treaty partner.
*** Such provisions are in Article 10(2) of the DTAA.
**** Such provisions are in Article 21(5) of the DTAA.
***** Such provisions are in Article 21(4) of the DTAA.
****** Such provisions are in Article IV(2) of the DTAA.
******* Such provisions are in Article 22(4) of the DTAA.
******** Such provisions are in Article 24(4) of the DTAA.
@ Indonesia's Dispute Resolution Profile (last updated on 1 September 2016) states that rollback of APA is not permissible under the Indonesian APA programme. However, under the revised Ministry of Finance Regulation No. 22/PMK.03/2020, rollback is available in Indonesia.

3.25 APA REGIME IN US

535. The US has had an APA programme since 1991. The CA in charge of the APA programme in US is Advance Pricing and Mutual Agreement (APMA) office, under the Large Business and International (LB&I) Division of the Internal Revenue Service (IRS). The relevant provisions in regard to the implementation of the APA programme in US are contained in the Revenue Procedure 2015-41[202] and Guidance available on the APMA office website.[203]

536. Unilateral, bilateral, and multilateral APAs are available in the US. Although the appropriate APA term is determined on a case-by-case basis, an APA request typically proposes at least five prospective years, unless the taxpayer states a compelling reason to include fewer years. Additionally, in the interest of principled, effective, and efficient tax administration, APMA typically seeks to set the APA term so that there are at least three unexpired years (i.e., years that have not yet ended) remaining in the APA term upon the execution of the APA (in the case of a unilateral APA) or upon the execution of the underlying CA resolution (in the case of a bilateral or multilateral APA). APMA may require that the taxpayer agrees to extend the APA term in order to achieve that

202. Refer Rev. Proc. 2015-41 https://www.irs.gov/pub/irs-drop/rp-15-41.pdf accessed on 17 February 2021.
203. Refer DLA Piper – APA and MAP Country Guide 2019 https://www.dlapiper.com/en/us/insights/publications/2019/03/apa-and-map-country-guide-2019/ accessed on 11 August 2020.

goal. In the case of a bilateral or multilateral APA, any proposed term extension is coordinated with the relevant foreign CAs.

537. APA filing fee (user fee) is required to be paid under the US APA regime, as under:

- General fee: USD 60,000.
- Renewal fee: USD 35,000.
- Small cases fee: USD 30,000.
- Each amendment to a current unilateral, bilateral, or multilateral APA: USD 12,500.

538. If multiple APA requests are filed by the same controlled group within a sixty-day period, the maximum total fee charged will be USD 60,000, plus USD 30,000 for each foreign CA involved (if any) beyond the first two.

3.25.1 Rollback of APA

539. An APA may cover one or more rollback years. Taxpayers are required to include a rollback request as part of its APA request. APMA may consider implementing a rollback even in the absence of a request. The rollback request must include the same kind of information regarding the proposed rollback years that is required to be submitted regarding the proposed prospective years. After coordinating and collaborating with other offices within the IRS, APMA will inform the taxpayer whether its rollback request has been accepted for consideration. Except in unusual circumstances, APMA does not agree to cover a closed filed year with a rollback of a unilateral APA request. For a rollback that is requested in conjunction with a bilateral or multilateral APA request, APMA agrees to cover:

- an open filed year only if it would agree to accept a CA or accelerated competent authority procedure (ACAP) request covering such year, and
- a closed filed year only if it would agree to accept a CA or ACAP request covering such year and only if the applicable US tax treaty(ies) allows the corresponding CA resolution to be implemented in that filed year.

540. Regardless of whether the taxpayer pursues a rollback request, APMA reserves the right to coordinate with applicable IRS offices to pursue a rollback to any or all of the taxpayer's open back years. In general, APMA will consider taking such action where there is sufficient similarity in relevant facts and circumstances across the proposed prospective years and the taxpayer's open back years. APMA informs the taxpayer in writing, either before the APA process begins or at any time during the APA process, whether it will pursue a rollback and the back years it will seek to cover. If the taxpayer refuses to accept a rollback, and after considering the taxpayer's reasons for the refusal, APMA may decline to initiate the APA process or may suspend or terminate the process if it has already begun.

3.25.2 APA Team[204]

541. As of 22 December 2018, the APMA Program included fifty-six team leaders, twelve economists, six managers and three assistant directors. Each assistant director oversees two managers who lead teams comprised of both team leaders and economists. The APMA Program's main office is in Washington, DC, and it also has a significant presence in San Francisco and the Los Angeles area.

3.25.3 APA Process

542. In the APA process, the taxpayer is required to undertake the following:

- meet the pre-filing requirements, as applicable;
- submit a complete APA request;
- pay the correct user fee;
- supplement its APA request and provide updated information.

Throughout the APA process, the taxpayer and the IRS will execute consent agreements as necessary to extend the period of limitations for assessment of tax for each proposed APA year (including both proposed prospective years and proposed rollback years).

3.25.5 Pre-filing Meeting

543. APMA may require the taxpayer to meet in a pre-filing conference and submit a pre-filing memorandum. Both optional and mandatory pre-filing memoranda must be accompanied by an APMA pre-filing conference request form, available on the IRS website. Pre-filing meeting is also available on an anonymous basis.

544. A mandatory pre-filing memorandum that identifies the taxpayer must be filed if:

(1) the taxpayer wishes to file a unilateral APA request to cover an issue that could be covered under a bilateral or multilateral APA under the pertinent tax treaty(ies);
(2) the taxpayer seeks permission to file an abbreviated APA request; or
(3) the covered issue(s) proposed by the taxpayer will, or could reasonably be expected to, involve any of the following:
    - the licence or other transfer of intangibles in connection with, or the development of intangibles under, an intangible development arrangement;
    - a global trading arrangement;

204. Refer Announcement and Report Concerning Advance Pricing Agreements dated 22 March 2019 of the Secretary of the Treasury, USA https://www.irs.gov/pub/irs-drop/a-19-03.pdf accessed on 4 August 2019.

- a business restructuring, or the use of intangibles whose ownership changed as a result of a business restructuring; or
- unincorporated branches, pass-through entities, hybrid entities, or entities disregarded for US tax purposes.

545. A taxpayer may voluntarily submit an optional pre-filing memorandum in cases other than those set forth above. Although not required, APMA generally recommends that a pre-filing memorandum be submitted for APA requests that may present novel or complex substantive or procedural issues, and APA requests for which APMA could reasonably have concerns regarding interrelated matters.

546. A mandatory pre-filing memorandum must have a length and content appropriate to the size and complexity of the covered issue(s) proposed by the taxpayer, and must be primarily in memorandum form but may be accompanied by diagrams, slides, spreadsheets, and similar supporting materials. An optional pre-filing memorandum must have a length and content appropriate to the substantive or procedural issues the taxpayer wishes to raise with APMA. Whether mandatory or optional, a pre-filing memorandum must do the following:

(1) state whether the taxpayer seeks a pre-filing conference and, if so, the issues the taxpayer wishes to discuss;
(2) propose at least three possible dates for a pre-filing conference that normally would be at least two weeks after the date that the pre-filing memorandum is submitted, if either the pre-filing memorandum is mandatory (whether or not the taxpayer seeks a pre-filing conference, which might be required by APMA) or the pre-filing memorandum is optional and the taxpayer seeks a pre-filing conference;
(3) include covered issue diagrams if the pre-filing memorandum is mandatory;
(4) if mandatory pre-filing and if submitted to seek permission to file an abbreviated APA request, the memorandum must:
    - specify any information, documents, or other materials the taxpayer proposes to omit from its APA request;
    - present the taxpayer's arguments that the information, documents, or other materials the taxpayer proposes to omit from its APA request are not necessary for APMA's evaluation of the APA request, including if applicable the taxpayer's arguments that the applicable law, facts and circumstances, economic conditions, proposed covered issue(s) and method(s), and other factors relevant to the proposed APA years are substantially the same as those relevant to the current APA or the CA resolution as the case may be; and
    - in the case of a proposed renewal APA, summarize in a table the results and adjustments under the current APA, in absolute and (as applicable) percentage terms (e.g., operating margin), with

comparison to any arm's-length points or ranges specified in the APA, and also summarize any proposed changes in terms from the current APA.

(5) list the name and contact information of the taxpayer, and authorization for the taxpayer's representatives and points of contact to inspect or receive confidential tax information (unless the pre-filing memorandum is submitted on an anonymous basis); and

(6) identify all open back years and which, if any, are under investigation by the IRS.

547. Two printed copies and one electronic copy of the pre-filing memorandum are required to be submitted to APMA. APMA notifies the taxpayer whether it accepts or declines a request to hold a pre-filing conference, and may require a conference even where one has not been requested for. If APMA decides to hold a pre-filing conference, the conference is supposed to address procedural and substantive issues pertinent to the APA request. During the conference, the taxpayer is required to be prepared to discuss the relevant facts and circumstances surrounding the issue(s), method(s), and terms and conditions it proposes to cover in the APA, and (if applicable) the taxpayer's justification for its request to file an abbreviated APA request. If APMA decides against holding a pre-filing conference, it will direct the taxpayer to proceed with its APA request. Unless the taxpayer has submitted a mandatory pre-filing memorandum, which requires identification of the taxpayer, or has otherwise identified the taxpayer, a pre-filing conference may be held on an anonymous basis. APMA generally recommends, however, that pre-filing conferences be held on a named basis to facilitate a more informed discussion of procedural and substantive issues that may arise during the APA process.

548. APMA's interest and preference are for bilateral and multilateral APAs over unilateral APAs. To minimize taxpayer and governmental uncertainty and administrative cost, bilateral and multilateral APAs are generally preferable to unilateral APAs. If a taxpayer requests a unilateral APA to cover any issue that could be covered under a bilateral or multilateral APA under the applicable tax treaty(ies), the taxpayer must explain in a pre-filing memorandum as to why it believes that a unilateral APA is appropriate to cover that issue. Reasons which the taxpayer may have for not pursuing BAPA/MAPA could be that there is no APA process with the treaty country, or that the taxpayer's proposed covered issues involve so many treaty countries that bilateral APAs or a multilateral APA would be impractical. After taking into account the taxpayer's views expressed in the memorandum (and in a pre-filing conference), APMA will inform the taxpayer whether it will accept a unilateral APA request. APMA may reject a taxpayer's unilateral APA request for various reasons, particularly when accepting it would contravene procedures and practices established with particular treaty partners.

3.25.6 APA Application

549. The US APA programme provides that all APA requests must contain a request letter, as well as the following twenty-two exhibits:

(1) contents of exhibits - provide a table or similar comprehensive list of the exhibits submitted, indicating the form in which they have been submitted;
(2) authorization forms - for representatives of the taxpayer (e.g., an enrolled agent, lawyer or certified public accountant), and/or for those authorized to inspect or receive confidential information about the taxpayer;
(3) protective claim - for bilateral or multilateral APAs, a statement affirming whether the request is to serve as a protective claim;
(4) waiver of ex parte communication - if the APA involves rollback years, a waiver of the taxpayer's right to be present during communications between the IRS Appeals and the APMA team;
(5) consent to disclosure - for disclosure of an APA request to any applicable foreign tax authorities;
(6) consents regarding period of limitations - any executed consents to extend the period of limitations for assessment of tax;
(7) 'penalties of perjury' declaration - a declaration signed by the taxpayer that the APA request and supporting documentation contain all relevant facts, and that such facts are true, correct and complete;
(8) user fee receipt - obtained after paying required APA user fee;
(9) documents submitted to foreign CAs - a list of all documentation or written submissions provided to foreign tax authorities in connection with the APA request;
(10) pre-filing submissions - any pre-filing memoranda submitted in connection with the APA request;
(11) covered issue diagrams - including the controlled group's legal structure, tax structure, business units, the value chain of the proposed covered group, and organizational charts;
(12) APAs - the most recent APA, if any, that the taxpayer has entered into with the IRS or foreign tax authorities;
(13) selection process - a report on results of applying criteria for selecting comparable agreements or independent comparable companies or other market data, including tables or matrix showing reasons for rejecting agreements, independent companies or other market data;
(14) information on selected comparables - a detailed discussion of the contractual terms of selected comparable agreements, as applicable;
(15) proposed draft APA - submitted in a form similar to APMA's current model APA (available on the APMA website or on request) and a 'redline' version of the same showing the differences between the model APA and the proposed draft APA;
(16) application of APA template - for APA requests that involve an application of the comparable profit method or the TNMM, taxpayers are required to

provide income statement data for the previous five taxable years and balance sheet data for the previous six taxable years for the relevant members of the proposed covered group, using the template provided by the IRS;

(17) federal income tax filings - Forms 1120, 5471, 5472, 8858 for each of the three most recent filed years of the taxpayer;

(18) financial statements - full income statements, balance sheets, cash flow statements for the most recent three back years, specifying accounting standard used;

(19) section 6662 documentation - documentation prepared in consideration of the transfer pricing penalty under IRC section 6662(e) for each relevant member of the proposed covered group for each of the most recent three back years;

(20) regulatory filings - Securities and Exchange Commission filing by the controlled group for each of the most recent three back years;

(21) APA annual reports - for renewal requests only; and

(22) intercompany agreements - copies of intercompany contracts or agreements between the taxpayer and other members of the covered group within the scope of the covered issues.

550. A taxpayer is required to file an APA request within the time prescribed for filing its federal income tax return for the first proposed APA year. In order to better coordinate the timing of discussions on bilateral and multilateral APAs with foreign CAs, the taxpayer is required to file a complete bilateral or multilateral APA request no later than sixty days after a corresponding bilateral or multilateral request proposing to cover substantially the same coverable issue(s) and APA years has been filed with a foreign CA. For this purpose, the filing of a corresponding request with a foreign CA shall be understood to mean the filing of a substantive request with that foreign CA rather than the mere filing of a notice of intent to file a substantive request.

551. APMA will consider an APA request to be complete if it:

- is accompanied by payment of the correct user fee;
- contains all the information required (subject to any exceptions agreed to by APMA); and
- proposes covered methods that provide a reasonable basis on which to consider resolution of the proposed covered issues.

For this purpose, a subsequent remedy of minor deficiencies, made promptly under the circumstances, will relate back to the time of original filing. In exceptional circumstances, APMA may also allow a subsequent remedy of substantial deficiencies, made promptly under the circumstances, to relate back to the time of original filing. APMA's decision of whether, and when, a complete APA request is filed or considered filed is not subject to administrative review.

552. Submission of a complete APA request does not, in itself, suspend examination or enforcement proceedings. Although APMA coordinates within the IRS to minimize duplicative requests in conducting its due diligence, the taxpayer duly remains obligated to respond to information document requests issued, and according to deadlines set, by other IRS offices in any examination or enforcement proceedings.

3.25.7 Abbreviated APA Request

553. An abbreviated APA request is the one in which information, documents, or content required for a complete APA request has been truncated or omitted, in pursuance of explicit authorization from APMA. The taxpayer must obtain prior permission from APMA to file an abbreviated APA request. An abbreviated APA request that the taxpayer files without such permission will not be considered a complete APA request. An abbreviated APA request might be appropriate in the following situations (as described in Revenue Procedure 2015-41):

- for expansion of a CA request under Revenue Procedure 2015-40 into APA years under certain circumstances described in section 5.01(2);
- for APA renewals under certain circumstances described in section 8;
- for APA requests eligible for the small case user fee in certain circumstances as specified in section 3.04 of the Appendix; and
- in other exceptional circumstances.

554. In evaluating the taxpayer's request to file an abbreviated APA request, APMA will consider that in most cases it can most efficiently process an APA request when the APA request itself contains all documents reasonably needed to evaluate that request, even if some of those documents have been submitted before to the IRS. Before requesting permission to file an abbreviated APA request, the taxpayer should consider whether the documents that it proposes to omit from the APA request could alternatively be provided as exhibits to that request.

555. To request permission to file an abbreviated APA request that is not eligible for the small case APA user fee, the taxpayer must file a pre-filing memorandum. After reviewing the pre-filing memorandum and (if applicable) holding a pre-filing conference, APMA will inform the taxpayer either that APMA will accept an abbreviated APA request (in which case APMA will instruct the taxpayer on the content of the request), or that APMA will require a complete APA request.

556. To request permission to file an abbreviated APA request that is eligible for the small case APA user fee, the taxpayer may contact APMA informally to discuss the proposed contents of the request. After discussion with the taxpayer and consideration of any written material submitted by the taxpayer, APMA will inform the taxpayer either that APMA will accept an abbreviated APA request (in which case APMA will instruct the taxpayer on the content of the request) or that APMA will require a complete APA request.

3.25.8 Corrected and Updated Information to Be Filed by Taxpayer

557. After the APA request is filed, any material errors or material omissions in the APA request or in supplemental submissions are required to be promptly corrected or remedied by the taxpayer. The taxpayer is required to timely notify APMA of all material changes and updates to information previously submitted in connection with the APA request. The taxpayer is also required to submit any information or documents discovered or created during the APA process that is material to the APA request. Any financial data that are produced in connection with the APA request during the APA process, and that relate to the application of the proposed covered methods to the proposed covered issues, are required to be updated annually or on a schedule that is mutually acceptable to the taxpayer and to APMA. In addition, the APA request is required to be supplemented with a demonstration of the application of the proposed covered method(s) to the actual financial results of the applicable members of the proposed covered group for each taxable year completed while the APA request is pending. Such a supplemental submission is required to be provided within 180 days of the close of the taxpayer's taxable year, or by a date that is mutually acceptable to the taxpayer and to APMA. APMA recognizes that additional time may be appropriate if the covered methods require data from foreign parties that have different taxable years than the taxpayer. APMA may, at its discretion, grant an extension or modify these requirements if the taxpayer provides written notification before the date the supplemental submission would otherwise be due.

3.25.9 Evaluation of Application

558. In evaluating a bilateral or multilateral APA request, the APA team considers requests from, and may invite or require, the taxpayer to make presentations jointly to the APA team and to the foreign CAs. The provision of such information simultaneously to all CAs could facilitate efficient case processing. The APA team consults as needed with the foreign CAs as to its interest in joint presentations, and notifies the taxpayer accordingly. During the APA process, the APA team may also request teleconferences or in-person meetings with the taxpayer to discuss questions or concerns the APA team may have about the taxpayer's APA request, or to discuss the APA team's provisional views on the request or aspects of the request. The APA team may also invite the taxpayer to provide written responses to memoranda discussing such issues.

559. The APA team may reach a point in the APA process when it prepares to formally present its view on the APA request to the foreign CAs. At this point, the APA team conveys the substance of its views to the taxpayer, generally in a paper or memorandum having a length, content, and format appropriate to the scope and duration of the APA process and to the size and complexity of the proposed covered issue(s) and method(s) and other relevant facts and circumstances surrounding the case. In some cases, the APA team may present the paper or memorandum to the taxpayer for its comment before the APA team formally presents its views to the foreign CAs. In other cases, the APA team may issue the paper or memorandum simultaneously to the taxpayer and to the foreign CAs. The taxpayer is then invited to provide its comments to both the APA team and the foreign CAs for their discussion and consideration towards reaching a CA resolution. The decision as to which approach is taken is within the discretion of the APA team.

560. Many of the steps involved in the evaluation and presentation stage of the APA process as applied to unilateral APA requests are similar to those relating to bilateral and multilateral APA requests. For example, at various points, the APA team may invite the taxpayer to respond, either orally or in writing, as appropriate, to its questions or concerns about, or provisional views on, the APA request. The primary difference is that, in the case of a unilateral APA request, the APA team and the taxpayer will proceed directly to finalize an APA after the APA team has completed its due diligence and evaluation of the APA request and the APA team and the taxpayer have agreed to the APA's covered issue(s), covered method(s), and terms and conditions.

3.25.10 Withdrawal of APA Request

561. The taxpayer may withdraw its APA request at any time before it executes the APA. APMA generally does not refund user fees if the taxpayer withdraws its APA request after APMA has begun its due diligence.

3.25.11 Denial or Discontinuation of the APA Process

562. APMA may decline to enter into or continue with the APA process, either at the outset by rejecting the APA request or by terminating or suspending the APA process after it has accepted the APA request. APMA may take such actions if, for example, there is failure to include the materials required by this revenue procedure in the APA request or the materials requested by the APA team during the APA process. APMA also terminates the APA process for a requested unilateral APA if agreement cannot be reached on the APA's terms. For requested bilateral and multilateral APAs, APMA may terminate the APA process if a CA resolution is not reached; however, in some cases, APMA and the taxpayer might then agree to execute a unilateral APA. APMA's decision to decline to initiate, or to suspend or terminate, the APA process is not subject to administrative review.

3.25.12 Advance Pricing Agreement

563. With regard to either a unilateral APA or a bilateral or multilateral APA, the agreement will become effective on the date when it is has been executed by both the IRS and each entity included within the definition of the taxpayer, and the APA then will have effect as provided therein. When an APA's covered group includes a member of a consolidated group other than the common parent, the common parent must sign the APA. The person who signs an APA for a corporation must be an authorized officer of that corporation, have personal knowledge of the APA's covered issue(s), covered method(s), and terms and conditions, perform duties not limited to obtaining letter rulings or determination letters from the IRS or entering into APAs, and have authorization to sign that corporation's income tax return pursuant to section 6062 of the Code. An APA for a non-corporate taxpayer must be signed by an individual who has personal knowledge of the APA's covered issue(s), covered method(s), and terms and conditions, and who is authorized to sign that taxpayer's income tax return pursuant to section 6061 or 6063 of the Code, as applicable. In the case of a partnership, APMA may additionally require that some or all partners sign the APA.

564. The following are the legal effects of an APA:

- Binding Agreement – An APA is a binding agreement between the taxpayer and the IRS.
- Effect of Compliance – If the taxpayer complies with the APA terms and conditions, the IRS will not contest the application of the covered method(s) to the covered issue(s) of the APA except as provided in the revenue procedure. The taxpayer remains otherwise subject to US income tax laws and applicable US tax treaties.
- Scope of Agreement – Except as otherwise provided, an APA will have no legal effect except with respect to the taxpayer, taxable years, and issues to which the APA specifically relates.
- Use as Evidence – Unless provided otherwise by written agreement or regulations, the IRS and the taxpayer may not introduce the APA or non-factual oral and written representations made in conjunction with the APA request as evidence in any judicial or administrative proceeding regarding any tax year, issue, or person not covered by the APA. This paragraph does not preclude the IRS and the taxpayer from agreeing to roll back the APA's covered method(s), or the IRS' use of any non-factual material otherwise discoverable or obtained other than in the APA process merely because the parties considered the same or similar material in the APA process.
- Use as Admissions – Unless provided otherwise by written agreement or regulations, the IRS and the taxpayer may not introduce a proposed, cancelled, or revoked APA, or any non-factual oral or written representations or submissions made during the APA process, as an admission by the other party, in any judicial or administrative proceeding regarding any taxable year of the requested APA term. This paragraph does not preclude the IRS' use of any non-factual material otherwise discoverable or obtained other than in the APA process merely because APMA and the taxpayer considered the same or similar material in the APA process.

3.25.13 Annual Report

565. On signing the APA, the taxpayer is required to provide an annual report for the duration of the APA, demonstrating compliance with the APA terms and conditions, and any adjustments. The taxpayer is required to document how the conforming adjustment for any APA primary adjustment is made, including the relevant amounts, timing, and manner of all payments and deemed payments, and is required to disclose these facts in the APA annual report for the APA year to which the APA primary adjustment relates. The report is required to be filed with APMA by later of the following:

- the fifteenth day of the twelfth month following the close of the APA year, or
- ninety days after the effective date of the APA.

APMA may agree to alternative filing dates if requested by the taxpayer. For bilateral and multilateral APAs, APMA may require the taxpayer to simultaneously file a copy of the Annual Report with the applicable foreign CAs.

566. APMA requires the following documentation to be enclosed as part of the Annual Report:

- a statement regarding any material differences between business operations during the APA year and the description of business operations contained in the APA request;
- a statement concerning any material changes to the taxpayer's accounting methods and classifications, and methods of estimation from those described in the APA request;
- any changes to the taxpayer notice information;
- a description of any failure to meet critical assumptions;
- a statement identifying whether or not any material information submitted while the APA request was pending is discovered to be false, incorrect or incomplete;
- the amount, reason for, and financial analysis of any compensating adjustments for the APA year;
- the amounts, description, reason for, and financial analysis of any book-tax difference relevant to the TP method for the APA year;
- a statement regarding whether the taxpayer intends to request a renewal, modify or cancel the APA;
- financial statements, analysis and accounting details to demonstrate compliance with the TP method;
- an organizational chart;
- a copy of the APA and any amendments; and
- a penalty of perjury statement.

3.25.14 Renewal of APA

567. Taxpayers may seek renewal of an APA, and the renewal process generally follows the same process as APA requests unless the IRS permits the submission of an abbreviated APA request. An abbreviated APA request may be filed if the taxpayer can show that the applicable law, facts and circumstances, economic conditions, proposed covered issues and methods and other relevant factors are reasonably expected to be substantially the same as those in the proposed renewal APA years. Taxpayers are encouraged to file a request to renew a current APA at least nine months before the expiration of the final APA year.

3.25.15 Revision of APA

568. An APA may be revised by agreement of the parties, and any such revision is effective upon the date of the execution of the revision. APMA may agree to revise an APA in lieu of cancelling or revoking it. If APMA is willing to agree to a revision proposed by the taxpayer to a bilateral or multilateral APA, it will seek the consent of the applicable foreign CAs with respect to the revision. If the US and foreign CAs agree to such revision, or agree to another revision acceptable to the taxpayer, then APMA will agree with the taxpayer to revise the APA. If the US and foreign CAs cannot so agree, the APA remains in force without revision. However, in some cases, APMA and the taxpayer may then agree, for US domestic purposes, to:

- revise the APA with respect to one or more APA years, or
- cancel the APA as of a specific date.

3.25.16 Cancelling or Revoking the APA

569. APMA's cancellation of an APA generally is effective as of the beginning of the taxable year in which the critical assumption failed or the beginning of the taxable year to which the misrepresentation, mistake regarding a material fact, failure to state a material fact, or non-compliance relates. If, however, the cancellation results from a change in case law, statute, regulation, US tax treaty, or coordination agreement, the cancellation generally is effective at the beginning of the year that contains the effective date of the change in case law, statute, regulation, US tax treaty, or coordination agreement. APMA may cancel an APA *inter alia* under the following situations and circumstances:

(1) due to fraud or malfeasance or disregard by the taxpayer in connection with the APA, involving:
    - material facts in the request or subsequent submissions (including an annual report) or
    - lack of good faith compliance with the APA terms and conditions.

(2) due to the taxpayer's misrepresentation, mistake with respect to a material fact, failure to state a material fact, failure to file a timely annual report, or lack of good faith compliance with the APA terms and conditions.
(3) unless the parties agree to revise the APA, APMA will cancel an APA in the event of a failure of a critical assumption or a material change in governing case law, statute, regulation, or applicable treaty.

570. If APMA revokes an APA, the revocation relates back to the first day of the first APA year.

3.25.17 Confidentiality of Information

571. An APA, any background information relating to an APA, and the taxpayer's APA request and any supplementary materials submitted in conjunction with the APA request are return information and are confidential.

3.25.18 Statistics[205]

572. The details of applications filed in the past years are as below:

	Unilateral	*Bilateral*	*Multilateral*	*Total*
Filed in 1991-1999				401
Filed in 2000-2017	570	1,364	11	1,945
Filed in 2018	35	161	7	203
Total Filed in 1991-2018				2,549

573. Details of executed and pending APA applications are as below:

	Unilateral	*Bilateral*	*Multilateral*	*Total*
Total Executed in 1991-2017	590	1,108	15	1,713
Total Executed in 2018	24	81	2	107
Total Executed in 1991-2018	**614**	**1,189**	**17**	**1,820**
Total Pending as of 31/12/2018	**58**	**387**	**13**	**458**
Renewals Executed in 2018	15	45	2	62
Renewals Pending	36	158	1	195

205. Announcement and Report Concerning Advance Pricing Agreements dated 22 March 2019 of the Secretary of the Treasury, USA https://www.irs.gov/pub/irs-drop/a-19-03.pdf accessed on 4 August 2019.

574. Consistent with prior years, roughly 40% of the APAs executed in 2018 were new APAs (i.e., not a renewal of a prior APA). Over half of the bilateral APAs executed in 2018 involved mutual agreements with either Japan or Canada. The number of pending requests continues to rise largely due to the increase in the number of requests filed. As of 31 December 2018, over half of the pending bilateral APA requests involved either Japan or India.

575. Details of APAs revoked or cancelled and applications withdrawn are as below:

	Unilateral	*Bilateral*	*Multilateral*	*Total*
Revoked or Cancelled in 2018	0	0	0	0
Total Revoked or Cancelled in 1991-2018				11
Applications Withdrawn in 2018	7	14	0	21
Total Applications Withdrawn in 1991-2018				253

576. Details of APAs executed industry-wise were found to be as below:

Industry	*Number*
Manufacturing	48
Wholesale/Retail Trade	35
Management	8
Services	7
Finance, Insurance, and Real Estate	4
All Other Industries	5

577. Consistent with prior years, in 2018, the primary TPM used for both the sale of tangible property and the use of intangible property was the comparable profits method/transactional net margin method (CPM/TNMM). The CPM/TNMM was used for 86% of transfers of tangible and intangible property, while all other methods combined accounted for the other 14% of such transactions.

578. The average time taken (in months) in the year 2018 to complete new or renewal of APAs was as below:

	Unilateral		*Bilateral*		*Unilateral & Bilateral*	
	Average	*Median*	*Average*	*Median*	*Average*	*Median*
New	35.4	30.7	47.8	43.2	45.5	41.7
Renewal	32.4	36.3	43.9	42.0	40.8	40.1
New & Renewal	33.4	33.5	45.6	42.1	42.8	40.2

579. Statistics on the number of APA requests received and resolved in various years in US are provided in Figure 12.

Figure 12 Number of APA Requests Received and Resolved in Various Years in United States of America

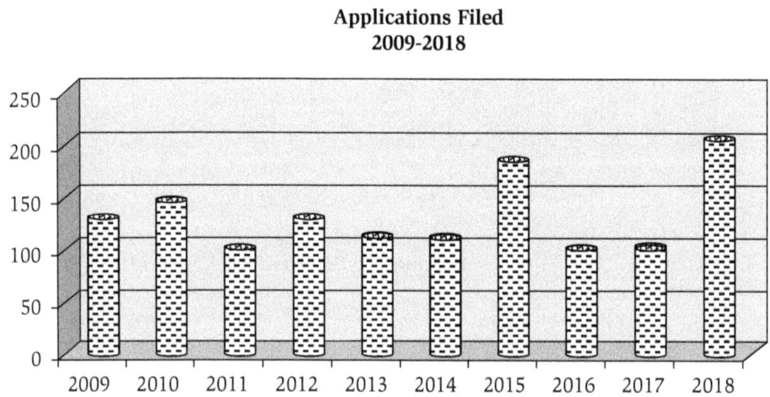

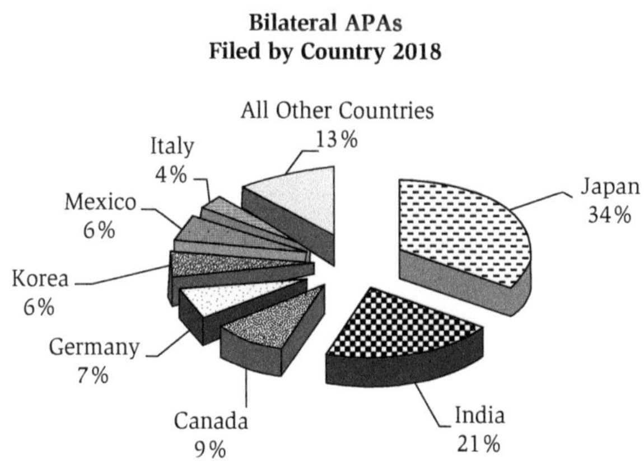

APAs Executed
2009-2018

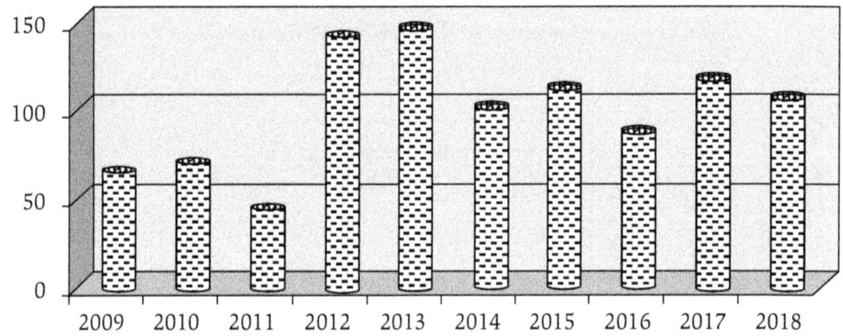

Bilateral APAs
Executed by Country 2018

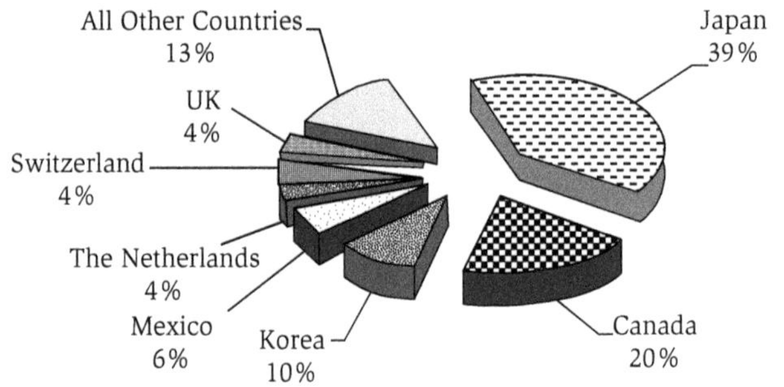

Source: Announcement and Report Concerning Advance Pricing Agreements dated 22 March 2019 of the Secretary of the Treasury, USA https://www.irs.gov/pub/irs-drop/a-19-03.pdf.

3.25.19 Ready Reckoner on Availability of Article 9(2), BAPA and Rollback Provisions

580. US allows unilateral, bilateral and multilateral APAs, as well as rollback of APAs. A ready reckoner on existence of Article 9(2) to relieve economic double taxation in DTAAs between US and various countries and the presence of BAPA and rollback provisions in the legislation of US's treaty partners is provided in Table 26 by analysing the following database:

- status of Article 9(2) as provided under OECD MTC, 2017 in the DTAA[206] between US and respective treaty partner;

206. Refer IBFD Tax Research Platform https://research.ibfd.org accessed on 17 February 2021.

- if not already present, Article 9(2) shall not get introduced through the MLI[207] in such DTAAs, as US is not a signatory to the MLI as of now;
- the country MAP/Dispute Resolution profiles[208] of the respective treaty partners available on the OECD website.

Table 26 Ready Reckoner on Availability of Article 9(2), BAPA and Rollback Between United States of America and Treaty Partners

S. N.	*Treaty Partner*	*Date of Signature of DTAA*	*Does Article 9(2) Already Exist?*	*If No, Will It Come Through MLI?**	*Does the Treaty Partner Have BAPA?*	*Does the Treaty Partner Have Rollback?*
1	Australia	06.08.1982	Yes	NA	Yes	Yes
2	Austria	31.05.1996	Yes	NA	Yes	Yes
3	Belgium	27.11.2006	Yes	NA	Yes	Yes
4	Bulgaria	23.02.2007	Yes	NA	No	No
5	Canada	26.09.1980	Yes **	NA	Yes	Yes
6	China	30.04.1984	Yes ***	NA	Yes	Yes
7	The Czech Republic	16.09.1993	Yes	NA	Yes	No
8	Denmark	19.08.1999	Yes	NA	Yes	Yes
9	Egypt	24.08.1980	Yes ****	NA	No	No
10	Finland	21.09.1989	Yes	NA	No formal programme. But can be considered based on MAP article	Can be considered
11	France	31.08.1994	Yes	NA	Yes	No
12	Georgia	20.06.1973	No	NA	No	No
13	Germany	29.08.1989	Yes	NA	Yes	Yes
14	Greece	20.02.1950	No	NA	Yes	No
15	Hungary	04.02.2010	Yes	NA	Yes	Yes
16	Iceland	23.10.2007	Yes	NA	No	No
17	India	12.09.1989	Yes	NA	Yes	Yes
18	Indonesia	11.07.1988	Yes *****	NA	Yes	Yes @
19	Ireland	28.07.1997	Yes	NA	Yes	Yes

207. Refer OECD – Signatories and Parties to the MLI http://www.oecd.org/tax/treaties/beps-mli-signatories-and-parties.pdf accessed on 17 February 2021.
208. Refer MAP profiles on www.oecd.org https://www.oecd.org/tax/dispute/country-map-profiles.htm accessed on 17 February 2021.

S. N.	*Treaty Partner*	*Date of Signature of DTAA*	*Does Article 9(2) Already Exist?*	*If No, Will It Come Through MLI?**	*Does the Treaty Partner Have BAPA?*	*Does the Treaty Partner Have Rollback?*
20	Israel	20.11.1975	Yes ******	NA	No formal programme. But can be considered based on MAP article	No
21	Italy	25.08.1999	Yes	NA	Yes	No
22	Japan	06.11.2003	Yes	NA	Yes	Yes
23	Kazakhstan	24.10.1993	Yes *******	NA	Yes	No
24	Mexico	18.09.1992	Yes	NA	Yes	Yes
25	The Netherlands	18.12.1992	Yes	NA	Yes	Yes
26	New Zealand	23.07.1982	Yes	NA	Yes	Yes
27	Poland	13.02.2013	Yes	NA	Yes	No
28	Portugal	06.09.1994	Yes	NA	Yes	No
29	Romania	04.12.1973	Yes	NA	Yes	No
30	Russia	17.06.1992	Yes *******	NA	Yes	No
31	Slovenia	21.06.1999	Yes	NA	Yes	Yes
32	South Africa	17.02.1997	Yes	NA	No	No
33	Spain	22.02.1990	Yes	NA	Yes	Yes
34	Sweden	01.09.1994	Yes	NA	Yes	Yes
35	The Swiss Confederation	02.10.1996	Yes	NA	Yes	Yes
36	Thailand	26.11.1996	Yes	NA	Yes	Yes #
37	Turkey	28.03.1996	Yes	NA	Yes	Yes
38	United Kingdom	24.07.2001	Yes	NA	Yes	Yes
39	Vietnam	07.07.2015	Yes	NA	Yes	No

* Article 9(2) shall not get introduced through the MLI in any of the DTAAs, as US is not a signatory to the MLI as of now.

** Such provisions are in Article 9(3) of the DTAA.

*** Such provisions are in Article 8(2) of the DTAA.

**** Such provisions are in Article 10(2) of the DTAA.

***** Such provisions are in Article 10(3) of the DTAA.

****** Such provisions are in Article 11(2) of the DTAA.

******* Such provisions are in Article 7(2) of the DTAA.

@ Indonesia's Dispute Resolution Profile (last updated on 1 September 2016) states that rollback of APA is not permissible under the Indonesian APA programme. However, under the revised Ministry of Finance Regulation No. 22/PMK.03/2020, rollback is available in Indonesia.
# On perusal of Thailand's Dispute Resolution Profile (last updated on 1 June 2020), it is mentioned that rollback of APAs is provided for in the bilateral APA programme. However, Guidance on APA process issued by the Revenue Department of Thailand is silent on this issue.

3.26 APA REGIME IN VIETNAM

581. In Vietnam, APA is defined as a written agreement between a tax administration and a taxpayer, or between Vietnamese tax administration, taxpayer, and a tax administration of a country or territory with which Vietnam has concluded a tax treaty, for a certain period of time, where the basis of tax calculation, pricing methodologies, or market prices are determined in advance.

582. The CA in charge of the APA programme in Vietnam is General Department of Taxation under the Ministry of Finance or an authorized representative. The relevant provisions in regard to the implementation of the APA programme in Vietnam are contained in Circular No. 201/2013/TT-BTC.[209] The Circular is effective from 5 February 2014.

583. Unilateral, bilateral and multilateral APAs are available in Vietnam. The APA is effective for a five-year maximum term. There is no filing fee for APAs in Vietnam.

3.26.1 Salient Provisions of the Circular

584. Some of the prominent provisions on implementation of APAs contained in Circular No. 201/2013/TT-BTC (hereinafter 'Circular')[210] issued by the tax authorities in Vietnam are *inter alia* as below:

(1) Any consultation before official submission of the application shall be held at the request of the taxpayer to determine the suitability of the APA application. Paragraph 2 of Article 8 of the Circular *inter alia* provides for situations for consultation before official submission of the APA application, as below:

   a) The taxpayer intends to enter into an APA (whether it is the first APA application or an application for additional transactions covered by an effective APA);

209. Refer DLA Piper – APA and MAP Country Guide 2019 https://www.dlapiper.com/en/us/insights/publications/2019/03/apa-and-map-country-guide-2019/ accessed on 11 August 2020.
210. Refer Circular No. 201/2013/TT-BTC https://vanbanphapluat.co/circular-no-201-2013-tt-btc-application-of-advance-pricing-agreements-to-tax-administration accessed on 26 March 2021.

b) The taxpayer shall submit the application for renewal of the APA when the expiration of the current APA is approaching;
c) A taxpayer that has signed a unilateral APA with a tax administration wishes to switch to a bilateral/multilateral APA, and vice versa.

(2) Paragraphs 5, 6 of Article 8 of the Circular *inter alia* provide procedure and information to be submitted for consultation before official submission of the application, as below:

5. During the consultancy, the taxpayer must provide information, explanation, data, and documents for the General Department of Taxation to decide whether to allow the official submission of the application for APA.
6. Every consultation shall be recorded in writing. Within 30 working days from the end of the consultation, based on the consultancy record and conditions of tax administrations, the General Department of Taxation shall notify the taxpayer of the approval or disapproval of the official submission of the APA application.

(3) Paragraph 1 of Article 9 of the Circular *inter alia* provides for official submission of the APA application, as below:

1. An APA application shall be sent to the General Department of Taxation within 12 days from the day on which the taxpayer receives the written approval for official submission of the application for application from the General Department of Taxation.
If the taxpayer is not able to submit the application on schedule due to justifiable reasons, a written request for deadline extension shall be submitted to the General Department of Taxation. The extension shall not exceed 30 days from the deadline.

(4) Article 10 of the Circular *inter alia* provides the procedure for evaluating APA application, as below:

1. The APA application shall be evaluated by the General Department of Taxation within 90 days from the day on which it is officially submitted by the taxpayer. If the evaluation exceeds 90 days, the General Department of Taxation shall notify the taxpayer in writing of such extension. The extension shall not exceed 60 days.
2. Within 15 days from the day on which it is officially submitted by the taxpayer, the General Department of Taxation and the taxpayer shall hold a meeting to reach an agreement on the plan and order for taking the next steps to process the APA application.
3. The General Department of Taxation may take the following measures during the evaluation of the APA application if necessary:
   a) Request the taxpayer and relevant entities to provide information, explanation, or work with taxpayers to confirm the information and data related to the APA application;
   b) Carry out an inspection at the premises of the taxpayer (including the business establishments at various locations of the taxpayer).
4. The evaluation of the APA application for APA includes assessment and determination of the sufficiency and objectivity of the information

provided by the taxpayer so that the tax administration can make an assessment of the method for market price determination as the basis for negotiation with the taxpayer and the foreign tax administration (where necessary). The evaluation consists of:

a) Finding, assessing, and comparing the information and data provided by the taxpayer with the information and data about the business, capital investment, accounting, etc.;

b) Finding, assessing, and collecting information and evidence for analysis of functions, assets (including but not limited to the use of infrastructure serving the business, allocation of fund, payment for general expenses, etc.) and the risks taken by the taxpayer during the business (including but not limited to determination of the scope, risk of unsold goods, risk to credit and payment, etc.);

c) Finding, assessing and collecting information and evidence for comparability analysis (including finding information about customers, suppliers, and competitors of the taxpayer); finding and selecting the method for market price determination that is suitable for the nature of the taxpayer's business;

d) Finding, checking, and assessing the information and data collected from third parties (including exchange of information with foreign tax administrations);

dd) Collecting information and assessing the reasonability of critical assumptions.

5. The record on the consultation or survey at the premises of the taxpayer shall be made by the tax administration and the taxpayer.
6. Where the APA applied for is bilateral or multilateral, if the foreign tax administration requests the taxpayer to provide information and explanation (whether the information is in the initial or additional application), the taxpayer is responsible for providing such documents to the tax administration to ensure that all competent officials of the tax administrations participating in the APA are provided with similar information which is sufficient for processing the application.
7. If the General Department of Taxation needs to exchange information with the foreign tax administration while processing the application, the taxpayer shall also be informed of the information exchanged, the information used as documents and evidence during the APA negotiation and conclusion, unless the information must be kept secret from the taxpayer according to information exchange clauses of the tax treaty.

(5) Paragraphs 3-5 of Article 12 of the Circular *inter alia* provide the procedure for conclusion of the APA, as below:

3. If the APA is unilateral, the final draft shall be sent by the tax administration together with a written notification of its official conclusion; the legal representative of the taxpayer shall add a signature and seal to the final draft APA, then send it back to the tax administration.
4. If the APA is bilateral or multilateral, the General Department of Taxation shall make the final draft based on the terms and conditions agreed by the General Department of Taxation and the foreign tax administration, then send it to the taxpayer and request the taxpayer to

make a written response stating their assent to the contents of the final draft. Representatives of relevant tax administrations and the legal representative of the taxpayer shall add their signatures and seals to the bilateral or multilateral APA. The General Department of Taxation shall announce bilateral and multilateral APAs.

5. The official language of APAs is Vietnamese language; if an APA is bilateral or multilateral, an English translation may be used.

(6) Article 14 of the Circular provides procedure and order of priority of use of data and information selected for comparability analysis to determine interquartile range, as below:

1. The data and information selected for comparability analysis to determine standard market price range are the data announced in accordance with law, such as:
   a) Audited financial statements;
   b) Information about the industry; the information announced in accordance with the regulations on securities market;
   c) The information announced or provided on request by state agencies, research institutes, associations and professional organizations accredited by the State;
   d) Information from licensed information providers;
   dd) Other official sources.
2. Follow the following order of priority when selecting an independent entity for comparability analysis and determination of inter quartile range:
   a) Domestic entities;
   b) The entities in regional countries that have similar economic conditions;
   c) The entities in ASEAN countries;
   d) The entities in Asia-Pacific;
   dd) The entities in other parts of the world.

(7) Article 15 of the Circular provides procedure of participation of independent experts, as below:

The tax administration and the taxpayer may invite or hire independent experts who possess skills and knowledge suitable for the APA contents to participate in the discussion, negotiation, provision of explanation for relevant issues. The opinions offered by independent experts shall be used by the tax administration for reference and thus are not legally binding. Independent experts are entitled to access the documents and information while the APA application is being processed, and are responsible for maintaining the confidentiality of information under the law and contract between the experts and the taxpayer or tax administration.

(8) Article 19 of the Circular provides for submission of application form and procedures for implementation of BAPA and MAPA, as below:

1. The taxpayer who is a resident of Vietnam wishes to enter into a bilateral or multilateral APA and needs support from the tax administration shall submit an application for initiation of mutual agreement

procedures under the relevant tax treaty (form No. 4/APA-MAP), specifying:

a) The name, address, tax code (if any) of the taxpayer of the foreign country participating in the APA, the relation between the parties to the APA (including the organization diagram);
b) Names and addresses of foreign tax administrations where the foreign taxpayers pay tax;
c) Explanation for the request for bilateral or multilateral APA;
d) Brief description of the necessity of the support from the tax administration;
dd) Relevant documents circulated by foreign tax administrations (including but not limited to decisions to collect tax arrears, adjust tax liabilities that may lead to double taxation on incomes derived from related transactions).

An APA application together with the prescribed information shall be sent to the General Department of Taxation.

2. Within 30 days from the receipt of the request for initiation of mutual agreement procedures and the official APA application, competent officials of the General Department of Taxation shall contact competent officials of the foreign tax administration in accordance with mutual agreement procedures in the relevant tax treaty.
Within 15 days from the receipt of the response from the foreign tax administration, the tax administration shall notify the taxpayer of the result and instruct the taxpayer to fulfill the requirements mutually agreed by competent officials.
3. Competent officials of the Vietnamese tax administration are the Minister of Finance and the persons authorized by the Minister according to the tax treaty.
Competent officials are the points of contact (who receive and send documents and notifications) between the Vietnam tax administration and foreign tax administrations during processing of applications and supervision of implementation of bilateral and multilateral APAs.

(9) Article 23 of the Circular provides for effects of an APA upon conclusion, as below:

1. A concluded APA is binding upon both the tax administration and the taxpayer once the terms and conditions in the APA are strictly observed by the taxpayer.
2. An APA is effective for up to 05 years. The effect begins no sooner than the day the taxpayer submits the APA application.

3.26.2 Rollback of APA

585. Rollback is not available to prior years under the APA programme of Vietnam.

3.26.3 APA Team

586. Under the APA programme of Vietnam, in accordance with Article 6 of the Circular, the various authorities involved in the entire APA process are as below:

1. The Ministry of Finance shall approve the plan for negotiating, concluding, amending, renewing, revoking, and invalidating APAs.
2. The General Department of Taxation shall receive applications, hold negotiations, conclude, amend, renew, revoke, invalidate APAs, supervise and inspect the implementation of APA.
3. Departments of Taxation of provinces shall negotiate and implement APAs within their duties.

3.26.4 APA Process

587. In accordance with Article 7 of the Circular, an APA application shall be processed in the following order:

a) Consultation before official submission of the application;
b) Official submission of the application;
c) Evaluation of the APA application;
d) Negotiation of the APA;
dd) Conclusion and use of the APA.

3.26.5 Pre-filing Meeting

588. In accordance with Article 8 of the Circular, the consultation before official submission of the application shall be held at the request of the taxpayer to determine the suitability of the APA application. Taxpayer is required to file Form No. 1/APA-TV and include the following with its request for consultation:

- the name and address of the taxpayer, and names and addresses of parties to the related transaction(s);
- the type of APA sought;
- any relevant foreign jurisdiction(s) that will be party to the negotiations;
- a description of the related transaction(s) to be covered and not covered (if any) by the APA and an explanation for their inclusion, or exclusion;
- the value of the related transaction(s);
- the desired duration of the APA;
- an analysis of the functions, assets, and risks during the business of the taxpayer and related parties to the transaction(s) covered;
- the proposed TP method including comparables, benchmarking, calculation methods, arm's-length range, and adjustments of material differences (if any);
- critical assumptions;
- general information on enterprises, such as the business scope and size, the taxpayer's controlled transactions, and its associated parties relevant to the controlled transaction(s) to be covered by the APA;
- organizational structure;
- a summary of any tax audits;

- disclosure of whether any APAs have been concluded with any other foreign jurisdiction(s) or similar covered APA transactions;
- positions of any relevant foreign tax authorities;
- a proposed timeline for the APA application;
- process, and forms of communication; and
- any other information or documentation relevant to the APA application or as requested by the tax authorities.

589. The tax authorities in Vietnam notify the taxpayer within thirty working days from the last pre-filing meeting about the outcome of the pre-filing consultation. Anonymous pre-filing is not available under the APA programme of Vietnam.

3.26.6 APA Application

590. In accordance with Article 9 of the Circular, taxpayers are required to submit a formal APA application in Form No. 2/APA-CT to the tax authorities within twelve days of receiving written approval after the pre-filing consultation (a thirty-day extension is possible in certain circumstances). The APA application is required to include the following information and documents:

- information about the taxpayer and parties to the related transaction(s) covered by the APA;
- the name and address of the taxpayer, and names and addresses of parties to the related transaction(s), including any foreign tax authorities;
- tax codes of the taxpayer and addresses of business locations;
- information about the primary lines of business of the taxpayer and related parties;
- type of related transaction(s), scope and the covered period intended under the APA;
- the related transactions covered and not covered (if any) under the APA and an explanation for their inclusion, or exclusion;
- value of the related transaction(s);
- the type of APA sought;
- general information about the taxpayer and organization, including a brief history, business model, and organizational structure;
- a description of the group's value chain and the position of the related transaction(s) covered by the APA in that value chain;
- a detailed description of the transaction flow related to the transaction(s) covered by the APA and similar related transactions made in other jurisdictions (if any);
- the capital structure, associated relationship (including but not limited to direct or indirect investments, loans, and the ratio of investment among the partners);

- characteristics of business activities and main business areas of associated parties;
- a description of the business strategy of the corporation and any impact on the taxpayer;
- a description of the business strategy intended to be employed by the taxpayer during the covered period, including a business plan for the period of five years following the APA application, and performance over the previous three years;
- an analysis of the taxpayer's industry and tendencies that might affect the business of the taxpayer;
- detailed functions, risks and assets analysis of the taxpayer and any associated party to the APA, including allocation of resources and facilities if shared by associated parties (for assets including intellectual property (IP) or intangibles, it is necessary to state clearly the ownership, usage, any protection status, IP registration date, and the value of intangibles in price settings of goods/services covered by the APA);
- financial statements including any audits, annual reports and enterprise income statements from the three years prior to filing the APA application;
- proposed TP method, the source of data and information used for comparable analysis and, calculation method of product prices, gross profitable ratios, and PLIs related to the controlled transaction(s) covered by the APA;
- critical assumptions;
- information on the settlement of corporate income tax in any relevant foreign jurisdiction(s) and the relationship between the domestic laws and relevant DTAA provisions;
- copies of any existing APAs with foreign tax authorities for similar covered APA transaction(s);
- copies of any contracts or other legal agreements between the taxpayer and related parties that affect the transaction(s) covered by the APA, including agreement on ownership, rights of usage, sale, distribution of services, and development studies; and
- any other information or documentation relevant to the APA application or as requested by the tax authorities.

591. The APA applicants are required to submit three copies of the APA application to the tax authorities.

3.26.7 Evaluation of APA Application

592. On receipt of the APA application, the tax authorities shall notify the taxpayer of the outcome within ninety days of receiving the formal APA application. The tax authorities may extend the evaluation stage by no more than sixty days and notify the taxpayer in writing if such an extension is required.

593. The tax authorities may request to carry out a site visit of the taxpayer's premises during the evaluation of the APA application.

594. Article 11 of the Circular *inter alia* provides the procedure for APA negotiation and discussion, as below:

> The APA may be negotiated and discussed through direct meetings or indirect meetings via telephone, online video, or mail.
>
> 1. *Unilateral APA*: The negotiation revolves around the APA drafted by the tax administration. The draft APA may be sent to the taxpayer in advance.
> 2. *Bilateral or multilateral APA*: The representative of the tax administration who is a competent official shall inform the competent official of the foreign tax administration of the contents of the APA negotiation according to mutual agreement procedures of the relevant tax treaty. During the bilateral or multilateral negotiation among relevant tax administrations, the taxpayer may send a representative to provide additional information, documents, or explanation for related issues if agreed by competent officials and tax administrations. The tax administration may briefly inform the taxpayer of the negotiation progress and result, and may request the taxpayer to provide additional information, data, or explanation for related issues.

3.26.8 Withdrawal from APA Process

595. In accordance with Article 16 of the Circular, an applicant has the privilege and liberty to withdraw its APA application or terminate the APA negotiation at any time before the APA is concluded. The taxpayer is required to send a written request for the withdrawal of application or termination of negotiation to the General Department of Taxation.

3.26.9 Denial or Termination of APA Proceedings

596. In accordance with Article 16 of the Circular, the General Department of Taxation may terminate the negotiation process in the following circumstances:

> a) The related party transactions covered by the APA and the tax liabilities under dispute are due to administrative violations by the applicant pertaining to tax management;
> b) The related party transactions covered by the APA are arranged for the purpose of tax evasion, tax avoidance, or misusing the tax treaty;
> c) The taxpayer fails to provide sufficient documents and information or provides none at all, following the request of the tax administration;
> d) The taxpayer provides inaccurate information for the tax administration;
> dd) Other cases in which the tax administrations mutually agree to terminate the negotiation of the bilateral or multilateral APA.

597. The General Department of Taxation shall notify the taxpayer and foreign tax administration (if the APA is bilateral or multilateral) of the termination of the APA negotiation.

3.26.10 Advance Pricing Agreement

598. In accordance with Article 12 of the Circular, the contents of the APA are as below:

- Names and addresses of related parties to the APA.
- Description of the related transactions covered by the APA.
- The method for price market determination as the basis for calculation of tax, prices, gross profit margin, and net profit margin to determine taxable prices related to the related party transactions covered by the APA (including interquartile range if suitable).
- Critical assumptions that can significantly affect the implementation of the APA (including the analysis and forecasts).
- Regulations on responsibilities and obligations of the taxpayer.
- Regulations on responsibilities and obligations of tax administrations.
- The effect of APA.
- Other regulations conformable with the laws on fulfilment of tax liabilities related to the APA.
- Appendices, if any (including but not limited to interpretation of terms, additional explanation, etc.).

3.26.11 Annual Report

599. Taxpayers are required to submit an APA annual report together with their annual final statement of corporate income tax. Taxpayers with an APA are subjected to an APA compliance audit, but are exempted from a transfer pricing audit. In accordance with Article 17 of the Circular, the Annual Report in Form No. 3/APA-BC shall consist of the following:

- Description of the changes in the functions, assets, and risks to the taxpayer's business, the calculation of prices, gross profit margin, net profit margin (if any) using the method stated in the APA as the basis for stating tax on related transactions.
- Description of the compliance with the APA (including the update or change of critical assumptions).
- Description of the changes to the taxpayer's tax liabilities according to the signed APA: changes of the indicators that lead to an increase or decrease of tax liabilities.
- Opinions of the taxpayer on preserving or changing APA terms and relevant issues (including but not limited to new issues, relevant disputes over tax, etc.).

3.26.12 Renewal of APA

600. In accordance with Article 24 of the Circular, taxpayers may extend an existing APA for up to five additional years. An application for extension is required to be submitted at least six months before the expiry of the existing APA. The application for APA extension shall be processed similarly to the APA application. An APA may be extended in the following circumstances:

(a) No critical changes to the scope of related party transactions and related parties are made.
(b) No critical changes to critical assumptions are made.
(c) Interquartile range or gross profit margin or net profit margin used for comparability analysis is stable throughout the extension period.

3.26.13 Revision of APA

601. In accordance with Article 25 of the Circular, the APA may be adjusted/revised at the request of the taxpayer or tax administration. The circumstances in which the APA may be adjusted/revised are as under:

(a) Critical assumptions have changed.
(b) Changes have been made in law which affect the APA.
(c) CA of the foreign tax administration requests the adjustment and such request is agreed by the General Department of Taxation.
(d) Other cases (such as consensus among the parties to the APA).

3.26.14 Cancellation of APA

602. Article 26 of the Circular provides for cancellation of the APA. The General Department of Taxation is required to make a written announcement of APA cancellation, specifying the reasons for cancellation and the cancellation date. The circumstances in which the APA may be cancelled are as below:

- The taxpayer or any affiliate to the related party transactions fails to comply with APA terms and conditions.
- The taxpayer makes grave mistakes in the APA application, APA annual report, or any other unscheduled report sought by the tax administration.
- The taxpayer fails to provide sufficient documents and information in the annual or any unscheduled report at the request of the tax administration.
- The taxpayer and the tax administration fail to reach an agreement on adjustments to the APA.

- The foreign tax administration requests the APA cancellation and such request is agreed by the General Department of Taxation.
- The taxpayer applies for APA cancellation for legitimate reasons.

3.26.15 Withdrawal or Revoking of the APA

603. Article 27 of the Circular provides for withdrawal or revoking of the APA. The General Department of Taxation is required to make a written announcement for withdrawal or revoking the APA, specifying the reasons for withdrawal or revoking the APA and the withdrawal date (which shall be the first day of the covered period). The circumstances in which the APA may be withdrawn are as below:

- The taxpayer deliberately provided false information when reporting or requesting APA amendments.
- The foreign tax administration requested the APA withdrawal and such request is agreed by the General Department of Taxation.

3.26.16 Confidentiality

604. In accordance with Article 20 of the Circular, tax administrations and taxpayers are responsible for the confidentiality of the information and data throughout the APA process (including all procedures for assessing documents, discussion, negotiation, conclusion, and use of the APA) in accordance with Clause 3, Article 6 of the Law on Tax Administration. Where the APA negotiation is terminated, the APA application is withdrawn or cancelled, the information and data provided by the taxpayer in the official APA application and provided on request, the APA annual reports and unscheduled reports shall not be used by the tax administration as evidence in support of inspection or imposition of tax upon the taxpayer.

3.26.17 Statistics

605. Vietnam has had an APA programme since 2014. As per Vietnam's Dispute Resolution Profile (last updated on 17 February 2020),[211] statistics on APAs are not publicly available.

3.27 SYNOPSIS OF FEATURES OF APAs IN VARIOUS JURISDICTIONS

606. A striking feature noticed in the APA regime in various countries is that the procedures and provisions are similar in most countries with minor variations, as

211. Refer Vietnam's Dispute Resolution Profile https://www.oecd.org/tax/dispute/vietnam-dispute-resolution-profile.pdf accessed on 26 March 2021.

elaborately discussed in the foregoing paragraphs. This has enabled CAs of various jurisdictions to execute bilateral or multilateral APAs in a seamless manner under provisions corresponding to Articles 9 and 25 of the OECD MTC. In addition, CAs are found to be flexible in their approach during the course of APA negotiations so as to reconcile the minor procedural variations, if any. Some of the prominent features of the APA programme in various jurisdictions discussed in this chapter are summarized in Table 27.

Table 27 Synopsis of Features of APAs in Various Jurisdictions

Jurisdiction	*Types of APAs Available*	*Is Filing Fee to Be Paid?*	*Is Pre-filing Available?*	*Is Pre-filing Available on Anonymous Basis?*	*Term of APA*	*Rollback of APAs*	
						Is Rollback Available?	*Number of Prior Years Covered*
Australia	Unilateral, bilateral, multilateral	No	Yes	No	Up to 5 years	Yes	ATO decides on a risk assessment basis
Canada	-do-	Yes	Yes	Yes	3-5 years	Yes, but not for UAPA	Open prior years covered
China	-do-	No	Yes	No	3-5 years	Yes	10 years
France	-do-	No	Yes	No specific guidance	3-5 years	No	NA
Germany	Bilateral, multilateral*	Yes	Yes	Yes	3-5 years	Yes	No specific guidance
India	Unilateral, bilateral, multilateral	Yes	Yes	Yes	Up to 5 years	Yes	4 years
Indonesia	-do- #	No	No @	No	Up to 5 years	Yes @	No specific guidance
Ireland	Bilateral, multilateral	No	Yes	Yes	Up to 5 years	Yes	Subject to the applicable time limits of the jurisdictions involved in the APA
Japan	Unilateral, bilateral, multilateral	No	Yes	Yes	Up to 5 years	Yes, but not for UAPA	6 years

Jurisdiction	*Types of APAs Available*	*Is Filing Fee to Be Paid?*	*Is Pre-filing Available?*	*Is Pre-filing Available on Anonymous Basis?*	*Term of APA*	*Rollback of APAs*	
						Is Rollback Available?	*Number of Prior Years Covered*
Korea	-do-	No	Yes	Yes	Up to 5 years	Yes	Up to 5 years for BAPA, MAPA & up to 3 years for UAPA @@
Mexico	-do-	Yes	Yes	Yes	Up to 5 years **	Yes	Immediately preceding year in which application is made **
The Netherlands	-do-	No	Yes	Yes	Up to 5 years	Yes	No specific guidance
New Zealand	-do-	Yes	Yes	No	Up to 5 years	Yes	No specific guidance
Nigeria	-do-	No	No specific guidance		Up to 3 years	No specific guidance	
Poland	-do-	Yes	Yes	No specific guidance	Up to 5 years	No	NA
Portugal	-do-	Yes	Yes	No specific guidance	4 years	No	NA
Romania	-do-	Yes	Yes	No	Up to 5 years	No	NA
Russia	-do-	Yes	Yes	No	Up to 3 years	No specific guidance	
Singapore	-do-	No ***	Yes	No	3-5 years	Yes, but not for UAPA	2 years ****

Jurisdiction	*Types of APAs Available*	*Is Filing Fee to Be Paid?*	*Is Pre-filing Available?*	*Is Pre-filing Available on Anonymous Basis?*	*Term of APA*	*Rollback of APAs*	
						Is Rollback Available?	*Number of Prior Years Covered*
Spain	-do-	No	Yes	No	4 years	Yes	Applicable for previous periods which are not statute-barred and there is not a final assessment in place
Sweden	Bilateral, multilateral	Yes	Yes	No	3-5 years	Yes	Decided on a case-by-case basis
Thailand	Bilateral	No	Yes	No	3-5 years	Yes ##	No specific guidance
United Kingdom	Unilateral, bilateral, multilateral	No	Yes	No	3-5 years	Yes	Decided on a case-by-case basis
United States	-do-	Yes	Yes	Yes	At least 5 prospective years	Yes	1 or more rollback years
Vietnam	-do-	No	Yes	No	Up to 5 years	No	NA

* Unilateral binding statements from the tax authority in Germany can be obtained in the form of advance tax rulings which are available only under exceptional circumstances.

** Validity period may be extended for bilateral and multilateral APAs negotiated under the MAP provisions of a DTTA, and at the discretion of the relevant CAs involved.

*** IRAS does not impose any fee for APAs except for administrative fee/charges for unilateral APAs where the related party transactions involve a jurisdiction with which Singapore does not have a DTAA.

**** Depending on the facts and circumstances of each request, IRAS may exercise its discretion to vary the number of rollback years.

Indonesia basically does not have a multilateral APA programme. However, if the covered transactions and covered entities are from more than two countries, the APA can be conducted by applying multiple BAPAs with the countries concerned.

@ In Indonesia, vide Ministry of Finance Regulation No. 22/PMK.03/2020, there is no longer a prelodgement (pre-filing) process, and rollback of APA has been introduced.

On perusal of Thailand's Dispute Resolution Profile (last updated on 1 June 2020), it is mentioned that rollback of APAs is provided for in the bilateral APA programme. However, Guidance on APA process issued by the Revenue Department of Thailand is silent on this issue.

@@ For APAs submitted on or after 1 January 2021, rollback period for BAPAs is increased to seven years (from five years) and for UAPAs, the period is increased to five years (from three years).

607. An important requirement for executing APAs worldwide, particularly bilateral and multilateral APAs, is that the procedures, provisions and features need to be as uniform as possible. Table 27 captures a bird's-eye view of salient APA provisions applicable in various jurisdictions discussed in this chapter, and it is observed that these provisions are broadly similar in most countries with minor variations which are adequately addressed by the respective CAs in the course of bilateral or multilateral negotiations.

Chapter 4

Experience Sharing on Key Issues in India's APA Programme

Implementation of APA programme in India has brought into the limelight some conspicuous elements as below:

- Constituents/components of cost base in respect of captive entities performing functions solely for AEs.
- Handling of complex issues on intangibles pertaining to Advertisement, Marketing and Promotion (AMP) and such brand promotion activities involving Development, Enhancement, Maintenance, Protection and Exploitation (DEMPE) functions.
- PE related transactions.
- Location Savings.
- Best practices, like joint site visits.
- Practice adopted by appellate authorities in applying APA rulings to non-APA years (period).

608. Implementation of APA programme in India has brought into the limelight some conspicuous elements which are discussed in detail hereunder.

4.1 CONSTITUENTS/COMPONENTS OF COST BASE IN RESPECT OF CAPTIVE ENTITIES PERFORMING FUNCTIONS SOLELY FOR AEs

609. In pursuance to the spawning of Information Technology (IT)/Information Technology-Enabled Services (ITeS) industry in India, there has been a proliferation in setting-up of captive units which render services exclusively to their overseas AEs and, in turn, get remunerated on cost plus mark-up remuneration basis. APA authorities have been consistently following the policy that all the costs that are integral to the business of the Indian entity should be included in the cost base of the Indian entity. In view of this policy, any cost of goods or services or tools or any other tangible or intangible benefit, i.e., employee incentives like Employee Stock Option Plan (ESOP), cost of communication, secondment of employees by AEs, training cost incurred on employees of the taxpayer, etc. that may be provided by the AEs free of charge is included in the cost base of the entity (applicant) to determine the service revenue of the Indian entity. Accordingly, the cost base of the Indian entity is required to be revised to the extent of such costs. The reasons for increasing the cost base are *inter alia* stated as below:

(a) It is expedient to include all costs (whether allocated or not allocated by the AEs) so that the 'plus' factor, i.e., mark-up on costs, which essentially is the income of the taxpayer from the services rendered to the overseas AEs, is appropriately and commensurately captured.
(b) Appropriate capturing of cost base is essential as the taxpayer is rendering services to the AEs on captive basis, and the remuneration model gets vitiated if the cost base is artificially reduced.
(c) Since remuneration by the AEs to taxpayer in India is based on arm's-length principle, any decrease in cost base, for whatever reason, shall lead to decrement in remuneration to the taxpayer in India and vitiate the arm's-length principle.

610. In the initial years of India's APA programme, the taxpayers did not agree to increase in the cost base; however, they agreed later on, appreciating the above-mentioned arguments of the APA teams in India.

611. In view of the above, definitions of base elements comprising 'operating expense' and 'employee cost' *inter alia* defined in Rule 10TA of Income Tax Rules, 1962 were also amended with retrospective effect from 1 April 2017, by specifically providing that 'ESOPs provided for by the AEs to the applicant's employees; reimbursement to AEs of expenses incurred by the AEs on behalf of the applicant; amounts recovered from AEs on account of expenses incurred by the applicant on behalf of those AEs and which relate to normal operations of the applicant and depreciation and amortization expenses relating to the assets used by the applicant (provided free of cost by the AEs)' shall be included in the definition of 'operating expenses'. Further, the 'employee cost' shall *inter alia* include additional elements pertaining to expenses incurred on contractual employment of persons performing tasks similar to those performed by the regular employees, outsourcing expenses, recruitment expenses, relocation expenses, training expenses, etc. The definitions of 'operating expense' and 'employee cost' now read as below:

- 'operating expense' means the costs incurred in the previous year by the assessee in relation to the international transaction during the course of its normal operations including costs relating to Employee Stock Option Plan or similar stock-based compensation provided for by the associated enterprises of the assessee to the employees of the assessee, reimbursement to associated enterprises of expenses incurred by the associated enterprises on behalf of the assessee, amounts recovered from associated enterprises on account of expenses incurred by the assessee on behalf of those associated enterprises and which relate to normal operations of the assessee and depreciation and amortisation expenses relating to the assets used by the assessee, but not including the following, namely: –

(i) interest expense;
(ii) provision for unascertained liabilities;
(iii) pre-operating expenses;
(iv) loss arising on account of foreign currency fluctuations;
(v) extraordinary expenses;
(vi) loss on transfer of assets or investments;
(vii) expense on account of income-tax; and
(viii) other expenses not relating to normal operations of the assessee:

Provided that reimbursement to associated enterprises of expenses incurred by the associated enterprises on behalf of the assessee shall be at cost:

Provided further that amounts recovered from associated enterprises on account of expenses incurred by the assessee on behalf of the associated enterprises and which relate to normal operations of the assessee shall be at cost;

– 'employee cost' includes,

(i) salaries and wages;
(ii) gratuities;
(iii) contribution to Provident Fund and other funds;
(iv) the value of perquisites as specified in clause (2) of section 17 of the Act;
(v) employment related allowances, like medical allowance, dearness allowance, travel allowance and any other allowance;
(vi) bonus or commission by whatever name called;
(vii) lump sum payments received at the time of termination of service or superannuation or voluntary retirement, such as gratuity, severance pay, leave encashment, voluntary retrenchment benefits, commutation of pension and similar payments;
(viii) expenses incurred on contractual employment of persons performing tasks similar to those performed by the regular employees;
(ix) outsourcing expenses, to the extent of employee cost, wherever ascertainable, embedded in the total outsourcing expenses:
Provided that where the extent of employee cost embedded in the total outsourcing expenses is not ascertainable, eighty per cent of the total outsourcing expenses shall be deemed to be the employee cost embedded in the total outsourcing expenses;
(x) recruitment expenses;
(xi) relocation expenses;
(xii) training expenses;
(xiii) staff welfare expenses; and
(xiv) any other expenses related to employees or the employment.

4.2 HANDLING OF COMPLEX ISSUES ON INTANGIBLES PERTAINING TO ADVERTISEMENT, MARKETING AND PROMOTION AND SUCH BRAND PROMOTION (DEMPE) ACTIVITIES

612. India is now home to almost all the major brands of the world that have set up shop in India. Most MNCs have manufacturing facilities in India, whereas the rest sell in India through distribution channels. Predominantly, these MNCs function through their subsidiaries set up in India. The parent MNCs own valuable IP rights (know-how, copyrights, patents, etc.) and other commercial or marketing intangibles (brands, trademarks, etc.) and are involved in complex product development, manufacturing and brand development operations. The subsidiaries in India incur expenditure on Advertisement, Marketing and Promotion (AMP) and such brand promotion activities to promote the brand/trade name which is owned by the AE. Such expenditure has resulted in brand building and increased awareness of the products bearing the AEs' brand/trade name in India. The expenditure incurred by the taxpayer is for the advantage of its AE since the brand/trade name is owned by the AE. In such a situation, the taxpayer (Indian subsidiary) should be suitably compensated by the AE. Compensation by the AE for AMP expenditure becomes all the more expedient in situations where the subsidiary pays brand royalty to its AE. Amendments made by the Finance Act 2012[212] to section 92B of Income Tax Act, 1961 provide that incurring of AMP expenditure is to be treated as an international transaction. In the course of TP audits on the said issue in India, it has been invariably observed by the tax authorities as below:

(a) The well-established doctrine of 'substance over form' indicating that transfer pricing regulations are to be applied keeping in mind the overall scheme of the taxpayer's business arrangement. The Indian subsidiary, in its own right, owns significant marketing intangibles in the form of trademarks, trade names, customer lists, customer relationships, distribution channels, and proprietary market and customer data that is used or aids in marketing and selling goods or services to customers.
(b) The brand building vision, procedures and course of action are all dictated at global level. The AE sets the tone and path for building the brand in India, but the expense is exclusively borne by the taxpayer in India for which no compensation is provided by the parent AE.
(c) The parent AE hand-holds the global associate entities on the path of advertising and marketing of the products, which is then adopted/implemented uniformly worldwide, including in India.
(d) While some intangibles may be identified separately and transferred on a segregated basis, other intangibles may be transferred only in combination

212. Refer section 35 of Finance Act 2012 https://www.incometaxindia.gov.in/Pages/acts/finance-acts.aspx accessed on 12 August 2019.

with other business assets. Therefore, separate transferability is not a necessary condition for an item to be characterized as an intangible for transfer pricing purposes.

613. Most taxpayers hold the view that AMP compensation required to be provided by the AE is not an international transaction per se and no additional compensation/attribution is called for in case benchmarking at entity level (all international transactions including AMP aggregated) gives favourable results. Whereas tax administration in India holds the view that Amendments made by the Finance Act 2012[213] to section 92B of Income Tax Act, 1961 provide that incurring of AMP expenditure is to be treated as an international transaction and TP law in India prescribes transaction-by-transaction approach (benchmarking in segregated manner), thereby implying that even if economic analysis at entity level is satisfied, compensation/attribution for AMP expenses by the AE to its subsidiary in India is still called for.

614. The Hon'ble Courts in India have decided in the cases of *Maruti Suzuki India Limited,*[214] *Whirlpool of India Limited,*[215] *Bausch & Lomb Eyecare (India) Private Limited*[216] and *Honda Siel Power Products Limited*[217] that as the respective taxpayers are risk-bearing manufacturers, attribution of AMP expenses to the AEs is not called for, whereas in the case of distributors,[218] the courts have taken a contra view and have upheld AMP attribution. At this juncture, the matter is sub judice in the Hon'ble Supreme Court of India.

615. Actions 8-10[219] Report of the OECD/G20 BEPS Project has recognized that 'brand' is an intangible and represents a combination of intangibles and/or other items, including among others, trademarks, trade names, customer relationships, reputational characteristics, goodwill and any action or spend which enhances goodwill, also leads to brand building. Any spend on advertisement leads to build-up of intangibles, and such spend should be capitalized for proper reflection in the Balance Sheet. Failure to do so calls for compensation by the AE for the significant economic value created for the AE's brand by such advertisement spends. The OECD has also recognized that characterization of an intangible for general tax purposes may not hamper or distort its true characterization of being an intangible. Thus, OECD has reinforced the view that advertisement spend by the taxpayer in India leads to creation of an intangible and

---

213. *Id.*
214. ITA No. 110/2014 and 710/2015, Delhi High Court dated 11/12/2015.
215. ITA No. 610/2014, Delhi High Court dated 22/12/2015.
216. ITA No. 643/2014, Delhi High Court dated 23/12/2015.
217. ITA No. 346/2015, Delhi High Court dated 23/12/2015.
218. ITA No. 5140/DEL/ 2011 – Ruling by three-member Special Bench of Income Tax Appellate Tribunal (ITAT), Delhi upheld partially by the Delhi High Court in the case of *Sony Ericsson Mobile Communications India Private Limited v. Commissioner of Income* (ITA No. 16/2014) 276 CTR 97 (Delhi).
219. Refer BEPS Actions 8-10 Report https://read.oecd-ilibrary.org/taxation/aligning-transfer-pricing-outcomes-with-value-creation-actions-8-10-2015-final-reports_9789264241244-en#page1 accessed on 12 August 2019.

whatever characterization has been given by the taxpayer in India for such advertisement spend for general tax purposes will not impact the creation of an intangible by the taxpayer in India for its AE, which needs to be commensurately compensated with a markup (to compensate for the services rendered/additional functions performed by the taxpayer for its AE for brand building). To add to the argument in support of attribution, a taxpayer in India is to be compensated based on the value it creates through functions performed, assets used and risks assumed in the development, enhancement, maintenance, protection and exploitation (DEMPE) of intangibles for its AE in India. Hence, a key consideration is that taxpayer in India that contributes to the DEMPE of intangibles legally owned by another member of the group must receive arm's-length compensation for the functions they perform, the risks they assume, and the assets they use. In evaluating whether a taxpayer in India that performs functions or assumes risks related to the DEMPE of intangibles has been compensated on an arm's-length basis, it is necessary to consider (i) the level and nature of the activity undertaken; and (ii) the amount and form of compensation paid. In assessing whether the compensation provided in the controlled transaction is consistent with the arm's-length principle, reference should be made to the level and nature of activity of comparable uncontrolled entities performing similar functions, the compensation received by comparable uncontrolled entities performing similar functions, and the anticipated creation of intangible value by comparable uncontrolled entities performing similar functions.

616. Considering the actions of the TPOs in India, diverse court rulings on the subject and Actions 8-10 Report of the OECD/G20 BEPS Project, few taxpayers have filed APAs (mainly UAPAs) so as to obtain certainty on this issue. In the course of APA proceedings, where AMP is the only covered international transaction, the most appropriate TP methodology identified is 'Other Method' prescribed in clause (f) of subsection (1) of section 92C[220] of Income Tax Act, 1961, read with Rule 10AB[221] of Income Tax Rules, 1962. As a next step, the amount of expenditure incurred by the tested party (taxpayer) on AMP is computed. Expenditure incurred on 'Point of Sales' marketing, sales promotion, dealer incentives, discount to customers, etc. is excluded for this purpose. The nature of expenditure to be considered is the pure brand marketing expense that leads to promotion and development of brand (i.e., Brand Marketing expense). As an illustration, the following heads of expenditure are treated as expenditure for brand promotion:

- All types of payments made to advertising agencies.
- Purchase of air time on TV.
- Purchase of air time on radio.
- Advertising on Internet.

220. Refer section 92C(1)(f) https://www.incometaxindia.gov.in/Pages/acts/income-tax-act.aspx accessed on 15 August 2019.
221. Refer Rule 10AB https://www.incometaxindia.gov.in/_layouts/15/dit/Pages/viewer.aspx?path=https://www.incometaxindia.gov.in/Rules/Income-Tax%20Rules/103120000000007188.htm&IsDlg=0 accessed on 15 August 2019.

- Advertising in cinema halls.
- Outdoor advertising in public places, like airports, railway stations, bus stands, malls, public transportation, through large billboards, etc.
- Advertising in print media of all kinds, i.e., newspapers, magazines, etc.
- Expenses incurred on conducting all kinds of events for consumers.
- Market research expenses.
- Expenses incurred on sponsorships/contracts/rights for organizing sports tournaments.

Thereafter, ratio of expenditure on brand promotion (AMP) to sales of the tested party is calculated which is tested against AMP/Sales ratio of third-party comparables engaged in a similar line of business as the tested party (taxpayer). AMP/Sales ratio of third-party comparables is treated as a 'bright line'. Bright line is a tool to bifurcate the AMP expenses between routine and non-routine AMP expenses so as to identify the expenditure incurred towards brand building. Expenditure of the tested party below the bright line is treated as routine AMP expenditure which any business entity is expected to incur to promote its sales, whereas any expenditure above the bright line is the non-routine AMP expenditure which the tested party (taxpayer) has excessively incurred to promote the brand value of the AE and the same is required to be compensated by the AE to the taxpayer, along with a markup. Markup is necessitated as it is the compensation for the services rendered/additional function performed by the taxpayer for the AE in regard to promotion of the brand of the AE.

617. In cases under APA where covered international transactions are payment of brand royalty to the AE and incurring of AMP expenses also, the APA resolution varies from case to case. Depending on facts of the case and negotiations involved, in some cases, payment of brand royalty to the AE is not allowed at all, but AMP expenses are allowed to be borne by the taxpayer in India, subject to certain limit based on certain percentage of operating profits/revenue or no such limit, as the facts of each case demand. In other cases, both royalty and AMP expenses are allowed to be incurred, but they are restricted to a ceiling based on certain percentage of operating profits/revenue of the tested party (taxpayer in India). It would be worthwhile to state here that APA authorities get encouraged to allow brand royalty/AMP expenses in cases where the tested party (taxpayer in India) has robust operating profits. There has been an instance where the tested party (taxpayer in India) was in losses for many years (rollback years) and the projected profits in the APA period were very minimal. In this case, in the APA, allowability of brand royalty/AMP expenses was considerably reduced on the premise that there appears to be excess diversion of profits to the AE at the expense of taxpayer's profitability/operations.

618. In some APA cases of manufacturing entities, where covered international transactions with AEs relate to purchase/sale, brand royalty payment and AMP, the resolution is somewhat different. In such cases, one of the mechanisms for resolution is that the taxpayer is guaranteed cost-plus remuneration for sale/purchase function, wherein cost may include a component of AMP expenses, and in respect of brand royalty, the residuary profits are split between the taxpayer and the AE based on their respective FAR. As stated above, it may be reiterated that such resolutions are case specific and based on negotiations.

619. Based on the above discussions, it can be seen that in respect of a highly litigated issue concerning AMP in India, APAs have provided a platform to the taxpayers to reach an amicable resolution with tax authorities and obtain tax certainty.

4.3 TREATMENT OF PE-RELATED INTERNATIONAL TRANSACTIONS

620. A few taxpayers have filed UAPAs in India to obtain tax certainty concerning the international transactions between a non-resident entity and its branch office in India. The latter is a PE in India of the non-resident. By virtue of section 92F(iii) of the Income Tax Act, 1961,[222] an enterprise includes a PE, and computation of ALP under section 92 of the Income Tax Act, 1961 can be carried out in respect of international transactions (meaning of international transaction is provided in section 92B of the Income Tax Act, 1961) between two AEs (meaning of AE is provided in section 92A of the Income Tax Act, 1961). Application of TP regulations in APAs in respect of international transactions between the non-resident AE and its PE in India is confined to determination of ALP of international transactions undertaken by them. It may be noted that application of TP regulations for such transactions is not for profit attribution alone since the same would be in conflict with India's stand on Authorized OECD Approach[223] (AoA) on profit attribution to PEs. It has been India's position[224] that AoA puts reliance upon functions, assets, and risks for profit attribution to a PE, which represents only the supply side and neglects the demand or sales side of activity. While the AoA approach may be favourable to the interests of certain countries that are net exporters of capital and technology, it is likely to have a very significant adverse impact on all other stakeholders, especially the developing economies like India, which are primarily importers of capital and technology. For India and other developing countries which are net importers of capital and having a huge market/consumption capacity, apportionment of profits to a PE based on FAR, as advocated by the AoA, does not approximate the proper contribution that should be allocated to such countries. Instead, these countries should be compensated with a fair share of income based on factors which have direct correlation with the situations prevailing in the market economy. Therefore, it has been India's suggestion that a new three-factor apportionment method to attribute profits to PEs in India should be adopted, giving equal weight to sales, manpower (employees and wages), and assets. Further, in the case of digital businesses, a fourth factor of 'users' should also be added. India's approach can also be read into paragraphs 3 and 4 of Article 7 of the UN Model Double Taxation Convention

222. Refer https://www.incometaxindia.gov.in/Pages/acts/income-tax-act.aspx accessed on 16 August 2019.
223. Refer 2010 Report on the Attribution of Profits to Permanent Establishments https://www.oecd.org/ctp/transfer-pricing/45689524.pdf accessed on 16 August 2019.
224. Refer Article by Madhan N titled 'Proposed India profit attribution rules reject OECD approach, add "sales" and "users" as apportionment factors' https://mnetax.com/proposed-india-profit-attribution-rules-reject-oecd-approach-33521 accessed on 16 August 2019.

and some of the Indian tax treaties as well as Rule 10[225] under the Income Tax Rules, 1962, wherein India applies the 'fractional apportionment method' which is different from the 'formulary apportionment method' as the former does not seek to consolidate the profits of the enterprise from different jurisdictions, instead only considers and seeks to apportion profits derived by the enterprise from India.

621. It would be worthwhile to clarify here that under APAs in India, prior to 1 April 2020, tax certainty to a PE concerning TP provisions only was provided and the same was achieved through determination of ALP of international transactions undertaken between the parent AE and its PE based on FAR of the two entities. As per domestic law, the PE in India is a non-resident entity and may be subjected to regular audit by the AO holding jurisdiction over such PE in respect of its business income in India, wherein it may be assessed by applying domestic regulations applicable to non-residents, *inter alia* including section 44C[226] of the Income Tax Act, 1961. Thus, any disallowance/addition to PE's total income in India made by the AO by applying domestic law used to be over and above the determination of ALP under TP regulations. However, through Finance Act, 2020 (with effect from 1 April 2020), in order to provide greater certainty to APA applicants, section 92CC of the Income Tax Act, 1961 has been amended so as to provide that the government may enter into an APA with any person, including by or on behalf of that person, being a non-resident, i.e., a PE, determining the income referred to in clause (i) of subsection (1) of section 9, or specifying the manner in which said income is to be determined, as is reasonably attributable to the operations carried out in India. With this amendment, instead of determining the price, APA entered into under section 92CC is now determining the income of the PE itself, which would represent not only the supply side but also the demand or sales side of activity. Hence, the AO need not carry out any further action post entering into the APA by the government in respect of a PE, under the amended provisions of section 92CC which will apply to an APA entered into on or after 1 April 2020.

4.4 LOCATION SAVINGS

622. Features of the geographic market in which business operations occur can affect comparability and ALPs. Difficult issues can arise in evaluating differences between geographic markets and in determining appropriate comparability adjustments. Such issues may arise in connection with the consideration of cost savings attributable to operating in a particular market. Such savings are sometimes referred to as location savings.[227]

225. Refer https://www.incometaxindia.gov.in/Pages/rules/income-tax-rules-1962.aspx accessed on 16 August 2019.
226. Refer https://www.incometaxindia.gov.in/Pages/acts/income-tax-act.aspx accessed on 17 August 2019.
227. Refer para. 1.139 of OECD Transfer Pricing Guidelines for Multinational Enterprises and Tax Administrations (July 2017).

623. During the course of APA proceedings, on the issue of location savings, the applicants invariably state that they use independent local Indian companies as comparables to determine the ALP of covered international transactions. These companies also operate in the same market as the APA applicants and hence have access to the location-specific advantages (LSAs) of India, if any. The net operating margins earned by Indian comparable service providers include the impact of LSAs, and therefore, no separate/additional compensation is required on account of location savings. On this issue, the Tax Tribunal[228] has held that no separate or additional allocation is required on account of location savings if local Indian comparable companies are used to determine ALP.

624. The APA teams in India are of the view that if local third-party comparables performing similar functions are available, the location saving gets captured in the margin of these comparables. To illustrate, let us consider that there are independent third-party companies providing IT services in India. If the average margin of these companies is 20% on full cost, then this margin includes the location saving. In a free economy, each of these independent companies would try to maximize its profits keeping in mind the following facts that:

(i) the foreign companies are saving costs by outsourcing the provision of services to India;
(ii) there is competition in India and there are other companies who could perform similar functions; and
(iii) the foreign company could also have an option to get these services from outside India.

Thus, the price quoted by these independent companies (third-party comparables) would factor in location saving enjoyed by foreign company and the competition within and outside India to take advantage of that location saving. From the foreign company's perspective, the cost saving from relocating to India would also be temporary since there would be other companies who would have already been outsourcing similar services to India or other low-cost countries and the competition within these foreign companies, in a free economy, would have already reduced the location saving. In fact, the situation may have been that this foreign company had to relocate the provision of services to India or other low-cost countries just to survive.

625. Accordingly, the market forces would ensure that margin earned by independent third-party comparables in India reflects the location saving. Now, if the tested party is performing similar functions as these independent third parties, then these independent third parties can be taken as comparables for the tested party, and after that no separate adjustment for location saving would be needed. On the contrary, if these independent third parties are not performing similar functions or suitable local comparables are not available, then location saving is an issue which will have to be considered while benchmarking. Hence, view of the APA teams in India is that when

228. Refer Delhi Income Tax Appellate Tribunal (ITAT) order in the case of *GAP International Sourcing India P Ltd v. ACIT* (ITA 5147/Del/11 & 228/Del/12).

good local comparables are available, the comparability takes care of locational advantage. This view of the APA teams aligns with the OECD's[229] viewpoint that where reliable local market comparables are available and can be used to identify ALPs, specific comparability adjustments for location savings should not be required.

4.5 BEST PRACTICE LIKE JOINT SITE VISITS

626. In BAPA cases, on the issue of joint site visit by representatives of CAs involved, OECD's[230] viewpoint is that it may be more efficient in appropriate cases to have some degree of joint fact-finding. This could take a variety of forms ranging from an occasional joint fact-finding meeting or site visit to the preparation of a joint report by delegated caseworkers.

627. Under India's APA programme, site visits form an integral part and are mandated under Rule 10L(2)(iii)[231] of the Income Tax Rules, 1962. While processing BAPA applications, representatives of the CA in India and some treaty partners like, US, UK, the Netherlands, Finland, Korea, and others have been conducting joint site visits at the premises of the applicants in India and their respective AEs in above-stated countries. The joint site visits are being conducted in select cases, chosen carefully by the two CAs involved by taking into consideration the nature of international transactions, their complexity, materiality of transactions, etc. These joint site visits have been quite advantageous as both CAs obtain a similar set of information during site visit while interacting with the top management of the BAPA applicants, and thus, they are able to develop common understanding of the case, which, in turn, helps in expediting APA resolutions. It has also been experienced that in some cases, the CA of treaty partner could appreciate Indian CA's concern on FAR of the taxpayer in India much better post joint site visit in India. BAPA applicants have also welcomed the concept of joint site visits, and it is expected that this practice will become more popular for faster BAPA resolutions. Due to COVID-19-induced restrictions, since physical site visits have more or less got stalled, tax authorities and taxpayers will need to devise an alternate mechanism to organize joint site visits online, till normalcy returns.

4.6 PRACTICE ADOPTED BY APPELLATE AUTHORITIES IN APPLYING APA RULINGS TO NON-APA YEARS (PERIOD)

628. The APAs signed between the tax administration and the taxpayers in India, *inter alia*, contain the following provisions:

229. Refer para. 1.142 of OECD Transfer Pricing Guidelines for Multinational Enterprises and Tax Administrations (July 2017).
230. Refer para. 58 of Annex II of Chapter IV of OECD Transfer Pricing Guidelines for Multinational Enterprises and Tax Administrations (July 2017).
231. Refer https://www.incometaxindia.gov.in/Pages/rules/income-tax-rules-1962.aspx accessed on 17 August 2019.

- term of the agreement clearly mentioning the years to which the agreement shall apply;
- the TPM, as described in the agreement, will be consistently applied throughout the term of the agreement for the covered transactions;
- ALP, PLI for specific years covered under the agreement;
- depending upon the facts of the case, some agreements duly mention that the agreement shall apply or not apply to rollback years;

629. Despite the APAs clearly mentioning the years (period) to which they will apply, taxpayers have been citing them before courts in support of their past years under dispute, which are years prior to the covered period under the agreement. Surprisingly, courts have taken cognizance of such APAs while imparting their verdicts and have invariably held that the ALP agreed in the APA may be applied to the years (period) under dispute. Some of such court verdicts are mentioned hereunder:

(a) The Hon'ble ITAT, Delhi, India has observed/held in the case of *FIS Global Business Solutions India Private Limited*[232] for Financial Year 2009-2010 as below:

> Hon'ble Delhi High Court in the case of PCIT vs. Ameriprise India Pvt. Ltd. held that when under the APA entered into between the taxpayer and the CBDT under section 92CC aforementioned cost-plus pricing methodology has been implicitly accepted, the APA has persuasive value to the dispute in question for other years.
> We are of the considered view that when in the APA entered into between the taxpayer and the CBDT though for the roll back years and subsequent years, application of most appropriate transfer pricing method and arm's length price of these transactions have already been agreed upon between the taxpayer and CBDT and there is no change in the FAR and nature of international transactions entered into during the year under consideration vis-à-vis earlier years and subsequent years, principle laid down in the APA for benchmarking the international transactions in question shall have a guidance value. More so these days, it is endeavour of the Union of India to stop avoidable litigations and this case falls in the category of cases where litigation can be minimized.

(b) The Hon'ble ITAT, Delhi, India has observed/held in the case of *Springer [India] Pvt Ltd*[233] for Financial Year 2011-2012 as below:

> Even though the year under consideration is not covered under APA and risk profile as claimed by the ld. counsel for the assessee is consistent with APA years and, therefore, the ld. counsel for the assessee has prayed for adoption of the method and computation mechanism adopted in the APA to determine the ALP of the international transactions in dispute.
> We direct TPO to consider the FAR of the year under consideration with FAR of the years in APA. The assessee is directed to produce all necessary

232. ITA No. 422/Del./2019 and ITA No. 423/Del./2019, Delhi ITAT dated 18.06.2020.
233. ITA No. 6708/DEL/2016, Delhi ITAT dated 28.08.2020.

> documents in compliance with APA and the Assessing Officer/TPO is directed to decide the issue in light of APA in respect of international transactions in dispute in the present appeal and adopt the same methodology which has been directed to be adopted in the APA.

(c) The Hon'ble ITAT, Kolkata, India has observed/held in the case of *Cookson India Pvt Ltd*[234] for Financial Years 2008-2009, 2010-2011 & 2011-2012 as below:

> The question arises as to whether, when the factual matrix including the functional and risk profile of the assessee with respect to these three years under appeal is similar, to the factual matrix and functional profile of the assessee considered by the CBDT while determining the ALP in the APA, for the five Financial years 2015-16 to 2019-20 and for the rollback period i.e. FY 2012-13 to 2014-15. In our view the ALP determined and agreed to in the APA should necessarily be applied as the ALP, on the international transaction of IGS and R & D services for the assessment year in appeal. While holding so, we have considered the various judgments one of which is passed by the Hon'ble Delhi High Court in the case of Ameriprise India Pvt. Ltd. in ITA 206/2016.
> Direct the Assessing Officer to adopt the ALP determined in the APA as the ALP of the international transaction of MSSF for IGS and R & D services for all the impugned assessment years.

630. The verdicts of Hon'ble courts to adopt the ALP agreed in the APAs as the ALP of the international transactions undertaken in the non-APA years are unwarranted on account of the following reasons:

(i) Section 92C(2) of Income Tax Act, 1961 read with Rule 10B(4) of Income Tax Rules, 1962 provides that for the computation of ALP, the most appropriate transfer pricing method is to apply. In respect of the financial years to which these court verdicts pertain, Rule 10B(4) *inter alia* provides that the data to be used in analysing the comparability of an uncontrolled transaction with an international transaction shall be the data relating to the financial year (referred to as the 'current year') in which the international transaction has been entered into. Quite clearly, the APA years are not equivalent to the 'current year' of cases under dispute, and the courts have completely ignored the fact that the ALP in the years in which the international transaction has been entered into was to be computed based on comparability with third-party comparables, as clearly provided in law.

(ii) There is violation of the provisions of section 92CC(4) of the Income Tax Act, 1961 which provides that the agreement shall be valid for such period not exceeding five consecutive previous years as may be specified in the agreement. This implies that the agreement cannot be valid for years not specified in the agreement. The court verdicts, therefore, have enlarged the

234. ITA Nos 633 & 442/Kol /2016, ITA No. 387/Kol/2017, Kolkata ITAT dated 20/11/2020.

scope of periods covered in the APAs without any statutory backing and support. It requires appreciation on the part of taxpayers and courts that the APA scheme is a dispute prevention scheme and need not be made subject matter of litigation.

(iii) Such verdicts open opportunities for the taxpayers to further use the APAs to their undue advantage and may encourage them to even not proceed for renewal of APAs, as courts appear to be more than willing to apply an APA ruling to non-APA years, which could be past years or future years.

(iv) APAs on IT/ITeS have provisions to increase the cost base in respect of covered years. The courts have ignored to increase the cost base in such non-APA years and have restricted themselves in holding that the rate or PLI agreed in APAs only may be applied to non-APA years. Thus, the courts have rendered their verdict in a one-sided manner, without understanding the nuances of APA programme in totality.

631. It would be pertinent to state here that on analysing the APA regime in Ireland,[235] it is observed that in negotiating bilateral APAs, the Irish Revenue considers that each case is unique and is based on a specific set of facts and circumstances. The APA terms agreed between Irish Revenue and the foreign tax administration do not create a precedent for transactions involving the same taxpayers for any years other than those years included in the APA period (including any rollback period) or for transactions involving taxpayers other than those specified in the APA. On the contrary, the courts in India are transgressing the established international principles and norms on APAs being diligently followed by regimes the world over, i.e., to not apply APAs to non-APA years (period).

632. The unwarranted reliance on APAs by courts in India has started a trend which tantamount to interference in a self-contained regime which was meant to be a dispute prevention mechanism in the first place. By citing APAs in courts, the taxpayers themselves are making APAs an area of litigation. The APAs signed in India *inter alia* also contain provisions stating that the agreement and the information, data and documents related to this agreement are subject to the same rules of confidentiality as any information under the Income Tax Act, 1961 and also not to reveal taxpayers' identities. By citing their APAs in courts, the taxpayers themselves are compromising on the confidentiality of their agreements. This is a classic example where an efficacious and a well-intentioned programme is getting diluted and being made subject matter of litigation, when in the first place, the primary purpose of this programme is to prevent litigation.

235. Refer Ireland's Bilateral Advance Pricing Agreement Guidelines 2016, Part 35-02-07 https://www.revenue.ie/en/tax-professionals/tdm/income-tax-capital-gains-tax-corporation-tax/part-35/35-02-07.pdf accessed on 19 March 2021.

CHAPTER 5

Key Features in APA Programme of Various Countries

Implementation of APA programmes the world over involves the following key elements:

- Rollback available compulsorily on Risk Assessment basis under the Australian APA Programme.
- Flexibility allowed under the Canadian APA programme to relieve double taxation.
- APAs for small businesses under the Canadian APA programme.
- Treatment of LSAs in China.
- APAs for SMEs under the French APA programme.
- APAs for SMEs and abbreviated procedure for renewal of APAs under the German APA programme.
- APAs for PEs under the Irish APA programme.
- APAs for SMEs under the Korean APA programme.
- APAs for SMEs under the APA programme of the Netherlands.
- Significance of economic nexus prior to grant of APAs and release of anonymized APA summaries in the Netherlands.
- Unilateral APAs for domestic affiliated entities under the APA programme of Poland.
- APAs for certain domestic transactions under the APA programme of UK.
- APAs for small businesses and abbreviated APAs under the US APA programme.

633. Implementation of APA programme in various jurisdictions has in its domain certain conspicuous elements which are discussed in detail hereunder.

5.1 ROLLBACK AVAILABLE COMPULSORILY ON RISK ASSESSMENT BASIS UNDER THE AUSTRALIAN[236] APA PROGRAMME

634. Transfer pricing issues that arise in income years prior to the commencement of the APA, i.e., rollback years, are treated as collateral issues. The existence of collateral issues (e.g., the possible applicability of anti-avoidance rules) may make it inappropriate for the ATO to proceed with an APA. A collateral issue, as defined by ATO in PS LA 2015/4, is as below:

- an administrative or tax issue in relation to the taxpayer's affairs;
- in addition to the cross-border dealings the subject of the APA;
- relevant to, and can potentially affect, the outcomes of the APA.

635. Where the principles developed in concluding an APA provide a reasonable basis, one approach to dealing with such issues may be to apply the principles or method used in the APA to the prior income years (rollback). The APA team leader considers whether the principles developed in concluding an APA provide a reasonable basis for a rollback. This would depend on the availability of all relevant information in respect of the prior years and whether there are any material changes in the taxpayer's circumstances in those years. Any decision on whether rollback is available for years prior to an APA is made on a risk assessment basis. APA team leaders considering rollback, subject to the facts and circumstances of the particular case, are required to be cognizant of the following:

- not seek rollback where the transfer pricing issues for prior years are rated as low risk under ATO risk assessment procedures;
- be more likely to seek rollback for a lesser number of years in the case of a voluntary APA request than it would be for a case resulting from ATO compliance activity;
- be more likely to seek rollback for issues rated as high risk.

636. The APA team leader, the taxpayer and, where applicable, the audit team leader should agree how and when the prior years' issues should be resolved. ATO staff treat as a voluntary disclosure any amendment to prior years arising from rollback where the following are satisfied:

- the ATO has not initiated compliance or risk activity with respect to the prior-year returns;
- there is a need to amend a prior-year return as a result of providing information for an APA.

236. Refer ATO-PS LA 2015/4 https://www.ato.gov.au/law/view/document?DocID=PSR/PS2015 4/NAT/ATO/00001&PiT=99991231235958#P21.

637. If there are any unresolved non-transfer pricing related issues arising in prior years, these are addressed through an active compliance product (risk review or audit). Thus, rollback is not available in a routine manner and decided on a case-by-case basis (on risk assessment basis) by the Australian Tax Authorities.

5.2 FLEXIBILITY ALLOWED UNDER THE CANADIAN[237] APA PROGRAMME TO RELIEVE DOUBLE TAXATION

638. Under the Canadian APA programme, preference is provided to BAPA and MAPA. The purpose of pursuing a BAPA or MAPA is to avoid double taxation between the APA applicant and a non-resident entity, which on the other hand may remain when only a unilateral APA is in place. The APA process achieves maximum benefits for the APA applicant when the CAs of two or more countries reach a BAPA or MAPA. If the CAs cannot reach a BAPA or MAPA, the APA team may, nevertheless, provide a unilateral APA.

639. When the Canadian CA agrees to pursue a BAPA or MAPA with the CA of one or more treaty partners, there will be a mutual exchange of information with those treaty partners concerning all aspects of the APA process, including any subsequent revisions, cancellations, revocations, or requests for APA renewal, in accordance with the relevant tax treaties. The final TPM agreed on by the CAs in a BAPA or MAPA may differ from the TPM proposed by the applicant in its APA submission. If for any reason a BAPA or MAPA could not be concluded, and applicant and the CCRA have concluded a unilateral APA, the applicant retains its rights to pursue the MAP available under the relevant tax treaty. However, if double taxation occurs on the transactions covered by the unilateral APA, the Canadian CA may, under the MAP article of the relevant tax treaty, deviate from the terms and conditions in the unilateral APA to resolve the matter with the relevant treaty partner. If the applicant and the non-resident entities accept the settlement negotiated by the Canadian CA and the relevant foreign CA regarding the parties and transactions specifically covered by the unilateral APA, such resolution under MAP will prevail over the terms and conditions of the said unilateral APA. This facility in the Canadian APA and MAP regime that is allowed to the APA applicants demonstrates the extent to which the Canadian tax authorities are willing to go in order to relieve their taxpayers from double taxation.

237. Refer IC 94-4R dated 16 March 2001 https://www.canada.ca/en/revenue-agency/services/forms-publications/publications/ic94-4/international-transfer-pricing-advance-pricing.html accessed on 9 February 2021.

5.3 APAs FOR SMALL BUSINESSES UNDER THE CANADIAN[238] APA PROGRAMME

640. Since the APA Program was introduced in Canada in July 1993, the majority of cases addressed transfer pricing issues for large MNCs. However, the CRA received a number of requests to make the APA Program more accessible to a broader group of taxpayers with non-arm's-length transactions. These taxpayers contended that they had been unintentionally screened out of the APA Program for the following reasons:

- the demand for information and company time may exceed the capability of a small business to comply; and
- the fees charged by both the CRA and external advisors to pursue the APA process may be too high given the small size of the business.

641. To address these issues, the CRA implemented the procedures outlined in a special release of IC No. 94-4R. Canada introduced special procedures for small business taxpayers to improve access to the CRA's APA Program. An APA may be used to cover these transactions for a period of up to five years. As the taxpayer and the CRA gain comfort with the issue through the Small Business APA Program, the taxpayer may wish to renew the arrangement as a bilateral APA under the traditional APA Program.

642. In order to address the particular concerns of small business taxpayers, the CRA has adopted a number of procedures that are designed to reduce the time and cost of the APA process. Taxpayers applying for the Small Business APA programme must accept these procedures in their entirety and cannot opt out of one or more procedures in favour of the approach taken under the traditional APA Program. Key elements of the Small Business APA programme are summarized as follows:

- The CRA's CASD administers the programme.
- The programme has a fixed non-refundable administrative fee of CAD 5,000.
- Taxpayers must have gross revenues of less than CAD 50 million or a proposed covered transaction of less than CAD 10 million to be considered for the programme. The gross revenue and transaction thresholds are based on the taxpayer's reported prices for the most recent taxation year prior to the request and not the prices that may ultimately be determined to be at arm's length. A taxpayer may request that the APA covers multiple transactions of dissimilar products or services provided that the threshold is met for each transaction.
- The programme only covers transactions of tangible goods (which have not been bundled with non-routine intangibles) and routine services.

238. Refer Information Circular No. 94-4R (Special Release) dated 18 March 2005 https://www.canada.ca/en/revenue-agency/services/forms-publications/publications/ic94-4rsr/advance-pricing-arrangements-small-businesses.html accessed on 9 February 2021.

- Site visits are not performed. The only material CASD requires the taxpayers to submit is a functional analysis. The functional analysis should contain information about the proposed covered transaction, including: an organizational structure depicting the transaction flows/entities involved; the terms and conditions of the transaction; the functions performed, property used or contributed, and risks assumed by the entities involved in the transaction; the assumptions, strategies, and policies in respect of the transaction; detailed financial data for the most recent three fiscal years for the relevant entities; a history of the business; the names of direct competitors; industry background information (including critical success factors); as well as a description of transactions with unrelated parties that the CRA could potentially consider to be comparable.
- Only requests for a unilateral APA, without rollback, are accepted into the programme.
- Annual reporting under the programme is limited to stating, in writing, whether the critical assumptions have or have not been breached.

643. The goal of the Small Business APA Program is to conclude an APA within one year of the date of receipt of the request. Every effort is made to deal with Small Business APA requests as expeditiously as possible and taxpayers are duly informed of any unusual delay.

644. The main differences between the traditional APA programme and the Small Business APA programme are summarized as below:

(a) *Small Business APAs do not have site visits* - Under the traditional APA programme, APA site visits are routinely undertaken as part of the CRA's due diligence prior to establishing its position on a transfer pricing issue. Under the Small Business APA programme, site visits do not take place at all. If the taxpayer is selected for audit by TSO, the facts relevant to the transactions covered by the Small Business APA will be verified. Any concerns the TSO has regarding the proposed or finalized APA will be fully discussed with CASD staff prior to any action being taken. If the CRA determines that there has been a material omission or misrepresentation in the statement of relevant facts submitted by the taxpayer or the taxpayer's authorized representative, the CRA has the right to revoke the APA.

(b) *Small Business APAs only require a functional analysis* - Under the traditional APA programme, the CRA asks taxpayers to provide both a functional and an economic analysis. Under the Small Business APA programme, the CRA only requires a functional analysis. If the taxpayer has existing transfer pricing documentation which contains a complete and accurate functional analysis for the proposed covered transactions, the CRA accepts this documentation as the functional analysis for the Small Business APA request. A functional analysis must contain the records or documents listed under paragraph 247(4)(a) of the Income Tax Act, except for subparagraph 247(4)(a)(v) 'data and methods considered'. The CRA, then, performs an economic analysis based on the functional analysis provided by the taxpayer as well as responses to supplemental questions. The economic analysis determines an ALP for the transactions based on the most reliable data available. As part of the Small Business APA programme, taxpayers may still choose to prepare an economic analysis and may elect to submit this material to the CRA. However, the CRA bases its conclusion on its own economic analysis. The CRA presents its conclusion in draft format to the taxpayer for comment and may modify its conclusion when persuaded by factual evidence. This should not be misconstrued as a negotiation process as the CRA does not negotiate APAs with taxpayers.

(c) *Small Business APAs are unilateral and without rollback* – Under the traditional APA programme, a taxpayer is encouraged to request a bilateral APA and may also request a rollback of the results to prior taxation years. Under the Small Business APA programme, the taxpayer can only request a unilateral APA and does not have the option of requesting a rollback. This policy is intended to reduce the time and cost of completing the taxpayer's APA request, and to preclude the possibility of the APA leading to unresolved double taxation in a rollback year. Should any taxation authority reassess a transaction covered by the Small Business APA, taxpayers maintain a right to seek relief from double taxation pursuant to the pertinent provisions of the relevant bilateral Income Tax Convention.

(d) *Small Business APAs have a reduced cost recovery amount (filing fee)* – Under the traditional APA programme, the taxpayer agrees to cover CRA expenses for APA-related travel. Under the Small Business APA programme, there are no site visits and no travel is required for CA negotiations as the process will be unilateral. A fixed administrative fee of CAD 5,000 is charged by the CRA for this programme and is to be paid when the taxpayer makes its official Small Business APA request. Once the Small Business APA request has been accepted by the CRA, the administrative fee is non-refundable.

(e) *Small Business APAs have a reduced reporting requirement* – Under the traditional APA Program, taxpayers are required to file an annual report describing the taxpayer's compliance with the terms and conditions of the arrangement. Under the Small Business APA Program, the administrative burden of preparing an annual report is greatly reduced. All that is required is an annual statement saying that the critical assumptions have been reviewed for the APA year and that they have or have not been breached.

5.4 TREATMENT OF LOCATION-SPECIFIC ADVANTAGES (LSAs) IN CHINA

645. Location savings are the net cost savings derived by an MNE when it sets up its operations in a low-cost jurisdiction. Net cost savings are commonly realized through lower expenditure on items such as raw materials, labour, rent, transportation and infrastructure even though additional expenses ('dis-savings') may be incurred due to the relocation, such as increased training costs in return for hiring less-skilled labour. Market premium (equivalent to location savings) relates to the additional profit derived by an MNE by operating in a jurisdiction with unique qualities impacting the sale and demand for a service or product. In dealings with Chinese taxpayers, the Chinese tax administration has adopted a four-step approach on the issue of LSAs:

- identify if an LSA exists;
- determine whether the LSA generates additional profit;
- quantify and measure the additional profits arising from the LSA; and
- determine the TPM to allocate the profits arising from the LSA.

646. Both industry analysis and quantitative analysis are critical in determining LSAs and their impact on transfer pricing. The Chinese tax authorities believe that automotive industry, contract R&D services, luxury goods and pharmaceuticals are sectors where there are many LSAs that have led to extraordinarily high profits accruing to Chinese taxpayers.

647. Given that taxation should follow value creation, the Chinese SAT takes the view that the additional profits should be taxed in China if they are derived from the unique characteristics of the Chinese market. For example, the Chinese subsidiaries of some luxury brands have undertaken significant promotion activities to educate Chinese customers who had known nothing about the brands before. With more and more Chinese customers now familiar with the brands and products, sales revenue has experienced a great increase for the Chinese subsidiaries. On the other hand, deterred by the high prices set by the MNE groups in the Chinese stores, some Chinese customers who would have gone to luxury stores in China have instead chosen to go abroad. The money spent by Chinese shoppers in overseas luxury stores has been growing at a steady rate of more than 50% in recent years and has constituted a sizeable portion of the sales revenue of overseas affiliates. In the case of one brand (as an example), the products sold to Chinese nationals in stores located in countries other than China accounted for 12% of the total sales generated in these areas for the brand. This portion of the sales revenue and the profits realized should be attributed to the marketing contribution made by Chinese subsidiaries and taxed in China.[239]

5.5 APAs FOR SMEs UNDER THE FRENCH APA PROGRAMME

648. As the standard APA procedure can be burdensome, a simplified APA procedure[240] for SMEs is available from 28 November 2006 onwards. The simplified procedure proposed by the FTA includes the following:

239. Refer section D.2.4.4 of the United Nations Practical Manual on Transfer Pricing for Developing Countries (2017) accessed on 11 August 2019.
240. Refer Note issued by PwC on Transfer Pricing in France https://www.pwc.com/gx/en/international-transfer-pricing/assets/france.pdf accessed on 9 February 2021.

- Less transfer pricing documentation is required for the APA request. The documentation is limited to a legal chart of the group, the list of transactions and prices between related parties, functional analysis, description and justification of the TPM, and the financial statements of the foreign companies involved in the transactions.
- The FTA assists in the preparation of the functional analysis and in the choice of the appropriate TPM.
- An economic analysis is also requested.
- Simplified content of the ACR requested in the follow-up years of the APA (e.g., details of the computation of the remuneration and a statement on the substantial changes to the activity conditions described in the APA request, such as activities, functions performed, risks borne, assets used, accounting methods).

649. A simplified APA application process is available in France[241] to SMEs that meet the following criteria:

- less than 250 employees and a turnover of less than EUR 50 million (approx. USD 56.5 million), or total assets worth less than EUR 43 million (approx. USD 48.6 million); and
- 25% or more of the capital or voting rights are not held by one or more companies that do not meet the first condition.

These thresholds relate to the financial year preceding the one in which the APA is requested.

5.6 APAs FOR SMEs AND ABBREVIATED PROCEDURE FOR RENEWAL OF APAs UNDER THE GERMAN APA PROGRAMME

650. Simplified APA procedures[242] are available on request for applicants that meet the small taxpayer criteria as set out below:

- taxpayers with intercompany tangible goods transactions below EUR 5 million (approx. USD 5.7 million); and
- other intercompany transactions below EUR 500,000 (approx. USD 567,000).

241. Refer DLA Piper – APA and MAP Country Guide 2019 https://www.dlapiper.com/en/us/insights/publications/2019/03/apa-and-map-country-guide-2019/ accessed on 9 February 2021.
242. Refer Ministry of Finance Ordinance of 5 October 2006 – Information on bi or multilateral mutual agreement procedures under double taxation agreements for reaching Advance Pricing Agreements ('APA') in Germany, section 8 https://www.oecd.org/ctp/dispute/47655669.pdf accessed on 9 February 2021.

651. Simplified APA procedures are provided as long as no threat is posed to the objective of the APA, i.e., to create legal certainty for the applicant that is based on clear facts, and there is agreement with the relevant foreign tax authorities.

652. An APA may be renewed if the renewal request is duly filed, there is consent from the relevant foreign tax authorities, and it can be proved that the underlying facts in the future will continue to match those on which the existing APA is based. An abbreviated procedure[243] without submission of the documents required in an initial request is possible in such circumstances.

653. These processes are taxpayer-friendly measures and act as an enabler to accelerate the APA programme to a substantial extent.

5.7 APAs FOR PEs UNDER THE IRISH APA PROGRAMME[244]

654. The bilateral APA programme in Ireland applies to transfer pricing issues, including the attribution of profits to a PE. An application for a bilateral APA may be made by a company which is tax resident in Ireland for the purpose of the relevant double tax treaty and also by a PE in Ireland of a non-resident company in accordance with the provisions of the relevant treaty. In the latter case, an application may be made by a taxpayer for an APA in respect of transactions between parts of the same business enterprise operating in different countries (e.g., between a head office and a PE or between two separate PEs), subject to the provisions of the relevant double tax treaty.

655. It may be noted that a case which would require determining whether or not a PE exists for tax purposes will not qualify for admission into the APA programme in Ireland. However, where there is agreement between the taxpayer and both tax administrations that a PE does exist, the attribution of profit to that PE may be the subject of an APA in Ireland.

5.8 APAs FOR SMEs UNDER THE KOREAN APA PROGRAMME

656. A simplified APA application process is available to SMEs with annual revenue of less than KRW 50 billion (approximately USD 46 million). Eligible taxpayers can expect to complete the APA application process within one year.[245]

657. Under the APA programme existing prior to 2015, the in-depth review of NTS was necessary to examine the transactional and functional profile of transaction parties,

243. Refer DLA Piper – APA and MAP Country Guide 2019 https://www.dlapiper.com/en/us/insights/publications/2019/03/apa-and-map-country-guide-2019/ accessed on 9 February 2021.
244. Refer Ireland's Bilateral Advance Pricing Agreement Guidelines 2016, Part 35-02-07 https://www.revenue.ie/en/tax-professionals/tdm/income-tax-capital-gains-tax-corporation-tax/part-35/35-02-07.pdf accessed on 19 March 2021.
245. Refer DLA Piper – APA and MAP Country Guide 2019 https://www.dlapiper.com/en/us/insights/publications/2019/03/apa-and-map-country-guide-2019/ accessed on 9 February 2021.

and application of the most appropriate TPM. This used to cause the APA evaluation process to be prolonged to more than two years. Consequently, this added to the burdens on the taxpayer with incremental time and cost. Thus, the existing APA programme had become a tool mostly utilized by large MNEs. In response, the simplified APA programme was created to help streamline the process for SMEs. The simplified APA programme was launched in January 2015 and has been made available to SMEs in manufacturing, wholesale/retail, and service industries and gradually be made available to the remaining industries. The results of the simplified APA would be exemption from the NTS tax audit on the covered transaction for the evaluation period which is the covered period of APA. In addition, the MNE would be able to resolve the issue of uncertain tax risk for the covered period.[246]

5.9 APAs FOR SMEs UNDER THE APA PROGRAMME OF THE NETHERLANDS

658. A process designed to accommodate small businesses and specific support from the APA/ATR team for providing comparable data on independent enterprises is available for taxpayers that meet the following requirements:

- the value of assets is not more than EUR 6 million (approx. USD 7 million);
- the net turnover for the financial year does not exceed EUR 12 million (approx. USD 14.1 million); and
- the average number of employees for the financial year is less than fifty (not available for entities engaging in financial service activities without a real economic presence in the Netherlands).[247]

659. In order to decrease the administrative burden for smaller companies, the tax authorities, to the extent possible, give comparable financial information of independent enterprises. This assistance makes it easier for relatively small companies to file an APA request, as many small companies are reluctant to enter the APA process due to the administrative burden and related costs. The taxpayer still must provide, for example, the necessary information on the organization and functional analysis of the company, as well as the rationale for the proposed TPM and mechanisms.[248]

246. Refer Article by Gil Won Kang, Seung Mok (William) Baek and Sang Hoon Kim titled 'BEPS and transfer pricing in Korea' (15 July 2016) https://www.internationaltaxreview.com/article/b1f7nfymf94b9y/beps-and-transfer-pricing-in-korea accessed on 9 February 2021.
247. Refer DLA Piper – APA and MAP Country Guide 2019 https://www.dlapiper.com/en/us/insights/publications/2019/03/apa-and-map-country-guide-2019/ accessed on 9 February 2021.
248. Refer Note issued by PwC on Transfer Pricing in The Netherlands https://www.pwc.com/gx/en/international-transfer-pricing/assets/netherlands.pdf accessed on 4 March 2021.

5.10 SIGNIFICANCE OF ECONOMIC NEXUS PRIOR TO GRANT OF APAs AND RELEASE OF ANONYMIZED APA SUMMARIES IN THE NETHERLANDS

660. Since 1 July 2019, the formal procedure in the Netherlands for granting a tax ruling in a cross-border situation requires a second review, approval, and signature by a newly composed team of specialists within the Dutch tax authorities (DTAs): the College International Tax Certainty. This team, consisting of seven experts in transfer pricing and international tax, could therefore be considered as a second assessment team. Alongside the tightened internal procedure, one of the other most significant changes is the introduction of eligibility requirements for entitlement to prior consultation with the Dutch tax ruling team to obtain a tax ruling with an international character. As a result of these changes, the requirements to be eligible to enter into prior consultation have become stricter and more extensive.[249] Hence, rulings shall only be granted if the taxpayer has 'economic nexus' with the Netherlands. This means that operational activities in the Netherlands (or the plans to bring these to the Netherlands) are required for a ruling.

661. On 22 June 2020, the Dutch State Secretary of Finance published a new decree relating to mutual agreement procedures (MAP Decree) which also provides an option to a taxpayer to request the Dutch CA to enter into BAPA or MAPA discussions with other jurisdictions as a means to prevent or solve (potential) tax disputes based on the applicable tax treaty.[250] The said decree continues with the principles enacted in the Dutch tax ruling of July 2019 that no (advance) certainty will be provided if:

- there is no relevant economic nexus in the Netherlands;
- the sole or decisive purpose of the relevant case or structure is to reduce Dutch or foreign taxes; or
- entities involved are established in non-cooperative tax jurisdictions (EU list) or in a low-taxed jurisdiction (jurisdictions with a corporate income tax rate below 9%).

249. Refer 'An in-depth analysis of published anonymized APA and APA request summaries under the revised Dutch Tax Ruling Practice (Intertax, vol. 49, 2021, issue 3) by Koen Bolink (Houthoff)' http://kluwertaxblog.com/2021/02/18/an-in-depth-analysis-of-published-anonymized-apa-and-apa-request-summaries-under-the-revised-dutch-tax-ruling-practice-forthcoming-intertax-vol-49-2021-issue-3/ accessed on 5 March 2021.

250. Refer 'Netherlands issues new MAP decree' https://taxnews.ey.com/news/2020-1684-netherlands-issues-new-map-decree accessed on 5 March 2021.

5.10.1 Analysis of Published Anonymized Summaries[251]

662. During the period from 1 July 2019 to 30 June 2020, the first year after the introduction of the revised Dutch Tax Ruling Practice, the DTA assessed and published sixty-six anonymized summaries of APA requests and granted APAs. The most salient conclusions are as follows:

- All of the summaries have been properly anonymized since they cannot be traced back to the respective individual taxpayer in any way.
- The anonymized summaries provide valuable insight into which types of cases will and will not be granted certainty by the DTA and therefore contain useful and valuable information for stakeholders such as tax policymakers, non-governmental organizations, academics, transfer pricing practitioners, advisers and taxpayers who envisage obtaining an APA.
- In the vast majority of the published anonymized APAs, the TNMM was considered the most appropriate TPM for the circumstances of the case and, as such, has been approved by the DTA and applied by the taxpayer. Under the TNMM, the remuneration agreed in the APA is the median of a value close to it of a benchmarking study that is conducted and provided to the DTA. However, almost all of the anonymized summaries only provide the lower quartile and upper quartile of the conducted TNMM benchmarking study while the median value is not disclosed.
- In order to deal with the stricter eligibility requirements for preliminary consultation, a potential solution to meet the economic nexus requirement could be hiring staff from a group payroll company or having a limited number of employees employed by a Dutch group company and hiring the rest from a third-party employment agency.
- It is worth noting that even if there are transactions with a group company in a low-tax country or non-cooperative jurisdiction, an APA can still be obtained for the remuneration of the group companies in the 'other' countries. Only the transactions with the group company in the low-tax or non-cooperative jurisdiction will be excluded from the APA.

251. Refer 'An in-depth analysis of published anonymized APA and APA request summaries under the revised Dutch Tax Ruling Practice (Intertax, vol. 49, 2021, issue 3) by Koen Bolink (Houthoff)' http://kluwertaxblog.com/2021/02/18/an-in-depth-analysis-of-published-anonymized-apa-and-apa-request-summaries-under-the-revised-dutch-tax-ruling-practice-forthcoming-intertax-vol-49-2021-issue-3/ accessed on 5 March 2021.

5.11 UNILATERAL APAs FOR DOMESTIC AFFILIATED ENTITIES UNDER THE APA PROGRAMME OF POLAND[252]

663. A prominent characteristic of APA programmes the world over has been that they provide certainty in respect of TP issues involving cross-border transactions undertaken by AEs. An additional feature in the Polish APA programme has been that this certainty has been extended to domestic affiliated entities also. Article 20a of the Tax Ordinance Act 1997 provides that unilateral APA can be entered into at the request of a domestic entity so as to recognize the correctness of the selection and the application of the method for setting the transaction price between domestic entities affiliated with each other. Further, Article 20m of the Tax Ordinance Act 1997 provides that the APA filing fee shall be 1 % of the value of the transaction that is the object of the agreement, whereas in the case of a unilateral agreement that refers only to domestic entities, it shall amount to no less than PLN 5,000 and no more than PLN 50,000.

5.12 APAs FOR CERTAIN DOMESTIC TRANSACTIONS UNDER THE APA PROGRAMME OF UK[253]

664. Since April 2004, UK-to-UK transactions have been subject to transfer pricing legislation, but HMRC does not generally see such transactions as likely to warrant an APA. However, some UK-to-UK transactions, for example oil-related ring-fenced trades, are specifically provided for in legislation, i.e., in Part 5 of section 218(2)(f) of TIOPA.

665. Subsection (2) of section 206 of TIOPA states that activities carried on by a person are an 'oil-related ring-fence trade' carried on by that person if subsection (3) or (4) applies to the activities, as below:

> (3) This subsection applies to the activities if –
>
> (a) they are carried on by the person as part of a trade, and
> (b) in accordance with section 16(1) of ITTOIA 2005 or section 279 of CTA 2010 (oil-related activities), they are treated for any tax purposes as a separate trade distinct from all other activities carried on by the person as part of the trade.
>
> (4) This subsection applies to the activities if –
>
> (a) they are carried on by the person as a trade, and
> (b) in accordance with section 16(1) of ITTOIA 2005 or section 279 of CTA 2010 they would, if the person did carry on any other activities as part of the trade, be treated for any tax purposes as a separate trade distinct from all other activities carried on by the person as part of the trade.

---

252. Refer The Tax Ordinance Act, Poland https://supertrans2014.files.wordpress.com/2014/06/the-tax-ordinance-act.pdf accessed on 4 March 2021.
253. Refer Policy paper issued by HM Revenue and Customs – Statement of Practice 2 (2010) – Updated 12 July 2019, para. 18 https://www.gov.uk/government/publications/statement-of-practice-2-2010/statement-of-practice-2-2010 accessed on 17 February 2021.

5.13 APAs FOR SMALL BUSINESSES AND ABBREVIATED APAs UNDER THE US[254] APA PROGRAMME

5.13.1 APAs for Small Businesses

666. Taxpayers that are eligible for the small cases APA may submit a complete APA request together with the fee, or may contact APMA to discuss filing an abbreviated APA request. The pre-filing requirements do not apply to such APA requests. In order to be eligible for small cases APAs in US, the following conditions are required to be satisfied:

- sales revenues must be less than USD 500 million in each of the most recent three tax years;
- the aggregate value of the proposed covered issue(s) cannot be expected to exceed USD 50 million in any given year for the duration of the APA;
- the aggregate value of any transfer of rights in, or rights to use, intangibles cannot be expected to exceed USD 10 million in any given year for the duration of the APA; and
- no proposed covered issue can involve intangible property arising from, or otherwise relate to, an intangible development arrangement.

5.13.2 Abbreviated APAs

667. Under the US APA programme, taxpayers may seek renewal of an APA, wherein the renewal process generally follows the same process as APA requests unless the IRS permits the submission of an abbreviated APA request. An abbreviated APA request is the one in which information, documents, or content required for a complete APA request has been truncated or omitted, in pursuance of explicit authorization from APMA. An abbreviated APA request may be filed if the taxpayer can show that the applicable law, facts and circumstances, economic conditions, proposed covered issues and methods and other relevant factors are reasonably expected to be substantially the same in the proposed renewal APA years, as in the APA already signed.

668. These processes are taxpayer-friendly measures and act as an enabler to accelerate the APA programme to a substantial extent.

254. Refer DLA Piper – APA and MAP Country Guide 2019 https://www.dlapiper.com/en/us/insights/publications/2019/03/apa-and-map-country-guide-2019/ accessed on 17 February 2021.

CHAPTER 6

Way Forward

The success of the APA programme is an outcome of the collaborative process between the tax department and the taxpayers. Suitable suggestions have been made to usher into an era of accelerated APA conclusions. Recourse to APAs is destined to increase in the post-BEPS era. Also, APAs will be provided more impetus and would be a preferred dispute prevention recourse for MNCs with more opening up of economies.

6.1 FACTORS INFLUENCING SPEEDIER PROCESSING OF APAs

669. Success of APAs programme gets accentuated if the taxpayers are equally forthcoming and willing to provide details in time to tax authorities. Taxpayers need to be cognizant of the fact that the APA process can be time-consuming and resource intensive. Therefore, taxpayers are expected to evaluate their own situations and apply for APAs only if:

(a) the incidence of double taxation is certain or highly probable for the years to be covered by APA;
(b) they have a robust basis and TP documentation to justify their TPMs;
(c) they have the necessary resources to support APA process; and
(d) they have evaluated the suitability of APAs by conducting an in-depth cost-benefit analysis for their tax situations.

670. Tax authorities get energized for an early completion/resolution of APA proceedings if taxpayers:

(a) act in good faith throughout the process;
(b) comply with all the requirements pertaining to pre-filing meetings and application processes;

(c) provide access to TP documentation;
(d) be forthcoming in providing complete and reliable information and good quality analysis relating to APA applications;
(e) adhere to all the stipulated timelines when providing any clarification, information and analysis that may be requested by the relevant foreign CAs;
(f) update tax administrations on all information that they have provided to or received from the relevant foreign CAs on a timely basis; and
(g) provide the same set of information to the relevant CAs involved in the BAPA or multilateral APA.

671. The success of bilateral and multilateral APA process also depends on the agreement between the relevant CAs involved. Taxpayers are not expected to assume that the CAs would always be able to reach agreement for all BAPA cases. There may be valid constraints such as:

(a) lack of cooperation from taxpayers;
(b) transfer pricing adjustment cannot be varied due to domestic tax law or the adjustment has already been finalized through the domestic tax appeal process or litigation; and
(c) lack of suitable data to analyse the transactions for future years.

6.2 SUGGESTIONS ON IMPROVEMENT IN THE APA PROGRAMME

6.2.1 Recommendations in OECD Transfer Pricing Guidelines (2017)

672. The key recommendations[255] for improving the APA programme as stated in the OECD Transfer Pricing Guidelines (2017) are summarized as below:

(a) *Equitable access to APAs for all taxpayers*: The nature of APA proceedings may de facto limit their accessibility to large taxpayers. The restriction of APAs to large taxpayers may raise questions of equality and uniformity since taxpayers in identical situations should not be treated differently. A flexible allocation of examination resources may alleviate these concerns. Tax administrations also may need to consider the possibility of adopting a streamlined access for small taxpayers. Tax administrations should take care to adapt their levels of enquiry, in evaluating APAs, to the size of the international transactions involved.
(b) *Developing working agreements between CAs*: Between those countries that use APAs, greater uniformity in APA practices could be beneficial to both tax administrations and taxpayers. Accordingly, the tax administrations of such countries may wish to consider working agreements with the CAs for the

255. Refer Part F.5 under Chapter IV of the OECD Transfer Pricing Guidelines (2017).

undertaking of APAs. These agreements may set forth general guidelines and understandings for the reaching of mutual agreement in cases where a taxpayer has requested an APA involving transfer pricing issues.

6.2.2 Procedural Improvements[256]

673. In addition to suggestions made above, certain procedural changes are also a need of the hour to make the APA programme more efficient. Some of the recommendations are as below:

(a) *Using e-filing mechanism*: Various governments have already moved to e-filing mode for various compliances, be it annual tax return filing, withholding tax return filing, etc. Recently, India also commenced e-assessment procedure, and allowed online filing of all submissions to tax authorities during an audit process. In most countries, with few exceptions, the APA programme currently requires all filings to be done on paper, be it the initial application or the subsequent information such as responses to questionnaires or other submissions. Sometimes, these filings are in multiple copies. All these create a huge burden even on record-keeping and record maintenance. It will thus be perfectly in line with the current government programmes of most countries to allow e-filing of APA applications and subsequent documents.

(b) *Augmenting APA teams*: The inventory of APA applications continues to be large. Such large inventory puts undue pressure on existing APA teams and often delays the process. APA renewal cases also seem to suffer due to these reasons. This has created challenges for taxpayers, and surely for the governments. With more applications coming for bilateral APAs, as the shift in APA filings trend suggests, the responsibility to deliver them timely for meaningful engagement with treaty partners would present another set of challenges for the APA authorities.

(c) *Appropriate skill and stability of tenure*: Augmenting the number of officers in the APA team is necessary, but certainly not sufficient. For effective outcomes, tax officers with requisite skill sets and experience in transfer pricing cases should be appointed and for a stable/longer tenure.

(d) *Multiple subject matter experts*: Transfer pricing analysis is anchored in functions, assets and risks (FAR) of the business and economic analysis of the business and transactions provides requisite analysis on ALP of international transactions. Transfer pricing is far from a settled, business-as-usual area of tax. The new understanding gaining ground, particularly after BEPS recommendations and its implementation through multilateral instrument (MLI), is

256. Refer Deloitte Tax Policy Paper 2 (October 2018) https://www2.deloitte.com/content/dam/Deloitte/in/Documents/tax/in-tax-apa-evaluation-way-forward-noexp.pdf accessed on 11 August 2019.

of understanding the value chain of the transactions within the MNE group. Only a handful of tax administrations involve subject experts in the APA process. Hence, it would be desirable if more governments involve various subject matter experts to handle complex cases either permanently or on advisory basis to assist APA teams in arriving at better and commercially justifiable APA outcomes.

6.2.3 More Suggestions

674. Similarly, there are some procedural improvements which are suggested for implementation by the taxpayers and tax administrations. The taxpayers claim that their business transactions/interactions with their AEs are at arm's length. The said intention is seen to be true more in 'letter' than in 'spirit'. This inference is drawn from the observation made during the course of processing of UAPA applications that even for submitting responses/letters to queries raised by the APA teams, taxpayers invariably seek AEs' prior approvals. Needless to say, for agreeing at a markup in UAPAs, taxpayers do not come forward without taking internal approvals from their AEs. There have been instances where UAPA applications did not move forward for months together, even in routine IT/ITeS cases, as taxpayers failed to obtain any instructions from their AEs abroad. This has led to inordinate delays in signing of UAPAs. In response, tax administrations have introduced broad timelines in the past to be followed at each step of UAPA processing, but taxpayers have failed to adhere to such timelines. It may be noted that under BEPS Action 14 report articulated in the OECD/G20 BEPS Project, Element 1.3 provides that countries should commit to a timely resolution of MAP cases and countries have committed to resolve MAP cases within an average time frame of twenty-four months. Hence, not only for MAP APAs but also for UAPAs, a timeline for completion of each step of the APA process is essential. In fact, some jurisdictions have already provided significant importance to this aspect in their laws and guidance. There is precedence to this effect in Korea, where unilateral APAs are mandated by the LCITA to be completed within two years from the application date. Similar overall timelines have been prescribed under the APA programme of Poland, Portugal, Romania and Spain also.

675. A key characteristic of an APA is that it is discretionary, involving confidential tax ruling negotiated between the MNE and a tax authority. In terms of more suggestions[257] to dispel doubts involving secrecy, as this programme is held in closed doors, the following are brought on the table for consideration:

257. Refer Article titled 'Transfer pricing and state aid: the unintended consequences of advance pricing agreements' (Authors: Lorraine Eden and William Byrnes) https://unctad.org/en/PublicationChapters/diae2018d4a3.pdf accessed on 11 August 2019.

(a) At present, few countries publish their APA statistics. This practice should increase and more and more countries should come forward in making full statistical disclosures on an annual basis about their APA programmes.
(b) Bilateral APAs where two or more tax authorities develop and agree to a transfer pricing arrangement involving one MNE should be encouraged where possible. Bilateral APAs mean more governments are at the table and involved in the bargaining process. Having two governments at the table should trigger less room for State aid (APAs can be viewed as hidden, discretionary policies that can be misused by governments to attract or retain inward foreign direct investment by offering individual MNEs preferential tax treatment).
(c) Tax authorities need to develop clear internal documentation of their APA negotiations, methodologies, and outcomes.

6.2.4 Scheme for Simplified Process of Unilateral APAs in China[258]

676. APA applicants in China have encountered challenges under the APA process, such as cumbersome negotiation and signing procedures for APA applications and a long period of time for acceptance and review of the APA applications by the tax authorities. In the regions of Shenzhen and Guangdong, pilot projects under a unilateral APA simplified process were completed. In order to improve the efficiency of unilateral APA negotiations, the SAT has proposed to implement the unilateral APA simplified process on a nationwide basis, based on the findings from the pilot projects in Shenzhen and Guangdong. Accordingly, the SAT issued on 19 March 2021 a draft consultation document and a corresponding policy interpretation that would simplify the unilateral APA process in China.

677. Under the simplified process for unilateral APAs, the draft consultation document *inter alia* contains the following provisions:

(1) Clarifies that the simplified procedures would only be applicable with regard to unilateral APAs, and could not be applied to bilateral and multilateral APAs.
(2) Targets for the simplified procedures are companies with 'high tax compliance' defined as an enterprise that:
    (a) in the three tax years before the company's APA application period, the amount of connected transactions that occur each year is greater than RMB 40 million; and
    (b) one of the following three elements is satisfied:

258. Refer KPMG report dated 22 March 2021 titled 'China: Proposal for simplified process for unilateral APAs' https://home.kpmg/us/en/home/insights/2021/03/tnf-china-proposal-for-simplified-process-for-unilateral-apas.html accessed on 29 March 2021.

- at least three months before applying for the simplified procedure, the enterprise provides the tax authorities a report of contemporaneous information management (pursuant to Announcement No. 42 of 2016) for the most recent three tax years;
- an APA has been in place for the past ten tax years, and there has been compliance with that APA; or
- the enterprise over the past ten tax years has been subject to special tax investigation and adjustment by the tax authority, and the case has been closed.

678. Under the unilateral APA simplified process, the process steps would be reduced. The APA process under the general procedure is divided into six stages – preparatory meeting, negotiating intention, analysis and evaluation, formal application, negotiation and signing, and monitoring execution. The simplified APA process would reduce these six steps to three steps, and thus would be expected to accelerate the progress of the APA review. The simplified APA process also would set clear deadlines for the tax bureau's procedures for accepting applications and then for evaluating and negotiating the APA. It is expected that taxpayers shall be able to complete the process of applying for the negotiation and signing of the agreement within a nine to twelve-month period.

679. Considering the pendency of cases and the fact that under the general procedure, the Chinese tax authorities aim to conclude unilateral APAs within twelve to twenty-four months of the submission of formal applications, this is a very positive response on the part of the SAT, China. It is expedient that the simplified scheme is implemented as early as possible for the overall acceleration of the APA programme in China.

6.2.5 Proposal for Procedural Changes in India's APA Programme

680. *Framework agreement*:[259] The Indian Government entered into a framework agreement with the US in 2015 with the objective of resolving large pendency of MAP cases of IT and ITeS companies. The two countries set out several financial parameters and the cost-plus margins that may be applied to each case. The framework agreement played a very positive role in resolving close to four hundred MAP cases, resulting in a significant reduction in the inventory of pending MAP cases between India and US. There has been a demand from tax intermediaries that similar mechanism could also be attempted for the pending unilateral APAs for IT/ITeS cases in India keeping in mind the management of large pending IT/ITeS cases; therefore, CBDT may consider devising a framework of various quantitative and qualitative parameters; range of ALPs between which the negotiation can be done by the APA authorities with the taxpayers in such cases. It can be argued that such an arrangement would result in making APA somewhat akin to safe harbour rules. Tax intermediaries contend that it

259. Refer Deloitte Tax Policy Paper 2 (October 2018) https://www2.deloitte.com/content/dam/Deloitte/in/Documents/tax/in-tax-apa-evaluation-way-forward-noexp.pdf accessed on 11 August 2019.

is a matter of being practical so that the large inventory of APA applications can be liquidated quickly. In order to effectuate implementation of this arrangement, tax intermediaries contend that the CBDT may do so for IT/ITeS cases wherein quantum of covered international transactions is below a threshold limit. It is also argued that based on experience gathered by CBDT over a period of time since APA programme was introduced in India, a comprehensive, flexible and broad framework may increase the pace of UAPA resolutions.

681. Though the idea is well intentioned, it needs to be borne in mind that the pace of APA resolutions in India is already at a fast clip relatively. The pendency in routine IT/ITeS cases in India is not a huge cause for concern, as APA scheme is inherently not meant for such routine cases. CBDT has not put any embargo in admitting/pursuing such routine IT/ITeS cases in UAPA, which some tax administrations have already done. Main reason thereof has been to not give a signal that CBDT is restricting recourse to UAPAs in any case or manner whatsoever. On the contrary, CBDT has increased the number of APA teams to process cases faster. Since the APA regime is collaborative, backlog in cases may have numerous reasons which cannot be attributed to administrative delays alone. APAs have their own well-established process of resolution and any dilution as suggested is not warranted at this stage. However, peer learning and study of APA regimes in various countries demonstrates that 'APA schemes for small businesses' prevalent in Canada, France, Germany, Korea, the Netherlands and US and 'abbreviated procedure for renewal of APAs' in practice in Germany and US may be considered for introduction (with suitable modifications to align with the ongoing programme) to further accelerate the APA process in India.

6.2.6 Granting of APAs in Nigeria May Be Speeded Up

682. According to Regulation 7 of the TP regulations (2012), a taxpayer may approach the FIRS to enter into an APA to establish an appropriate set of criteria for determining whether the taxpayer has complied with the arm's-length principle for certain future controlled transactions undertaken by the taxpayer over a fixed period of three years. The revised TP regulations (2018) retain the general provisions of APAs as under the TP regulations (2012).[260] Despite APAs being in place in Nigeria since 2012, no APAs have been concluded so far in Nigeria.[261] Thus, so far, Nigeria has failed to enjoy the benefits of an APA programme as being availed in other jurisdictions. Undoubtedly, this trend needs to be reversed.

260. Refer Article by Victor Adegite titled 'Nigeria - Evaluation of Transfer Pricing in Nigeria (2012-2020)' paras 3.5 and 5.4, Published online on 10 June 2020 in Volume 27 of International Transfer Pricing Journal, 2020 (Volume 27), No. 4 https://research.ibfd.org/#/doc?url=/collections/itpj/html/itpj_2020_04_ng_1.html accessed on 26 March 2021.

261. Refer Nigeria - Transfer Pricing - Country Tax Guides - 17. Dispute Resolution (Last Reviewed: 18 October 2020) https://research.ibfd.org/#/doc?url=/linkresolver/static/tp_ng_s_17.&refresh=1616919768981#tp_ng_s_17. accessed on 26 March 2021.

6.2.7 Impact of Policy Changes in Poland

683. It has been observed that policy decisions issued by tax authorities have an immediate and direct impact on the popularity of the APA programme. A case in point is Poland.[262] There was an introduction in 2019 in the Polish tax law of a peculiar provision for associated companies. This new law limited deductibility for royalty payments and intangible services payments. At the same time, the new provision left the door open for full deductibility, but under the condition of receiving a positive APA regarding these transactions. As the limits for deductibility were set extremely low, most companies with such business models involving indicated payments were forced to apply for APAs. This resulted in a rapid increase in APA applications, whereas the pace of APA signings could not match this increase. Also, as per Polish regulations, most companies entering into the APA programme are seldom audited from a transfer pricing perspective. That is why every application makes it incumbent upon the APA team to make a meticulous assessment of what is presented by the taxpayer in the APA process. This factor has increased the time period in processing and signing of an APA, which in turn has led to increase in pendency in APA applications. The total number of pending APA cases was 429 in 2020, which means that some applicants could be waiting for an APA for more than ten years, despite the fact that Poland has stipulations in place to complete APAs within a fixed period of time. This situation called for an introduction of a scheme to accelerate the Polish APA programme.

684. In order to address the issue of rising APAs' pendency, a draft bill that addresses dispute resolution of double taxation issues and APAs was published on 22 March 2019 on Poland's legislative centre website to introduce 'simplified APA' into the Polish system. According to the draft bill, 'simplified APAs' would be unilateral; the procedures for concluding a 'simplified APA' would be completed within three months of the application. Once concluded, a 'simplified APA' would apply for a maximum period of three years, with the possibility of renewal for the next three years (provided that there are no substantial changes to the taxpayer's situation or the information relating to the 'simplified APA'). Taxpayers could apply for a 'simplified APA' if one of the following conditions or types of transactions is involved:

- Low value-added services.
- Fees for right to use a trademark or knowledge related to the experience gained, which could be used in industrial, commercial, scientific or organizational activities, or in other words, 'know-how'.[263]

The Polish President signed the Act on Resolving Double-Taxation Disputes and Concluding Advanced Pricing Agreements (DMR Act) on 5 November 2019. Unfortunately, contrary to earlier information and the communications from the Polish

262. Refer Article by Dr Monika Laskowska titled 'Poland APA statistics reveal alarming trends' https://mnetax.com/poland-apa-statistics-reveal-alarming-trends-42382 accessed on 16 February 2021.
263. Refer Poland: Proposals for 'simplified APA' https://home.kpmg/xx/en/home/insights/2019/04/tnf-poland-proposals-for-simplified-apa.html accessed on 6 March 2021.

Ministry of Finance, the Act does not contain provisions allowing taxpayers to sign APAs in a simplified procedure.[264] Considering the substantial backlog, Polish authorities need to expeditiously introduce the required mechanism(s) to accelerate the disposal of APA applications.

6.3 APA PROGRAMME IN THE PIPELINE

685. *Discussion paper on APAs released in South Africa*: Historically, South Africa's transfer pricing regime has not allowed APAs. To date, South African Revenue Service (SARS) has not offered tax rulings on transfer pricing. The Davis Tax Committee recommended the introduction of an APA programme in South Africa and presented various suggestions regarding how an APA regime could be implemented. The SARS has released a discussion paper on APAs. Given the current economic climate and the importance of transfer pricing for international trade, the need to find reliable and consistent methods to address uncertainty is viewed as critical if South Africa intends to increase foreign trade and investment. Observers believe it will be important for South Africa to introduce an effective APA programme as a matter of priority, and the opportunity to allow stakeholders to provide comments to the discussion paper is seen as demonstrating such good intentions.[265]

6.3.1 Maldives Issues APA Regulations[266]

686. As of now, Maldives has the distinction of being the latest jurisdiction to introduce the APA Regulations with effect from 16 March 2021. The Third Amendment to the Tax Administration Regulation granted the Maldives Inland Revenue Authority (MIRA) the right to enter into APAs with taxpayers or other tax administrations with the purpose of providing certainty and clarity in the domain of transfer pricing. The Advance Pricing Regulation (2021/R-42) was published by the MIRA on 16 March 2021 stipulating the procedures to be followed for entering into an APA with the MIRA. The Regulation provides for unilateral, bilateral or multilateral APAs. MIRA may enter into an APA for a maximum period of five years with a possibility for rollback. APAs can be applied by tax residents as well as PEs established in Maldives who enter into international transactions or arrangements with related parties. MIRA may charge a non-refundable application fee before proceeding with APA negotiations. The taxpayer is also required to reimburse the cost of essential travel incurred by the MIRA in relation to APA negotiations.

264. Refer Article dated 03.12.2019 by Michał Sojka https://www.roedl.net/pl/en/hot_news/transfer_pricing_in_poland/apa_costs_may_be_deducted_only_until_the_end_of_the_year.html accessed on 6 March 2021.
265. Refer Report by KPMG dated 12 November 2020 titled 'South Africa: Discussion paper on APAs' https://home.kpmg/us/en/home/insights/2020/11/tnf-south-africa-discussion-paper-apas.html accessed on 29 March 2021.
266. Refer Report of IBFD dated 6 April 2021 titled 'Maldives Issues Advance Pricing Arrangement Regulations' https://research.ibfd.org/#/doc?url=/data/tns/docs/html/tns_2021-04-06_mv_1.html accessed on 17 April 2021.

687. *Pre-filing consultation*: A person proposing to enter into an APA is required to make a request for a pre-filing consultation, which aims to determine the scope of the agreement, identify transfer pricing issues, determine the suitability of international transaction for the agreement, and discuss broad terms of the agreement.

688. *APA application*: The APA application must contain, among others, the following information:

(1) a description of the transactions or arrangements which are proposed to be included in the APA, and the proposed scope and period of the APA;
(2) details of how the transfer price will be determined via the APA, including:
   - comparability analysis of the transaction or arrangement;
   - elected TPM and the basis for such election;
   - critical assumptions; and
   - worldwide organization structure, history of and information about products, functions, tangible assets and intangible assets of the AE.
(3) place of residence of the AE; and
(4) jurisdiction or jurisdictions which the person proposes to be party to the APA.

689. *APA*: An APA signed between MIRA and the applicant shall include but is not limited to the following information:

- The names and addresses of the enterprises covered by the APA.
- Transactions, arrangements and agreements covered by the APA and the periods covered by the APA.
- A description of the agreed TPM and other related matters such as agreed comparables or a range of expected results.
- Critical assumptions upon which the transfer pricing is based, the breach of which would trigger renegotiation of the agreement.
- Definitions of relevant terms and phrases used in the APA.
- The conditions determined by MIRA, if any, other than those specified above.

690. *ACR*: A person with whom MIRA enters into an APA is required to submit an ACR together with the Income Tax Return for that tax year by 30 June of the following tax year, for the duration of the APA. The report must provide, among others, the following information:

- details of activities carried out by the person during the tax year;
- evidence of compliance with the APA; and
- assurance that critical assumptions and conditions stipulated in the APA remain unchanged.

691. *Termination of APA*: MIRA may terminate an APA under the following circumstances (the termination shall have effect from the first day of the first tax year to which the APA relates):

- intentional misrepresentation, omission or provision of incorrect information on an APA application or a compliance report;
- non-submission of the compliance report by the due date without reasonable cause; or
- material breach of a principal condition stipulated in the APA.

692. *Discontinuation of APA*: MIRA may discontinue an APA under the following circumstances (the discontinuation shall have effect from a date determined by MIRA with reference to the reasons for the discontinuation):

- unintentional misrepresentation, omission or provision of incorrect information on an APA application or a compliance report;
- non-submission of the compliance report by the due date with reasonable cause;
- material breach of a condition stipulated in the APA;
- material breach of a critical assumption; or
- change to an advance pricing related provision in a tax law, tax convention or international agreement.

6.4 RECOURSE TO APAs TO GET ENERGIZED IN POST-BEPS ERA

693. The complexities of establishing a transfer price for inter-affiliate cross-border transactions according to the arm's-length principle are universally acknowledged to be manifold. Adding to this complexity, the changes made to the OECD Transfer Pricing Guidelines (2017) by the BEPS Final Report on Action 7[267] on 'Preventing the Artificial Avoidance of Permanent Establishment Status' and Actions 8-10[268] regarding 'Aligning Transfer Pricing Outcomes with Value Creation' have introduced an entirely new dimension to the thought process of MNEs.

694. BEPS Action 7 report includes the changes that will be made to the definition of PE in Article 5 of the OECD MTC so as to restore taxation in a number of cases where cross-border income would otherwise go untaxed or would be taxed at very low rates. BEPS Action 7 report *inter alia* addresses these concerns in Article 5 of the OECD MTC as below:

(i) A commissionaire arrangement is frequently used by MNEs to escape from invocation of PE provisions in the source state. It may be loosely defined as

267. Refer Action 7: BEPS 2015 Final Report, OECD/G20 Base Erosion and Profit Shifting Project http://www.oecd.org/tax/beps-2015-final-reports.htm.
268. Refer Actions 8-10: BEPS 2015 Final Report, OECD/G20 Base Erosion and Profit Shifting Project http://www.oecd.org/tax/beps-2015-final-reports.htm.

an arrangement through which a person sells products in a State in its own name but on behalf of a foreign enterprise that is the owner of these products. Through such an arrangement, a foreign enterprise is able to sell its products in a State without technically having a PE to which such sales may be attributed for tax purposes and without, therefore, being taxable in that State on the profits derived from such sales. Since the person that concludes the sales does not own the products that it sells, that person cannot be taxed on the profits derived from such sales and may only be taxed on the remuneration that it receives for its services (usually a commission). A foreign enterprise that uses a commissionaire arrangement does not have a PE because it is able to avoid the application of Article 5(5) of the OECD MTC, to the extent that the contracts concluded by the person acting as a commissionaire are not binding on the foreign enterprise. Since Article 5(5) relies on the formal conclusion of contracts in the name of the foreign enterprise, it is possible to avoid the application of that rule by changing the terms of contracts without material changes in the functions performed in the source state. Similar strategies that seek to avoid the application of Article 5(5) involve situations where contracts which are substantially negotiated in a State are not formally concluded in that State because they are finalized or authorized abroad, or where the person that habitually exercises an authority to conclude contracts constitutes an 'independent agent' to which the exception of Article 5(6) applies even though it is closely related to the foreign enterprise on behalf of which it is acting.

(ii) Artificial avoidance of PE status through the specific exceptions, generally considered to be of a preparatory or auxiliary nature, in Article 5(4) of the OECD MTC has been on the rise due to dramatic changes in the way business is conducted. Depending on the circumstances, activities previously considered to be merely preparatory or auxiliary in nature may nowadays correspond to core business activities. In order to ensure that profits derived from core activities performed in a country can be taxed in that country, Article 5(4) is modified to ensure that each of the exceptions included therein is restricted to activities that are otherwise of a 'preparatory or auxiliary' character. BEPS concerns related to Article 5(4) also arise from what is typically referred to as the 'fragmentation of activities'. Given the ease with which MNEs may alter their structures to obtain tax advantages, it is important to clarify that it is not possible to avoid PE status by fragmenting a cohesive operating business into several small operations in order to argue that each part is merely engaged in preparatory or auxiliary activities that benefit from the exceptions of Article 5(4).

(iii) The exception in Article 5(3) of the OECD MTC, which applies to construction sites, has given rise to abuses through the practice of splitting up contracts by an enterprise or between closely related enterprises. These abuses are being addressed through recommendations of the BEPS Action 7 report.

695. On the other hand, Actions 8-10 reports deal with transfer pricing rules and have focused on three key areas to ensure that the transfer pricing rules secure outcomes that see operational profits allocated to the economic activities which generate them. Work under Action 8 looked at transfer pricing issues relating to transactions involving intangibles since misallocation of the profits generated by valuable intangibles has contributed to BEPS. Members of the MNE group are to be compensated based on the value they create through functions performed, assets used and risks assumed in the DEMPE functions involving intangibles. Work under Action 9 addressed the level of returns to funding provided by a capital-rich MNE group member, where those returns do not correspond to the level of activity undertaken by the funding company. Work under Action 10 focused on other high-risk areas, including the scope for addressing profit allocations resulting from transactions which are not commercially rational for the individual enterprises concerned (re-characterization), the scope for targeting the use of TPMs in a way which results in diverting profits from the most economically important activities of the MNE group, and neutralizing the use of certain types of payments between members of the MNE group (such as management fees and head office expenses) to erode the tax base in the absence of alignment with value creation.

696. The measures developed under Action 14[269] of the BEPS Action Plan (minimum standard) aim to strengthen the effectiveness and efficiency of the MAP process. They aim to minimize the risks of uncertainty and unintended double taxation by ensuring the consistent and proper implementation of tax treaties, including the effective and timely resolution of disputes regarding their interpretation or application through the MAP. Through the adoption of this Report, countries have agreed to important changes in their approach to dispute resolution, in particular by having developed a minimum standard with respect to the resolution of treaty-related disputes, committed to its rapid implementation and agreed to ensure its effective implementation through the establishment of a robust peer-based monitoring mechanism. As part of its focus on robust controversy management tools, Action 14 also recommended as a best practice that countries should implement BAPA programmes. Specifically, in regard to APAs, the BEPS Action 14 report *inter alia* recommends as below:

- Element 2.7 - Countries with BAPA programmes should provide for the rollback of APAs in appropriate cases, subject to the applicable time limits.
- Best Practice 1: Countries should include paragraph 2 of Article 9 of the OECD MTC in their tax treaties. This best practice is being implemented through Article 17 of MLI.
- Best Practice 4: Countries should implement bilateral APA programmes.
- Best Practice 11: Countries' published MAP guidance should provide guidance on multilateral MAPs and APAs.

269. Refer Action 14: BEPS 2015 Final Report, OECD/G20 Base Erosion and Profit Shifting Project.

697. There has been an increased interest[270] in bilateral and multilateral APAs in recent years on the part of both taxpayers and tax authorities, in response to greater risks of increased disputes and double taxation in the wake of the OECD/G20 BEPS Project and the ensuing changes to long-established rules. The response from tax authorities has been varied at global level, mainly due to resource constraints and consequent need to consider APAs in light of a cost-benefit analysis. Nevertheless, a heightened level of enthusiasm for APAs is reflected in the willingness of more and more administrations to negotiate APAs. The time and cost involved in negotiating a bilateral or multilateral APA remain an ongoing problem, but both taxpayers and tax authorities need not only to evaluate carefully the benefits of APAs in themselves but also to consider these agreements in light of the time and cost involved in alternative controversy resolution mechanisms, which may afford fewer advantages. The following validation offered by the OECD Transfer Pricing Guidelines (2017) in paragraph 4.173 is clearly applicable:

> A bilateral APA carries less risk of taxpayers feeling compelled to enter into an APA or to accept a non-arm's-length agreement in order to avoid expensive and prolonged enquiries and possible penalties. A bilateral APA also significantly reduces the chance of any profits either escaping tax altogether or being doubly taxed. Moreover, concluding an APA through the mutual agreement procedure [MAP] may be the only form that can be adopted by a tax administration which lacks domestic legislation to conclude binding agreements directly with the taxpayer.

698. With the adoption and implementation of BEPS Action 7 Report titled 'Preventing the Artificial Avoidance of Permanent Establishment Status' through the MLI, definition of PE in various tax treaties in Article 5 (as per the OECD MTC) shall be modified so as to restore taxation in a number of cases where cross-border income would otherwise go untaxed or would be taxed at very low rates. In order to obtain certainty in regard to income attributable to a PE as far as operations carried out in a particular market economy like India are concerned, MNCs are expected to increase filing of APA applications, as with effect from 1 April 2020, section 92CC of the Indian Income Tax Act, 1961 has been amended so as to provide that the government may enter into an APA with any person, including by or on behalf of that person, being a non-resident, i.e., a PE, determining the income referred to in clause (i) of subsection (1) of section 9, or specifying the manner in which said income is to be determined. Similarly, in other jurisdictions which allow access to APAs for PEs, as is the case in Canada, Indonesia, Ireland, Japan, Poland, Spain, UK and others (including Maldives, the latest entrant to the APA club), APA filings are expected to increase.

699. Transfer pricing of intangibles or IP has always been a major challenge for MNEs and tax administrations, and it is expected to remain challenging in light of the Actions

270. Refer Article by Michelle Markham titled 'OECD/International – Are Advance Pricing Agreements Experiencing a Renaissance as a Dispute Resolution Mechanism in the Era Following the OECD/G20's Base Erosion and Profit Shifting Initiative?' https://research.ibfd.org/#/doc?url=/collections/bit/html/bit_2020_01_o2_5.html#d18e253 accessed on 2 September 2020.

8-10 reports since the challenges that arise for both taxpayers and tax administrations in implementing the key DEMPE functions approach still remain. In order to reduce the level of subjectivity of tax administrations in assessing the outcome of TP analyses by corporates related to intangibles, taxpayers are expected to have greater access to APAs so as to have certainty in advance.[271]

700. While it may have been hoped by the visionaries behind the BEPS Project that it would lead to harmonious laws and interpretations, it would be expedient to state here that it appears that the opposite may be happening in many countries, more so, with many countries abstaining from wholeheartedly accepting the entire package of BEPS Action Reports. The importance of APAs, or perhaps a new generation of bilateral or multilateral agreements, remains at least as vital as in prior periods. But the enactment of unilateral regimes that differ from international norms frames serious issues that will have to be addressed in the future by tax administrations and MNCs alike. Accordingly, interest in APAs should continue to strengthen in the face of the increasing challenges faced on all sides of the international tax landscape.[272]

701. The ability to alleviate risk and access certainty on a prospective basis through negotiations at bilateral or multilateral level highlights expediency of multiparty APAs as a leading controversy management practice for the future. Consequently, tax administrations may ponder on whether more resources should be diverted to APA programmes to prevent transfer pricing disputes on an upfront basis, rather than, adopting an *ex post* approach and waiting for disputes to reach a MAP.

6.5 RECOURSE TO APAs TO INCREASE WITH MORE OPENING UP OF ECONOMIES

702. With the diversification of economies of developing countries and further opening up of the market, it is expected that the number of APAs involving the service industry and other types of industries could increase further in future.

703. What marks APAs as an unusual procedural device in the tax system is the fact that they permit the taxpayer and the government to discuss and resolve substantive tax issues voluntarily, prior to the transactions occurring, and to reach agreement on their tax treatment. Unlike an audit or settlement agreement, the primary function of the APA is to cover future transactions. APAs are different for several reasons:

271. Refer Article by Vikram Chand and Giovanni Lembo titled 'Intangible-Related Profit Allocation within MNEs based on Key DEMPE Functions: Selected Issues and Interaction with Pillar One and Pillar Two of the Digital Debate' published online on 6 November 2020 in International Tax Studies, 2020 (Volume 3), No. 6 https://research.ibfd.org/#/doc?url=/collections/itaxs/html/itaxs_2020_06_o2_1.html accessed on 3 April 2021.

272. Refer Article by Mark Thomas, Kristina Novak and Cym Lowell titled 'United States – Evolution of Advance Pricing Agreement Processes: Current and Future Experience in the United States' https://research.ibfd.org/#/doc?url=/collections/itpj/html/itpj_2018_02_us_1.html accessed on 2 September 2020.

- the issues are intensely factual (and the facts very complex) and require significant negotiation between the government and taxpayer;
- the agreements can cover a number of years;
- the agreements involve foreign countries; and
- the terms of the agreements are confidential with no redacted versions released to the public.

704. Most MNE taxpayers are drawn to the APA process because of current audit difficulties. The APA process, with its possibility for rollback application, can be an attractive alternative for dealing with existing and future problems, saving interest, penalties and current dispute costs. MNE taxpayers in a particular industry may consider the APA Program, with its ability to rely on treaty authority (in bilateral and multilateral APAs), as a useful way to combat serious gaps or irrationalities of current transfer pricing rules.

705. The APA Program is found attractive by MNEs as it has introduced three basic changes to the way the tax administration and taxpayers interact over transfer pricing:

- First, the APA Program changed the timing of the interactions. TP audits address transfer pricing issues after the transaction has occurred. In the APA process, however, the taxpayer and government(s) confront the transfer pricing questions at the outset, before the transactions occur.
- Second, the APA changed the participants. Traditionally, the initial government participant in a transfer pricing issue is the field office, when it audits the taxpayer. This stage is followed by an internal administrative appeal. Ultimately, if the case fails to be resolved through these channels, it moves to the courts. The APA, however, brings together all of the potentially interested parties (taxpayer, field office, domain experts, CA, foreign governments) in the upfront process. Rather than sequential involvement, if any, the APA Program facilitates the contemporaneous interaction of the full set of actors ultimately involved in a transfer pricing issue.
- Third, the APA changes the mission and 'scope of power' of the government in handling the individual taxpayer's transfer pricing problem. In the traditional audit context, the field authority is constrained in terms of flexibility and creativity. In the APA programme, the APA team possesses a greater degree of flexibility due to a variety of factors, including its place in the administrative hierarchy and its reliance on treaty power in reaching certain results with other countries.[273]

706. Cross-border business between foreign affiliated parties of multinational corporate company groups is of increasing importance in today's business world. Depending

273. Refer Article by Diane M. Ring titled 'On the Frontier of Procedural Innovation: Advance Pricing Agreements and the Struggle to Allocate Income for Cross Border Taxation' published in Michigan Journal of International Law, Volume 21, Issue 2 https://repository.law.umich.edu/cgi/viewcontent.cgi?article=1384&context=mjil accessed on 20 February 2021.

upon the countries involved, a large share of the total cross-border exchange of business transactions is coordinated within the boundaries of MNEs. With respect to today's global business structures, intra-group transfers of technology, management services, and financial loans move around within the MNE family. Intermediate goods (parts, components, and subassemblies) flow downstream for further processing within the boundaries of the MNE (or coordinated by it) before a final sale to third parties. At the same time, some affiliates may provide shared services to group business services (legal, accounting, advertising, IT, etc.) on behalf of the group, or its headquarters. For tax purposes, the pricing of intra-group transactions should align with the arm's-length principles based upon TPMs. With respect to the comparability of related party transactions and market transactions and given the limitations in comparable data availability, the combination of ALP and TPMs provides much room for interpretation, discretionary power, and transfer price manipulation affecting the tax base allocation. In this scenario, it becomes difficult for taxpayers and tax authorities to identify a perfect or near to perfect ALP of complex cross-border business transactions among associate enterprises. This is where APAs may address such special cases, namely complex related party transactions of multinationals for which standard transfer pricing technique may not apply or might be viewed differently by the parties involved, i.e., taxpayers and tax administrations of countries involved.

707. An APA is featured as a cooperative arrangement between the tax administration and the MNE taxpayer and, if bilateral or multilateral, between other states' tax administration and the MNE affiliates present in those States. The agreement determines, ideally in advance of controlled related party transactions within the boundaries of an MNE, an appropriate set of criteria for the determination of transfer pricing for these transactions over a fixed period of time. As the role of transfer pricing between related party corporations of a multinational group dramatically increases in the globalizing business world, the taxpayer and the tax authorities face complex problems of tax base allocation. APAs are intended to supplement the traditional administrative, judicial, and treaty mechanisms for resolving transfer pricing issues and tax base allocation. They are assumed to be most useful when traditional mechanisms to allocate income of related party business within the multinational group fail or are difficult to deploy because of a lack of institutionalization in international taxation and the transfer pricing system. International tax policies are inclined to consider that cooperative, non-adversarial mechanisms, such as APAs, can be a helpful tool to resolve transfer pricing and tax base controversies which could otherwise not be governed properly.[274]

708. Over the past decades, globalization of markets and firms was accompanied by development of powerful IT and efficient communication systems. The era of globalization that we live in and on whose journey the world embarked upon a couple of decades ago, albeit with a bit of trepidation, is almost irreversible. The new world trade

274. Refer IIMA Working Paper No. 2005-12-01 by Markus Brem titled 'Globalization, Multinationals and Tax Base Allocation: Advance Pricing Agreements as Shifts in International Taxation?' https://papers.ssrn.com/sol3/papers.cfm?abstract_id = 874567 accessed on 20 February 2021.

order ushering in globalization has resulted in a considerable increase in foreign institutional investments and a huge expansion in the production and service base leading to a multiplicity of international transactions. International taxation is hence assuming increasing importance, wherein the spectrum of transfer pricing is a major component. Transfer pricing is one of the most litigious subjects the world over. APA is one of the mechanisms to avoid Transfer Pricing disputes and is therefore destined for an exponential increase.[275]

6.6 IMPACT OF COVID-19 ON APAs

709. The unforeseen onset of COVID-19 has sent shivers down the spines of major economies of the world, with weaker developing countries having to face the brunt of the pandemic. None of the world economies, whether big or small, has been left untouched. However, impact of the pandemic industry-wise has been varied, with some sectors of industry, like IT/ITeS, e-retail, pharmaceuticals, seeing an exponential increase in business, while some others, like aviation, hospitality, commercial real estate, have really struggled. In the context of transfer pricing, such challenges include how to realign existing supply chain arrangements in order to adapt to the changed environment and how to undertake arm's-length comparability or benchmarking analyses in the absence of contemporaneous comparable data.

710. Release of Guidance on the transfer pricing implications of the COVID-19 pandemic by the OECD[276] has been very timely. This Guidance was developed and approved by the 137 members of the OECD/G20 Inclusive Framework on BEPS. It clarifies and illustrates the practical application of the arm's-length principle as articulated in the OECD Transfer Pricing Guidelines to the unique fact patterns and specific challenges implied by the COVID-19 pandemic. Four priority issues were identified and are covered in the Guidance:

(1) comparability analysis;
(2) losses and the allocation of COVID-19 specific costs;
(3) government assistance programmes; and
(4) APAs.

711. In respect of APAs, the OECD Guidance is *inter alia* as below:

- existing APAs and their terms should be respected, maintained and upheld, unless a condition leading to the cancellation or revision of the APA (e.g.,

275. Refer Article by Jabiulla titled 'Advance Pricing Agreement in India: Empirical evidence from corporate respondents' http://www.tjprc.org/publishpapers/2-41-1472021079-2.%20IJECR%20-%20ADVANCE%20PRICING%20AGREEMENT%20IN%20INDIA.pdf accessed on 16 February 2021.
276. Refer Guidance on the transfer pricing implications of the Covid-19 pandemic by the OECD dated 18 December 2020 https://www.oecd-ilibrary.org/social-issues-migration-health/guidance-on-the-transfer-pricing-implications-of-the-covid-19-pandemic_731a59b0-en.

breach of critical assumptions) has occurred. Taxpayers and tax administrations cannot automatically disregard or alter the terms of existing APAs due to the change in economic circumstances;

- a mere change in business results during the period affected by the COVID-19 pandemic would not, however, result in a breach of a critical assumption (unless the particular APA had a critical assumption regarding changes in business results). Where tax administrations establish that the critical assumptions of an APA have not been breached, the existing APA, as agreed, must continue to be respected, maintained and upheld. If a taxpayer believes that the terms of the APA are no longer appropriate, it should not seek unilaterally to breach critical assumptions deliberately or fail to comply with the terms or conditions of the APA, and it should avoid making unreliable price adjustments or taking other actions that are not consistent with (or otherwise fail to comply with) the terms of the APA that it may view as not appropriate. Instead, where taxpayers have concerns, they should approach the relevant tax administration in a transparent way to discuss their concerns;
- when considering the consequences of the failure to meet critical assumptions, tax administrations and taxpayers should consider the (i) terms of the APA; (ii) any agreement between relevant tax administrations as to how to deal with the failure; and (iii) any applicable domestic law or procedural provisions. A breach of critical assumption with the APA could have three potential outcomes:
  - Revision, which means that the taxpayer and tax administrations still have the benefit of the APA for the whole of the proposed period, albeit that different terms apply before and after the revision date.

    Revision would be the appropriate response where there has been a material change in conditions noted in a critical assumption in the APA and the tax administration and the taxpayer agree on how to revise the APA. The revision of an existing APA would have the effect of changing the previously agreed terms of an APA. Under this approach, it is likely that the original terms of the APA would remain in force for the period up to FY 2020, with revised terms applying for FY 2020 and any subsequent year(s) subject to the economic circumstances derived from the COVID-19 pandemic. In some circumstances, it may be possible to retain some of the terms set out in an APA, but revise specific provisions for which the breach in the critical assumptions is relevant. For example, an APA may cover a series of controlled transactions for which the agreed methodology for only one specific transaction required revision. In other circumstances, more general revisions may be required, depending on the specific facts and circumstances of a case, where allowed by domestic law. For example, tax administrations could consider evaluating the results of the transfer pricing methodology specified by the APA over the period of the APA, rather than on an annual basis, i.e., a 'term test'. This approach would aggregate the financial results of FY 2020, which may be exceptional, with the more normal results of prior and future years. In combination with this, tax administrations could also consider extending the period covered by an APA. Tax administrations could consider segregating the terms of the APA between financial years affected and unaffected by COVID-19, or cancelling an existing APA for FY 2020 and then renewing the APA in a future period, potentially on revised terms. Alternatively, tax administration could also consider aggregating the financial results from a series of covered transactions covered separately under an APA and assessing whether on aggregate they deliver an outcome consistent with the terms of the APA;

  - Cancellation, which means the APA is treated as being effective and in force but only up to the cancellation date and not for the whole of the proposed period.

    In the context of the COVID-19 pandemic, there are two situations which may lead to cancelling an APA when it is established that: in FY 2020 (i) there is a material breach in an APA's critical assumption as a result of a change in economic circumstances; or (ii) the taxpayer failed to materially comply with any term or condition of the APA. Cancellation would not, however, be automatic and the tax administration may waive cancellation under certain circumstances. Cancellation would have the effect of ending an APA on an agreed date or from a particular tax year or accounting period (e.g., after FY 2019);
  - Revocation, which has the effect that the taxpayer is treated as if the APA had never been entered into.

    Revocation may be considered where: (i) there is a misrepresentation, mistake or omission that was attributable to the neglect, carelessness, or wilful default of a taxpayer when filing an APA request and submission, the annual reports, or other supporting documentation or in supplying any related information; or (ii) the participating taxpayer (or taxpayers) fails to materially comply with a fundamental term or condition of the APA. The pandemic has not altered that standard;
- the timing for addressing the terms of APAs impacted by COVID-19 is important. Where material changes in economic conditions lead to the breach of one or more of the critical assumptions, taxpayers should notify the relevant tax administrations as soon as practicable after the change occurs, or the taxpayer becomes aware of the change. Early notification is encouraged in order to give the affected parties more time to try to reach agreement on revising the APA, thereby reducing the likelihood of cancellation;
- where the critical assumptions of an APA are breached, it is important that taxpayers collect and provide tax administrations with relevant supporting documentation. When engaging with tax administrations, it is important that taxpayers are transparent and disclose all relevant information in a timely manner. In so doing, they will help to maintain the non-adversarial spirit and environment that is vital to the success of APA negotiations;
- when considering the consequences of non-compliance with terms and conditions of an existing APA, tax administrations should adopt a similar approach to situations where there is a failure to meet critical assumptions. For example, when determining their response, tax administrations should consider (i) the terms of the APA; (ii) any agreement between relevant tax administrations as to how to deal with non-compliance; and (iii) any applicable domestic law or procedural provisions;
- in respect of APAs under negotiation, where taxpayers and tax administrations are negotiating APAs that are intended to cover FY 2020, all parties are encouraged to adopt a flexible and collaborative approach to determine how to take into account the current economic conditions. For example, consideration could be given to agreeing to a short period APA covering the period affected by the COVID-19 pandemic and a separate APA covering the post-COVID period. Another solution could be to conclude the APA for the whole period (e.g., APA period of 2020-2024) with a condition that the relevant impacts of the COVID-19 pandemic will be analysed and reported annually once they are known, and retrospective amendments to the APA made accordingly, when appropriate. Another solution could be to extend the period of the APA to mitigate the short-term effect of the pandemic, depending on the magnitude and the length

of such effect. Additionally, the use of a cumulative or term test throughout the APA period could be given consideration. In this context, it is important that taxpayers be transparent and disclose all relevant information concerning the impact of the COVID-19 pandemic on the covered transactions in a timely manner.

712. With margins under pressure due to COVID-19-led business discontinuity, multinationals are looking to exit or renegotiate APAs. Many multinationals and captive centres of MNEs have reached out to tax experts seeking a legal opinion on how they can exit or renegotiate APAs signed with tax authorities.[277] Here, a careful consideration has to be provided by tax authorities, as any relaxation in terms or margins agreed under the APA cannot be blanket, but must focus on a particular business/industry, as not all companies have been adversely impacted by COVID-19. Some taxpayers may face challenges applying existing APAs under the economic conditions resulting from the COVID-19 pandemic. In those instances, taxpayers are within their rights to adopt a collaborative and transparent approach by raising these issues with the relevant tax administrations in a timely manner. Taxpayers should not seek to resolve them unilaterally without consulting with the relevant tax administrations. Where taxpayers notify tax administrations of the failure to meet critical assumptions, tax administrations may want to consider waiting for a reasonable period until data and information on the magnitude and longevity of the economic impact of COVID-19 are available before determining how to respond to a breach. By deferring their response, until more data and information is available, tax administrations may find it easier to revise, rather than cancel, an APA.

277. Refer Article published on 29 April 2020 titled 'Covid 19 impact: MNCs look to exit, renegotiate APAs' https://economictimes.indiatimes.com/news/company/corporate-trends/mncs-look-to-exit-renegotiate-apas/articleshow/75436398.cms?from=mdr accessed on 20 February 2021.

CHAPTER 7
Conclusion

An exhaustive view of the taxpayer position, which is made possible by the APA programme, enables a proper understanding of the transaction, proper determination of arm's-length pricing methodology and helps collect a fair amount of taxes without any dispute. Filing of a large number of APA applications by the taxpayers is a testimony of their confidence in the APA Program. In terms of BEPS Action 5 minimum standard, exchange of APA rulings has provided another dimension to the benefits of APA programme, as availability of timely and targeted information about such rulings has immense potential to better equip tax authorities to quickly identify risk areas in their respective jurisdictions so as to curb BEPS. This augurs well for the APA programme and is another milestone in its evolution process. APAs have provided jurisdictions with an excellent platform to fostering a non-adversarial tax regime in their fight against BEPS.

713. The European Parliament[278] took cognizance that the scale of tax evasion and avoidance as estimated by the Commission is up to EUR 1 trillion a year, while the OECD estimated the revenue loss at global level to be between 4% and 10% of all corporate income tax revenue, representing between EUR 75 and EUR 180 billion annually, at 2014 levels. It is also reported that in 2016, 60% of all world trade was conducted through intra-group transactions and therefore subject to TPMs, with 70% of all profit shifting having been done through transfer pricing. To prevent international tax issues, many States initiated a robust development of transfer pricing and APA practices, with the main purpose being to protect tax revenue, while at the same time providing certainty for their stakeholders. As per OECD Work on Taxation (2018-19),[279] intra-group trade accounts for approximately 50% of global transactions. Out of these global transactions, the developing countries are likely to have a significant proportion of cross-border transactions within the MNE groups and hence,

278. Refer European Parliament, Report on tax rulings and other measures similar in nature or effect (2016/2038(INI)) (2016) http://www.europarl.europa.eu/sides/getDoc.do?type=REPORT&reference=A8-2016-0223&language=EN accessed on 10 August 2019.
279. Refer OECD Work on Taxation (2018-19) http://www.oecd.org/tax/centre-for-tax-policy-and-administration-brochure.pdf accessed on 10 August 2019.

these transactions shall be subjected to transfer pricing regulations and resultant litigation. Tax uncertainty, particularly, in the field of Transfer Pricing, has been an area of immense concern to the MNEs. Various measures for providing certainty to MNEs have been taken by tax authorities across the world to ameliorate the situation, so as to facilitate economic activity and seamless transfer of investments and technologies. Among various steps taken, introduction of APA scheme has attracted tremendous interest among the MNEs. The developing countries have greater exposure to BEPS risks due to being capital and technology importing countries. This requirement potentially increases the usefulness of an effective TP dispute prevention mechanism like APA. Intensive examination of APA applications and in-depth analysis of international transactions and documents enable a better appreciation of transfer price set by the applicant and their compliance with the arm's-length principle. The 360° view of the taxpayer position, which is made possible by the APA programme, enables a proper understanding of the international transaction(s), proper determination of arm's-length pricing methodology(ies) and helps collect a fair amount of taxes without any dispute.

7.1 SUMMARY OF ANALYSIS OF APA PROGRAMMES UNDER CHAPTER 3

714. Countries have implemented APAs in their legal or administrative procedures as a bilateral resolution mechanism to avoid double taxation. Many countries have introduced APA procedures in their domestic laws through different legal forms. For example, in certain countries, an APA may be a legally binding engagement between taxpayers and tax authorities, while in other countries it may be a more informal arrangement between the tax authorities and the taxpayer. Out of the twenty-five jurisdictions analysed in detail in Chapter 3, namely, Australia, Canada, China, France, Germany, India, Indonesia, Ireland, Japan, Korea, Mexico, the Netherlands, New Zealand, Nigeria, Poland, Portugal, Romania, Russia, Singapore, Spain, Sweden, Thailand, UK, US and Vietnam, it was observed that fifteen jurisdictions have introduced APAs through its inclusion under their respective tax code or law, whereas ten jurisdictions have issued guidelines, circulars and notifications for their implementation, as provided in detail in Figure 13.

Figure 13 Introduction of APA Through Tax Code or Through Guidelines in Various Countries

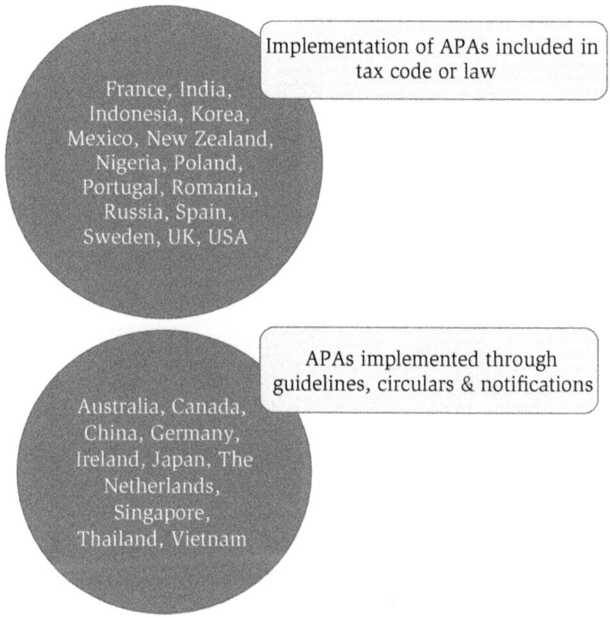

715. Out of the twenty-five jurisdictions which have been analysed in detail, twenty-one have unilateral, bilateral and multilateral APAs in their respective programmes. Three countries have bilateral and multilateral APAs, whereas only one has bilateral APAs. The distribution of types of APAs in various jurisdictions is provided in Figure 14.

Figure 14 Types of APAs Available in Various countries

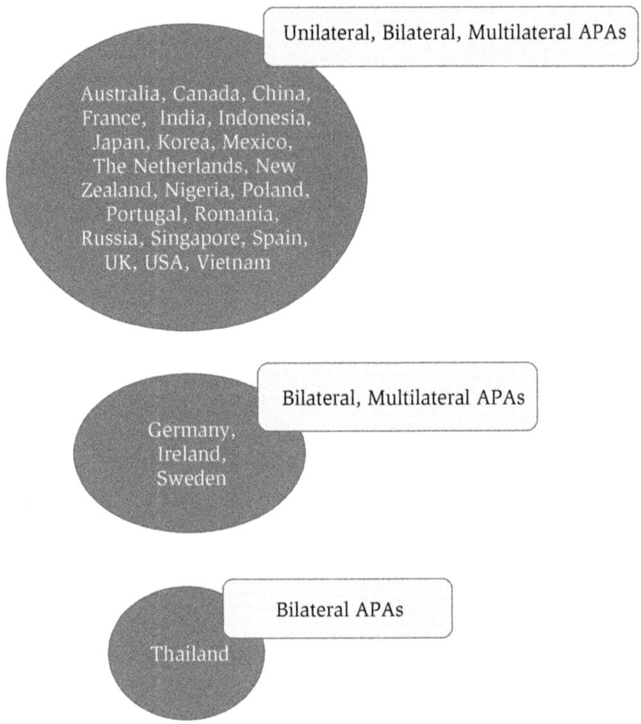

716. In regard to the term of the APA period under the APA programme in each country, twenty-one jurisdictions have the provision to execute APAs with a term up to five years, two jurisdictions have the provision to execute APAs with the term of four years, whereas two jurisdictions execute APAs for a term of three years, as provided in Figure 15.

Figure 15 Term of APAs Available in Various Countries

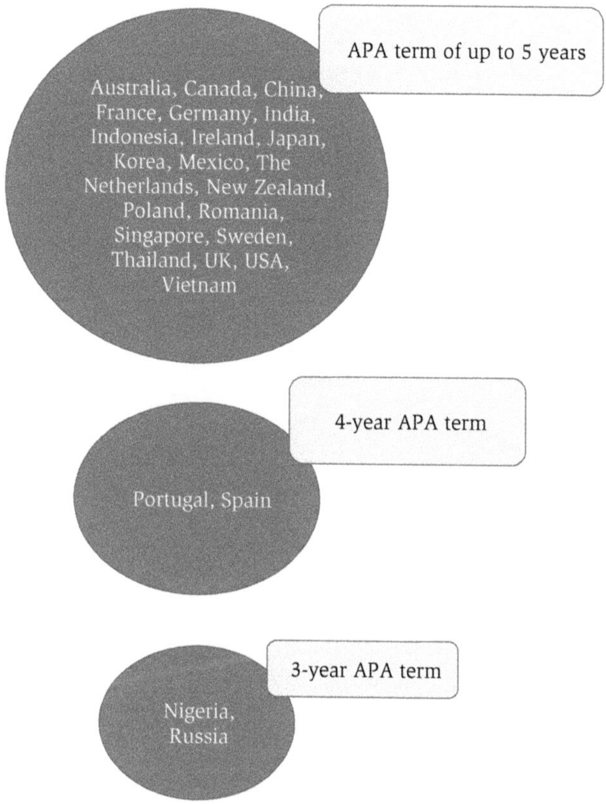

717. In regard to the requirement of payment of filing fee to avail the benefits of the APA programme in each country, eleven jurisdictions have this requirement, whereas in fourteen jurisdictions, there is no such stipulation of payment of filing fees as provided in Figure 16.

Figure 16 Requirement to Pay Filing Fee in Various Countries

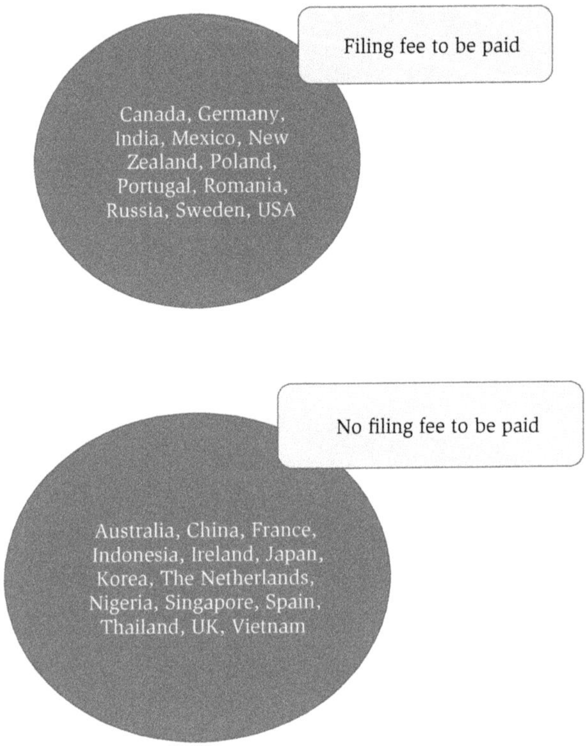

718. In regard to availability of pre-filing in the APA programme in each country analysed in Chapter 3, twenty-three jurisdictions have this facility, whereas in one jurisdiction, there is no such stipulation and in one jurisdiction, there is no specific guidance to this effect, as provided in Figure 17.

Figure 17 Availability of Pre-filing in Various Countries

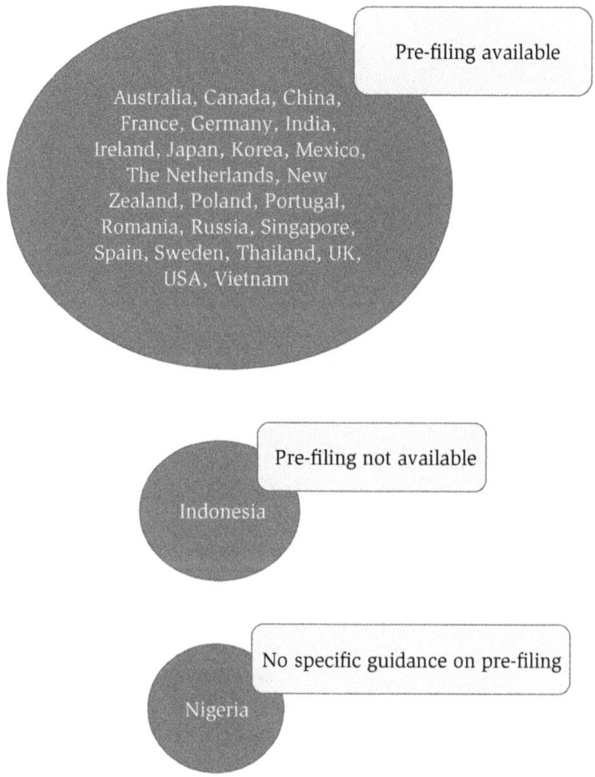

719. In regard to availability of pre-filing in the APA programme on an anonymized basis in each country analysed in Chapter 3, nine jurisdictions have this provision, whereas in twelve jurisdictions, there is no such stipulation, and in four jurisdictions, there is no specific guidance to this effect, as provided in detail in Figure 18.

Figure 18 Availability of Pre-filing on an Anonymised Basis in Various Countries

720. In regard to availability of rollback of APA in the APA programme in each country analysed in Chapter 3, eleven jurisdictions allow rollback of APA, whereas in five jurisdictions there is no such mandate; in seven jurisdictions rollback is available for BAPA, MAPA and not for UAPA, and in two jurisdictions, there is no specific guidance to this effect, as provided in Figure 19.

Figure 19 Availability of Rollback of APA in Various Countries

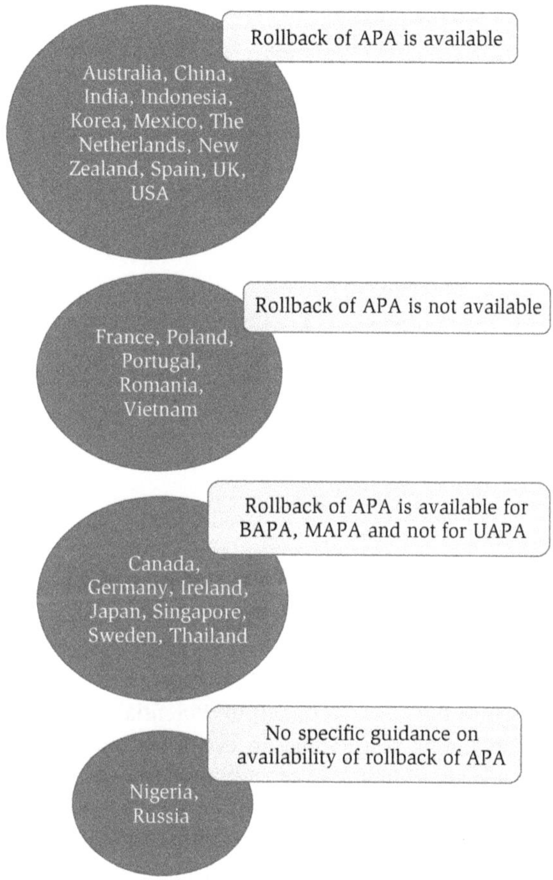

721. Renewal of APAs is an important constituent of APA programme of any jurisdiction. Renewal is facilitated when there is not any change in FAR, economic situation and the terms and conditions of the existing APA have been fully complied with. Incorporation of provisions in regard to renewal of APAs demonstrates the intent of a jurisdiction to provide a long-term and stable APA programme. In regard to availability of renewal of APA in the APA programme in each country analysed in Chapter 3, twenty-two jurisdictions allow renewal, whereas in three jurisdictions, there is no specific guidance to this effect, as provided in Figure 20.

Figure 20 Availability of Renewal of APAs in Various Countries

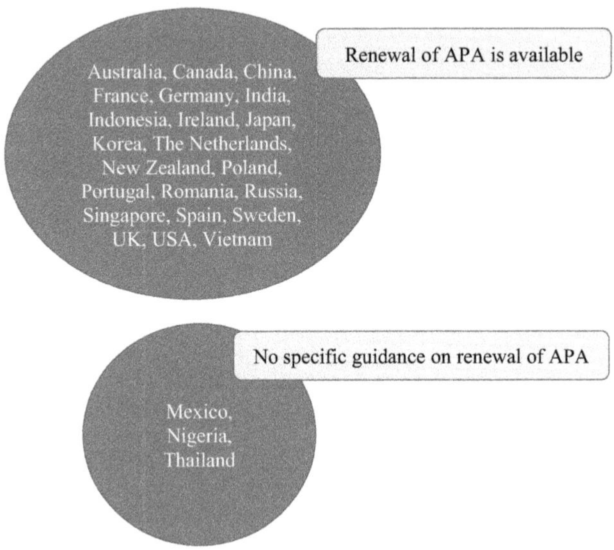

7.2 CHANGE IN MUTUAL INTERACTIONS BETWEEN TAX ADMINISTRATIONS AND TAXPAYERS

722. The COVID-19 pandemic has presented practical difficulties for tax administrations and taxpayers currently negotiating APAs. Potential challenges may arise for a number of reasons, including restrictions on domestic and international travel; enforced or voluntary working from home; or additional resource pressures as a result of efforts to manage responses to the COVID-19 pandemic. Despite these potential challenges, the value of achieving advanced certainty and effective dispute prevention through APAs remains compelling. A number of tax administrations and taxpayers have identified a variety of ways to adapt working practices in order to overcome any practical impediments to working APAs. Tax administrations and taxpayers should recognize that rigid adherence to pre COVID-19 working practices may unduly lead to significant delays in APA negotiations. Instead, innovative and flexible approaches to ensure collaborative working in order to minimize delays in concluding APAs under negotiation should be encouraged. Effective use of tax administration and taxpayer resources is crucial during the period of the COVID-19 pandemic and the following facilities/options may be explored:

- virtual tax administration and taxpayer case conferences in place of physical meetings (e.g., through telephone and videoconferences);
- virtual functional interviews with taxpayer's employees;
- virtual taxpayer site visits in place of physical visits (so long as the performance of adequate due diligence is not compromised);

- electronic documentation sharing (via encrypted emails or electronic sharing platforms).

7.2.1 Outcome on APAs' Disposal Due to Online Working

723. A silver lining that has emerged as a result of modification in procedural improvements in the APA programme has been reported in Poland,[280] wherein, because of the COVID-19 perturbations, the Polish APA team was required to shift to an online style of work. The team managed this change very fluently and was available for applicants throughout the year. They were very active with respect to collaboration and cooperation with other countries' CAs. As a result of this effort, there was a slight growth in the number of completed APAs. In 2020, the number of APAs finalized was eighteen, including eleven unilateral APAs and as many as seven bilateral APAs, the best record since launching the programme in 2006.

7.3 EXCHANGE OF APA RULINGS: A TOOL TO TACKLE BEPS CONCERNS

724. The BEPS Action 5 minimum standard on the compulsory spontaneous exchange of information on tax rulings (the 'transparency framework') provides tax administrations with timely information on rulings that have been granted to a foreign related party of their resident taxpayer or a PE, which can be used in conducting risk assessments and which, in the absence of exchange, could give rise to BEPS concerns. The transparency framework requires spontaneous exchange of information on five categories of taxpayer specific rulings:

(i) rulings related to certain preferential regimes;
(ii) UAPAs or other cross-border unilateral rulings in respect of transfer pricing;
(iii) rulings providing for a downward adjustment of taxable profits;
(iv) PE rulings; and
(v) related party conduit rulings.

In practice, tax rulings can be an effective way to provide certainty to taxpayers and reduce the risk of disputes. Rather, the need for transparency on rulings is that a tax administration's lack of knowledge or information on the tax treatment of a taxpayer in another jurisdiction can impact the treatment of transactions or arrangements undertaken with a related taxpayer resident in its own jurisdiction and thus lead to BEPS concerns. The availability of timely and targeted information about such rulings is intended to better equip tax authorities to quickly identify risk areas. This framework was designed with a view to finding a balance between ensuring that the information exchanged is relevant to other tax administrations and that it does not

280. Refer Article by Dr Monika Laskowska titled 'Poland APA statistics reveal alarming trends' https://mnetax.com/poland-apa-statistics-reveal-alarming-trends-42382 accessed on 16 February 2021.

impose an unnecessary administrative burden on either the country exchanging the information or the country receiving it. In regard to the exchange of UAPA rulings, under OECD's Harmful Tax Practices – 2019 Peer Review Reports on the Exchange of Information on Tax Rulings,[281] only the following observations were made, indicating an overall efficiency in the practice of exchange of rulings:

(1) Botswana was recommended to apply the best efforts approach to identify all potential exchange jurisdictions for APA and PE rulings and to put in place a review and supervision mechanism, as soon as possible.
(2) India was recommended to continue its efforts to ensure that all information on future APAs is exchanged as soon as possible.

725. Apart from the above, in December 2015, an EU Directive was adopted which requires certain information to be exchanged between Member States of the EU on advance cross-border rulings and APAs (exchange of unilateral, bilateral and multilateral APAs) issued by its Member States. Council Directive (EU) 2015/2376 of 8 December 2015[282] amended Directive 2011/16/EU, as regards mandatory automatic exchange of information in the field of taxation provides for the mandatory automatic exchange of information on advance cross-border rulings and APAs. Under the Directive, Member States are obliged to automatically exchange basic information in relation to APAs with the other Member States of the EU and to communicate a subset of this information to the EC. EU Member States are required to apply the provisions of the Directive with effect from 1 January 2017. Following the exchange of such information, a Member State may request its counterparts in EU to provide additional information including the full text of the APA. Under the Directive, where a Member State enters into an APA with a non-EU country under a double tax treaty and the provisions of that treaty do not permit disclosure of the information received under the treaty to a third-party country, that Member State is still obliged to exchange certain information. The information to be exchanged with other Member States and the EC is based on the taxpayer's request that led to the issuance of the APA rather than the APA itself.

726. Exchange of APA rulings has provided another dimension to the benefits of APA programme, as availability of timely and targeted information about such rulings has immense potential to better equip tax authorities to quickly identify risk areas in their respective jurisdictions so as to curb BEPS. This augurs well for the APA programme and is another milestone in its evolution process.

281. Refer OECD's Harmful Tax Practices – 2019 Peer Review Reports on the Exchange of Information on Tax Rulings https://www.oecd-ilibrary.org/docserver/afd1bf8c-en.pdf?expires=1616235727&id=id&accname=guest&checksum=3F84496DCD3EE5B70B9F8007E002E8C5 accessed on 20 March 2021.
282. Refer Council Directive (EU) 2015/2376 of 8 December 2015 https://eur-lex.europa.eu/legal-content/en/TXT/?uri=CELEX%3A32015L2376 accessed on 20 March 2021.

7.4 CONCLUDING REMARKS

727. Filing of a large number of APA applications by the taxpayers across various jurisdictions is a testimony of their confidence in the APA programme. The experience suggests that applicants have, by and large, provided cooperation in the APA process leading to the logical conclusion of the process and signing of agreements. The APA teams around the world have had a good experience in dealing with the applicants and tax intermediaries, barring certain exceptions where APA teams are not able to process some applications due to non-cooperation from the taxpayers like non-furnishing or delayed furnishing of information.

728. The APA process is very open and transparent, and its success depends on the mutual faith among the stakeholders. It has been experienced that the quality of information filed, FAR analysis, and economic analysis submitted in the applications has improved over the years. On the other hand, as evident from the statistics on APA programme of various countries, a large number of applications have been filed, but average time taken in processing these cases is gradually increasing. It has been experienced at the ground level that the APA teams are able to dispose of applications with speed when taxpayers furnish comprehensive FAR, robust economic analysis in tandem with filing of the APA applications and are equally forthcoming/prompt in filing replies to queries of APA teams in the course of processing of APA applications. Few examples of very early conclusion of APAs can be seen in China,[283] where five of the nine newly signed bilateral APAs in 2019 were concluded within only one year of formal application. In addition, in the period 2018-2019, two UAPAs in India[284] were signed within twelve months of filing of APA applications and in the period 2017 in Romania,[285] the average time taken to complete BAPA was eighteen months only.

729. The APA programme has so far been successful in resolving pending transfer pricing disputes and providing a realistic solution to potential problems. Many types of difficult issues and complex cases involving AMP compensation, PE-related matters, transactions involving use and transfer of intangibles have been resolved. With the adoption and implementation of BEPS Action 7 Report titled 'Preventing the Artificial Avoidance of Permanent Establishment Status' through the MLI, definition of PE in various tax treaties in Article 5 (as per the OECD MTC) shall be modified so as to restore taxation in a number of cases where cross-border income would otherwise go untaxed or would be taxed at very low rates. In order to obtain certainty in regard to income attributable to a PE as far as operations carried out, for example, in India are concerned,

283. Refer China's APA Annual Report, 2019 https://home.kpmg/us/en/home/insights/2020/11/tnf-china-annual-apa-report-statistics-2019-future-considerations.html accessed on 10 February 2021.
284. Annual Report (2018-19) by Central Board of Direct Taxes on Advance Pricing Agreement (APA) Programme of India, November 2019 – refer Table B.4(1) https://www.irsofficersonline.gov.in/Documents/OfficalCommunique/129112019165648.pdf accessed on 13 December 2019.
285. Refer Statistics on APAs in the EU at the end of 2017 https://ec.europa.eu/taxation_customs/sites/taxation/files/statistics_on_advance_pricing_agreements_2017_en.pdf.

MNEs are expected to increase filing of APA applications, as with effect from 1 April 2020, section 92CC of the Indian Income Tax Act, 1961 has been amended so as to specifically provide that the government may enter into an APA with any person, including by or on behalf of that person, being a non-resident, i.e., a PE, determining the income referred to in clause (i) of subsection (1) of section 9, or specifying the manner in which said income is to be determined. Similarly, other jurisdictions which allow access to APAs for PEs, as is the case in Canada, Indonesia, Ireland, Japan, Poland, Spain, UK and others (including Maldives, the latest entrant to the APA club), APA filings are expected to increase. In addition, transfer pricing of intangibles or IP is expected to remain challenging in light of the BEPS Actions 8-10 reports since the challenges that arise for both taxpayers and tax administrations in implementing the key DEMPE functions approach still remain. In order to reduce the level of subjectivity of tax administrations in assessing the outcome of TP analyses by corporates related to intangibles, taxpayers are expected to have greater access to APAs so as to have certainty in advance.

730. Undertaking site visits at the premises of the APA applicants has been a regular feature to understand FAR of the applicants and all taxpayers have appreciated this feature contained in APA programme. Further, joint site visits in BAPA cases, as mutually agreed by the CAs of the two sides and the taxpayers, have also now become an integral feature of processing of many APA applications. Notwithstanding the unforeseen disruption caused by COVID-19, it is expected that site visits shall continue to perform their crucial role in enabling tax administrations to better understand and appreciate FAR of the AEs involved.

731. The programme has provided desired certainty to the taxpayers on transfer pricing issues and at the same time has managed to collect the much-needed revenue for the governments running this programme. The programme has made a noticeable change in the taxpayer's perception of tax systems and tax administrations. The hallmark of APAs has been the certainty obtained by taxpayers for a number of years from TP-related litigation. Signing of one APA agreement in China may potentially resolve fifteen transfer pricing years (five APA years and ten rollback years), whereas in Japan, it may resolve eleven potential transfer pricing years (five APA years and six rollback years), in Korea, it may resolve ten potential transfer pricing years (five APA years and five rollback years) which may increase to twelve years as for APAs submitted in Korea on or after 1 January 2021, the rollback period for BAPAs shall increase to seven years and in India it may resolve nine potential transfer pricing years (five APA years and four rollback years). Signing of more APAs has immense potential to reduce pendency of cases with administrative and judicial authorities and shall go a long way in reducing litigation. The governments running this programme are committed to its effective implementation and have adopted a solution-oriented approach for providing certainty to the taxpayers as far as the issues regarding transfer pricing are concerned. Statistics of various jurisdictions discussed in Chapter 3 amply demonstrate that in most countries which have adopted the APA programme, it has been appreciated domestically and internationally for being able to address complex transfer pricing issues in a fair and transparent manner. This amply demonstrates that most jurisdictions are committed to fostering a non-adversarial tax regime in their fight against BEPS.

Bibliography

APA Program Report 2007, National Tax Agency http://www.drtp.ca/wp-content/uploads/2015/02/APA_Program_Report_2007.pdf accessed on 11 August 2019.

2010 Report on the Attribution of Profits to Permanent Establishments https://www.oecd.org/ctp/transfer-pricing/45689524.pdf accessed on 16 August 2019.

Adjustment of International Taxes Act (AITA) https://www.global-regulation.com/law/korea/643987/adjustment-of-international-taxes-act.html.

Administrative Guidelines https://bofip.impots.gouv.fr/bofip/1053-PGP.html/identifiant=BOI-SJ-RES-20-10-20180718 accessed on 11 August 2020.

Advance Pricing Arrangement – Program Report – 2019 by Canada https://www.canada.ca/en/revenue-agency/services/tax/international-non-residents/competent-authority-services/advance-pricing-arrangements/2019-apa-program-report.html accessed on 10 February 2021.

An in-depth analysis of published anonymized APA and APA request summaries under the revised Dutch Tax Ruling Practice (Intertax, Volume 49, 2021, Issue 3) by Koen Bolink (Houthoff) http://kluwertaxblog.com/2021/02/18/an-in-depth-analysis-of-published-anonymized-apa-and-apa-request-summaries-under-the-revised-dutch-tax-ruling-practice-forthcoming-intertax-vol-49-2021-issue-3/ accessed on 5 March 2021.

Announcement and Report Concerning Advance Pricing Agreements dated 22 March 2019 of the Secretary of the Treasury, USA https://www.irs.gov/pub/irs-drop/a-19-03.pdf accessed on 4 August 2019.

Annual Report (2018-19) by Central Board of Direct Taxes on Advance Pricing Agreement (APA) Programme of India, November 2019 https://www.irsofficersonline.gov.in/Documents/OfficalCommunique/129112019165648.pdf accessed on 13 December 2019.

APA Annual Report, 2019 published by NTS https://www.bdo.global/en-gb/microsites/tax-newsletters/corporate-tax-news/issue-57-january-2021/korea-transfer-pricing-advance-pricing-agreement-updates accessed on 13 February 2021.

Apple Computers Australia Pty Ltd, Historic transfer pricing agreement reached between Apple Computer, the Australian Taxation Office and US Internal Revenue Service, Media Information, Frenchs Forest NSW (5 March 1991).

Article 18.9 of Corporate Income Tax Law (Law 27/2014 of 27 November) https://www.global-regulation.com/translation/spain/1447828/law-27-2014-november-27%252c-from-corporate-income-tax.html accessed on 24 March 2021.

Article 105.19. of Tax Code of the Russian Federation (Part One) dated 31 July 1998 N 146-FZ (as amended on 17 February 2021) http://www.consultant.ru/document/cons_doc_LAW_19671/a0c86ac1c3ab260f92c469dd683ec981bb527d8d/ accessed on 18 March 2021.

Article 105.20. of Tax Code of the Russian Federation (Part One) dated 31 July 1998 N 146-FZ (as amended on 17 February 2021) http://www.consultant.ru/document/cons_doc_LAW_19671/0a4a5495b27af9f5435f41171b72cd7a51995712/ accessed on 18 March 2021.

Article 105.21. of Tax Code of the Russian Federation (Part One) dated 31 July 1998 N 146-FZ (as amended on 17 February 2021) http://www.consultant.ru/document/cons_doc_LAW_19671/9aaeef7f31107ccf62dff8dd28d6908771fc1caf/ accessed on 18 March 2021.

Article 105.22. of Tax Code of the Russian Federation (Part One) dated 31 July 1998 N 146-FZ (as amended on 17 February 2021) http://www.consultant.ru/document/cons_doc_LAW_19671/1c15cd7143ee3b88cf1e4fb4fc0ef2ae6bd6ff85/ accessed on 18 March 2021.

Article 105.23. of Tax Code of the Russian Federation (Part One) dated 31 July 1998 N 146-FZ (as amended on 17 February 2021) http://www.consultant.ru/document/cons_doc_LAW_19671/88ba2afecdf8ef18d72de5ec3b144603d438307b/ accessed on 18 March 2021.

Article 105.24. of Tax Code of the Russian Federation (Part One) dated 31 July 1998 N 146-FZ (as amended on 17 February 2021) http://www.consultant.ru/document/cons_doc_LAW_19671/365218d7ebf2ae01c908521ee759d0e314ceeef9/ accessed on 18 March 2021.

Article 105.25. of Tax Code of the Russian Federation (Part One) dated 31 July 1998 N 146-FZ (as amended on 17 February 2021) http://www.consultant.ru/document/cons_doc_LAW_19671/6db5fd4c7ad795e2d227b23b7f3dedf7e73fa065/ accessed on 18 March 2021.

Article 138 of the IRC Code https://info.portaldasfinancas.gov.pt/pt/informacao_fiscal/codigos_tributarios/CIRC_2R/Pages/irc138.aspx accessed on 22 March 2021.

Article 5 of Public Notice of the SAT [2017] No. 6 http://www.chinatax.gov.cn/download/pdf/20171122.pdf accessed on 10 February 2021.

Article 52 of the Law No. 207/2015 on the Fiscal Procedure Code https://static.anaf.ro/static/10/Anaf/cod_procedura/Cod_Procedura_Fiscala_cu_norme_2016.htm#__RefHeading__3257_1651101228 accessed on 16 March 2021.

Article authored by Vikas Vasal, Grant Thornton India. Updated: 16 March 2018 https://www.livemint.com/Opinion/wsAuF2Ea39oCEfmz6JpdEO/How-advance-pricing-agreement-helps-India-Singapore-business.html accessed on 11 August 2019.

Article by Madhan N titled 'Proposed India profit attribution rules reject OECD approach, add "sales" and "users" as apportionment factors' https://mnetax.com/proposed-india-profit-attribution-rules-reject-oecd-approach-33521 accessed on 16 August 2019.

Article by Anurag Soan and Shreya Ganju titled 'India – Advance Pricing Agreements' https://research.ibfd.org/#/doc?url=/collections/aptb/html/aptb_2014_01_in_1.html#d18e337 accessed on 2 September 2020.

Article by Ashwin Vishwanathan published on 17 December 2020 titled 'Advance pricing agreement: Certainty in uncertain times' https://www.financialexpress.com/opinion/advance-pricing-agreement-certainty-in-uncertain-times/2151462/ accessed on 20 February 2021.

Article by Christian R. Natera titled 'Getting an APA in Mexico' https://www.natera.com.mx/euromoney/Transfer_Pricing_2011-12.pdf accessed on 13 February 2021.

Article by Cyril Maucour, Emmanuel du Douët and Jérôme Granotier, Bignon Lebray titled 'Transfer pricing in France: overview' https://uk.practicallaw.thomsonreuters.com/w-007-3859?transitionType=Default&contextData=(sc.Default)&firstPage=true accessed on 21 February 2021.

Article by Diane M. Ring titled 'On the Frontier of Procedural Innovation: Advance Pricing Agreements and the Struggle to Allocate Income for Cross Border Taxation' published in Michigan Journal of International Law, Volume 21, Issue 2 https://repository.law.umich.edu/cgi/viewcontent.cgi?article=1384&context=mjil accessed on 20 February 2021.

Article by Dr Monika Laskowska titled 'Poland APA statistics reveal alarming trends' https://mnetax.com/poland-apa-statistics-reveal-alarming-trends-42382 accessed on 16 February 2021.

Article by Evgenia Veter titled 'Russia's 20-year evolution of transfer pricing practices' https://www.internationaltaxreview.com/article/b1g76x4kthy1r0/russias-20-year-evolution-of-transfer-pricing-practices accessed on 18 March 2021.

Article by Gil Won Kang, Dong Kwan Kim and Pius Tae Hyun Park titled 'Korea: Navigating transfer pricing issues: Korean perspectives' (14 March 2014) https://www.internationaltaxreview.com/Article/3319660/Korea-Navigating-transfer-pricing-issues-Korean-perspectives.html?ArticleId=3319660 accessed on 3 August 2019.

Article by Jabiulla titled 'Advance Pricing Agreement in India: Empirical evidence from corporate respondents' http://www.tjprc.org/publishpapers/2-41-1472021079-2.%20IJECR%20-%20ADVANCE%20PRICING%20AGREEMENT%20IN%20INDIA.pdf accessed on 16 February 2021.

Article by Mark Thomas, Kristina Novak and Cym Lowell titled 'United States – Evolution of Advance Pricing Agreement Processes: Current and Future Experience in the United States' https://research.ibfd.org/#/doc?url=/collections/itpj/html/itpj_2018_02_us_1.html accessed on 2 September 2020.

Article by Michelle Markham titled 'OECD/International – Are Advance Pricing Agreements Experiencing a Renaissance as a Dispute Resolution Mechanism in the Era Following the OECD/G20's Base Erosion and Profit Shifting Initiative?'

https://research.ibfd.org/#/doc?url=/collections/bit/html/bit_2020_01_o2_5.html#d18e253 accessed on 2 September 2020.

Article by Taiwo Oyedele, Anthony Curtis, Elizabeth Sweigart and Robert Smallwood titled 'The Impact of Nigeria's New Transfer Pricing Rules on Multinational Enterprises' https://pwcnigeria.typepad.com/files/nigeria-tp-article_lexisnexis.pdf accessed on 7 March 2021.

Article by Victor Adegite titled 'Nigeria – Evaluation of Transfer Pricing in Nigeria (2012-2020)' paragraphs 3.5 and 5.4, Published online on 10 June 2020 in Volume 27 of International Transfer Pricing Journal, 2020 (Volume 27), No. 4 https://research.ibfd.org/#/doc?url=/collections/itpj/html/itpj_2020_04_ng_1.html accessed on 26 March 2021.

Article by Vikram Chand and Giovanni Lembo titled 'Intangible-Related Profit Allocation within MNEs based on Key DEMPE Functions: Selected Issues and Interaction with Pillar One and Pillar Two of the Digital Debate' published online on 6 November 2020 in International Tax Studies, 2020 (Volume 3), No. 6 https://research.ibfd.org/#/doc?url=/collections/itaxs/html/itaxs_2020_06_o2_1.html accessed on 3 April 2021.

Article by Zahra Mulachella titled 'International – Improving the Effectiveness of the International Advance Pricing Agreement Process' https://research.ibfd.org/#/doc?url=/collections/itpj/html/itpj_2018_02_int_3.html accessed on 2 September 2020.

Article dated 03.12.2019 by Michał Sojka https://www.roedl.net/pl/en/hot_news/transfer_pricing_in_poland/apa_costs_may_be_deducted_only_until_the_end_of_the_year.html accessed on 6 March 2021.

Article published on 3 April 2015 http://www.thehindubusinessline.com/economy/cbdt-signs-3-more-advance-pricing-agreements/article7065018.ece accessed on 11 August 2019.

Article published on 29 April 2020 titled 'Covid 19 impact: MNCs look to exit, renegotiate APAs' https://economictimes.indiatimes.com/news/company/corporate-trends/mncs-look-to-exit-renegotiate-apas/articleshow/75436398.cms?from=mdr accessed on 20 February 2021.

Article published on 29 November 2019 titled 'The legislative amendment creates new opportunities for using advance pricing agreement (APA) solution and offers a chance for quicker resolution of disputes relating to double taxation in Poland' https://www.cms-lawnow.com/ealerts/2019/11/the-legislative-amendment-creates-new-opportunities?cc_lang=en accessed on 20 February 2021.

Article published on 9 September 2019 titled 'Advance pricing agreements in Indonesia' https://www.lexology.com/library/detail.aspx?g=6e1910bb-5612-480b-a4b9-92b4b9412c82 accessed on 20 February 2021.

Article titled 'Transfer pricing and state aid: the unintended consequences of advance pricing agreements' (Authors: Lorraine Eden and William Byrnes) https://unctad.org/en/PublicationChapters/diae2018d4a3.pdf accessed on 11 August 2019.

ATO-PS LA https://www.ato.gov.au/law/view/document?docid=PSR/PS20111/NAT/ATO/00001#P6 accessed on 11 August 2019.

ATO-PS LA 2015/4 https://www.ato.gov.au/law/view/document?DocID = PSR/PS20154/NAT/ATO/00001&PiT = 99991231235958#P21.

BEPS Action 14 Report – www.oecd.org http://www.oecd.org/tax/beps/beps-actions/action14/ accessed on 4 August 2019.

BEPS Action 5 Report https://read.oecd-ilibrary.org/taxation/countering-harmful-tax-practices-more-effectively-taking-into-account-transparency-and-substance-action-5-2015-final-report_9789264241190-en#page1 accessed on 11 August 2019.

BEPS Action 7 Report, OECD/G20 Base Erosion and Profit Shifting Project http://www.oecd.org/tax/beps-2015-final-reports.htm.

BEPS Actions 8-10 Report https://read.oecd-ilibrary.org/taxation/aligning-transfer-pricing-outcomes-with-value-creation-actions-8-10-2015-final-reports_9789264241244-en#page1 accessed on 12 August 2019.

Chanakya_Niti-Shastra http://www.krishnapath.org/Library/Chanakya_Niti-Shastra.pdf accessed on 11 August 2019.

Chapter VII of Corporate Income Tax Regulations (CIT R), as drafted by Royal Decree 634/2015 https://www.global-regulation.com/translation/spain/615992/royal-decree-634-2015%252c-july-10%252c-which-approves-the-regulation-of-tax.html accessed on 24 March 2021.

China's APA Annual Report, 2019 https://home.kpmg/us/en/home/insights/2020/11/tnf-china-annual-apa-report-statistics-2019-future-considerations.html accessed on 10 February 2021.

Circular No. 10/2015 dated 10 June 2015 www.incometaxindia.gov.in.

Circular No. 201/2013/TT-BTC https://vanbanphapluat.co/circular-no-201-2013-tt-btc-application-of-advance-pricing-agreements-to-tax-administration accessed on 26 March 2021.

Clarification of India's position on the acceptance of MAP and bilateral APA in cases of countries where Article 9(2) of OECD Model Tax Commentary is absent (27 November 2017) http://pib.nic.in/newsite/PrintRelease.aspx?relid = 173885 accessed on 6 August 2019.

Council Directive (EU) 2015/2376 of 8 December 2015 https://eur-lex.europa.eu/legal-content/en/TXT/?uri = CELEX%3A32015L2376 accessed on 20 March 2021.

Degree Project – Business Administration by Maria Alm and Helena Ehrstedt titled 'Advance Pricing Agreements-The concept and its implementation in Swedish tax law' section 7.3.2.3 http://hj.diva-portal.org/smash/get/diva2:419020/FULLTEXT01 accessed on 25 March 2021.

Deloitte Tax Policy Paper 2 (October 2018) https://www2.deloitte.com/content/dam/Deloitte/in/Documents/tax/in-tax-apa-evaluation-way-forward-noexp.pdf accessed on 11 August 2019.

DLA Piper – APA and MAP Country Guide 2019 https://www.dlapiper.com/en/us/insights/publications/2019/03/apa-and-map-country-guide-2019/ accessed on 11 August 2020.

Doing Business in The Netherlands 2020-2021 by Baker McKenzie https://www.bakermckenzie.com/-/media/files/insight/publications/2020/02/doing-business-in-the-netherlands-20202021_v2.pdf accessed on 4 March 2021.

European Parliament, Report on tax rulings and other measures similar in nature or effect (2016/2038(INI)) (2016) http://www.europarl.europa.eu/sides/getDoc.do?type=REPORT&reference=A8-2016-0223&language=EN accessed on 10 August 2019.

Executive summary by EY https://www.ey.com/en_gl/tax-alerts/nigeria-releases-new-transfer-pricing-regulations accessed on 7 March 2021.

Finance (No. 2) Bill, 2014 https://www.incometaxindia.gov.in/Pages/budget-and-bills/finance-bill.aspx.

Finance Act of India, 2001 https://www.incometaxindia.gov.in/Pages/acts/finance-acts.aspx accessed on 10 August 2019.

Finance Bill, 2012 https://www.incometaxindia.gov.in/Pages/budget-and-bills/finance-bill.aspx.

Form No. 3CEC https://www.incometaxindia.gov.in/Pages/downloads/forms.aspx.

Germany Dispute Resolution Profile https://www.oecd.org/tax/dispute/Germany-Dispute-Resolution-Profile.pdf accessed on 11 August 2020.

Government Regulation-74 of 2011 https://www.pajak.go.id/sites/default/files/2019-03/PP-74-2011%20%28EN%29.pdf accessed on 3 March 2021.

Guidance on APAs, published on 9 April 2016 by HMRC https://www.gov.uk/hmrc-internal-manuals/international-manual/intm422000 accessed on 17 February 2021.

Guidance on Pricing announcement (APA) https://www4.skatteverket.se/rattsligvagledning/edition/2021.5/339233.html?q=apa accessed on 25 March 2021.

Guidance on the transfer pricing implications of the Covid-19 pandemic by the OECD dated 18 December 2020 https://www.oecd-ilibrary.org/social-issues-migration-health/guidance-on-the-transfer-pricing-implications-of-the-covid-19-pandemic_731a59b0-en.

Guidelines on Mutual Agreement Procedure (MAP) in Nigeria No. 2019/01 dated 21 February 2019 https://assets.kpmg/content/dam/kpmg/ng/pdf/tax/FIRS-guidelines-on-the-mutual-agreement-procedure-in-Nigeria.pdf accessed on 7 March 2021.

IBFD Tax Research Platform https://research.ibfd.org accessed on 8 February 2021.

IC 94-4R dated 16 March 2001 https://www.canada.ca/en/revenue-agency/services/forms-publications/publications/ic94-4/international-transfer-pricing-advance-pricing.html accessed on 9 February 2021.

IIMA Working Paper No. 2005-12-01 by Markus Brem titled 'Globalization, Multinationals and Tax Base Allocation: Advance Pricing Agreements as Shifts in International Taxation?' https://papers.ssrn.com/sol3/papers.cfm?abstract_id=874567 accessed on 20 February 2021.

Information Circular No. 94-4R (Special Release) dated 18 March 2005 https://www.canada.ca/en/revenue-agency/services/forms-publications/publications/ic94-4rsr/advance-pricing-arrangements-small-businesses.html accessed on 9 February 2021.

IRAS e-Tax Guide: Transfer Pricing Guidelines (Fifth Edition), https://www.iras.gov.sg/irashome/uploadedFiles/IRASHome/e-Tax_Guides/etaxguide_Income%20Tax_Transfer%20Pricing%20Guidelines_5th.pdf accessed on 9 August 2019.

Ireland's Bilateral Advance Pricing Agreement Guidelines 2016, Part 35-02-07 https://www.revenue.ie/en/tax-professionals/tdm/income-tax-capital-gains-tax-corporation-tax/part-35/35-02-07.pdf accessed on 19 March 2021.

Japan Dispute Resolution Profile (Last updated: 1 August 2019) https://www.oecd.org/tax/dispute/Japan-Dispute-Resolution-Profile.pdf accessed on 11 August 2020.

Japanese transfer pricing 2018 dated 23 August 2018 – Update https://www.tpweek.com/articles/update-on-japanese-transfer-pricing-2018/arkkxtkp accessed on 4 August 2019.

Korea's Dispute Resolution Profile https://www.oecd.org/tax/dispute/Korea-Dispute-Resolution-Profile.pdf accessed on 13 February 2021.

KPMG report dated 22 March 2021 titled 'China: Proposal for simplified process for unilateral APAs' https://home.kpmg/us/en/home/insights/2021/03/tnf-china-proposal-for-simplified-process-for-unilateral-apas.html accessed on 29 March 2021.

Law (2009:1289) on Advance Pricing Agreements Regarding International Transactions https://www4.skatteverket.se/rattsligvagledning/321837.html accessed on 25 March 2021.

Law 43/1995 established on 27 December 1995 on Corporations Tax https://www.global-regulation.com/translation/spain/1461190/law-43-1995%252c-of-27-december%252c-the-corporate-income-tax.html accessed on 24 March 2021.

Law for the Coordination of International Tax Affairs https://transferpricing.com/pdf/Korea_LCITA.pdf accessed on 13 February 2021.

MAP profiles on www.oecd.org https://www.oecd.org/tax/dispute/country-map-profiles.htm accessed on 8 February 2021.

Mexico's Dispute Resolution Profile https://www.oecd.org/tax/dispute/Mexico-Dispute-Resolution-Profile.pdf accessed on 13 February 2021.

Ministry of Finance Ordinance of 5 October 2006 – Information on Bi or multilateral mutual agreement procedures under double taxation agreements for reaching Advance Pricing Agreements ('APA') in Germany https://www.oecd.org/ctp/dispute/47655669.pdf accessed on 11 August 2020.

Ministry of Finance Regulation No. 7/PMK.03/2015 in Indonesia https://www.pajak.go.id/sites/default/files/2019-03/PMK-7-2015%20%28EN%29.pdf accessed on 11 August 2020.

Ministry of Finance Regulation No. 22/PMK.03/2020 in Indonesia https://pajak.go.id/sites/default/files/2020-08/REGULATION%20OF%20THE%20MINISTER%20OF%20FINANCE%20NUMBER%2022PMK.032020.pdf accessed on 28 February 2021.

Mutual Agreement Procedures Report 2019 by NTA https://www.nta.go.jp/english/MAP-Report/2019.pdf accessed on 12 February 2021.

Netherlands issues new MAP decree https://taxnews.ey.com/news/2020-1684-netherlands-issues-new-map-decree accessed on 5 March 2021.

New Zealand – Compliance Focus – 2019 https://www.ird.govt.nz/-/media/project/ir/home/documents/international/multinational-enterprises---compliance-focus-documents/compliance-focus---2019.pdf accessed on 6 March 2021.

New Zealand's Dispute Resolution Profile (updated on 19 July 2019) https://www.oecd.org/tax/dispute/New-Zealand-Dispute-Resolution-Profile.pdf.

Nigeria – Transfer Pricing – Country Tax Guides – 17. Dispute Resolution (Last Reviewed: 18 October 2020) https://research.ibfd.org/#/doc?url=/linkresolver/static/tp_ng_s_17.&refresh=1616919768981#tp_ng_s_17. Accessed on 26 March 2021.

Nigerian Transfer Pricing Regulations of 2018 https://taxaide.com.ng/files/Income%20Tax%20(Transfer%20Pricing)%20Regulations%202018.pdf accessed on 7 March 2021.

Note by KPMG dated 6 May 2018 titled 'Russian Ministry of Finance publishes Order on advance pricing agreements involving Russian and foreign tax authorities' https://home.kpmg/ru/en/home/insights/2018/05/ru-eng-tax-tp-alert-order.html accessed on 18 March 2021.

Note issued by PwC on Transfer Pricing in France https://www.pwc.com/gx/en/international-transfer-pricing/assets/france.pdf accessed on 9 February 2021.

Note issued by PwC on Transfer Pricing in Germany https://www.pwc.com/gx/en/international-transfer-pricing/assets/germany.pdf accessed on 9 February 2021.

Note issued by PwC on Transfer Pricing in Indonesia https://www.pwc.com/gx/en/international-transfer-pricing/assets/indonesia.pdf accessed on 9 February 2021.

Note issued by PwC on Transfer Pricing in New Zealand https://www.pwc.com/gx/en/international-transfer-pricing/assets/new-zealand.pdf accessed on 4 March 2021.

Note issued by PwC on Transfer Pricing in Poland https://www.pwc.com/gx/en/international-transfer-pricing/assets/poland.pdf accessed on 4 March 2021.

Note issued by PwC on Transfer Pricing in Portugal https://www.pwc.com/gx/en/international-transfer-pricing/assets/portugal.pdf accessed on 22 March 2021.

Note issued by PwC on Transfer Pricing in Romania https://www.pwc.com/gx/en/international-transfer-pricing/assets/romania.pdf accessed on 16 March 2021.

Note issued by PwC on Transfer Pricing in Russia https://www.pwc.com/gx/en/international-transfer-pricing/assets/russia.pdf accessed on 18 March 2021.

Note issued by PwC on Transfer Pricing in Sweden https://www.pwc.com/gx/en/international-transfer-pricing/assets/sweden.pdf accessed on 25 March 2021.

Note issued by PwC on Transfer Pricing in The Netherlands https://www.pwc.com/gx/en/international-transfer-pricing/assets/netherlands.pdf accessed on 4 March 2021.

OECD – Signatories and Parties to the MLI http://www.oecd.org/tax/treaties/beps-mli-signatories-and-parties.pdf accessed on 8 February 2021.

OECD Releases 1999 update to OECD Transfer Pricing Guidelines for Multinational Enterprises and Tax Administrations http://www.oecd.org/tax/transfer-pricing/guidelinesforapa.htm accessed on 11 August 2019.

OECD Transfer Pricing Guidelines for Multinational Enterprises and Tax Administrations (July 2017).

OECD Work on Taxation (2018-2019) http://www.oecd.org/tax/centre-for-tax-policy-and-administration-brochure.pdf accessed on 10 August 2019.

OECD, Transfer Pricing and Multinational Enterprises (OECD 1979), International Organizations' Documentation IBFD.

OECD's Harmful Tax Practices – 2019 Peer Review Reports on the Exchange of Information on Tax Rulings https://www.oecd-ilibrary.org/docserver/afd1bf8c-en.pdf?expires = 1616235727&id = id&accname = guest&checksum = 3F84496DCD3EE5B70B9F8007E002E8C5 accessed on 20 March 2021.

OECD's Transfer Pricing Guidelines, 1995 http://www.oecd.org/officialdocuments/publicdisplaydocumentpdf/?cote = OCDE/GD(95)31&docLanguage = En accessed on 11 August 2019.

Ordinance No. 620-A/2008 https://dre.pt/pesquisa/-/search/394311/details/maximized accessed on 22 March 2021.

Paragraph 2 of Article 5 of Circular No. 201/2013/TT-BTC https://vanbanphapluat.co/circular-no-201-2013-tt-btc-application-of-advance-pricing-agreements-to-tax-administration accessed on 26 March 2021.

Poland: Proposals for 'simplified APA' https://home.kpmg/xx/en/home/insights/2019/04/tnf-poland-proposals-for-simplified-apa.html accessed on 6 March 2021.

Policy paper issued by HM Revenue and Customs – Statement of Practice 2 (2010) – Updated 12 July 2019 https://www.gov.uk/government/publications/statement-of-practice-2-2010/statement-of-practice-2-2010 accessed on 4 August 2019.

Press Release by Press Information Bureau, Government of India dated 1 October 2019 https://pib.gov.in/newsite/PrintRelease.aspx?relid = 193539 accessed on 13 December 2019.

Private Binding Rulings under Chapter 5A of the TAA https://www.legislation.govt.nz/act/public/1994/0166/latest/DLM348343.html accessed on 4 March 2021.

Public Notice of the SAT [2016] 64 http://www.chinatax.gov.cn/n810341/n810755/c2292979/content.html accessed on 10 February 2021.

Report by KPMG dated 12 November 2020 titled 'South Africa: Discussion paper on APAs' https://home.kpmg/us/en/home/insights/2020/11/tnf-south-africa-discussion-paper-apas.html accessed on 29 March 2021.

Report by KPMG dated 14 January 2021 titled 'Russia: First bilateral APA is concluded' https://home.kpmg/us/en/home/insights/2021/01/tnf-russia-first-bilateral-apa-concluded.html accessed on 29 March 2021.

Report dt 17 February 2021 by KPMG titled 'Korea: Transfer pricing-related amendments in tax legislation' https://home.kpmg/us/en/home/insights/2021/02/tnf-korea-transfer-pricing-related-amendments-tax-legislation.html accessed on 29 March 2021.

Report from IBFD correspondent Mr Romulus Badea, Bucharest dated 28 August 2006 titled 'Romania – Amendments to transfer pricing legislation' https://research.ibfd.org/#/doc?url = /data/tns/docs/html/tns_2006-08-28_ro_1.html accessed on 16 March 2021.

Report from IBFD correspondent Romulus Badea, Soter & Partners, Bucharest dated 23 August 2007 titled 'Romania – Procedure for APAs and individual tax rulings established' https://research.ibfd.org/#/doc?url = /data/tns/docs/html/tns_2007-08-23_ro_1.html accessed on 16 March 2021.

Report of IBFD dated 6 April 2021 titled 'Maldives Issues Advance Pricing Arrangement Regulations' https://research.ibfd.org/#/doc?url = /data/tns/docs/html/tns_2021-04-06_mv_1.html accessed on 17 April 2021.

Revenue Procedure 2015-41 https://www.irs.gov/pub/irs-drop/rp-15-41.pdf accessed on 17 February 2021.

Rule 10AB https://www.incometaxindia.gov.in/_layouts/15/dit/Pages/viewer.aspx?path = https://www.incometaxindia.gov.in/Rules/Income-Tax%20Rules/103120000000007188.htm&IsDlg = 0 accessed on 15 August 2019.

Rules 10A-10E of the Income Tax Rules, 1962 https://www.incometaxindia.gov.in/Pages/rules/income-tax-rules-1962.aspx.

Rules 10F-10T and 44GA under Income Tax Rules, 1962 https://www.incometaxindia.gov.in/Pages/rules/income-tax-rules-1962.aspx.

Section 92C(1)(f) https://www.incometaxindia.gov.in/Pages/acts/income-tax-act.aspx accessed on 15 August 2019.

Sections 92-92F of the Income Tax Act, 1961 https://www.incometaxindia.gov.in/Pages/acts/income-tax-act.aspx.

Sections 92CC and 92CD of the Income Tax Act, 1961 https://www.incometaxindia.gov.in/Pages/acts/income-tax-act.aspx.

Snapshot: advance pricing agreements in Indonesia https://www.lexology.com/library/detail.aspx?g = b4d63ed8-373b-4632-8f16-3a0b647b70da#: ~ :text = Indonesia%20basically%20does%20not%20have,BAPAs%20with%20the%20countries%20concerned. Accessed on 3 March 2021.

Statistics on APAs in the EU at the end of 2017 https://ec.europa.eu/taxation_customs/sites/taxation/files/statistics_on_advance_pricing_agreements_2017_en.pdf.

Tax News Update by EY dated 10 October 2019 titled 'Portugal amends transfer pricing regulations' https://taxnews.ey.com/news/2019-1801-portugal-amends-transfer-pricing-regulations#: ~ :text = 119%2F2019%20on%2018%20September,General%20Regime%20for%20Tax%20Infractions. Accessed on 22 March 2021.

Tax Payers Information Series – 43 www.incometaxindia.gov.in.

Thailand's Dispute Resolution Profile https://www.oecd.org/ctp/dispute/thailand-dispute-resolution-profile.pdf accessed on 26 March 2021.

Thailand's Guidance on APA process https://www.rd.go.th/publish/fileadmin/download/GUIDANCE-ON-APA-PROCESS-EN.pdf accessed on 26 March 2021.

TPM-11 dated 28 October 2008 https://www.canada.ca/en/revenue-agency/services/tax/international-non-residents/information-been-moved/transfer-pricing/11.html accessed on 10 February 2021.

Unit IIa, Articles 20a-20r of the Tax Ordinance Act, Poland https://supertrans2014.files.wordpress.com/2014/06/the-tax-ordinance-act.pdf accessed on 4 March 2021.

United Nations Practical Manual on Transfer Pricing for Developing Countries (2017).

USTransferPricing.com http://www.ustransferpricing.com/APA.html accessed on 11 August 2019.

Vietnam's Dispute Resolution Profile https://www.oecd.org/tax/dispute/vietnam-dispute-resolution-profile.pdf accessed on 26 March 2021.

Table of Cases

Name of the Party/Case Page(s)

List of Statutes

Name of the Statute Page(s)

Index

F

G

H

I

J

K

L

www.ingramcontent.com/pod-product-compliance
Ingram Content Group UK Ltd.
Pitfield, Milton Keynes, MK11 3LW, UK
UKHW020846290926
15470UKWH00004B/1574

9 789403 535517